THE SOCIOLOGIST'S EYE

KAI ERIKSON

The Sociologist's Eye

REFLECTIONS ON SOCIAL LIFE

Yale

UNIVERSITY PRESS

NEW HAVEN AND LONDON

Published with assistance from the Louis Stern Memorial Fund.

Yale University Press books may be purchased in quantity for educational,
business, or promotional use. For information, please e-mail sales.press@yale.edu
(U.S. office) or sales@yaleup.co.uk (U.K. office).

"Under Which Lyre: A Reactionary Tract for the Times" from *W. H. Auden
Collected Poems,* by W. H. Auden, copyright © 1976 by Edward Mendelson,
William Meredith, and Monroe K. Spears, Executors of the Estate of W. H.
Auden. Used by permission of Random House, an imprint and division of
Penguin Random House LLC. All rights reserved.

Excerpt from "Little Giddings" from *Four Quartets* by T. S. Eliot. Copyright
1936 by Houghton Mifflin Harcourt Publishing Company; Copyright © renewed
1964 by T. S. Eliot. Copyright 1940, 1942 by T. S. Eliot; Copyright © renewed
1968, 1970 by Esme Valarie Eliot. Reprinted by permission of Houghton Mifflin
Harcourt Publishing Company. All rights reserved.

Set in Times Roman and Scala Sans types by IDS Infotech Ltd.
Printed in the United States of America.

ISBN 978-0-300-10667-1 (hardcover : alk. paper)

Library of Congress Control Number: 2016962072

A catalogue record for this book is available from the British Library.

This paper meets the requirements of ANSI/NISO Z39.48-1992
(Permanence of Paper).

10 9 8 7 6 5 4 3 2 1

For
Keith Erikson
and
Christopher Erikson

Every sentence of this book
was written with them in mind

CONTENTS

PLACES

PROCESSES

Introduction: A Way of Looking

I HAVE NEVER QUITE KNOWN WHAT TO SAY when someone asks: "And what is sociology, anyway?" That is a perfectly fair question, of course, but it is harder to answer than one might suppose. Other sociologists I have spoken to share the same sense of hesitancy, not only in everyday conversation but in the classroom.

I taught a large lecture course at Yale University for many years. It was listed in the university catalogue in the same way as introductory offerings in other fields—philosophy, chemistry, psychology, ancient history. But I never used the word *Introduction* in the title of the course as a matter of deliberate choice, and I noticed years later that I never used the word *Sociology* either.

The titles I can remember using are *Perspectives on the Social Order, The Social Fabric, Individual and Society,* and *Human Societies.* I wanted those headings to indicate that the course would be an *approach* to social life itself rather than to the kinds of subject matter that introductory courses and introductory textbooks usually include: the methods specialists generally use to extract data from the world around them, the theories they draw on to orient themselves as they go about it, and so on. That is what I hope to accomplish in this book as well—to offer a sense of what the social world looks like when viewed with a sociological eye.

One reason for the difficulty so many of us experience in coming up with a crisper definition of our discipline is that the intellectual terrain we cover is so vast. We tend to regard the whole of human experience as our natural subject matter. No activity involving the lives of human beings is so remote in time, so

1

distant in space, so far removed from the range of practical concern that it can be said to exist outside the borders of the field. In a gathering of sociologists that took place several decades ago—an annual meeting in which members of the profession share information about the research they are doing and the ideas they are mulling over—the following topics were discussed *in the first hour* of a five-day meeting. These are the actual titles of the papers presented:

Nineteenth-Century English Villages
Modern Catholicism
The Social Meaning of the Handshake
The Nature of Comedy
The French Working Classes
Drunken Driving Among Fundamentalist Christians
The Sociology of Natural Resources
The Sociology of Love
The Sociology of Ibn Khaldun

The range of subjects brought up in a more recent meeting—some fifty years after the one just cited—reflects the same breadth. Had you thumbed through the program, you would have come across papers entitled:

Nigerian Beauty Pageants
Coalfield Residents of Central Appalachia
Household Inequalities in Rural Honduras
Vietnamese Cafes
Women Longshoremen
Turkish Industrial Designers
Witchhunting
A Royal Moroccan Harem
Old-Time Fiddling in Interior Alaska

It would be easy to make fun of these titles. Old-time fiddling in Alaska? But these papers are not meant as curiosities—interesting life sketches from a rich, varied cultural landscape. They serve as examples of broader and more abstract aspects of social life, and together they cover an almost impossible range of human experiences in the near and distant past, in the near and distant future, and in every corner of the world. And the question then becomes: How can one draw boundaries around a discipline in which so much is going on?

The fact is that most sociologists regard their field as an *approach* rather than as a subject matter, a *perspective* rather than a body of knowledge. What differentiates us from other observers of the human scene is *how* we look out at the world—the way our eyes are focused, the way our intellectual reflexes are set, the way our imaginations are tuned. We scan the same landscapes as historians or poets or economists or anyone else, but we select different details to attend to closely and we sort them in different ways. So it is not only *what* we see but the *way we look* that gives the field its distinction.

The shelves of university libraries are full of textbooks with straightforward titles like *Introduction to Sociology* and *Principles of Sociology*. But the titles of many of them strike quite different chords: *The Sociological Worldview, The Sociological Orientation, Sociological Wonderment, The Sociological Way of Looking at the World, You May Ask Yourself*. Other volumes can be found on the same introductory shelves, although they are not really texts, with names like *Sociological Insight, Social Things, The Sociologically Examined Life, Thinking Sociologically, The Forest and the Trees*. The two best known titles on that part of the shelf are *Invitation to Sociology* and *The Sociological Imagination*.

Titles like these seem altogether natural to sociologists, but consider how odd they might look if used to introduce other fields in the social or natural sciences. How about *The Chemical Imagination* or *The Mathematical Way of Looking at the World?* How about *The Linguistic World View* or *Geological Insight* or *Economic Wonderment?* In that respect, sociology is a different sort of intellectual undertaking than many of the other disciplines into which human knowledge is usually divided.

The pages to follow are divided into four sections. Each of them contains three chapters and a visit to the field—a social portrait that is meant both to illustrate and give dimension to subjects raised in the chapters that precede it and to serve as a bridge to the chapters that follow. The field visits are every bit as important as other chapters and are not meant to be approached as an interlude or some other diversion from the business at hand.

Each section covers a lot of ground in historical time and in geographical space, so the topics gathered there may look like a mixed assortment at first glance. The chapters in *Approaches* are three separate efforts to convey how the sociologist's eye is focused and what one can see with it. The chapters that make up *Beginnings* cover an almost reckless span of time, but their object is to offer a rough sense of the lay of the land when sociology first made an appearance a hundred and fifty years ago. *Places* deals with various locations on the surface of the earth where people gather into social clusters. And *Processes,* finally, discusses the passages and other forms of change we experience as human beings growing up and becoming active participants in the social order that swirls about us. Three of the field visits to follow draw on studies I have done over the years, and the fourth issues from an earlier experience of mine as an apprentice sociologist.

I mention that because a book like this is almost sure to have a somewhat personal edge to it. It will turn to topics that the author knows best, finds most interesting, considers most important, and cares the most about. So let me pause for a moment to give you a sense of where the voice you will be listening to comes from.

When I was an undergraduate in the early 1950s, the only ambition I can remember taking very much to heart was to see more of the world and perhaps to write about it for a living. I used to say "journalism" when asked about my future plans, but that was really a way of evading a question I did not know how to answer. I took courses on a wide variety of subjects, and when the time came for me to declare a major, I chose sociology. This was not because it appealed to me more than philosophy or history or anthropology but because it seemed to me to contain elements of them all.

I followed that path of reasoning straight into graduate school. I did not see myself as preparing for a career in sociology. I was just continuing my education and still citing "journalism" when circumstances required me to say something.

So my mind was not very well-focused, even by the more relaxed standards of that time. But things sometimes happen to the ill-focused that do not happen to persons who are already in motion down established career tracks. So as I look back over the path I seem to have drifted along, I am surprised to note how large a role sheer chance played in it. Four events in particular strike me now as having made a special difference in my life, and, thus, in this book of reflections.

At the University of Chicago, where I enrolled for graduate study, one of the first professors I encountered was a wondrous man named Everett Cherrington Hughes. I told him in what I hoped would sound like a casual tone of voice that I was interested in "doing field work." I was not altogether sure what the term meant, but he replied that if that were the case I should "forget the classroom" for the time being and "get a feel for the streets." He did not mean it literally, I would later learn. That was just his way of making a point. But I did not understand that then, so I spent a good part of the next few months immersing myself in a section of South Chicago where mass was offered in Polish and where signs in the nearby steel mills were printed both in Polish and in English. That experience of the "feel of the streets" made a deep impression on me, and it played a far greater role than I realized at the time in influencing my sense of what "social life" really is and how one might go about studying it. Hughes looked at me a bit warily when I reported back to him about my recent adventures, and he teased me for years in his gentle way about my awkward introduction to field study.

Two years into graduate study I was drafted into the U.S. Army, and after a month of basic training was assigned to the Department of Military Psychiatry at Walter Reed Army Institute of Research in Washington, DC. I was a Private then, the lowest rank possible, but someone in a distant office must have been looking for enlisted personnel qualified to assist in research. I became part of a team studying army squads that had recently lost a member because he had been diagnosed as severely disturbed and committed to a psychiatric ward. One might suppose that the other squad members would be glad to lose so inept a comrade, but it soon became clear that they had tried to shield their colleague from medical attention and wanted him back. He was almost spectacularly incompetent, which of course was one of the reasons he came to medical attention in the first place, and the squad as a unit paid a considerable cost for protecting him and making up for his disabilities. He obviously meant something quite special to the rest of the squad, and the research team wondered why. We interviewed a number of squads at considerable length in an effort to find that out.

I returned to graduate study after a two-year tour of duty with that question still very much in mind and fully persuaded by then that I was serious about becoming a sociologist. I also brought with me a cardboard carton full of typed transcripts of the squad interviews we had undertaken in the hope that I might find a way to convert them into material for a Ph.D. dissertation. What had those soldiers gained from having sheltered so unlikely a comrade in their ranks? By their own reports, they did not particularly like him or even relate to him in the way they did one another. He was usually the only squad member not listed as "buddy" by the others when they were asked to fill out a questionnaire on that topic. It was as if the squad had formed a protective layer *around* him without really *including* him.

I was toying with what was at first a remarkably shapeless idea—that social groups might actually profit from having visible examples of deviant behavior within their midst—and I was at the same time hoping that the material I had brought back with me would serve as an illustration of it. But I could not figure out how I might use that data to throw light on the idea. The problem was that so few places in the United States kept public records in a fashion that would allow one to calculate something like a "rate of deviance," and if I were to find the kind of data I needed, I would have to look elsewhere.

I considered a canton in Switzerland, but I had never visited that part of the world and would have had to learn a new language even to begin. I also considered fairly remote islands off the coast of Scotland like the Shetlands or the Outer Hebrides. I had never visited one of them, either, but a friend named Erving Goffman—whom you will meet before long—had not only been there but had written brilliantly about it in his own dissertation, and he said in his blunt way that it was not for me.

I was still looking at maps for a viable research setting when it occurred to me that I could reach back into the American past for the data I was looking for, since records were kept very differently then. So I rounded out my time in graduate school (as well as my early years in academic posts) writing a dissertation on crime and other forms of deviant behavior in 17th-century New England. I knew the language this time—or a version of it, at least—but even so it took me six years to complete the dissertation because I knew so little about the historical era I had decided to enter. It gave me a taste for historical records that also made a decided impression on me.

My first academic position upon leaving graduate school was in the Department of Psychiatry at the University of Pittsburgh. It was a logical next step for me in the sense that my Master's thesis and my first published paper were both based on research I had done at a private mental hospital in Massachusetts on the social dimensions of mental illness. I had also spent several months, notebook in hand, wandering through the wards of an immense state hospital in Chicago, an asylum for the desperately ill in an age before drugs had been developed that could take the stark edge off the look of madness. And, of course, I had served two years with the Army's Department of Military

Psychiatry. So my joining a medical faculty seemed to fit well with what was beginning to look like the early trajectory of a professional career.

My role in Pittsburgh was to bring a sociological perspective to bear on the study and treatment of the mentally ill, and to pass relevant parts of that perspective on to psychiatrists, nurses, psychologists, social workers, and other clinical personnel on the staff. The faculty I joined was interdisciplinary to a degree that is exceedingly rare anywhere in the social and behavioral sciences now. It included individuals with training in anthropology, linguistics, animal ethology, philosophy, social psychology, medical specialties of a number of different stripes, and, of course, sociology so settings like that are a thing of the past, but this one worked a real spell on me. My second appointment, too, was in a department of psychiatry, this time at Emory University in Atlanta, so I had a fairly broad exposure to psychiatry and to clinical ways of thinking quite early in my career.

After I had moved to Yale University a few years later and joined a department of sociology, I received a phone call from an attorney I did not know who was about to file suit on behalf of something like 650 residents of a coal mining community in West Virginia called Buffalo Creek. A huge wall of black water, full of coal waste and other debris, had pounded its way down a narrow mountain hollow, destroying a majority of the homes in the upper valley and killing some 125 persons. The flood left survivors deeply traumatized—exhausted, demoralized, numbed, feeling at times as though they were more dead than alive. The attorney was calling to ask whether I would recommend a graduate student who might be willing to spend a semester or two on Buffalo Creek in an effort to get some idea of the damage done to the community there.

I told him over the phone that I could make a more informed recommendation if I saw the site myself. I was intrigued, of course, as anyone reading this paragraph might be, and that was certainly one of my reasons for responding as I did. But my main concern was that I had to know more about what was at stake before I could match student with scene. I made the trip. I had not been in Buffalo Creek more than a few hours when I volunteered for the assignment myself. I had never seen or even imagined anything remotely like that—desolate, dark, a scene of such heavy, muted pain that I have a hard time finding words to capture it decades later. I was drawn to the place as if by a compulsion. When I spoke to the attorney about my reaction, he simply nodded without a trace of surprise. He had half expected it. That was what had drawn him there, too.

That exposure to Buffalo Creek resulted in a major shift of focus for me. In the next four decades I visited a number of communities in which people had been damaged by a catastrophic event of one kind or another. The list includes an Ojibwa Indian band in sub-arctic Canada, a group of migrant farm workers from Haiti camped at the edge of the Everglades in Florida, a neighborhood of families in the shadow of a failed nuclear reactor at Three Mile Island in Pennsylvania, several communities in Colorado exposed to toxic leakages of varying kinds, Native villagers who lived in the path of an immense oil spill in Alaska, Serb and Croat neighbors caught up in the tides of a savage civil war in what had recently been Yugoslavia, and a group of islanders on one of the most remote atolls in the South Pacific who had lived for fifty years with a deep and lingering fear of having been exposed to radioactive fallout from a nuclear test.

I mention this now because you will see glimpses and hear echoes of a number of the different peoples I have encountered in my own research endeavors in the chapters to follow—Appalachian coal miners, Puritan settlers, Polish immigrants to America, Army recruits, migrant farm workers from Haiti, Alutiiq fishers and trappers from Alaska, and survivors of civil war in Yugoslavia. In that respect, threads from my own research experience will appear now and then in the weave of the larger fabric. I will be offering a vision of human life here. It is probably fair for me to suggest that most other sociologists share that vision in at least its broader contours, but it is in the nature of our craft that sociologists will differ on matters of emphasis and of accent. What topics warrant the most detailed attention? What examples are most likely to come to mind when referring to them? What kinds of data should be taken as compelling? Those differences are likely to stem from individual reflexes as well as from scholarly positions, from habits of mind as well as from schools of thought. But they matter.

So let me take a moment to speak of some of the more individual accents that I am most aware of in my own approach to the study of social life.

For one thing, I have spent a lot of time over the years studying and thinking about people who live in villages and neighborhoods and other smaller clusters, and that exposure has persuaded me that a sense of community plays a critical role in human life generally. Most social scientists would agree with that assertion, but not all of them would give it the same amount of attention I do.

For another, it will be evident in what follows that I have a special respect for (and comfort with) field studies, perhaps dating back to my original exposure to the streets of South Chicago and continuing through those years visiting scenes of disaster.

Social scientists have spent a lot of time describing the academic borderlines that set sociology off from anthropology and history and other disciplinary neighbors. I understand why those borderlines are important, but I have wandered across them so often without quite knowing that I was doing so that I sometimes have a hard time seeing them at all. Historical examples come to my mind more easily than economic or political ones, and I reach into the anthropological literature so often for examples that I could well be charged with a kind of trespass. I would describe myself as almost carelessly interdisciplinary, but I would credit that as much as to personal temperament as to academic conviction.

Moreover, my early years dealing with the social dimensions of mental illness may have made me more attuned to and interested in the workings of the human mind than is the case for many other sociologists, and in what follows you may hear more about how social processes are registered in the mind than is usual for sociological work.

And, too, you will soon learn how often I refer to moments of disaster, both in the field visits that appear throughout the book and in the various chapters as well. Those are the familiar materials I have filed away in my own data bank and call on when the time comes for illustration.

To speak of the emphases that have influenced my way of looking out at the world, of course, is to acknowledge, without quite saying so, that other relevant emphases will be missing here. More on that to come.

Sociologists, then, have a rather distinctive way of looking out at the world. The key element in that way of looking is the search for *patternings* in social life, for those currents that gather human beings into social formations of various kinds.

A distinguished law professor is said to have told his students many years ago: "If you can think about the relationship between two objects rather than the objects themselves, then maybe you have a legal mind." I am not sure what that has to do with legal reasoning, but it describes the sociologist's angle of vision remarkably well. The eye of the sociologist is generally trained on the way individual persons relate to one another—the shape of their interaction, the ways in which the words they speak and the motions they make combine to form structures that are independent of, something other than, the individual personalities and intentions of the persons who are found there.

So sociologists tend to focus on *configurations* in the human world rather than the individuals who constitute it. On the *composition* of the larger social scene rather than the particular activities that make it up. On the social *fabric* rather than the threads woven into it. On the broader social *landscape* rather than the separate details spread out across it.

This section turns to three differing approaches to the sociological perspective. The first has to do with looking at social life as if from afar even when one is positioned at arm's length from it. The second is an effort to make clear that the social scene and the individual persons who compose it can be viewed as quite different entities. And the third considers how to view a wholly familiar social reality in the way a newcomer, a stranger, might.

View from the Fourteenth Floor

IMAGINE THAT YOU ARE WALKING DOWN A busy sidewalk in New York City at rush hour. You pass thousands of people in the space of a few minutes, all of them intent on their own private errands, absorbed in their own private thoughts, making their own way through the crowd. It is difficult to sense any pattern or order in that scene, for what the eye sees down there at ground level is a vast scatter of individuals moving to their own rhythms and living out their own lives. If you were looking for some element of human drama in that setting, you might find your attention drawn to the singular faces and the singular gaits of some of the people passing by. There, an old man muttering fiercely to himself. There, a child who looks as though she is about to do something really special. There, a couple in what seems to be an uncommon hurry. A thousand different people. A thousand different stories.

Imagine, however, that you climb to the fourteenth floor of a nearby office building and look down on that same scene. You are too distant at that height to see the expressions on individual faces or to venture guesses about the motives that are impelling people along their separate paths. From that point of vantage, the eye sees a mass of humanity in motion, a swarm of particles that weave in and out as if moving along invisible tracks. Thousands of people may pass down that strip of pavement in a matter of minutes without so much as a single collision, moving in currents that none of them appear to be aware of. If you are looking for an element of drama in *that* scene, it may occur to you that you are witnessing a remarkable act of coordination. The streams of people moving along the sidewalk appear to be patterned, organized, governed by rules. And the wonder of it is that no one down there can tell you how the trick is done. The chances are, in fact, that if you were to ask a few of those pedestrians to think about what they are doing—to ponder their own maneuverings—they might become self-conscious, lose their bearings, and even stumble into one another.

Sociologists can be said to look at social life from a point of vantage not unlike that gained at a fourteenth floor. The particular qualities of individuals seem less distinct at that height, for one can sense that there are forces out there in the world that give direction and shape to the flows of everyday human life in much the same way they give direction and shape to the flow of human traffic along a sidewalk. When sociologists speak of *the social,* then, they tend to be speaking of tides, forces, currents, pulls—something in the nature of social life that induces people to behave in fairly predictable ways at least part of the time. It becomes clear when one looks out at the social world from the equivalent of a fourteenth floor that there are consistencies in the way people think and act, consistencies in the way they move from one place to another, consistencies in the way they view the universe, consistencies in the way they relate to one another. Human life is subject to social forces that help give it form and pattern.

Sociologists tend to regard those forces as *things.* We cannot see them, of course, or reach out and touch them. But we study their properties by examining what happens to the human particles caught up in them—which is exactly how physicists study the properties of gravity or any other natural force. Human life occurs in an ordered context, and sociologists study the nature of that context in largely the same way that other specialists study galaxies, organisms, molecular structures, or any other kind of organized matter. Sociologists are not likely to argue that human clusters are *like* galaxies or molecules, of course. But we would nonetheless insist that the eye a sociologist trains on the social world is disciplined in much the same way as the eye a biologist trains on the natural world.

There is pattern in the way we humans grow up, become adults, select occupations, form families, raise children. There is pattern in the way we fall ill, commit crimes, think thoughts. There is pattern in the way we compete for the scarce goods of the world. There is pattern in the way we make common cause with some of our fellow human beings and pattern in the way we exploit, abuse, and sometimes slaughter others of them. Sociologists are as aware as anyone else that a society is made up of individuals who carve out their own separate paths through life and are moved by their own private visions. Everyone who lives is a unique personality, a rare and special being. But the view from the fourteenth floor suggests that there are commonalities in the midst of all those particularities that give social life its distinctive design. Every individual biography is at the same time a part of some larger historical sweep and is, to some extent, caught up in it. Every person is entirely original and yet is connected to every other by thousands of invisible threads. The poet Stanley Kunitz caught it perfectly:

> The supreme awareness we can have is that all existence is a continuous tissue, a gigantic web of interconnected filaments, so delicately woven that if touched at any point the whole web trembles.

Those patterns, those filaments are among the subject matters of sociology. They are a part of its challenge. They are a source of its intellectual excitement.

I once used the metaphor of the fourteenth floor in an article on another subject, and I was astonished when a colleague I admire wrote in a published comment on the article that I was "elevating" myself above street level and "looking down" on people rather than being "among them." That way of understanding the metaphor had never occurred to me before, and I want to be clear on that point. I am not suggesting that sociologists climb onto lofty perches above the human fray and view social life from there. It is the *way* we look and not the distance *from which* we look that is at issue here. Most of the sites I have visited in my own research only have a ground level. So the point that needs to be made here is not where one positions oneself but what one looks for and what one makes of one's observations. One of the most gifted sociologists of our time, Erving Goffman, observed human behavior from distances no greater than three or four feet when he was studying how people relate to one another when standing in elevators or sitting around gaming tables. Even then, though, his perspective was like that gained from a fourteenth floor in the sense that he was focusing on the *patterning* of those settings rather than on the individual idiosyncrasies of the persons who made them up, the *choreography* of the scene rather than the separate motives of those who gathered there.

Studying the Ordinary

When sociology was considerably younger than it is now, the complaint was widely heard, especially in literary circles, that it had the look of a discipline devoted to the study of the already evident. Sir Ernest Gowers, who served for many years as editor of Fowler's *Modern English Usage*—and must have imagined himself to be an official trustee of the English language—thought he knew the reason why. He wrote half a century ago:

> Sociology is a new science concerning itself not with esoteric matters outside the comprehension of the layman, as the older sciences do, but with the ordinary affairs of ordinary people. This seems to engender in those who write about it a feeling that the lack of any abstruseness in their subject demands a compensatory abstruseness in their language . . . [resulting in] a jargon which one is almost tempted to believe is deliberately employed for the purpose of making what is simple appear complicated.

Murray Kempton, an American and one of the most thoughtful commentators of those times, made a similar observation when he described a group of papers he had heard at a sociology convention as "the remorseless pursuit of proof for what everybody knew all along . . . the perfectly obvious."

One does not hear such scornful dismissals of the field as often now, but the thought itself is worth a moment's reflection. Compared to archeologists who dig below the visible surface of the earth, to psychologists who peer into hidden corners of the mind, to biologists who look through elaborate instruments at bits of tissue the unaided eye cannot make out, to historians who trace events back into a distant past—compared to them, sociologists often do focus on aspects of social life that have a rather familiar look. In that sense, we can justly be called seekers into the commonplace. We study unusual events, of course— revolutions and social movements, for example, or, as in my own case, human disasters. But even then it is usually what those events share in common with other events of the same general kind that attracts our notice.

But "the ordinary affairs of ordinary people" and "what everybody knew all along" can be the most elusive of all subject matters.

Looked at in the right way, the ordinary can be truly exciting and full of surprises. The fact is that people in general are not all that well informed about the commonplaces of their existence. We know more about the geological strata that make up the earth's crust than we know about the way human beings sort themselves into castes and classes and all the other layers into which social life is divided. We know more about the ways molecules interact than we do about the ways people interact. We know more about the behavior of the stars than we do about the behavior of our own kind. It may even be a reasonable rule of thumb that people generally know less about the realities that matter most to them than those of a more remote kind—not because we are indifferent to those realities, obviously, but because the cultures we mature in have already supplied us with working answers even to those questions that reach to the very core of our being. "Why?" "Because it is in our nature." "Why?" "Because the gods would have it so." "Why?" "Because it is written thus." It does not occur to most people out in the world to inquire further. They already know.

This is a different kind of frontier. Some of the deepest mysteries lie not in the skies or the composition of the natural universe but in what Henry James once called the "envelope of circumstances" in which people live out their days. The strangest of all lands is the one we traverse every day. The strangest of all beings are the ones we encounter in the mirror or across the dinner table. So people like Sir Ernest Gowers who think they already know the lay of their own land and the habits of their fellow humans have simply missed the point. Gowers would never have suggested, presumably, that physics should be easy for us to understand because we are all subject to laws of motion or that anatomy should be easy for us to understand because we all occupy human bodies. Human society may be the least well understood of those mysteries.

So if the thought occurs to you that you already know the important features of the social landscape you live on, you might pause for a moment and consider how strange your round of life and mine might appear to someone from a remote land. How odd that we eat three meals a day at appointed times, live with one mate at a time, and send our children off to something called *schools*. Where's the logic in that? How odd that we smile at strangers and reserve our darkest frowns for people we care the most about. How odd that our mood can shift from one of elation to one of deep distress in an instant because of what an athlete does on a field of play. How odd that we think nothing of being served a roasted leg of lamb but would feel revulsion at the thought of a boiled haunch of puppy. Or that we can chew a fried chicken in comfort but not a fried sparrow. Where's the logic in that? How odd, in short, that people say the things they do, think the thoughts they do, act the way they do, and—most peculiar of all—view those oddities as perfectly natural. And, so far, we have been dealing with mere details. If we turn to bigger questions such as the biblical inquiry "from whence come wars and fightings among you?"—as we shall in a later chapter—the ante goes way up.

It feels natural to us to live in pairs and to feel the gnawings of hunger when we do and to identify with athletes wearing the uniforms of the schools we attend or the cities we live in or the countries we are citizens of. These feelings surge up from within, as if from some natural core. But the fact is that most of them are a product of cultural conditioning, not a gift of nature, and sociologists generally take it as part of their scholarly assignment to learn where those feelings originated in the first place and how they managed to persist over time.

On Conflict and Disorder

To say that the social world has pattern does not suggest for a moment that it is an orderly, benign place. No one who pays attention to what is going on out in that world can possibly fail to be impressed by the amount of exploitation and abuse and outright cruelty that has darkened the human prospect for millennia.

Many observers have concluded from this that human society should be understood as a violent landscape across which class struggles, imperial wars, assertions of dominance based on gender and race, and other contests for control are fought out, and that, as a result, social scientists in general and sociologists in particular should focus most if not all of their intellectual energy on the nature of conflict.

I have no problem with that view when it is intended as a comment on—or even as a diagnosis of—the human condition. The chapters to follow offer many scenes of violence and malice and slaughter as well as long discussions of the inequalities that are so prominent a part of social life everywhere.

But whether or not a focus on the nature of *conflict* truly gets to the core of the issue is another matter. Here are two examples of what I mean by that.

It is an obvious fact that things of value are not shared equally among the peoples of the world. This is the case for tangible goods like gold, land, oil, livestock, and water, but it is also the case for less tangible goods like power and influence. Individuals who manage to acquire a disproportionate share of the world's supply of wealth and power often acquire the ability to coerce other people into acting as they want. This is domination, pure and simple, and it certainly qualifies as a form of conflict.

One of Karl Marx's most telling contributions to sociological thinking, however, as we will note later, is that the outlooks of the powerful are often imposed upon the powerless with such force that they are simply absorbed into the moral reflexes of both on some level of consciousness. So we are not just dealing with flat-out *coercion* here but with something closer to what observers of animal life call *imprinting*. If a poor and exploited peasant, for example, is taught by her parish priest and by every other influential person in her world to believe that God wants her to remain in her present station without even questioning her lot in life, she is expressing a view of things that obviously works to her disadvantage and just as obviously works to the advantage of her landlord (and perhaps to the men in her family)—this because they would presumably like nothing better than for her to remain reconciled to her present circumstance. If this is coercion, it is coercion of a special kind, because she has come to accept the views of her landlord and her priest with at least a part of her heart. Things do not always work that way, as we will have occasion to see later, but it is common enough to make us want to ask: How does such a thing come about? How do people come to accept ways of thinking and behaving that by any rational standard are contrary to their true self-interest? What is happening here cannot be viewed simply as a form of "conflict." It is more complicated, more subtle, more compelling—and, I would say, infinitely sadder. To be dominated by powerful persons is a terrible thing. To come to think like them, to be taken over by them, is more terrible yet.

The second example I would like to offer is that even when one group of persons is trying to impose its will on another by the stark use of force, the scene of conflict itself will almost always be elaborately patterned—and the patterning will usually be its most crucial feature. We will note when we turn to the chapter dealing with nationalism that scenes of conflict are never a war of *all against all,* as Thomas Hobbes supposed. They are always a war of *some against some.* When the world we look out at is teeming with class struggles, national quarrels, ethnic wars, and all the other storms that fill modern life with sound and fury, the mind naturally turns to conflict. But if we adjust our lens slightly and look at the way those hostilities are being acted out, other things soon come into focus.

How might one make narrative sense of the civil war in Yugoslavia of the 1990s (although any conflict in these turbulent times could serve the purpose as well)? At first glance, we might be impressed by the stunning ferocity with which the two armed camps attacked each other. "Conflict" would certainly seem like the story line here. At second glance, we might be impressed by the ability of each camp to sustain a deep sense of fellowship and communion despite the troubles pressing in on it. "Solidarity" would seem to be the story line here. At third glance, however—far wiser than the initial two—we might be impressed by the fact that the ferocity focused *outward* from each camp and the comradeship focused *inward* are reinforcing one another. The hostility and the affection—that is to say, the conflict and the fellowship—are really separate halves of the same whole. The emotional fuel that drives a combatant to attack with fierce intensity when he faces an enemy and the emotional fuel that draws him into warm companionship with his fellows within the camp come from the same human well.

It is hard to imagine a harsher or more chaotic scene—or one more torn by conflict—than the war zones of Yugoslavia in the 1990s. But the eye of the sociologist is likely to see structure even in the midst of that seeming disorder. They are cruel terrains, but they are patterned for all of that.

The Individual and the Social

WHEN SPECIALISTS BECOME INVOLVED IN THE STUDY of social life, they are very likely to divide the vast human landscape spread out before them into a number of component parts in order to get a better sense of how that whole works. This is a familiar strategy in all forms of inquiry. As we move further into this book, for example, the chapters will shift from one subject to another, and in doing so give the impression that the social world consists of separate segments like "cultures," "peoples," "ethnicities," "classes," and "faiths," and that the moral precepts people live by can be split into categories like cultural traditions, religious beliefs, ideological convictions, and the like.

It is important to keep this in mind for two reasons.

First, many if not most of the distinctions we sociologists draw in this manner should be understood as *designs of our making* rather than as *the work of nature*. The physical and natural sciences are often in a position to divide the world they study into fixed units like "elements" and "species," but sociologists are rarely in that position. We study the ever-shifting ways of human behavior, and when we do our partitioning, it is for the most part an intellectual device we employ to help us see better. That is what observers of all kinds do when they sort what the eye encounters at first glance into identifiable sections. That is what we all do when we select a particular set of details from the continuous array of them available to us in order to tell a story or to narrate a history.

Second, and more important for our purposes, most of the persons living in the human settings we study do not make the same distinctions we sociologists do when they try to make sense of their own circumstances. To them, the things of the world are part of an endless tissue, "a gigantic web of interconnected fila-ments," to quote Stanley Kunitz yet again. If we were to interview a skilled gatherer of berries, roots, and other foods out in the Canadian wilderness or a tiller of the land in a peasant part of the world and ask her whether she is being guided by inner instincts, religious views, teachings passed down to her from her ancestors, or her long experience of the ways of the land, she would have no idea in the world what we were talking about. It is all part of a vast weaving, all of a piece. The languages of the gatherer from Canada or the peasant from elsewhere do not even have words that can be used to convey what we more modern folk mean by "culture," "religion," "science," or anything of that kind.

Those gatherers and tillers are on the verge of passing from the scene, but the outlook I have been attributing to them is a good deal truer of those of us who live in modern times than we suspect. Most of us know what to say when asked by a pollster or a census taker about our "religion" or "political prefer-ence" or even our "class standing," but having a term for those categories can only take us so far. Few of us are able to say with any assurance which of those realms of thought figure most prominently in our own inner sense of who we are or from what chambers of the mind our sources of motivation come as we make our way through life. We may be aware of the segments into which sociologists divide up social reality, but we rarely know what their actual impact is on us. We really do not know how to answer the questions we asked those natives either.

Sociologists, then, like all inquirers, know how to approach their subject matter as an assembly of parts. But we are quite aware at the same time that the social world, in essence, is a is a continuous field of force—a thing of drifts and tides and currents and flows. For us, too, it is a vast, endless weaving.

We human beings are all caught up in those drifts and flows, often without knowing that to be so. They play a major role in helping shape how we behave and what we become. That is what sociologists concentrate on for the most part—and in doing so sometimes raise a compelling question: where, then, does the individual fit in?

When I was a student many years ago, there were a number of prominent critics who resented the way sociologists went about their scholarly tasks for fear that they were leaving out the individual—that unique creature who resides in all of us—in their eagerness to study larger social forces. One of the most respected poets of the time, W. H. Auden, wrote:

> Thou shalt not answer questionnaires
> Nor quizzes on world affairs
> Nor with compliance sit with statisticians
> Nor commit a social science

And e. e. cummings, who had an enormous following on American campuses then, caught the spirit of that complaint well:

> O sweet spontaneous
> earth how often have
> the doting
>   fingers of
> prurient philosophers pinched
> and poked
> thee
> , has the naughty thumb
> of science prodded
> thy
>   beauty.

Prurient philosophers? Well, maybe so. Sociologists are certainly in the business of prodding and poking, and we often sit with statisticians when we are not one ourselves. But most of us would insist that the majesty of the human spirit is not diminished by examining the way individuals behave any more than the majesty of the human body is diminished by examining the way its cells operate. To Auden and cummings and many others of that time the lessons of sociology seemed to impose a dark and unwelcome wisdom at first glance—that the social world is full of forces that impose upon us and shape us in certain ways. An old and respected college in New England did not appoint a sociologist to its faculty until well into the late 1960s, long after departments of sociology were standard fare elsewhere, and when the president of the college was asked why it had taken so long to catch up, he is said to have replied: "it's because we believe in free will." That may seem absurdly out of date to some, almost as if a college decided to avoid teaching physics because the law of gravity posed a limit on the human ability to soar at will. But not to all. Yale University gave serious thought to dropping its department of sociology—the oldest in the land—in the early 1990s, and that old reasoning, expressed in a less direct way, had a place in the discussions that took place then.

That was long ago. But the questions raised then still linger in one form or another—if no longer in the halls of New England colleges and universities then in other locations on the social map: Are you sociologists saying that we human beings drift in social currents like plankton in the sea? That we are held tight in the vise of custom? That we are herded this way and that by forces we cannot even see?

The answer to that one is a simple no. Wills are something that individuals possess, while social forces are a part of that larger gravitation field we call "society." The drama of human life is found in the way the two interact—the way individuals negotiate a path for themselves through that field of force and emerge from it with their own identity and their own form of humanity. In that sense, the *social setting* and the *individual person* found on it can almost be understood as different orders of being altogether.

The social forces that sociologists study are tendencies and probabilities of the kind that help shape the way people in the mass will move through life. They do not determine individual outcomes. Here is a deliberately trivial example. If I had access to a few scraps of information that could fit on the back of an envelope, I could probably predict within a small margin of error how many individuals will attend a football game scheduled for the upcoming season. I would want to see records of past attendance, and then supplement that with information on how the two teams are performing, the size of the stadium, whatever weather forecasts are available, and other details a seasoned athletic director would know far better than I. Those scraps of information can serve as a pale version of those drifts and pulls and tides I was referring to earlier that influence the way people behave.

But with all that information on hand I will still have no way of knowing whether you or I or any other individual person will be among the attendees. Perhaps even more to the point, if someone else had interviewed every person living within commuting distance of the game site and asked whether or not they planned to attend the game themselves, my estimate might well be the more accurate of the two.

A trivial example, to be sure, but a similar logic is at work in more complex social scenes as well. You and I (and all the other "you's" and "I's" that make up the social order) have our own individual reasons for behaving as we do, but the larger aggregates of which we are a part are patterned in ways that can be observed and even predicted. The behavior of the larger mass, that is, can be orderly even when the behavior of its constituent atoms, traced individually, are harder to follow. So ask of sociologists how many people are likely to get married or go to prison or immigrate or publish a poem in any given season, but do not ask whether you or a friend of yours will be among them. To paraphrase a famous line often attributed to William Blake: "worlds in motion have structure that is not reflected in grains of sand."

It may be uncomfortable for some to recognize that they are enmeshed in the folds of that unending fabric, but there is liberation in that knowledge all the same. Autonomy is not a quality gained by asserting it to be so ("we believe in free will"). It is a quality to be gained by becoming aware of and coping with the social forces that, for better or for worse, make up the world in which we find ourselves. C. Wright Mills, a pioneer of modern sociology, in an effort to describe what he called "the sociological imagination," wrote long ago (using the pronouns of that earlier time):

> The first fruit of that imagination—and the first lesson of the social sciences that embodies it—is the idea that the individual can understand his own experiences and gauge his own fate only by locating himself within his period, and that he can know his chances in life only by becoming aware of those of all individuals in his circumstances. In many ways it is a terrible lesson; and in many ways it is a magnificent one.

Knowing the Place for the First Time

We shall not cease from exploration
And the end of all our exploring
Will be to arrive where we started
And know the place for the first time.
—T. S. Eliot, "Little Gidding"

IT WOULD BE REASONABLE TO ASSUME THAT sociologists know more about the lay of their land than most others do. They spend a fair part of their working lives peering into various corners of the social world, after all, and to that extent they can be thought of as seasoned, knowing, experienced, maybe even a bit blasé about human life.

At the same time, however, sociologists can be viewed as strangers to the lands they study, for it is one of their tasks to look at the social world almost as if they were seeing it for the first time. So the sociological eye is at least in part a naïve eye. We may enter a new research setting with a highly elaborate set of methods and speak of what we find there with a vocabulary as technical as that of any engineer. But the questions we ask ourselves once there sound almost innocent if asked aloud. "What are people doing there?" "What do they expect to accomplish by acting as they do?" "What is the logic in it?" Those are the kinds of question a stranger asks.

It is sometimes the case that sociologists really *are* newcomers to the locations they study. Some of the wisest insights we have into the nature of urban life, for example, were the work of observers who came to the city from the rural countryside and were fascinated by its strange rhythms. Some of the wisest insights we have into the American political and cultural scene were the work of visitors from other shores who could see the land stretched out before them from a stranger's perspective. One of the most perceptive portraits of the United States on record was written by a touring Frenchman, Alexis de Tocqueville, almost two hundred years ago, and it is still the case today that when historians or social scientists look for intelligent commentary on the character of this country at different points in time they are likely to turn to the observations of other visitors who have followed him.

Most sociologists, however, are natives of the lands they take a professional interest in, and they have to *learn* to think and see as strangers do. Strangers are people who often feel at a loss, who are never quite sure what is going on, who find many things in everyday life problematic. Strangers are people who have to pay especially close attention to what is taking place around them because they do not have the kind of cultural reflex that permit them to move across social space without really paying attention to it. One of the keys to a sociological education, then, is for apprentices to mute those reflexes and to unlearn at least a part of what they acquired as charter members of their culture.

So the paradox (if that is not too grand a word for it) is that sociologists know more about human society than most other people do, and yet at the same time know less. I used to tell students near the beginning of the sociology course I mentioned earlier that if they left the classroom at the end of the semester knowing less than when they walked in, they might well have gained something. I was smiling as I did so, but the thought has merit all the same.

The best way to become a stranger in your own land, probably, is to spend a period of time looking at human life in a locale so far away and so unfamiliar that there is scarcely any choice but to ask naïve questions about it. One helpful outcome of such a sojourn, as teachers of anthropology have known for generations, is that travelers often return home to discover that their native land looks a good deal stranger than they remembered it. Having been perplexed by the ways of a people who live far away, they continue to be perplexed by the ways of a people they have known all their lives.

It is impossible to convey in print what an actual field experience of that sort would be like, but one may get a sense of it by glancing for a moment at a few distant places where the cultural logic governing everyday behavior is different than our own. A look at religious ceremonies or child-raising practices or any number of other subjects would serve for that purpose, but I was interested in crime and mental illness and other forms of misbehavior early in my career and propose to turn there now. If you feel just a bit more detached from old and familiar cultural surroundings after traveling across these pages, you may be able to appreciate more readily what could happen in a tour lasting months or even years.

Dealing with Deviant Behavior

To put things far too simply:

Every social order can be said to have its own basic notions as to what constitutes a proper and natural way to behave. These views are reflected in formal rules like laws and ordinances as well as in informal rules like customs and usages. Every social order, too, can be said to have its own ideas as to what constitutes a breach of those rules—conduct known as "crime" or "sin" or "madness" or something else. And every social order, finally, has its own ways of dealing with individuals who are judged to have violated those rules. In some lands, like our own, violators are locked up. In others they are flogged. In yet others they are exiled or shunned in some other way. But whatever the penalties imposed, every social order takes it for granted that there will always be times when some members of the larger collectivity become so unruly, so difficult, so unwilling, or so unable to adhere to the rules that something has to be done about them. Specialists on deviant behavior are quite aware that definitions of what is proper and what not will vary considerably from one location to another, from one social class to another, from one ethnic group to another within any given society, so the blunt way I put the matter above would need qualification under any other circumstance. But that need not worry us yet. Broad strokes will serve for our purposes now.

One of the surest ways to see how a society hangs together is to note what happens when its rules are infringed—which is, of course, among the reasons sociologists have been so drawn to the subject in the first place. To look at a society's procedures for dealing with deviation is to open a window into its inner workings, to get a look at its inner reasonings.

It is important to appreciate that people everywhere see their own ways of handling deviance not only as natural but as just and even compassionate. Their first reaction to the ways of others, on the other hand, is to see them as peculiar if not cruel or even barbaric. Most Americans in our time, for example, shrink in horror from the idea of cutting off the hand of a convicted felon in a public marketplace, as can happen in other corners of the world. But persons who would think nothing of amputating someone's hand, in their turn, can be stunned by the brutality of a society that can lock up fellow humans in stone prisons for years at a time. The most interesting thing about these variations in penal practice from a sociological point of view is not what they reveal about a people's *sense of humanity* or *level of civilization* but what they reveal about a people's *view of the world.* If our ways of dealing with deviant behavior appear to us natural and sensible and human, that is because they are—well, because they are *ours.* Most people who have lived in times past, as well as many of those alive today, would not be able to make any more sense of our penal system than we would of theirs. They look upon it as strange, outlandish, bizarre, even grotesque. How, then, should an observer from afar look upon it?

Most sociologists would suggest: Don't ask whether any given way of dealing with deviance makes sense. Ask what *kind* of sense it makes. What kind of mind could devise it? What worldview is reflected in it? What social circumstances is it a response to?

A Clearing in the Forest

Imagine that you have been moving through a dense forest in the middle of the night and break into a clearing just in time to witness the following:

Kenge, a young man, slipped one night into Manyalibo's hut to have intercourse with the latter's daughter. Unfortunately, Kenge awakened Manyalibo as he groped around in the dark hut, and the older man began to chase him across the camp hurling stones and invectives. Manyalibo took a position in the middle of the camp and denounced Kenge loudly, accusing him of incest among other things. Awakened members of the camp tried to remind Manyalibo that Kenge and the girl were such distant relatives that sexual relations would be acceptable according to custom. But Manyalibo countered with the charge that Kenge, in crawling across him to reach his daughter, had insulted him: the two should have quietly arranged to meet elsewhere. Kenge's response to all of that, meantime, was to laugh harshly at the older man and to call out: "You are making too much noise!" This only infuriated Manyalibo further, and he proceeded to decry Kenge's immorality and disrespect for elders, all the while stomping around the camp and rattling on huts in an effort to rally the community to his support.

Finally, one of the camp leaders named Moke took his place at the center of the encampment, the very spot on which Manyalibo had begun his tirade. With a low whistle Moke silenced the entire camp, and, after a pause, told Manyalibo that the noise was giving him a headache and that he wanted to sleep. The irate Manyalibo replied that the matter was more important than Moke's sleep, to which the latter said in a slow and measured way: "You are making too much noise. You are killing the forest. You are killing the hunt. It is for the older men to sleep well at night and not to worry about the youngsters. They know what to do and what not to do." Manyalibo, though disgruntled, returned to his hut. It was over.

What sense can be made of a scene like that? It was reported by an anthropologist named Colin Turnbull, and it took place thousands of miles away among the pygmies of the Ituri Rain Forest of West Africa sixty years ago. They were a hunting and gathering people who had no police officers or prisons or formal codes of law or courts or anything else that resembles the legal system we know.

Manyalibo does not seem to have been punished in any other way than being told he was wrong to behave as he did, so we are not dealing with anything here that would rank as a serious offense in that social setting. Very few behaviors would have. But rules had been infringed in that odd nighttime episode. Values had been challenged, put to the test. What were they?

It would appear that the participants themselves were not really sure how to answer those questions at first. But when the dust had settled—when Manyalibo went grumpily to bed and Moke took something for his headache and the two young people decided whether they were still in the mood—when night closed in again on the encampment, that is to say, there appears to have been a general understanding among the participants as to what had happened:

Kenge had been somewhat rude and more than a little awkward when he blundered into Manyalibo's hut, that much is clear; and it is possible, although the story does not give us enough to go on here, that the young couple may have been venturing close to forbidden territory so far as local rules governing incest were concerned. But Manyalibo was the true offender in the long haul, as even he seems to have finally acknowledged. Why? Because he had run the risk of killing the forest, of killing the hunt. That is the logic of the episode. The people of the Ituri Rain Forest depend for survival on the game they bring down with bows and arrows or manage to snare in rude nets, and they have no means for moving across hunting grounds other than their own feet. So any disturbance that scares game away from the vicinity of the camp can be serious indeed, which is just what Moke was pointing out to Manyalibo in so emphatic a way. For, as the pygmies say, a noisy camp is a hungry camp.

A Campsite on the Great Plains

The scene now switches from Africa of sixty years ago to Oklahoma of one hundred years ago:

> Once, when the Kiowa were at war with the Comanche, a man and his wife went hunting. The weather turned cold and they went into a cave for shelter. During the night, a man came in from the cold; and the next morning, when it became light, they saw that he was a Comanche. The two men struggled mightily, and the Kiowa, who had a strong hold on the Comanche, called to his wife to take a knife and kill his adversary. The Comanche was young and handsome, however, and the wife hesitated to do as she was told, even though her husband called her several times. Finally, after a terrific struggle, the Kiowa killed the Comanche without his wife's help and scalped him.
>
> When they returned to camp, the husband told the story to the other men gathered in the smoking tipi. The wife's brother asked: "Why didn't you kill her then?" The husband answered that he was afraid that her family would not believe the story. The wife's brother, however, had seen the scalp and reasoned that his brother-in-law spoke the truth. He got his bow and went to his sister's tipi. He called to her, and when she came through the door shot her dead without a word.

This is not a very pretty story by any standard, but it tells us a good deal about the ways of the people whose camp we just entered. We can begin by discarding the theory that the wife hesitated to strike because the Comanche was so young and so handsome: no one even made an effort to find out what she was thinking, it would seem, and any assumptions made about her motives were either an invention of the husband or, more likely, a flourish supplied by the teller of the story. What we learn about the Kiowa of those times, however, is that families were so central a unit of social life that they not only interpreted but enforced tribal law among their members. The family circle was the sanctuary people could count on for protection, but it was also the school in which Kiowa law was taught, the court in which it was adjudicated, and sometimes—as in the present case—the site in which its sentences were carried out.

The woman of the account would have been entitled as a matter of customary law to turn to her brother for protection from the cruelties of an abusive mate. That being so, her husband was only being prudent when he became concerned that his brother-in-law might not believe what was, after all, an incredible story. The brother was not an irresolute person, as he soon proved, so what might he have done if he came to the conclusion that his sister was the wronged party? But he did believe the story—why is another but very important question—and he felt shamed that a member of his family had behaved as he thought she had. If the story had indeed been accurate, her crime would have been a capital one, a form of treason. There were no courts or magistrates among the Kiowa, however, and the brother knew that he had to serve as executioner as well as judge. That would restore the dignity of the family, for one thing, but, far more important for the peace of the community, it would prevent what might otherwise have become an unending feud as one family felt obliged to avenge a death at the hands of another—a death which had been in its own turn an act of retaliation. The logic of this is a simple one. If the sister's death was inflicted by her own brother—the person pledged to protect her from all others—who else would have reason to seek redress? The proceeding was over the moment that arrow hit home.

Such a consideration is certainly not peculiar to the Kiowa. In many other parts of the world the kinfolk of a person adjudged to be guilty of an offense are asked to participate in carrying out the sentence for just that reason. Starling Lawrence, author of a fine novel entitled *Montenegro,* has one of his characters describe an execution "carried out at a lonely crossroads" by a firing squad that was composed of "one member from each of the several clans, so that the death could not be avenged via the interminable blood feud" that would almost surely have followed.

Why would members of the band come to accept a story as incredible as this one? The subject will come up later, but for now it is worth noting that the person who told the story in the first instance and the band members who re-told it later were men; that the persons who heard it in the smoking tipi and discussed its meaning were men; and that the principal actor in what followed was a man.

A Village on the Edge of a Desert

A man started running through the village wielding a knife and a hatchet. He climbed down into the kiva, where the women were holding a ceremony, and after some "strange talk" went up to his father and threw him roughly to the ground. The women were so frightened at this that they left the kiva, thus allowing an important ceremony to be interrupted. The man then wandered through the village for the rest of the day and night. In his wanderings he saw an old Chief sitting on his housetop. He called out that he was going to climb up and kill the Chief, and, in fact, he did mount the wall and deliver a glancing blow to the Chief's head with a hatchet. The old and feeble Chief was nonetheless able to fight for his life and somehow managed to push the younger man off the roof. He threw a rock after the "madman" (for that was what the people now called him) and so drove it into his house. The man stayed there until he had recovered. Although it was widely acknowledged that he had done a good deal of mischief, nothing was said to him afterward about the matter.

This event took place in New Mexico among the Hopi Indians of a few generations ago. Whatever else can be said about the people who figure in this tale, it is clear that they not only had a very different concept of mental illness than most of their fellow Americans but different ideas about human nature and how to treat "madmen." One can sense here an almost complete absence of the feeling, so familiar to most of the rest of us, that something drastic has to be done if a member of the community acts as oddly and as erratically as this person did. Someone runs crazily down the middle of the village with a deadly weapon, interrupts a sacred ceremony, attempts to kill a high-ranking village elder, terrifies everyone in sight, and . . . and nothing happens at all! What does that say about the Hopi? What does that say about the Kiowa? What does it say about whatever we mean by "us"?

We could multiply such examples endlessly. Anthropological field notes are full of them. But societies like the ones we just visited are far removed from our own experience, and the attitudes toward misbehavior and its punishment we see there are responses to very different social realities. The distance from their world and our own is almost an invitation to regard them as exotic.

So let us move one step closer to familiar territory by looking at a non-native people who lived on the eastern shores of what is now the United States three and a half centuries ago—the Puritans of New England.

A Village in Old New England

Imagine (once again) that you have broken into a clearing in the forest. It is daylight this time, and a criminal court is just about to convene. The village you have ventured into may even have a name you recognize—Providence,

Cambridge, New Haven—and most of the scenes that form around you will be at least vaguely familiar. The people you encounter may look as though they are wearing costumes, but the language they speak will be for the most part understandable, even if the accents sound a bit peculiar. The procedures you see in the courtroom itself will resemble the ones you would expect to find in modern Rhode Island, Massachusetts, or Connecticut. You are among people who conduct trials, observe common law, use constables to enforce the peace, and, in general, are concerned with many of the same kinds of issues handled in courts of law today.

Court opens. The first several people brought before the magistrates are a familiar cast of characters. A gray, wrinkled man, bleary-eyed and unsteady on his feet, is fined for public intoxication. An indignant woman who insists that a miscarriage of justice has just taken place is admonished for stealing a chicken. And as the day continues you encounter others—a wayfarer with no established home or calling, a seaman on shore leave who was involved in a brawl, a student beginning to feel foolish about some prank that that did not end well, a lady of the evening looking pale and drawn in the morning light.

Every now and then, however, that familiar rhythm is broken by charges so quaint and so trivial that you cannot help but wonder what kind of society you have stumbled into. This is how the court reporter, his quill pen scratching across a sheet of parchment, records such moments:

> Susan, wife of Philip Harden, for taking two quinces, treble damages.

> Mr. William Snelling fined for the following curse: "I'll pledge my friends for my foes, a plague on their heels and a pox on their toes," and despite his urgings that he intended only to declare a proverb of the West country, was fined.

> Wife of Anthony Needham, presented for absence from public ordinances, fined three pounds and fifteen shillings.

These are but minor moments in the court calendar, and they do not seem to interest other spectators in the courtroom very much. They are strange to us, but not to them. If you were to inquire discreetly into those odd goings-on you might learn some interesting things about Puritan society, which is one reason why scholars study such records. But we will not go into the matter now.

The parade of minor offenses would probably continue for a long time, some of them sounding quite familiar to the modern ear, and others, like the ones above, eliciting at least a moment of perplexity. If you attended those proceedings over a long enough stretch of time, however, the routine would be punctuated every now and then by words so cruel, so terrible, so fearsome, that you would be hard put to know what to make of them. The faithful quill pen writes it down:

> It is ordered that Philip Ratliffe shall be whipped, have his ears cut off, fined forty pounds, and banished out of the limits of this jurisdiction, for uttering malicious and scandalous speeches against the government and the churches of Salem.

> Benjamin Saucer, a soldier, was indicted September last for uttering the most profane and unheard of blasphemy, saying that Jehovah was the devil and that he knew no God but his sword. The bench and the jury differing in the verdict whether the crime was capital or not, the case came to this Court to be determined. The said Saucer appeared before the Court and pleaded not guilty. The evidences against him were heard. But before the Court came to a sentence, the said Saucer made an escape out of prison.

> Mrs. Hibbens was called before the bar; the indictment against her was read, to which she answered not guilty and was willing to be tried by God and this court. The evidences against her were read, the parties witnessing being present, her answers considered on, and the whole Court, having met together, by their vote, determined that Mrs. Hibbens is guilty of witchcraft, according to the bill of indictment. The Governor in open court pronounced sentence accordingly, declaring that she was to go from the bar to the place from whence she came, and from thence to the place of execution, and there to hang till she was dead.

If you were to conclude from witnessing a few court appearances of this kind that the Puritans could be quite harsh, you would of course be correct. But harsh to what purpose? What values could prompt a people to cut off someone's ears for speaking unkindly about a church? What moralities could prompt a people to think seriously about executing a soldier for uttering what must have been a fairly commonplace oath in the London alehouses where he probably learned it? What fears can prompt a people to sense the presence of witches in their midst and then to hang an old woman for being one of them?

While pondering such matters from the back of the courtroom, you might also notice that the magistrates now and then made use of punishments that also have a strange ring to the modern ear, and there, too, your sense of curiosity—and sometimes your sense of horror—would be aroused. Our kind knows countless ways to hurt and humiliate. Whatever else can be said about it, the human imagination has never been deficient in that regard. But it is essential to keep in mind that people do not punish their fellows solely to inflict pain. The penalties a society comes to use are part of an overall logic. They fit into a vision of life. They reflect a view of human nature. They are meant to *accomplish* something.

As you listen in on these court proceedings, then, ask yourself what the Puritans of New England meant to accomplish by the following—and remember as you do so that they were a decent, thoughtful people trying to find punishments appropriate not only to the crime but what they understood to be the larger harmonies of nature.

General Court referred the case of Thomas West, concerning burglary and stealing on the Lord's day, to this court, and he was found guilty. It being his first offense, he was ordered to be branded on the forehead with a "B."

Daniel Fairfield, upon his own confession, and other sufficient proof, is found by the judgment of this Court to have had carnal knowledge of, and so, in a most vile and abominable manner, to have abused the tender body of Dorcas, daughter of John Humphrey, Esquire. . . . The Court therefore agreed that this aforementioned Daniel Fairfield shall be severely whipped at Boston the next lecture day, and have one of his nostrils slit so high as may well be, and then to be seared, and kept in prison, till he be sent to Salem, and then to be whipped again, and have the other nostril slit and seared, then further he is to be confined to Boston neck, so as if he be found at any time during his life to be out of Boston neck he shall be put to death; and he is also to wear a hemp rope about his neck, and so often as he shall be found without it, he shall be whipped.

The wife of Robert Wilson, for her barbarous and inhuman going naked through the town, is sentenced to be tied to a cart's tail with her body naked down to her waist, and whipped from Mr. Gidney's gate till she come to her own house, not to exceed 30 stripes.

Sarah Rowe, for unlawful familiarity with John Leigh, and abusing her husband, was sentenced to the house of correction for one month, and to suffer the discipline thereof according to law, which the keeper is required to execute; and on the next lecture day to stand all the time of the meeting in Ipswich, on a high place where the master of the house of correction shall appoint, with a fair white paper written in fair capital letters FOR MY BAUDISH CARRIAGE, open to the view of the congregation.

One last entry, this time from the diary of a deeply devout elder from Plymouth. It is difficult for us not to laugh in a somewhat embarrassed way at the beginning of this account, protected as we are by a distance of nearly four hundred years. But the author of these lines, a man named William Bradford, would ask us to read them with particular solemnity, since they describe as sad a moment as ever visited New England.

> There was a youth whose name was Thomas Granger. He was this year detected of a buggery, and indicted for the same, with a mare, a cow, two goats, five sheep, two calves, and a turkey. Being upon it examined and committed, in the end he not only confessed the fact with the beast at that time, but sundry times before and at several times with all the rest of the forenamed in his indictment. And accordingly he was cast by the jury and condemned, and after executed about the 8th of September, 1642. A very sad spectacle it was. For first the mare and then the cow and then the rest of the lesser cattle were killed before his face, according to law; and then he himself was executed. The cattle were all cast into a great and large pit that was digged of purpose for them.

It has been a long day in court (a long half century, really, since the entries used here from old court records actually span several decades). And what portrait are we prepared to draw of the people of New England on the basis of this brief exposure? A brief review will have to do here. We did not enter that courtroom in the first place to answer questions about 17th-century New England but to raise questions about human behavior everywhere. But three themes should have emerged by now.

First, it would make sense to assume that the early immigrants to Massachusetts Bay were a people of deep religious inclination who drew their legal code directly from the Bible—believing, quite literally, that every statute necessary for human governing had been posted there in its eternal form. That is why Susan Harden had to repay three times the value of the quinces she stole. The Bible simply mandates it. That is why Thomas Granger, that strange and troubled young man, spent his last day on earth as he did. The year 1642, it should be noted, when Granger was executed, was one of terrible hardship for the people of Plymouth, and the loss of all that valuable livestock must have been a tremendous jolt. But the Bible is explicit on such matters and, as Bradford was careful to point out, everything that happened that dreadful day was "according to law." Death is the penalty for sodomy, that much was clear. And the livestock had to be slaughtered as well, for the text is clear on that topic too. Leviticus 20:15: "And if a man lie with a beast, he shall surely be put to death and ye shall slay the beast."

Second, it would have been easy to see during our time in the courtroom that serious crimes were treated rather differently than minor ones. I don't mean just that the penalties were harsher but that they were of a different kind. When members of the community were found guilty of a slighter offense, the normal punishment would be a fine or a scolding or a warning of some kind. The idea was to make Mr. Snelling think twice before "declaring a proverb of the West country" again, and to encourage Mrs. Needham to rejoin her neighbors at Sunday services. If the offense was a bit more severe, the culprits might be shamed in a conspicuous and sometimes painful way—placed in the stocks or pillory for a day, made to stand in front of the congregation with a "fair white paper" pinned onto their clothing, or flogged a specified number of stripes on the village green. When time passes, the offender is invited to rejoin the community afterwards, chastened but none the worse for wear.

When offenses were considered truly serious, though, as we have seen, punishment could be fierce and permanent—brands pressed into foreheads, ears sliced off, nostrils slit "so high as may well be" and then seared to prevent healing. These were mutilations, pure and simple, changing an individual's features forever as well as causing a good deal of pain. What is the cultural logic there? A people who can impose such punishments, presumably, have lost hope that the culprits involved will mend their manners anytime soon and become reliable members of the community, since they are now forever scarred with the mark of their crime. It was as if that indelible stigmata on the body was a terminal comment on the bearer's true status in this life. And on the next? The elders of New England appeared to assume that the undeserving miscreants gathered down there at the bottom rungs of society will never improve their position and might as well be identified as the scum they are. But they also believed in a form of predestination, so the unspoken reasoning at work here can perhaps be translated into something like this: to commit a truly heinous crime is to offer evidence of one's true nature, and for that reason disfigurement can serve as a permanent insignia of one's place not only in this world but in the one to come.

Third, a people who punish in the manner the Puritans did are not intending thereby to remove deviants from their midst. A few persons might be put to death, as happened to Mrs. Hibbens, or banished from the colony altogether, as happened to Philip Ratliffe. But the rest remained a part of the community physically, and the stigmata they bore acted as a kind of announcement—a warning, almost like the bells worn by lepers in the Middle Ages. Thomas West wore a "B" on his forehead because burglary was his crime, and, in a sense, his calling (though how he was supposed to be distinguished from a neighbor named John Crossman, whose "B" stood for blasphemy, I simply do not know). Daniel Fairfield, who abused the tender body of Dorcas, continued to breathe as best he could through that ruined nose of his and never left home without a loop of hemp rope around his neck. He and his fellow sinners had been set apart in the sense that they had to wear their badges of infamy for the rest of their days, but even so they continued to be functioning parts of the larger community.

If you were taking your children to a public execution one day when spring was soft in the air—a moral exercise you would have thought as bracing as any sermon—you might pass someone with a brand or a scar on an exposed part of his face, you might see someone with her head wedged into a pillory or her feet secured in the stocks, you might come across a flogging, you might even witness a hanging. The odds are that you would not have seen all that on a single stroll or even in a year of strolling. But if we consider how many scenes of that kind an individual might encounter in a lifetime, one can more easily appreciate this important feature of the Puritan way of life: deviant persons were an important part of the scenery, part of the pageant, part of the texture of everyday life.

We have been looking at social worlds that knew nothing of the penitentiary, nothing of the asylum, or any other place of long-term confinement. The idea itself had not yet been invented. The people of those societies—of *all* societies until recent times, for that matter—would have found the notion of imprisoning people for years in guarded buildings altogether incredible. There is nothing even vaguely like that in the Ituri Rain Forest or the Oklahoma plains. There was nothing like that in Europe until the 18th century, and nothing like it in the United States until the nineteenth. The Puritans of Massachusetts Bay maintained structures they called "houses of correction," you may have noticed, but their purpose was to hold suspects for appearances in court or perhaps to punish them for minor infractions. In the experience of most of the people who have lived in this world, the prison would have been regarded as a very odd way of dealing with crime, and it reveals as much about the society *we* live in now as that time in court and that stroll across the village green reveals about the ways of old New England.

The chapter will come to closure by reaching back to the incident with which it began. Moke, you might remember, was the wise elder who whistled everyone to silence in the middle of the pygmy camp and settled a heated dispute. Suppose that Moke came to the United States at the invitation of the anthropologist, Colin Turnbull, who witnessed and wrote about that scene in the forest, and suppose that Moke had recorded his impressions of our society in a journal he kept for his people at home in Africa. Alas, that did not happen. Moke could not write, for one thing. But we are supposing here, and it might be interesting to imagine what a person like Moke would have made of *our* ways of dealing with deviant behavior. Something like this, perhaps:

> These Americans think of misbehavior very differently than our ancestors have taught us to. I do not understand the reason of their way of doing yet, but I have noticed several things as I journey around their homeland.
>
> They have laws and customs, as we do, and they become quite upset, as we do, when those laws and customs are disobeyed. But their ways of rebuking the persons who misbehave are very puzzling.
>
> For one thing, it is considered improper in America for victims of a misdeed to seek revenge themselves. Instead, the matter is referred to personages who act in the name of the whole tribe. Chief among these are men and women known as "police officers," who carry weapons of war upon their persons and wear costumes unlike those of the rest of the populace. These police officers are sometimes aided by persons known as "psychiatrists," whose magic is thought to be so strong that they can relieve illnesses of the soul better than kin who have known the sufferers all their lives.
>
> They have different notions than we do about what is important and what is not important. People can say whatever they want to in America without reproach— blaspheming the gods, ridiculing ancestors, mocking clan totems. They sound like children who do not yet know the way of things. But they have strong rules as to what is right and what is wrong nonetheless. I give you this example. It is hard to understand, so I ask you to listen carefully. They think it is wrong for a person to have recourse to land that is staked out by someone else, whether that land is in use or not. I cannot make camp in a shelter staked out by someone else even if it is vacant and I am cold. This is called "trespass." I cannot hunt in a forest staked

out by someone else even if no one else is there and I have no food. This is also called "trespass" or "poaching."

The methods Americans employ to decide whether or not someone is guilty of a wrongdoing relate back to ancient legends written in books that only a few of the elders have ever read. It is very important here to ascertain what people actually *did*, as it is with us also, but it is even more important to find out whether it was in their hearts to do it or not. I was told of a woman who admitted that she had slain someone else but asked to be absolved of blame because she was confused of mind. I was told of a man who admitted that he had slain someone else but asked to be absolved of blame because he had acted in a moment of great passion. This is hard for a person of the forest to understand. The victim is not less dead. The victim's family is not less alone. The place in the tribal circle is not less empty.

In America, when people are accused of having transgressed a law, they may declare that they did not do it or that they should not be blamed for doing it. When that happens, a ceremony called "trial" is invoked. I was allowed to attend such a gathering. A woman known as "judge" sat at a table elevated above the rest of the hall wearing a long black gown and carrying a wooden scepter shaped like a small mallet. When she stood up, we stood up. When she sat down, we sat down. The person who was accused of transgressing the law and an invisible spirit called "the state" were both represented by champions who argued the merits of the case with great fire, even though neither of them were related to the accused or to the victim by blood, and therefore had no recognizable interest in the outcome at all. The orations of the champions sounded very eloquent, but when members of the audience expressed approval or disapproval of them, the judge looked at them sternly and rapped the table with the wooden mallet. When the champions had finished their arguings, a group called "jury"—chosen because they were completely ordinary in respect to wisdom, attainment, and knowledge of the proceedings—were allowed to leave the fenced-in enclosure in which they had been held and to retire from the hall into a separate chamber to decide whether the accused was guilty or not. No one was allowed to listen to this conversation, not even the judge, so no one knew whether or not the jury understood what the champions were talking about.

Many of the people found guilty of misdeeds are taken from their homes and held captive in special buildings or compounds called "prisons." This is hard to understand, too. Americans seem to think that misbehavior is caused by keeping evil company, yet they lock malefactors away in places where there is no other kind of company. When I ask them why they do as they do, they say that prisons are contrived to cure the persons held there of their bad habits. But I do not think they believe this to be so, for they seem to be very suspicious of the people who have spent time in such places of confinement. They are reluctant to employ them, for example, and they can become quite apprehensive at the suggestion that a son or daughter might contract marriage with one of them—no matter how large the dowry or the bride price.

I do not know what to conclude of these things. Americans must view the heart very differently than we do. They must think that miscreants are sinful to the center of their souls, for how else could they make sense of what they do? They must have a large surplus of hunters and warriors and builders of huts, for how else could they afford to lock away so many of their youngest and strongest people? I hope to know more of these things before I bring my sojourn here to an end. I am a simple creature of the rain forest, and perhaps my great longing for home has blurred my vision. I have visited several of these prisons, and my eyes see something that cannot be so. A large number of the persons one finds in them are black or poor or both. It is not a crime in America to be black or poor. When people try to explain this thing to me, I become confused. Maybe that is because I am black and poor and have been away too long from the voices of the forest.

I pray that my understanding will be stronger once I have seen more of this strange land.

It should come as no surprise that a visitor from so distant a land might be perplexed by the ways people here deal with "misbehavior." But the question for us almost has to be: is there insight to be gained here—wisdom to acquire—from this sort of naiveté? From a sociological perspective, Moke's questions should also be our questions. What *is* the social logic that governs these ways of dealing with misbehavior? What *kind* of sense do they make? The eye of the stranger and the eye of the sociologist converge here.

Disaster at Buffalo Creek

THE WESTERN FLANK OF THE APPALACHIANS IS made up of sharp mountain ridges slicing high into the air and narrow creek bottoms in the spaces between, looking like creases in the folds of the earth. Buffalo Creek, West Virginia, is one of those hollows. The creek itself measures seventeen miles in length as it curls its way down to the Guyandotte River. Some five thousand persons lived along the valley floor in the winter of 1972, gathered into small clusters of homes that were sometimes called "villages" and sometimes "camps."

Almost everyone along Buffalo Creek depended for a living on the mining of coal. The men worked in mines cut deep into the sides of the mountains that loomed above the creek bed, and everybody else lived off those wages, provided support services of one kind or another, or drew pensions as a result of disability or retirement or death. As coal camps went, Buffalo Creek was doing relatively well. Most of the residents had worked their way out of the hardship their parents had known in the coal fields of a generation earlier and the poverty their grandparents had known in the mountain reaches of Appalachia before that.

The men and women of Buffalo Creek called themselves *neighbor people* and were fond of telling outsiders that their neighbors were "just like kin" or that the community in general was "like one big family."

> We was like one big family. Like when somebody was hurt everybody was hurt. I don't know how to explain it. It's a good feeling. It's more than friends. If you lost a member of your family, everybody was around bringing you something to eat, trying to help. It's a deeper feeling.

A man named Wilbur, whom we will encounter again soon, tried to explain it:

> What's a neighbor? Well, when I went to my neighbor's house on Saturday or
> Sunday, if I wanted a cup of coffee I never waited until the lady of the house asked
> me. I just went into the dish cabinet and got me a cup of coffee or a glass of juice
> like it was my own home. They come to my house, they done the same. You see?

The people of Buffalo Creek remember those times as happy ones. But they
came to an abrupt end in the early morning of February 26, 1972.

The Day of the Black Water

Buffalo Creek is formed by three narrow forks meeting at the top of the
hollow, each contributing its own small flow of drainage to the larger stream.
The middle of these forks, reasonably enough, was known as Middle Fork, and
it had been for many years the site of an immense bank of mine waste. The
waste was there because it solved two important disposal problems for the
Buffalo Mining Company.

The first problem is that whenever one digs four tons of coal out of the
ground one also digs up a ton or so of "slag" or "gob"—a dense mixture of mine
dust, shale, clay, and a rich array of other impurities. The coal companies of
Appalachia had typically disposed of those wastes by depositing them wherever the laws of gravity seemed to suggest—spilling them down the sides of
mountains, piling them at the foot of slopes, and dumping them into nearby
hollows. That last was the solution taken by the Buffalo Mining Company.
Middle Fork was a steaming trough of waste 200 feet deep near the mouth of
the fork, 600 feet wide from side to side, and reaching 1,500 feet upstream. Slag
is as black as the coal from which it is separated. When dry, it is crumbly and
crisp, like cinders; when wet, it is viscous and slimy, like an oily batter of mud.
Wet or dry, it is full of combustible materials and may smolder for years on end
or even erupt suddenly in a moment of chemical irritation.

The second disposal problem is that it takes enormous quantities of water to
rinse off a carload of coal for shipment. The Buffalo Mining Company used
more than a half million gallons of water a day for that purpose, and the water,
when it had done its work, was black with coal dust and thick with other solids.
The coal company solved the problem of what to do with the water by storing

it in Middle Fork, where it could be used over and over again. This was accomplished by piling new wastes on top of the old in such a way as to create an enormous impoundment across the mouth of the hollow that trapped 132 million gallons of that thick black liquid behind it. The result was a lake twenty acres in surface size and forty feet deep—stored there, as a shrewd observer of mountain ways named Harry Caudill put it, "like a pool of gravy in a mound of mashed potato."

At one minute before eight on the morning of February 26th, the impoundment gave way. It became so saturated with moisture that it simply dissolved into a mass resembling wet paste and slumped down onto its foundation of silt and sludge. The entire lake surged through that breach in a matter of minutes. It was already too thick to be called "water"—*gravy* might not have been an exaggeration—and as it charged through the impoundment and landed on the banks of waste below, it scraped up thousands of tons of other material, the whole being fused into one vast liquid body that one witness called a "mud wave" and another described as "rolling lava." The wave set off a series of explosions as it drove a channel through the smoldering mass of waste, raising mushroom-shaped clouds high into the air and sending spatters of mud some 200 feet up to a haul road along the side of a hill where a few men were coming home from their shift in the mine. The debris dislodged by the explosions was soon absorbed into the mass as well. By now a million tons of solids were caught up in the flow.

All of this took a brief two minutes, and then the wave churned out of Middle Fork and landed on the village of Saunders below. Having no other word for it, witnesses called it a "flood." What the people of the village saw, however, was a good deal more than that. It was a churning maelstrom of liquid and mud and debris, curling around its own core and grinding relentlessly into Buffalo Creek. As the mass hit the valley floor with a sound that could be heard miles away, it destroyed a power line. The one surviving clock served by that line stopped at 8:01.

At about that time a woman who lived halfway down the hollow and out of earshot looked out her window and thought the world seemed strangely quiet. "There was such a cold stillness. There was no words. No dogs. No nothing. It felt like you could reach out and slice the stillness." But nine miles upstream the carnage had begun in earnest.

The wave demolished Saunders entirely. A miner who had been up on the haul road remembered:

I was about a hundred and fifty feet above where the water came out. It was
burning there, and when the water hit the fire it shot right through the air about two
hundred feet high, right through the air. And when we looked down there [toward
Saunders] and the water was down and the smoke had cleared up, we couldn't see
nary a thing, not a living thing, nothing standing.

The wave did not crush the village into mounds of rubble, then, but carried
most of it along with it—houses, trucks, trailers, storage tanks, a white church
spire that had pointed toward the slag pile for years—and scraped the ground as
cleanly as if scores of bulldozers had been at work. At this point the wall of
water and mud was fifteen or twenty feet high as measured from the flood plain
and thirty or forty feet high as measured from the creek bed. But it was erratic
in its course, pausing for one moment to develop into a great frothing pyramid
before plunging ahead toward another cluster of homes, lashing up one side of
the valley and then the other as it turned corners like a bobsled in a chute,
driving straight toward some helpless target only to change direction in a
shower of foam. No wonder that witnesses remembered that writhing mass of
water, driving structures before it as though they were "match boxes," bouncing
trucks on its crest "like beach balls," roaring like thunder and belching smoke
and sparks as it wrenched power lines apart—no wonder that survivors would
remember it as a living creature, a thing of almost uncanny whim and malice.
"I cannot explain that water as being water," said one individual: "It seemed
like the demon itself. It came, destroyed, and left." A neighbor said: "I felt as
though the water was a thing alive and was coming after us to get us all. I still
think of it as a live thing."

Those who managed to scramble up the sides of the hollow before the
water churned by witnessed the horror from points of vantage only a few yards
above it.

Well, there was one explosion, and that's when all the water came, and then
there was another big explosion, and everything come out—just like them
houses wasn't nothing, just like bowling pins when you roll a ball against
them.

When I looked back, I saw the houses coming. They just looked like toy boats
in the water, and they was abusting and hitting against each other and bringing the
power lines down there. But what scared me out of my mind was that debris up
against the bridge going sky high. I went to screaming.

It looked like the whole town just raised up and started moving down the hollow, just like it was sitting. I seen the first house hit the bridge, then the second, then the third and fourth. And then a mobile home hit those houses where they had done jammed up against the bridge, and I guess the pressure and the impact was rolling under and that mobile home just vanished underneath. I never did see no more of it. There were three women in it. They were standing in a big picture window and their mouths were moving. I gathered they were hollering.

When the last of the black water finally disappeared into the Guyandotte, an aching silence fell over the hollow. The survivors were huddled together on the hillsides, numbed with shock, afraid to move. "We were like a litter of puppies," said one woman, "wet and cold, with no place to go." And as they waited, soft flakes of snow curled into the valley, as if to accentuate the blackness below and to mock their misery.

The wreckage of hundreds of homes was strewn all over the flood plain, much of it splintered into unrecognizable piles of debris, and the entire hollow was coated with a thick layer of sludge. Trees that still stood had been stripped of their foliage and the contours of the land itself had been reconfigured. Miles of railroad tracks had been torn loose from their beds and were twisted around trees or bent into coils like barbed wire. "We looked out over that hollow down there and it just looked so lonesome. God forsaken. Dark. That was the lonesomest, saddest place that anybody ever looked at."

And scattered somewhere in those godforsaken ruins were 125 bodies, hanging from tree limbs, pinned in wreckage, buried under piles of silt, or washed up broken and limp on the banks of the creek.

A story like this one is probably best told by immersing the listener in a cascade of detail. That is certainly how the people of Buffalo Creek experienced it. But we only have space here for a sampling, so as you listen to these voices, each of them recounting a private horror in a private way, remember that they belong to a whole chorus of similar voices and that they speak of feelings common to an entire community.

I saw a housetop go by with a friend of mine on top. There was nothing we could do but watch and pray and wonder how long our house would stand. I saw four or five of our neighbors' homes go by. The water was thirty or forty minutes passing, but it seemed like it would never pass. Then finally it was gone and left a dead body lying on the hood of my car.

I walked to the company store to see if I could get some water and milk. They had just found my best friend. She was washed up against the side of the store. I can't forget the horrible expression in her eyes and on her face. She looked as though she was scared to death, not drowned.

Just as I come off the hill, I was fixing to step over something, and I looked down and said, "Oh, that looks like a doll." And a friend of mine says, "Uh-uh, that's not a doll, that's a child." So he moved the plank and it was a boy. He looked to be about five or six years old. You know those dolls with the big legs all bent out? His legs was like that. I grabbed my whole body and hugged myself together.

I went over to the post office and a smell was coming from the woodpile. I went over and started taking pieces of wood, and I found a body. It was Sarah Barlow. I picked up the back of her hair, what hair she had left. She didn't have no clothes on, and I turned her over and the blood and mud and water came out of her eyes and nose and mouth and ears. I had to go set down.

They just looked like somebody that had been dragged out of a sludge hole or something, clothes tore off and face skinned up. You couldn't recognize them because they was in such bad shape. Part of their scalps was gone. It was a horrible thing, I'll tell you it was. A man will never forget it. If I live to be a hundred years old, I will never forget it.

That is how the people of Buffalo Creek spent February 26, 1972.

Aftermath

One year after the disaster, when I first visited Buffalo Creek, most of the wreckage had been cleared from the valley floor and new layers of grass were beginning to cover the ugliest of the physical scars. The place where Saunders had been was now a silent, empty space. It was still the case that one could see "nary a thing" down there, "not a living thing, nothing standing." Down in the lower regions of Buffalo Creek, where the flood plain was broader and the devastation less drastic, there were vacant gaps in what had once been one row after another of carefully spaced cabins. "It's like teeth in an old folk's mouth down there now," one survivor said. It was easy to find other traces of what had happened there—half a brick chimney reaching stubbornly out of a grassy field, dark watermarks on the sides of still-standing buildings, doors and windows boarded over in mute witness to the fury of the past and the uncertainty of the present.

The worst damage, though, was done to the *minds* and the *bodies* of the people who survived the disaster, and it is there that one had to begin the search for scars.

Sociologists and other strangers are often drawn to street corners when they try to get a feel for new locations. The nearest thing to a street corner on Buffalo Creek was Charlie Cowan's gas station. I positioned myself there on my first morning in the hollow, watching coal trucks make their way up and down the scarred road and talking a bit self-consciously to people who came in to pass the time of day. At one point a leathery old man came in to get a soft drink, and we exchanged a few words on the weather. I looked out at a gray sky and remarked (with what I hoped would sound like country shrewdness) that a storm might be coming along to clear the air. He turned away with a fierce "Haw," his face tightened in anger, and limped off to his car without another word. One did not mention storms casually on Buffalo Creek, and one certainly did not appear to welcome them. I met the same man later at a large gathering of people, and he brought me a cup of coffee in what I took to be a shy act of penance. He did not say anything to me, but he must have known by then why I was in the hollow, and he was prepared to overlook my insensitivity.

The gathering itself involved a number of attorneys and other staff persons from the law firm collecting information from their new clients. Tables had been spaced at intervals across a gymnasium floor and the room was filled with people from the Creek awaiting their turn, lined along the walls on benches or standing around in quiet clusters. The whole scene looked to me as though it had been painted in shades of gray. The children neither laughed nor played. The adults behaved as if they were surrounded by a sheath of heavy air through which they could move or react only at the cost of a considerable effort. Everything seemed muted and dulled. I felt for a long moment as though I were in the company of persons so wounded in spirit that they might have come from a different cultural universe altogether, as though the language we shared in common was simply not sufficient to overcome the huge gap in experience that separated us. I got over those feelings before very long, but the sense of being in the presence of a deep and numbing pain has remained with me until this day.

I was driving down Buffalo Creek that evening when the storm I had predicted so thoughtlessly earlier in the day broke with mountain vengeance. I pulled over to the side of the road near one of the trailer camps along the creek and remained there as half the lights in the camp flashed on, the sound of children crying could be heard, and men trudged out into the darkness to begin a wet vigil over the stream. The mood of that camp reached across the creek to where I was parked, and for a brief moment I had to resist an urge to flee. I had been in Buffalo Creek less than twelve hours.

Years later, one still met adults whose faces paled in anguish as they told stories of "the water," and children who had not spent a single night in their own beds or who went to sleep fully clothed with a packed overnight bag nearby "just in case." The disaster was with them always. When the weather was good, they found themselves returning to it again and again in their minds as every minute of the day and every turn in the road produced a painful association. When the weather was bad, they expected the flood to reappear momentarily. And when they went to bed, poised on the edge of sleep, the black waters would crash and smoke through their minds again, an apt prelude to the dreams that would follow.

Individual Trauma: Damage to the Self

The case could be put simply. Almost every person who lived on the upper reaches of Buffalo Creek before the flood was damaged in one way or another by what happened to them. They had experienced something akin to a concussion of the spirit—a state of shock that reached to the very core of their being. They had lost kinfolk and neighbors, and they suffered from the feeling that a part of their own selves had been ripped away. They ached from the very human guilt of not being able to explain to themselves or anybody else why they had been spared while others had perished. Many of them had lost their homes and almost everything in them: mere "things," one is tempted to note, but they were things that the survivors had lived with and among for so long that they had truly become an extension of themselves. Many of them had lost the illusion, so essential to life, that the social order and even the natural order can be relied upon. They had seen the faces of death up close—not the sanitized faces that undertakers arrange for us, but terrible faces on which unblinking eyes stare out at nothing, wounds are jagged and open and full of oily black mud, and the horror of the moment of death is frozen there as if on a mask.

Worst of all, perhaps, they could not get any of those dark feelings and thoughts out of their mind for more than a brief moment. Those feelings crouched down inside them like malignant thoughts, and they reappeared without warning in the flashbacks that interrupted the day and the dreams that interrupted the night.

The survivors of Buffalo Creek, then, by which I mean those who had experienced the flood at close range, felt that something had gone very wrong in the order of things, that they had been harmed beyond easy repair, that they might never again feel quite at home in the world, that they had been forever changed. One woman said of her feelings on the day of the flood: "It was like something was wiped over me and left me different." She felt the same way several years later, and so did most of her neighbors.

> You don't forget something like that. As we stood in the rain and snow and saw what we saw coming down the hollow—houses washing down the creek, people crying and getting out of the creek naked and almost frozen to death, people begging for help which we could not give. I had about twenty of my kin killed in the disaster, and if those things won't crack a person up they sure are strong people.

> Well, you can't think straight. Your mind is muddled and you can't reason things out. People who went through this thing up there are so confused and so frustrated and so torn up that their lives will never be the same again. Nothing will ever be the same again. There's no way to describe the horror of that day. It changed our lives. It changed everything about us.

> Now, myself, there was months and months and months where I felt I was just sitting around waiting to die. That's the way I felt. I thought there's nothing to live for, and at that time I just didn't care, either. Everything's changed. Nothing's the same.

Specialists who came to the hollow with questions to ask and tests to perform called this "trauma," "depression," "anxiety," and gave it a number of other clinical names. But the people of Buffalo Creek knew it by its mountain names—sorrow, despair, hopelessness—an emptiness so deep and pervasive that it felt to some like a form of death.

> Well, I've got a nervous condition due to the flood. I am tense. I lose my temper easily. I have bouts of depression every now and then. I can't stand loud noises— they tear my nerves all to pieces. It seems like I've lost all confidence in myself. I am afraid to be alone. I'm afraid of storms. I have nightmares. I'm just not the same person I was before. . . . When I have these bouts of depression, everything seems dark. I feel like there is nothing to live for. I feel like I am already dead.

Wilbur

Let's pause for a moment here to let a survivor I will call "Wilbur" tell his own story of what happened that day. It is important to remember as you listen to Wilbur's voice that the experiences he relates, though a critical chapter in his own personal history, nonetheless reflect those of a whole community. This is everyone's story.

Wilbur was 50 years old at the time of the disaster. He had a strong mountain face, streaked with thin scars and a little out of line. "I was caught under a slate fall," he said in a matter-of-fact way, "and it busted my face up." He breathed in a careful, labored way, not as if he was gasping for air, but as if he was rationing his intake, making every breath count. He was suffering from "black lung," as was the case with many miners of his time, and he was to die from it, as he expected to, a few years after my conversations with him. Wilbur was a seasoned veteran of World War II. He landed at Normandy on D-Day, served with Patton's army all the way across Europe, and was then transferred to the Asian theater for another tour of duty in the Philippines. He was no stranger to either the look of danger or the look of death. Four of Wilbur's six children were at home when the flood struck.

In order for the following description to make sense, you need to know that the wall of water churning down Buffalo Creek swept a good deal of seepage before it, almost like an enormous broom. That is why a yard could be overrun with water and small debris before the wave itself hit.

Wilbur spoke of what happened to him in the slow, measured cadences of mountain talk. I can hear it clearly in the back of my mind now as I press the keys that convert it into print, and I hope that something of that voice comes through:

> For the sake of a little cigarette, I guess, is the reason we're here today. I woke up to get me a cigarette and my pack was empty. I got up and just put on my trousers and went out of the bedroom—me and my wife was sleeping downstairs with the baby, and the rest of the girls were upstairs. I came through the living room, through the hall, into the kitchen, and got me a pack of cigarettes. For some reason I opened the inside door and looked up the road. And there it came. Just a big black cloud. It looked like twelve or fifteen foot of water. It was just like looking up Kanawha River and seeing barges coming down four or five abreast.

Wilbur roused his wife and children with a scream, and the whole family managed somehow to leave the house in their night clothes, make it across the already flooded yard at a lurching run, and reach the train tracks a few yards away where some railroad cars ("gons," gondolas) were idling:

> My wife and some of the children went up between the gons; me and my baby went under them because we didn't have much time. My neighbor's house hit the gon that we was under while we were still under it and wrecked it, and that turned the big water down through the valley to give us a chance to get up into the woods. We got up into the woods and I looked around and our house was done gone. It didn't wash plumb away. It washed down about four or five house lots from where it was setting, tore all to pieces.

Wilbur watched from his new perch on the side of the hill as the homes of neighbors who lived upstream swept by. On the porch of one of them a mother held a baby in her arms and called out to Wilbur for help. He could not have done anything for her, obviously, but what he remembered the most even years later is that he "never even thought to go help that lady. I was thinking about my own family. I blame myself a whole lot for that yet. They all six got drownded in that house. She was standing in water up to her waist, and they all got drownded."

That was just the beginning:

> The first five houses above me, they was about fourteen drownded, and I saw every one of them in their homes as they floated by where I was at. Well, I looked back on down the valley, and everything had done washed out and gone. I didn't know where my [married] daughter was who lived down below me. And about that time I passed out. I just slumped down. It was around maybe nine o'clock, in that vicinity somewheres.

His family wrapped him in a blanket and friends helped put him in a nearby car because he had made his way through the water below without any clothing other than the trousers he had slipped on to go into the kitchen. No shoes. No shirt.

He recovered shortly and began to take stock of the situation.

> My house was washed down about five lots from where it had been setting. The whole back side of it was torn off, the porch was gone, the bathroom was gone, and mud and water and stuff was up to the upstairs window. I decided to go over there. I got over there and there was a little child had washed up in mine and my

wife's bed, and it was torn in half. It was laying there on the bed, looked like eight or ten years old by the size of it. There was a truck, a pickup truck, setting in our living room, and it had a dead body in it. There was two dead bodies washed up with the debris that was outside of our house, and I had to step over them to get into the house. I just turned and went back.

Wilbur's wife—we'll call her Deborah—had taken refuge in a neighbor's home and had a report of her own:

> We had three injured persons in the house with us. One of them was George Hardy. The other two was Mike Phillips and his little boy Kenneth. Mike's wife and baby was already killed. Little Kenneth was bruised and muddy and we didn't have any water to clean him up. We had to use Q-Tips to get the mud out of his eyes and ears. George Hardy, he was mashed in here [indicating lower chest]. He had a real large concussion to the top of his head. His hand was all bashed and cut up, and he was just out of his head. He wasn't unconscious or nothing like that, but he was just wild because he had rode that water for half a mile. Mike Phillips had jumped out a window and glass had cut the main artery in his arm. He was about to bleed to death. He had a tourniquet around his arm.

Wilbur, meantime, was looking for his married daughter. He began his search, as the grisly logic of the situation suggested he should, at the makeshift morgue:

> They had a temporary morgue set up over at South Man Grade School. Well, they brung those bodies over there and I went in. Some of them I knew, some of them I didn't, some of them you couldn't tell cause they'd be beat up and banged and bruised and cut up and they would be beyond recognition, that's all. Some of them were never identified by nobody.

Thus February 26, 1972, in the lives of Wilbur, Deborah, and their children. The narrative above does not tell us very much about their feelings during the events of that day. They were too numbed at the time to feel much of anything, probably, and too overwhelmed later to think that a few words could begin to convey the horror of that scene. But a year or two later, when I first met them, they were able to describe their feelings eloquently. Wilbur had a number of problems that he attributed to the disaster:

> This just puts on me a load I can't carry. It seems like I just got something bulging out my chest. I can't breathe like I should, and it just makes me feel that my chest weighs a hundred pounds. Just a big bulge in there.

What I went through on Buffalo Creek is the cause of my problems. The whole thing happens over to me even in my dreams, even when I retire for the night. In my dreams, I run from water all the time, all the time. The whole thing just happens over and over again in my dreams.

I have the feeling that every time it comes a storm it's a natural thing for it to flood. Now that's just my feeling, and I can't get away from it, can't help it. Seems like every time it rains I get that dirty old feeling that it is just a natural thing for it to become another flood. It don't even have to rain. I listen to the news, and if there's a storm warning out, why I don't go to bed that night. I tell my wife: "Don't undress our little girls; just let them lay down like they are and go to sleep and then if I see anything going to happen, I'll wake you in plenty of time to get you out of the house." I don't go to bed. I stay up. My nerves is my problem. Every time it rains, every time it storms, I just can't take it. I walk the floor. I get so nervous I break out in a rash. I'm taking shots for it now.

And this despite the fact that the family had by that time moved to a new house so high up the side of a hill that it would have taken a flood of biblical proportions to reach it.

Wilbur has been describing in gripping detail what a sudden blow like the flood can do to the human spirit. His account is a profile in trauma. But that was not the whole of it. Something else was tormenting Wilbur at the same time, and that "something" turned out to be a very important part of the Buffalo Creek story. Wilbur was a "neighbor person," like most of the people who lived along the hollow, but he now felt adrift and alone.

In the old days, there had been community:

We all just seemed in that vicinity like one big family. We raised our children with our neighbors' children, they was all raised up together, and if your children wasn't at my house on a weekend from Friday to Sunday, why mine was at your house with your children. And that's the way we raised our children. We raised them together, more or less like brothers and sisters. The whole community was that way.

Back before this thing happened, you never went up the road or down it but what somebody was ahollering at you. I could walk down the road on a Saturday morning or a Sunday morning and people would holler out their door at me, and maybe we'd go sit down and have us a cup of coffee or a cigarette or something. And there'd be half a dozen families would just group up and stand there and talk.

But now? "But now you never see nobody out talking to one another. They're not friendly like they used to be. It's just a whole different life, that's all."

> I don't want to get out, see no people. I despise even going to the store. I just want to be by myself, and the longer I stay there by myself, the better satisfied I am. I just set there and whittle. Don't want to see nobody. If anybody comes, I'll be good to them, just as good as I can. Offer them the best I got. But as far as going visiting, I just don't. Why, I don't know. I'm just a different person.

And at one point Wilbur blurted out: "And we don't have no neighbors, that's the whole lot of it."

In the years that followed the disaster, persons like Wilbur and Deborah were trying to come to terms with devastating losses. They had lost relatives and friends. They had lost a home to which they felt deeply attached. They had lost the feeling that they were secure in their surroundings. And—an essential element in that pattern of loss—they felt the absence of a meaningful community setting. Among their problems, that is to say, was the fact that the *community itself* lay in ruins around them. "No neighbors, that's the whole lot of it."

That is what the eye of the sociologist is supposed to be able to see. Wilbur, in his own wise way, had sensed it as well. Something had happened to the larger *fabric* in which the residents of the hollow had been enmeshed during the whole of their lives. That is the *socio-logic* of it.

Collective Trauma: Loss of Community

I first visited the hollow a year after the flood, and it was becoming clear then—and would become clearer yet as the first year gave way to a second and the second to a third—that things were not going well. It was a widely accepted assumption in psychiatric thought then that time heals all but the most devastating of traumatic wounds, but that prognosis was obviously not accurate for Wilbur or Deborah or the majority of their neighbors. Years later the feeling of despair and anguish was almost as deep, the sense of numbness and depletion almost as profound, the memories almost as searing, the grief almost as intense as they had been in the weeks following the disaster. And to complicate things further, people who had only been touched by the event in a glancing way sometimes appeared to be as distraught as a result of what had happened to them as people who had been caught up in the black waters and had seen death at its ugliest. Stranger yet, people who called Buffalo Creek home but had not even been there at all that fateful day sometimes appeared to be as affected as those who came close to losing their lives there.

The specialist retained by the coal company as an expert witness (a court action was under way, you may recall) could see as clearly as everyone else that many of the people of Buffalo Creek were deeply harmed. But he, too, assumed that victims should be recovering at a faster rate than appeared to be the case, and he concluded that virtually every plaintiff must have been suffering from some kind of mental disorder *before* the flood waters began their dread journey down the hollow. He knew no other way to account for the fact that the injured of Buffalo Creek had been so slow to get better. Now *that* would have made for an interesting day in court—a physician prepared to testify that almost every man, woman, and child in a plaintiff group of over 650 suffered from a pre-existing mental illness at the time of the flood. But that is how things can look when viewed through a poorly focused lens. His conclusion would probably have sounded a bit strange in a court hearing (I will admit that I was really looking forward to that scene), but it was in many ways a logical conclusion all the same. It made sense of a narrow sort.

It seemed evident that the people of Buffalo Creek suffered two different forms of trauma that cold February day. The first, clearly, was a blow to the bodies and the minds of people who survived the flood. That is what "individual trauma" means.

The second form of trauma, however, was a blow to *the larger community.* We can call that "collective trauma" and define it as what happens to people when the community of which they had long been an integral part is itself damaged by the force of some disastrous event. If the first trauma can be said to impair the tissues of the individual *mind,* the second can be said to impair the tissues of *social life.* That is why persons who were only exposed to the flood in a minor way or who were not even there at all could feel deeply traumatized. They, too, were suffering from loss of communality.

Collective trauma is a far more difficult concept to deal with at first glance. Part of the drama seems to drain out of the story when we turn to such matters, if only because "loss of community" sounds so abstract when contrasted with the raw immediacy of the disaster scene itself. Collective trauma works its way slowly into the awareness of those who suffer from it, so it does not have the quality of suddenness usually associated with "trauma." But it is a form of shock all the same, a gradual recognition that the community no longer exists as a source of support or solace. It leaves people isolated and very alone—as it did Wilbur, whittling by himself in the silence of his new home high above the creek. "It's like being all alone in the middle of a desert," said one former neighbor of Wilbur's, who had moved with her husband to a tight cluster of homes not far from her original home on Buffalo Creek. As she spoke, the voices of other people living nearby could be heard in the background. One can hear those voices now on the tape where the interview is recorded. But they were not *her* neighbors, not *her* people, and their physical nearness did not give her the sense that she was part of a nourishing human community. She was surrounded by other folk, but she was alone. She was not at home. The healing power that can come from belonging to a larger communal body was no longer available to her.

The two forms of trauma occur simultaneously in many large-scale disasters and are experienced as two halves of a continuous whole. But it is important to keep the distinction between them in mind for two reasons. First, it alerts us to the possibility that damage done to people in a place like Buffalo Creek might be a product of the second trauma as much as the first. Second, it lends emphasis to the vital point that people may find it much harder to recover from individual trauma when the community around them is in shreds. Time may be the greatest of healers, but there are good reasons to suppose that its magic only works in concert with a nurturing social setting. It is harder to warm the inner world when the outer world is numbed and frozen as well.

Another reason why *collective trauma* is a harder concept to come to terms with at first is that the people who experience it—so articulate when they describe the disaster itself and their reaction to it—are not sure how to express what their painful separation from the familiar tissues of community has meant to them. Communal linkages were experienced on Buffalo Creek as part of the natural order of things, and the people who lived out their lives there, like people everywhere, find it as hard to describe the nature of those bonds as they would the nature of the air they move around in or the gravity that keeps them anchored to the ground. It is just there, part of the atmosphere in which they live, and it is taken largely for granted.

So it is difficult for people to pin down or find words for this thing that is missing in their lives. Communality on Buffalo Creek is a state of mind shared among a gathering of people, and this state of mind, almost by definition, does not have an identifying name or a cluster of distinguishing properties. It is a set of understandings that float unnoticed in the air:

> It was like a family up there. We had a sort of understanding. If someone was away, then we sort of looked after each other's property. We didn't do a lot of visiting, but we had a general understanding. If we cooked something, we would exchange dishes. It was a close-knit type of thing.
>
> If you had problems, you wouldn't even have to mention it. People would just know what to do. They'd just pitch in and help. Everyone was concerned about everyone else.
>
> Before the disaster, the neighbors, we could look out and tell when one another needed help or when someone was sick or something was disturbing somebody. We could tell from the lights. If the lights was on late at night, we knew that something unusual was going on and we would go over. There was just things like that you wouldn't think about. If my car wouldn't start, all I'd have to do is call the neighbors and they would take me to work. If I was there by myself or something, if my husband was out late, the neighbors would come over and check whether everything was OK. So it was just a rare thing. It was just a certain type of relationship that you knew from people growing up together and sharing the same experiences.

That outer layer of tissue had for the most part disappeared. When people described Buffalo Creek as a "cemetery," "ghost town," or "graveyard," they were obviously thinking of the social landscape more than they were the physical one. "Buffalo Creek looks to me like a deserted, forsaken place," said one person, and others struck the same desolate chord: "A dreary hollow is how it seems to me."

> The people are changed from what they were. Practically everyone seems despondent and undecided, as if they were waiting for something and did not know what. They just can't reconcile themselves to the fact that things will never be the same.

Why does loss of community matter so much on Buffalo Creek and elsewhere in the human world?

For one thing, when people invest a part of themselves in the forms of community I have been speaking about here, it is almost as though they had deposited their own personal resources in a kind of communal bank, only to discover that when the bank was more or less washed away, they would find it very difficult to reclaim as their own the resources they had stored there. "There's a part of us all missing somewhere," said one man trying to explain that vague feeling. "There's a part of you gone and you can't find it," said another: "You don't know what part it is. It's just a part that's gone." In a sense, your capacity to care for others or to ask others to care for you, to share things with them, to relate to them, was so much a part of your generalized sense of communal atmosphere that you are not sure how to *act* the part of neighbor. You are not sure how the thing is done. And so, as you wander the hollow, numbed and alone, you discover that your emotional tank is simply empty, and that there are few reserves of warmth and concern left within you to draw upon. "It seems like the caring part of our lives is over," said one person, reflecting a thought heard up and down the valley.

> People don't visit or associate with each other. Most just speak and go on about their business. They seem to be in a daze, having deep thoughts or pressing problems with which they cannot cope.
>
> I am now back in the community that I lived in before the flood, but most of my close friends have moved away. Nothing is the same. No one visits. No children come to play. Everyone seems to be alone now, living only for themselves and no one else. Before, they were kind and helpful.
>
> We lost a community, and I mean it was a good community. Everybody was close. Everybody knowed everybody. But now everybody is alone. They act like they're lost. They've lost their homes and their way of life, the one they was used to. You haven't got nobody to talk to.

Moreover, to lose a sense of community in a place like Buffalo Creek is to become disoriented. Years after the flood, the hollow felt like alien terrain to many of those who continued to live there. The contours of the land itself had changed in a number of ways, of course, and everyday life had an unsettled quality to it. But the familiar hills were still there. The road curved up the narrow flood plain as it always had. The schools had reopened, the stores were back in business, the churches were functioning, the mines were in operation. By then, one would think, a certain equilibrium should have been restored. But along the length of the valley people felt that they were lost in "a strange and different place." Once again, it is obvious that they were speaking not simply of the physical landscape but of the social one as well. "We find ourselves standing, not knowing exactly which way to go or where to turn," said one person. "They should call this whole hollow the Bureau of Missing Persons," said another, "we're all just lost."

> We feel like we're in a strange land, even though it is just a few miles up Buffalo Creek from where we lived.
>
> We don't have a neighborhood anymore. We're just strange people in a strange place. I feel our lives have been completely turned inside out by what has happened.
>
> My lonely feelings is my most difficult problem. I feel as if we were living in a different place even though we are still in the same home as before. Nothing seems the same.

In general, then, people all over the hollow live with a sense of being out of place, uprooted, torn loose from familiar communal moorings, and that feeling, too, results from the loss of community as much as from the effects of the flood itself. The disorientation experienced by the survivors may have been sharper on Buffalo Creek than would have been the case in a setting where the sense of community was less strong, but that is only a matter of degree. Something of the sort happens whenever the force of some catastrophe not only damages the people caught up in it but also damages the social surroundings they have always looked to for support and comfort.

People everywhere learn who they are and where they are by taking soundings from their fellows. As if using a form of radar, they probe others in the world around them with looks and words and gestures, hoping to learn something about themselves from the signals they get in return. But when there are no longer any reliable others out there to bounce those exploratory probes off of, people have a difficult time learning where they stand in relation to the rest of the world. One woman caught that feeling perfectly:

> I feel that the disaster has affected almost everyone on Buffalo Creek emotionally. People have no sense of belonging anywhere. There are no existing community identities left, only desolation and indecision. People are not sure yet what to do or where to turn.

And others picked up the same refrain:

> I just don't feel like the same person. I feel like I live in a different world. I don't have no home no more. I don't feel normal anymore. I mean, sometimes I just

wonder if I'm a human being at all. I just feel like I don't have no friends in the world, like no one cares for me.

The flood in its own way destroyed my past in the mental sense. I knew everybody in the area. That's where I lived. That's what I called home. And I can't go back there anymore. I can't even think of it. I have no past.

We will leave the people of Buffalo Creek here, although we will return to many of the themes struck by their experience later. The moral of this sad story is that people are connected to one another by ties they are only vaguely aware of, if at all. Those ties become most apparent, sometimes, when they are ruptured by the force of some disaster. When that happens, the human particles of which social life is formed begin to look, at least for a time, as though they are drifting aimlessly in a dead gravitational field. And it is then, ironically, that one can most easily sense what the structures of society look and feel like.

I have visited Buffalo Creek a number of times in the years since my original stays there, most recently to attend a memorial service at the Saunders Free Will Baptist Church on the thirtieth anniversary of the disaster in 2003. I was one of the speakers. Many of the people who attended the service were by then elderly, and the ones I talked to afterward gave me the impression that they were still bearing the weight of a vast sorrow even though most reported that their lives had improved. But there were many young people there, too, and while I did not spend as much time talking to them, it seemed obvious that they were there not to ponder their own troubles but to honor those of their elders. The fact that they were not suffering in the way their parents and grandparents had suggests that a certain peace has returned to Buffalo Creek, and the fact that they were honoring a past that only their elders knew suggests that a sense of community had returned as well.

BEGINNINGS

This section consists of three chapters—three separate narratives, really—that reach across very different stretches of historical time and deal with very different subject matters. But they are all beginnings in the sense that each, in its own way, is a necessary prelude to an understanding of human social life.

The first, *Human Origins,* covers the history of our species on earth—millions of years—in part because we need at least a rough idea where we came from in order to see ourselves in perspective, and in part to stress the fact that we are *social* animals to the very core of our being. That might seem like so evident an observation that one might wonder why anybody would bother to make a point of it. But the fact is that a good part of Western philosophy, even up until the present time, has been based on a quite different set of assumptions.

The second chapter, *Discovering Society,* races recklessly across several centuries of Western social thought, since the study of human social life could not have begun in earnest until the *concept* of social order—the recognition that human life is not only governed in crucial ways by social forces but a product of them—took wider hold.

The title of the third chapter, *Coming to Terms with Social Life,* involves something of a play on words. The chapter focuses on the thought of three individuals who are widely known as the grand masters of sociological theory: Karl Marx, Émile Durkheim, and Max Weber. They came to terms with social life both in the sense that they found new ways to envision it and to understand it and in the sense that they were instrumental in devising the conceptual vocabulary—the terms—that we use even now to frame it.

The field visit with which this section closes, finally, *The Journey of Piotr and Kasia Walkowiak,* tells the story of peasants from rural Poland who entered a migrant stream around the turn of the 20th century that carried them (and tens of millions of others) across a number of clearly marked national borderlines as well as a number of unmarked cultural ones. In doing so, they changed both the face of Europe and the face of the United States.

Human Origins

"I will praise thee," sings David in a psalm of thanks to God,
"for I am fearfully and wonderfully made."
—Psalms 139:14

"What a piece of work is a man! . . . the beauty of the world,
the paragon of animals!"
—*Hamlet,* Act II, Scene II

Into the Mists of the Past

The first creatures who can be identified as ancestors of ours made their appearance on this earth a long time ago. It was, in many ways, a rather modest debut. Compared to the lumbering dinosaurs who had dominated the world in an age then past, or to the great cats who swept noiselessly over the plain, they were not a very impressive lot. They were weak of limb and slow of foot. They were protected from predators by as meager a complement of natural weaponry as could be found in the animal kingdom—no fangs or talons or claws, no hooves or antlers or beaks. They had thin skulls and brittle bones. They could not swim very well or fly at all. They could not burrow into the ground or scale cliffs. An observer looking in on that scene from some distant perch might have wondered how well suited for life in the forests and savannas of Africa animals with that kind of endowment could be.

Fearfully and wonderfully made? Paragon of animals? Not at first glance, anyway. But in many ways they turned out to be just that, for they had inherited a cluster of traits that would one day combine to make them the craftiest hunters, the most resourceful gatherers, and the most restlessly migratory creatures the world had ever seen. They stood upright and moved about on two limbs. They had a remarkably adept pair of hands. They had a large and inventive brain. And they knew how to do things together. They were social, as many other creatures on earth were then as now, and yet they were in the process of becoming so in new and special ways.

The story of human evolution opens a good deal earlier, although it is no easy matter to establish a starting date or to draw an easy narrative line across those immense stretches of time. We know how the story comes out, at least so far. But the evidence available to us is a spare collection of fossil remains dug out of the ground in widely scattered parts of the world, and a good deal of significance can be given each skull fragment or bone splinter or tooth. To trace the emergence of a species from such meager scraps of information must be a little like trying to map a continent from surveying a few inches of turf. A wise naturalist named Loren Eiseley—speaking of humankind in general—put the matter beautifully:

> Most of our knowledge of him—even in his massive-faced, beetle-browed stage—is now confined . . . to the last half of the Ice Age. If we pass backward beyond this point we can find traces of crude tools, stone implements, which hint that some earlier form of man was present here and there in Europe, Asia, and particularly Africa . . . but to the scientist it is like peering into the mists floating over an unknown landscape. Here and there through the swirling vapor one catches a glimpse of a shambling figure, or a half-wild primordial face stares back at one from some momentary opening in the fog. Then, just as one grasps at a clue, the long gray twilight settles in and the wraiths and the half-heard voices pass away.

It is hard to construct anything like a continuous narrative under such circumstances. There are too few reliable markers in the record to fix the story in place and time, and vast empty spaces fill the intervals in between them.

The best way for us to approach the topic, then, may be to look for those openings in the mist of which Eiseley spoke. These are but steps in a truly improbable journey, and we are tracing them to make a single point.

First Glimpse: A New Creature Appears

Let's suppose that the banks of fog part the first time for us around three and a half million years ago. The landscape we are now viewing was one of abrupt geological change. The thick layers of forest that had sheltered our primate ancestors for millions of years were giving way to open woodlands, and the woodlands, in their turn, were giving way to grassy plains and savannas. A species of spry little apes, less than five feet tall on the average and owning a brain less than a third the size of ours, began to drift out from under that thinning forest canopy. They were among the first of the *hominins*—meaning "manlike," a term used to refer to the lineages that eventually produced our kind—and they would be called *australopithecines* when their remains were found by paleontologists millions of years later. No one knows when they made their debut (or even what "debut" means when species are concerned), but they were well-established in East Africa at the time of this parting of the mists.

Among the key adaptations of those early hominins was the ability to walk upright for relatively long stretches of time, leaving their upper limbs free for other purposes. They had not yet abandoned the shelter of the forest (although that is how things would work out eventually). They had long, powerful arms that allowed them to scamper in the trees with other arboreal beings, and the forest was still their natural habitat. But they were expanding their range and adding to their repertory in response to a changing environment.

The process by which those creatures slowly straightened their curved bodies into an erect posture, with all the anatomical changes that had to have entailed, took many hundreds of thousands of years, but it offered them a number of advantages.

For one thing, standing and moving upright gave them a more commanding view of the surrounding terrain than would have been the case if they had needed all four limbs to maintain balance on the open ground. For another, it freed the upper limbs to carry things—food, for example, or infants—which allowed them to cover far longer distances. Moreover, they had eaten pulpy fruits and other forms of vegetation in the forests, but as they ventured out onto more open terrains they expanded their diet by becoming ground feeders as well, foraging for the grittier fare of the open grasslands—fibrous vegetables, roots, nuts, insects, small game. They had developed large, flat teeth for just that purpose, an earlier version of the efficient chewing arrangement that would one day become the human mouth. Standing upright also has the virtue of creating a natural cooling system for bodies no longer shaded by trees because it minimizes the amount of body surface exposed to the midday sun.

It would be a long time before our ancestors left the forest behind them altogether, but the *australopithecines* had pioneered a new *hominin* career on the ground—a new place in nature, a new way of life. Many millennia later, humankind would become master of the places its predecessors had entered so tentatively. But it is probably reasonable to suppose that in those early years they were as likely to be preyed upon as they were to pose a danger to other animal species with whom they shared the earth.

The major advantage they had, so far as one can tell across the huge distances that separate us in time, is that they were becoming social in a different way— and likely to have begun to develop specialized human ways of banding together in times of danger, sharing in times of scarcity, and caring for one another in times of need.

Second Glimpse: The First Humans Enter the Scene

The banks of fog separate a second time for us, let's say, about one and a half million years ago. A new genus, *Homo,* is now established in Africa and is about to spread out over a far wider range. Something distinctly human had now emerged from the various species of hominin that had been adapting to the changing landscape of Africa for several million years. The brains of these people (we can call them "people" now) had grown in capacity and were now somewhere between one-half and two-thirds the size of ours. Their bodies were similar to ours in many respects, but we would have eyed them a bit warily if we had encountered them on a stroll across the savanna, and they would surely have wondered about us. Their faces had not yet lost the heavy brow and the receding chin that had been one of the physical signatures of their primate ancestors. We may have thought them rather dim-witted, too. They did not have our capacity for abstract thought, or so it would have seemed to us, and their vocal equipment would probably not have permitted the complex forms of speech we have since inherited.

What most distinguishes these ancestors of ours from other animals, however, is not what they *looked like* but what they could *do.* They had been users of tools from the start, but they were by now *makers* of ever more complex ones.

They knew how to fashion crude mallets for cracking nuts to get at their meat and splitting bones to get at their marrow. They knew how to make implements for removing hides, scrapers for stripping them, choppers for breaking up large chunks of food, levers for prying roots and tubers out of the ground, and rude hand-axes for many other purposes.

Many of those tools were put to a single task—to process the flesh of other animals or to bring them down in the first place. Meat, then, whether obtained by scavenging or by active hunting, was becoming a principal source of protein for our ancestors, and that had a number of consequences—among them the fact that the eating of meat can help expand the size of a species' territorial range. We cannot draw a direct connection here, but we can at least note that increasing numbers of creatures who may have been our ancestors began to drift out of Africa and to make their way to places as far away as the Caucasus, China, and Southeast Asia.

One of the anatomical costs a lineage must pay for standing upright is to develop a narrower pelvis. And one of the anatomical costs it must pay for a better endowed brain is to develop a larger skull to house it. That, if you think about it for a moment, poses a serious dilemma, since an ever expanding skull will sooner or later have difficulty passing through an ever narrowing pelvis at time of birth. The evolutionary solution to that quandary has been for human offspring to emerge from the bodies of their mothers a good deal earlier in the developmental sequence than is the case for smaller-brained and more widely-beamed animals. The human body and the human brain have to do much of their expanding after birth. A colt is on her feet within hours of her birth. An osprey leaves his nest before the summer is out. The human infant, though, is helpless for a very extended period, which means that many forms of maturation that take place *within the womb* among other animals take place *within a social enclave* for us. The family circle, then, was quite literally becoming an extension of the womb, and other persons in the band had to arrange a pocket of safety for both mother and child.

The eating habits of those early humans were changing as well, and perhaps for that reason. More and more of them, no matter what their contribution to the larger food supply, were bringing it back to camp to be shared. That was no small matter. Most creatures who hunt or forage eat at the scene of their success. Pangs of hunger sent them prowling in the first place, and they satisfy that craving on the spot. Some animals store food for future use, of course, and most bring scraps of food home from their travels for hungry offspring. But humans come home to eat as a matter of routine, and that habit appeared relatively early in evolutionary time.

This much we know from fossil and archeological evidence, which is the source of these momentary breaks in the haze to begin with. Bones and artifacts tell their own story, and our ancestors inaugurated a lasting human habit by leaving garbage dumps in their wake—a much appreciated registry of what food they ate, what tools they used to prepare it, and how many of them assembled for the purpose.

But we may infer more. It seems evident from the kinds of food gathering they were engaged in that they depended on a good deal of cooperating and sharing in their work life. They assembled into organized troops, foraging together for roots and berries and grubs and small rodents, scavenging together for the carcasses of other animals, and, as time passed, hunting together for larger game they could not have managed to bring down individually.

Long before the emergence of our own species, it would appear, our ancestors had a well-developed sense of gathering around a central core—what we would later call "the hearth"—and the life they lived around that core has to have involved fairly elaborate systems of allocation, collaboration, and communication. They did not converse as we do, and would not be able to for some time yet, but they were obviously in touch with one another in ways unknown to creatures that had preceded them.

The changes being described here, of course, took place over enormous stretches of time. It is almost impossible for us to get a sense of what it means to say that some feature or other was shaped gradually over a few million years. Decades, centuries, even millennia are but flickering moments in geological time, and the terms we use to describe change on so vast a scale are bound to seem inadequate to the task.

The main thing to be learned from these glimpses through the fog is that some form of social organization had become a part of the hominin career very early in the game, long before any animals appeared on the scene looking or thinking like us. The significance of this can hardly be exaggerated. It means that all of the changes that have taken place in our lineage over the past two or three million years, and particularly the remarkable expansion of the human brain, were adaptations *to* an environment in which *social life was already a prominent feature*. It means that when modern humans emerged from those countless eons of natural selection, they had been *shaped by*—and in that sense were a *product of*—social life. We were not the first, by any means. What makes us distinct is not the fact that we came into the world adapted to social living but that we made something entirely new of it: language, culture, mind, and the other specializations we will be talking about in what follows.

We humans have been selected for living in social clusters in largely the same way that fish have been selected for living in water. So it is simply inaccurate, as we will have occasion to note later, to think of social life as a convenient arrangement, a kind of contract, created by fully evolved humans to make their everyday lives more orderly or comfortable. Our true biological niche—our natural habitat—is a vast tissue of families, tribes, peoples, communities, and other groupings. We are, quite literally, *made for* them.

Third Glimpse: Modern Humans

The mists part a third time. It is now 35,000 years ago—the day before yesterday in evolutionary time. Fossil and archeological evidence is a good deal more plentiful for this more recent dating than was the case earlier, but, even so, the data we now have on hand is so scattered about that it still seems as though we are peering through those banks of fog into the past. The creatures we are looking at now are known to specialists by different names: *modern Homo sapiens, Homo sapiens sapiens,* "anatomically modern humans," or simply *Homo sapiens.* But it no longer matters all that much. We are looking at ourselves.

These ancestors of ours did not speak any languages now in use, but they conversed fluently with one another. They were probably leaner and more muscular than we because they lived more active lives. But at the same time they were a good deal more susceptible to accidents and illness and died on the average a good deal younger.

There is much debate within the ranks of specialists as to how long modern humans had graced the scene before this glance at them, or, for that matter, what it really means to say that our lineage had crossed that invisible line separating older forms of humankind from more modern ones. But the important thing is to have a sense of what happened to those people in the million and a half years that elapsed since our last glimpse of them.

They had become experienced makers of tools, having learned not only how to shape natural materials to fit some template in their minds but to fasten those

shapes to pieces of bone or wood in such a way as to make them more efficient—hafting a good cutting stone to a wood handle to make an axe, for
example, or attaching a sharp stone tip to a pole to make a spear. They had also
become resolute hunters and fishers as well as enterprising gatherers of vegetable matter, at least in part because their ability to do things together, to collaborate, had grown dramatically with the gift of speech.

But their most important talent was an ability to exploit the riches of the land
around them by compensating for their own fragilities. They knew how to
convert a wide range of animal and vegetable matter into digestible protein by
preparing it over a fire. They knew how to use the furs and hides of better
endowed animals to protect them from the cold. And they were about to learn,
if they did not already know, how to harness the greater strength and endurance
of dogs and horses, oxen and camels, to their own purposes, and to use sails and
wheels and sleds and pack animals to transport them to places where their own
limited physiques were unequal to the task.

Other species can develop new strengths only through countless generations
of trial and error. But human beings simply borrow or invent them—capitalizing
on the hard-won adaptations of other creatures or drawing on other bounties of
the world to compensate for what nature has been slow to supply. So Inuit
hunters and fishers, for example, could learn in a slow moment of recognition
how to prepare for wintry cold by wrapping themselves in the same skins that
other arctic animals had taken thousands of generations to develop.

The brain that finally emerged from those millions of years of evolutionary
change is restless, cunning, inventive, curious. Its most important faculties—at
least so far as human survival is concerned—are its ability to *symbolize* and its
inclination toward *sociability*. We will pause for a moment on each of those
topics.

A symbol is a sound, a gesture, an object, a token, a signal that stands for—
serves as a reminder of—something else. When the mind is able to conjure up
an image or an idea as the result of seeing a sight or hearing a sound, it is
symbolizing. If you say "tree" to me, I will see the thing the word refers to in
my mind's eye. If you show me a swastika, I will be reminded of a profound
horror. This may not seem like a very difficult task for an advanced brain to
perform, but the fact is that human beings are the only creatures who can engage
in that mental activity in any sustained way. If any one characteristic can be said
to serve as the identifying signature of the human animal, this is likely it. Our

brains have the capacity to name things, to classify them, to call them to mind. And this allows us not only to store knowledge away in the vaults of our minds but to communicate it to other humans through the medium of language.

Other creatures communicate in the sense that they pass signals back and forth in prescribed ways. They squawk or growl or chirp or bark. They preen their feathers or fan their gills or puff out their jowls. They display colors or emit scents or thump the ground or go into elaborate ritual dances. Signals like these contain messages, of course, but they are for the most part steps in a program choreographed by nature. One creature senses that the time for mating has come and sends a signal that will elicit a satisfactory response from a chosen partner. Another creature senses a dangerous presence slithering through the grass or lurking in the underbrush and makes a sound that will alarm its fellows into flight. These signals convey information, of course, and they can be learned, but they are not the product of thought in the sense we generally use that term, and they do not involve much in the way of symbolizing. They are triggered by sensory mechanisms and have as their object to trigger similar reactions on the part of others. That is the dance of life.

For all practical purposes, however, modern humans are less reliant on those innate tour guides that help steer other creatures through the perplexities of existence. As our brain grew in size and complexity, it developed an ability to improvise that added appreciably to our repertory, and since then the basic organizing principle of human life has been in many ways different from that of other creatures. We collaborate with one another by the use of language. We ponder things. To put the matter too simply, we draw on the accumulated lore of the culture in which we mature more than on inclinations encoded in our gene plasm. For us, the dance of life is still in part a choreography devised by natural forces, but our *human* nature is largely shaped by social experience.

Our ancestors learned the ways of fire 400,000 years ago or so. It was a very important moment in the history of the lineage. Fire allowed people to turn the night into a shadowy version of the day, supplying light by which they could prepare foods or fashion tools or cure hides. It allowed them to recapture some of the warmth of summer in the cold of winter. It allowed them to soften the sinews of the toughest animal and the fibers of the toughest plant. And it offered them a new measure of security as well, since other animals proved to be instinctively wary of the fluttering light a fire projects.

It is easy to imagine, moreover, that fire did something to quicken the human sense of communion and fellow feeling. In our time, the hearth serves as a symbol of home and stead, and so it may have been long ago. It was where food was prepared and meals shared. It was where families huddled for protection from the cold and the dangers of the dark. It was where they clustered in sleep. It is common even now for persons gathered around a hearth or camp fire to tell stories, share memories, find ways of being in touch, and become more firmly a part of a communal whole. It is always a mistake to assume that individuals of another kind and another time reacted as we do now, and the only witnesses we can call on in the fossil and archeological record are silent objects. But we can wonder.

A good deal had happened to the people we are now looking at through that break in the mist 35,000 years ago. But it is important to appreciate that when we trace our lineage backward in time we have a tendency to assume that our ancestors cut a finer figure on the world's stage than they in fact did. An ancient naturalist looking in on those people without knowing what would happen to them (if we can imagine so strange a thing for the moment) may not have been able to see that these struggling folk would be so successful. It was still much too early for a David to boast of being fearfully and wonderfully made or for a Hamlet to muse that he and his kind were an amazing piece of work. But we were then on the verge of an explosion of growth that would soon make us the most dominant form of life the world had seen.

The continuing drama of our species has moved to the theater of social history as we make and remake the environment in which we live. The fate of our more distant ancestors was to change in barely perceptible phases over geological time as they adapted to a shifting environment. But human beings now store the experiences of the generations that precede them in a far more rapid manner than the processes of evolution are able to, and in that sense we invent our own fate.

Fearfully and wonderfully made? David did not know the half of it. We have arms that can pick up objects weighing hundreds of tons when we are at the controls of a crane. We have voices that can be heard thousands of miles away because we know how to operate telephones. We have eyes that can see stars hundreds of thousands of miles away because we know the ways of the telescope. We have wings that can fly across oceans in a matter of hours and teeth that can tear away the sides of a mountain in a matter of minutes. Evolution has provided us with brains that can bring about change far faster than any other natural processes are able to, and *those brains themselves are a product of social life.*

One Final Glimpse

At the risk of further oversimplifying a complex set of events, we will pause for a moment to construct a short bridge of words to help convey us into the terrain we will be considering in the next chapter.

No matter how we go about tracing our line of descent, all but a minuscule fraction of our ancestors were foragers. They wandered in search of grains, berries, nuts, roots, and other kinds of vegetable matter. They caught smaller and more agile game in artfully placed snares. They stalked larger game and brought it down with rocks or clubs, and, later, with spears or bows and arrows. As time passed, they ventured out into shallow water for fish as they learned to make boats, paddles, hooks, and nets.

They foraged as no other animals could, as we have seen. Still, they were like most other animals in that they had to pluck the bounty of the land from where it lay, trudging on foot to locales where plants grew full or game was plentiful. That was the only livelihood we humans knew throughout the history of our species, and it continued to be our principal source of subsistence well into modern times. To this day, in fact, anthropologists continue to study bands of nomadic hunters living in remote corners of the world—the Mbuti of the Ituri Rain Forest we met in an earlier chapter are an example—but that way of life is on the verge of extinction and probably should be spoken of in the past tense.

Foraging bands had to be nomadic, small, and compact because calories are usually spread too sparsely across the land to feed larger groups of people. And, too, members of the band had to carry with them everything they owned on their endless sweeps across the land. So possessions had to be spare—a few utensils, a few light tools and weapons, a few hides, a leather pouch containing herbs, strips of smoked meat, a handful of nuts, a religious emblem, or an insignia of office. No one could acquire a significant store of goods, so the band did not pay as much attention to status distinctions as we now tend to, even though someone might be recognized as having a gift for leading the hunt or for telling stories or for deciphering the portent of dreams or curing illnesses. One member of the band might be called "chief" and another "shaman," but those titles do not appear to have conferred much in the way of reward or even privilege. Moke was honored for his years of experience and his wisdom, but he worked the same hours as everyone else in the tribe and died as poor as he had been when he was born.

This was on the verge of changing. Not long after our third look into the past—18,000 years, ago, say—an ever-increasing number of settled communities began to appear on the human landscape in places rich enough in nutrients to sustain the persons gathering there. That would include: stretches of land where wild grains grew so plentifully that a single harvest could nourish those living nearby for long periods of time, ocean shores where tides deposited fresh food twice a day, open fields where flocks of migrating birds and herds of migrating animals known to pause on their journey elsewhere, river banks that overlooked waters full of fish and other aquatic creatures, and so on.

Persons who live in settled locations can employ a stratagem that is simply not available to foragers on the move—to store the surpluses that had been gathered in good times for use in more difficult times. This was the beginning of what is sometimes known as "storage economies," or even the "age of storage." So the readiness to settle down and the ability to store and preserve were important preludes to what would soon become the age of agriculture. Starting 12,000 years ago or so a vast shift began to take place in the way humankind derived its living from the land. The change was slow, scarcely perceptible as historical time is measured, and it took the form of a gradual shift to more settled forms of horticulture. People began to take advantage of the fact that they did not need to depend on the normal processes of nature to provide nourishment but could set those processes into motion themselves. They could plant seeds, tend the shoots that emerged, and harvest the issue. They could corral animals, gather them into herds, and draw on them as a reliable source of food. In a sense, they could reproduce the rhythms of nature themselves.

We have no way of knowing whether our ancestors welcomed this change in circumstance, as older generations of paleontologists took for granted—it was "progress," after all, a step forward in the steady advance of human prospects— or whether they turned to it grudgingly to accommodate changes in the environment or their own growing numbers. The process was so gradual over time that our best guess has to be that no one gave it a moment's thought. It was just one of those quiet drifts that mark human history.

Whatever its original inspiration, the idea itself was slow to take command. If we could view those transitional centuries on a speeded-up film, we would see band members begin to take a head or two of cattle with them on their nomadic rounds or perhaps start a rudimentary garden at the edge of some frequently visited base camp in anticipation of the next time the band passed that way. The rest of life, meantime, went on in the same way it had for millennia. As the centuries rolled by on our film, though, we would notice that the herds and the gardens were growing larger and that more and more people were settling into permanent compounds. Hunters and gatherers were becoming herders and growers. The process was gradual, but it was a true revolution nonetheless, as telling a shift in the human condition as has taken place in the history of the species.

For one thing, people who live in settled villages learn to place a different value on land, and since they no longer need to carry their possessions around with them everywhere they go, their inventory of goods can expand enormously. The result was that individuals who turned out to be particularly enterprising or unscrupulous or lucky could acquire larger parcels of land and other forms of wealth—surplus measures of grain, more richly crafted tools and weapons and dishware, larger herds, grander dwellings. Jean Jacques Rousseau, from whom we shall hear again shortly, wrote toward the end of the 18th century:

> The first man who, having enclosed a piece of land, bethought himself of saying "this is mine," and found people simple enough to believe him, was the true founder of civil society.

That is a bitter but shrewd observation. Where one finds surplus goods that can be hoarded as a form of wealth; where one finds possessions that come to have special value because of the materials from which they are made or the quality of the workmanship that goes into them; and, above all, where one finds individuals who draw property lines around parcels of land, get away with calling them "mine," and derive some measure of advantage from doing so—there one finds rank, inequality, and the beginnings of class structure. That has become a simple reality to most of us. But it would have been an amazing concept to Moke, for instance, who "owned" nothing but a net, a bow, a few arrows, and a small cache of other articles that he carried with him as he moved lightly through the forest. The very idea that one can be the master of trees or running water or stretches of land would have seemed preposterous to him. Indeed, if you were to inform him that you held title to a section of the Ituri

Rain Forest, he would look at you with the same bewilderment as if you had told him you owned a section of the sky.

Cultivating the land can result in a surplus if things go well, and that surplus, in turn, can alter the texture of human life completely. When growers produce more calories than are necessary for their own survival, the population is likely to grow, and the new stocks of people generally leave the farmlands in search of other livelihoods. So the land nourishes those who live on it and work it, but it also nourishes new classes of persons who are then free to turn their energies to other pursuits—to join bureaucracies or fight wars, to teach or preach or tell ancient tales, and to take up the other callings we associate with civilization. The point is not that it takes growers and herders to create a surplus. A successful group of hunters and gatherers can do that, and much easier. The point is that it takes a settled way of life to *store* a surplus and to make something of it.

Human history over the past ten thousand years is as much as anything the story of what our species has done with its surplus calories. If we were to return to our speeded-up film to follow the period between the earlier years of horti-culture and the dawn of modern times, we would probably notice two things. It would be evident at a glance that most of humankind remained in village communities through the whole of those thousands of years, bound to the soil or the seashores and largely unchanged. But our attention would soon be drawn to a few locations scattered here and there across the countryside in which people were gathering and commerce was growing. The pace of human activity was obviously picking up in those places—hesitantly throughout the early moments of our strip of film, but gaining so much momentum as the centuries passed before our eyes that it would appear to end in a blur of activity. Villages became towns and then cities. The holdings of tribal chiefs grew into feudal demesnes and then states.

At one point as the film spins by we will pass over that divide when knowl-edge of the past no longer depends on archeological remains but can be traced from written records as well. Human history is then no longer the story of a species groping toward survival but a story of ancient empires in Asia, dynas-ties in Egypt, city states in Greece and Rome—all of these being matters we will return to later when we discuss villages and cities.

But it should be pointed out as this discussion draws to a close that a deep and lasting dilemma was posed for humankind when those who worked the land learned how to produce enough calories to nourish those who did not.

Christian theologians speak of "original sin" when referring to the time Adam and Eve ate of the tree of knowledge and so learned about good and evil. From a sociological point of view, though, the ability to produce and retain a surplus can be seen as a kind of original sin as well. No one was at fault, really, so "sin" might be too judgmental a term here. But when people left the soil in sufficient number, new opportunities opened up for the expression of human intelligence, human restlessness, and, of course, human cruelty and greed. People perfected the art of exploiting nature and the art of exploiting one another. They found new ways to sort their fellows into inclusive "we's" for whom one cares with all one's heart and exclusive "they's" for whom one feels nothing other than contempt or pity. They invented new forms of cooperation and new engines of destruction. The surplus, in short, has brought us a mixed array of blessings—individuals who could devote all their ingenuity to killing and thieving and enslaving, as well as to art, poetry, medicine, philosophy, and science. And the world has been ever since a place of conflict and harmony, grace and malice, caring and cruelty, generosity and greed, division and communion—all of them subjects to be touched on in what follows.

Discovering the Social

A GRADUAL BUT DECISIVE SHIFT IN THE intellectual climate of Europe began to take hold about the time the 16th century yielded to the 17th. It took the form of a new sensibility, slow to make itself felt, that was made up in part of curiosity and wonder and skepticism—all of them crucial to the posing of serious questions. It was the dawn of a new age of investigation.

In the next chapter, we will meet three masters of the sociological tradition. In order to understand the nature of their contributions, however, we will have to appreciate that the milieu in which they lived and the conceptual lens through which they looked at the world were quite new to Western thought.

In the last chapter, we went on a hurried tour across the entire span of human existence on earth. In this chapter, we will take an equally hurried rush across several centuries of European history. The objective here, as was the case earlier, is not to offer a comprehensive review of a time or a subject matter but to draw attention to a few meaningful landmarks and other points of interest as we spin by.

The Medieval Temper

It is clear to our modern way of thinking that the human world is made up of individuals, meaning independent beings who respond to the promptings of their own hearts and construct a life for themselves suited to their own needs. It is also clear that those individuals are attached to one another in a hundred ways, gathered into families, parishes, communities, peoples, faiths, and a variety of other social formations. So we find it fairly easy to speak of something called "the individual" and something called "society." But it was not so long ago that people would have had a difficult time understanding what we mean by either of those terms.

Suppose that we had been transported by a time capsule to rural Europe in the middle of the 12th or 13th centuries. And suppose, further, that our objective in doing so was to study the cultural temper of the medieval mind in more or less the same way that an anthropologist might study the ethos of a distant people in our own time (Colin Turnbull in the Ituri Rain Forest, for example).

We would be undertaking this journey for largely the same reason Turnbull did. There is virtually nothing in the historical record about the people he went to study, nor is there about the people we now propose to visit. Chroniclers of the time were primarily concerned with the goings-on of courts and of battlefields. Diaries of the time were composed by the literate for the literate. The songs and myths and legends and stories of the time dealt primarily with the deeds of the powerful rather than the days of the working poor. So we know very little about them. What follows, then, belongs in the category of guesswork, although it is informed by at least a vague understanding of what those times were like.

Here is the report we might have filed upon our return from that strange journey into the past:

To most of those who lived there, the medieval world was something like a vast tapestry. The design of that tapestry was understood to have been conceived in the mind of God, and the millions of people who turned the soil for a living or worked in some related trade were taught to visualize themselves as something akin to the threads making up that tapestry. Each thread was embedded in the weave. Each was fixed in place. The lessons both of religion and of everyday experience told common people that the integrity of the tapestry and the coherence of the design depended on those threads remaining for the most part where they were—each contributing its own speck of color, its own grain of substance, to the larger whole. People were told that they had been brought into the world in order to follow an assigned calling, to occupy an assigned station, to fill a defined spot. Everyone had an established niche in the order of things, and that niche defined who they were.

If we were to ask a peasant working his field to identify himself—"who are you?"—he would very likely be astonished to hear so absurd a question, but once he recovered from the surprise he would probably speak of his position in the tapestry. He is attached to a particular portion of land, by which he means not only that *it belongs to him* in one sense or another, but that *he belongs to it.* He has a clearly defined location within a continuing lineage, and he feels a profound sense of responsibility both to those who went before him and those who are yet to come. He belongs to—truly *belongs* to—a family, a parish, a village, and his niche in life is where those differing connections meet in the weave. If he is torn away from that spot for any reason, he may feel so reduced in substance that he no longer sees himself as a complete person. He has lost his place, his calling, and, in some respects, his identity. That is why ostracizing people or exiling them from home villages was so fearful a penalty.

This kind of embeddedness was given a new meaning for me when I was interviewing migrant farm workers from Haiti in South Florida with the help of a skilled anthropologist who spoke Creole and was serving as my interpreter. When I asked the people I was interviewing "Where are you from?" in English— by which I meant "what part of Haiti do you call home?"—she seemed to me to be translating my question differently in Creole. When I asked her about that, she said, "I know what you are trying to find out, but your question will not get you there. So I am asking them 'Where are you a person?'" I think I learned more in that instant than I normally do in a decade. "Where are you a person?" That's it exactly. It's a long way from 13th-century Europe to contemporary Haiti, of course, but I will guess here that medieval peasants of long ago and their modern counterparts in Haiti share something of an understanding of the relationship between *place* and *identity.*

A particular cast of mind and sense of self would almost surely have accompanied that worldview. Our medieval villager, fixed in those tight knots of attachment, would have found it a good deal harder than we to imagine that he could have ideas or tastes or ambitions different from those of his neighbors. He would have found it harder to imagine himself in a calling other than the one he followed or in a locale other than the one he occupied. He would have found it difficult to imagine that he could do things differently now than they had been done in the past. He did not view himself as having a unique personality or an individual identity in the sense we use those terms now. If we were to ask him about his "lifestyle" or what he does to express his "individuality" or to protect his "personal space," he might very well hear it as if it were in an alien tongue.

This does not mean for a moment that those peasants were less knowing or less astute than we. They used their powers of reason to solve different kinds of problems and they filled their minds with different kinds of information. They knew the shape and even the feel of every inch of land in their dominion. They could read the motions of the sky, the stirrings of the land, and the habits of other living creatures as easily as we can read a page of text. We might wonder instead what people like that would think of us, so deeply lacking in intellect that we need calendars to tell us the time of year, clocks to tell us the time of day, maps to tell us where we are, and specialists in weather to forecast the most elementary motions of nature.

Nor did it mean that peasants always accepted their lot passively. Marc Bloch, the great medieval historian, spoke of "the patient silent struggles stubbornly carried on" by rural peasants—those quiet acts of sabotage and evasion that a distinguished political scientist of our time, James C. Scott, called "the weapons of the weak." But their place in the fabric remained as it was for the rest of their days.

The Age of Reason: Discovering the Individual

Near the beginnings of what we in the West find it convenient to call the modern age, this began to change. It was a slow process, and it is essential for us to avoid the mistake of thinking that it was as abrupt as our descriptions of it are bound to make it seem. The medieval tapestry appeared to be unraveling, the separate threads working their way loose from the larger weave. People no longer felt that they were held so firmly in place by ties of family, parish, and community—no longer so bound by old traditions and customs. It began to occur to people that they were entities unto themselves—individual agents who were propelled by a personal generator within rather than by forces pressing in from the outside.

As a political matter, the medieval church passed over that point in its long and steady decline where one could simply say that it no longer reigned as the prevailing source of authority in Christendom. The age of faith was far from over. People continued to believe fervently and worship energetically. But the waning of the church as a political force meant that a number of aging doctrines were becoming matters of open debate. How one should think or conduct oneself was no longer as clear as it once had been because old moralities and orthodoxies were losing a good deal of their meaning. So the king who quarreled with the Pope on matters of religious law, or the lords who quarreled with their king on matters of civil law, were entering mental territories that had been less familiar to their predecessors. People were being invited by the emerging spirit of the time to consider a different sense of possibilities on their own.

As a scientific matter, a quite different sense of how the physical world works marked the beginning of a new age. The findings of scientists like Copernicus, Kepler, Newton, and Galileo indicated that the universe operates in an altogether different manner than medieval scholars had supposed. This was not just a revolution in science, then, but a revolution in thought. It was the foundation of a new philosophy, a new morality, a new cosmology, a new way to apprehend not only the physical but the human world.

The new physics taught that the universe bore very little resemblance to a tapestry with millions of threads fixed tightly in place. On the contrary, it was a thing of constant movement, of action and reaction, of bodies orbiting one another in patterns of the most elegant synchrony. It was assumed that all of this had been arranged by God in the beginning, to be sure. It was His handiwork. Still, the cosmos now appeared as an immense and wondrous engine, an intricate clockwork that operated according to its own mechanical laws. This meant that the universe had an order and a logic that could be discerned by everyday mortals through the use of their own minds.

The new physics also taught that a person's place in the cosmos was altogether different than what theologians had been suggesting for a thousand years or more. Earth, far from being the center of the universe, was revealed to be a tiny, pale, insignificant planet. It was a fly-speck in endless oceans of space, an instant in the wash of time, a detail lost in the sweep of celestial bodies. One might suppose that this was a humbling thought, and so it may have been for some. But for others, the effect of this realization was to increase the amount of confidence they had in themselves. True, the universe had been exposed as immense, and humankind's place in it as pitifully small. But if one could really comprehend that immensity and discover its secrets, here indeed was reason for pride!

Thoughtful people, then, came to feel that they had space to stretch out in and talents to exercise. They could learn the ways of the stars and explore the uncharted surfaces of the earth. They could manufacture goods, create markets, establish institutions, and build nations. And so a new attitude began to develop that had a pronounced influence on what people thought when they contemplated themselves. They were far less likely to view themselves as scraps of tissue embedded in a family, a parish, a village, or any other collectivity—tesserae in a vast mosaic—and far more likely to view themselves as separate entities moving under their motive powers. They had minds, wills, personalities. They were individuals.

These faculties, moreover, came to be viewed as something inborn and innate, a part of human nature. And this notion contained within it the germ of a very important political theory. If a person's true nature is contained within her, is a part of her natural endowment as a human being, then it is only logical to argue that this nature can only be freely expressed when all the bonds that attach her to other people and particularly to other institutions are sliced away. That is, if the puppet proves to have a sound mind of its own, a motor that drives it from within, then both good sense and common decency would seem to insist that the strings pulling it this way and that be sheared. Old customs and obligations, that is to say, should be seen no longer as sources of security and direction but as obstacles that inhibit the expression of an individual's true nature.

It is hard to argue with this idea from an ideological point of view, for the major issue raised by it is one of human freedom. But, as we shall see shortly, it contains a deeply flawed theory of human nature. The Age of Reason was beginning, and with it a vision of social life that came to dominate European thinking for most of the 17th and 18th centuries and is still a prominent part of the intellectual climate in which we live now.

Among the key figures in the development of that vision were Thomas Hobbes (1588–1679), John Locke (1632–1704), and Jean Jacques Rousseau (1712–1778). The three thinkers could hardly have been less alike in political ideology or personal temperament, but they had a similar outlook on the origins of society and on the nature of human nature.

The Sociologies of Hobbes, Locke, and Rousseau

One of the first notes in what was to become a chorus was sounded by Thomas Hobbes. In his great work, *The Leviathan,* published in 1651, he proposed that the mental faculties of human beings are wholly natural, planted there by God, but that the social institutions in which people become enmeshed are mere inventions, contrivances, fancies.

People once lived in a state of nature, Hobbes supposed, without rules or governments or institutions of any kind. They just did what was in their hearts to do. That appears to have been an agreeable arrangement in many ways, but the problem that presented itself was that people in a state of nature, doing as they pleased, tended to be selfish, predatory, greedy, aggressive, and for that reason lived in a state of perpetual conflict, a "war of every one against every one." The outcome of this, as Hobbes delicately phrased it, was that their lives were "solitary, poor, nasty, brutish, and short."

These ancient ancestors of ours did not seem to have minded very much that their lives were nasty and brutish—this was, after all, their nature—but they took a decidedly dim view of the fact that their lives were short, so they gathered together into a social order to guard against the malice they knew to be in their hearts. They agreed to abide by common rules, to regulate property, to observe prohibitions against mayhem. The main provision of this contract, Hobbes assumed, was that people would yield their natural autonomy to a sovereign, and in the process forfeit their freedom for all time. It was the only arrangement they could think of for providing a rule of law.

The ideological significance of this philosophy is that it denies the divine right of kings—a deeply compelling issue of the time—in its claim that sovereigns derive their authority from a decision of the citizenry and not from an act of God. But it is at the same time an argument for authoritarian power, since the contract people agreed to in that long-forgotten past provided that the sovereign and his descendants, having once accepted a call from their people, are no longer accountable to them. A vote had been taken at the dawn of history, as it were, and that vote had settled the fate of the citizenry forever. Once they had voluntarily given up their natural liberty, they had given up the right to complain about the powers that ruled over them.

The sociological significance of Hobbes's philosophy, however, is his view that social institutions are not only invented out of thin air but accepted by the citizenry that created them with considerable reluctance. The human social order has no warrant in nature, and humankind has no natural need or even inclination to gather together into groupings. We do so only as a matter of calculation to protect individual self-interest.

The writings of John Locke, a young contemporary of Hobbes, reflect many of the same general themes, although with several crucial differences. Locke agreed that at some moment in the distant past people decided to submit to the authority of a sovereign and to join together in a social contract. But Locke thought that human beings in a state of nature, far from being nasty and brutish, tended on the whole to be a kindly, generous, and decent lot—like English gentry, one is tempted to suggest. Their main shortcoming was that they did not know how to regulate property, and as much as they admired their own liberty, it would seem, they yearned even more for an arrangement in which ownership of property could be registered and commerce could be transacted in an orderly fashion. So they, like Hobbes's unruly savages, invented civil society. The covenant they agreed to, however, differed from the one Hobbes had envisioned in a very important particular: the sovereign to whom the people decided to submit was himself a party to the agreement, and he is therefore accountable to his subjects.

The ideological significance of Locke's theory, then, is different from Hobbes's. Locke was arguing for democracy and even for the legitimacy of revolution, since when a ruler fails to live up to the terms of the covenant he has made with his subjects, they have the right to simply discharge him. It is the echo of Locke's voice, in fact, that can be heard in the opening sentences of the U.S. Declaration of Independence: "When in the course of human events . . ."

But the *sociological* significance of Locke's theory is essentially the same as Hobbes's. People may be sociable as a matter of natural temperament, but the institutions that govern them are an afterthought in human life—stratagems introduced to make the conduct of everyday life move more smoothly.

This brings us to Jean Jacques Rousseau, who was born eight years after Locke's death. Hobbes regarded human beings as naturally surly and dangerous, so he was inclined to view the social contract as a major gain for humanity. Locke regarded human beings as naturally kindly and neighborly, so he was inclined to see the social contract as a minor gain for humanity. But Rousseau regarded humankind in the state of nature as naturally perfect, without blemish, and he was inclined to view the social contract as a tragic loss to humanity. If Hobbes and Locke, each in his own way, were making an argument for human government, Rousseau was lashing out at the whole idea of civilization. "Man," he wrote, "is naturally good, and only by institutions is he made bad." He spoke with affection and even longing about "noble savages," referring not only to people who lived in the distant past but to contemporaries then roaming the forests and plains of the New World—a population that Europe as yet knew almost nothing about.

Why would such virtuous and content creatures agree to a binding social contract in the first place? Well, they could not figure out how to deal with property either, which, for all their innocence, they seem to have wanted to do quite badly, so they opted for human government as well. Rousseau was clearly not pleased with that decision. He said in a passage that we have already encountered:

> The first man who, having enclosed a piece of land, bethought himself of saying "this is mine," and found people simple enough to believe him, was the real founder of civil society.

Rousseau's vision of human history, then, is a dark and gloomy one. The noble savages become more entangled as the millennia roll by in an ever thicker web of customs and traditions, laws and ordinances, conventions and understandings, and in the process their natural faculties, their true selves, are stifled. The final blow is the formation of the state. The opening words of Rousseau's principal work on the subject (*Le Contrat Social* does not need to be translated here) struck that note sharply: "Man is born free, but everywhere he is in chains."

Hobbes, Locke, and Rousseau could hardly have been more unalike in their political and ideological readings of human history and in the conclusions they drew from it. But they shared a perspective on human nature and on human society that became one of the dominating ideas of the Age of Reason—the view that the human personality is naturally alien to the idea of society and that human instincts are either indifferent to or actively antagonistic to the bonds that draw people together into communal groupings. The actual nature of the human animal, then, is to be found in solitary freedom and not in the social institutions to which people become reluctantly attached.

The social contract theory and its various derivatives came under a good deal of strain as Europe emerged from the hopeful mood of the 17th and 18th centuries into the colder realities of the 19th. One of the lasting bequests of the Age of Reason was a commitment to rational forms of inquiry—to observation, investigation, experimentation—and before long it became apparent that some of the most telling philosophical conclusions of the age could not survive the findings of the scientific research it set into motion or the lessons of history it promoted. We will turn to those matters soon. Meantime, a brief detour.

A Note on the French Revolution

In order to understand the general intellectual texture of the 19th century, one almost has to begin with the last great event of the 18th century—the French Revolution. That tremendous moment changed the very flow of things. The leading thinkers of the Age of Reason, especially in France, had long nourished the hope that a new age was about to begin. The source of their hope was a logic that went something like this. If human beings are born with the natural power to reason things through by themselves, and if the social institutions in which they are ensnarled are nothing more than artificial contrivances, then what prevents them from reshaping the world according to the dictates of human reason? Nothing at all. The ability to create a perfect world lies in every human breast, and the way to free that innate ability, to give it room for expression, was to scrape away those crusts of tradition and do away with all the rest of the decaying debris of the old order. Alexis de Tocqueville wrote that the Revolution had a good deal more to do with "the regeneration of the human race than with the reformation of France."

So it was a profoundly hopeful time at first. Natural law would replace royal prerogative as the basis for government. Reason would replace power as its motive. Liberty would replace privilege as its objective. Persons everywhere would be cut loose from the old feudal moorings to which they had been so long held fast and be free to drift in the natural currents of the natural world.

That is not how the story unfolded, and the disappointment that followed the dimming of those hopes is an important part of the cultural and historical mood in which the study of society was soon to emerge. The new leaders, armed with philosophy and what appears to us now as a remarkably naïve confidence, could not rule. The power of reason soon proved to be an elusive quality at best. And the workings of the free market threatened to create as much disproportion and inequality and sheer human pain as the forces it had replaced. So it was becoming clear to observers at either end of the ideological spectrum that the experiment had worked only in part.

One lesson from the failed experiment—from a sociological point of view, at least—was that people do not always fare well when detached from tradition and community and the other secure niches that the English political philosopher Edmund Burke called the "inns and resting places" of the human spirit. Indeed, they sometimes resisted efforts to change the familiar fabric of custom with surprising obstinacy. Attempts on the part of the French to apply reason to the organization of everyday human life—to make it more measured, proportioned, orderly, sensible—appeared to fail more often than not. A logical new calendar was introduced and abandoned. A rational new way of partitioning France into more symmetrical parcels of land was proposed and forgotten. For it turned out that the manner in which people count their days and chart their lands is far more resistant to change than *les philososophes* had calculated. The human animal was a creature of custom after all!

Discovering the Social

In general, then, it became increasingly evident as the 19th century replaced the 18th that Enlightenment theories of human nature and human society did not well describe the realities they had drawn attention to. When thinking people cast a cool and discerning eye on the world around them, the social contract idea seemed more and more like a wistful fiction and less like an observation grounded in actual experience.

It was not plausible from a historical point of view, for one thing. Hobbes, Locke, and Rousseau might only have been employing a figure of speech when they wrote about the origins of the social contract, but in order for that parable to be converted into a workable theory, we have to be able to envision the framing of that agreement as an actual happening. And that is no easy matter. Was it signed in an open field like the famous Magna Carta? Not likely. Was it a more gradual and subtle arrangement, then? Presumably. But however we try to imagine it, the covenant could have been reached only if the partners to it already spoke the same language, had similar concepts of law and the nature of property, and shared other cultural understandings in common. Contracts are possible only among persons who already belong to a fairly advanced form of social order—an argument that Émile Durkheim, to whom you will be introduced soon, made with particular vigor. So human society had to have been in existence long before anyone could have met to confer about it.

Nor was it plausible from an anthropological standpoint. Hobbes, Locke, and Rousseau all thought that history moved from a condition of primitive freedom to a condition of civilized restraint. The "state of nature," for each of them, was characterized by an atmosphere of license, impulsiveness, and individual liberty. That was what so unnerved Hobbes and what so appealed to Rousseau.

But this vision of the human past could not survive the test of actual observation, because it was soon obvious that people who live in preliterate societies are so bound by custom and tradition that it makes little sense to think of them as uninhibited and free from the restraints of a social order.

Moreover, the optimism of the Age of Reason, already sobered by the aftermath of the Revolution and early findings from a new age of inquiry, was exposed to yet another source of disappointment; for Europe in the middle of the 19th century seemed to many to offer a dismal portrait of what would happen if individual people were left to the mercies of natural law and the free market. It was a period of increasing urbanization and industrialization, of movement and change. Large populations had drifted out from the confines of village and parish, and in doing so had distanced themselves from old traditions and obligations. They were free to flow with the benign currents of the market. They were free from the yoke of custom.

And what happened to them then? Vast numbers, as it turned out, left the countryside and drifted into growing cities like Lyon and Manchester and Dresden, where they lived in wretched hovels, worked fifteen hours a day, contracted diseases they had never even heard of before, and slumped into a state of numbed demoralization.

Imagine that you are a veteran of the several hundred years I have been speaking of here, having lived through all those excitements and hopes. It is 1850, let's say, and you are looking out over the grimy squalor of a city like Manchester, your mind no longer as sure as it once had been about the triumph of human reason. To some degree, at least, the pure air and clear water of the countryside might begin to look better to you despite the constraining obligations that go with them. The crofter's hut might begin to look a little better to you despite the dark shadow of the landlord. Village life, with its old simplicities and securities, might begin to look better to you despite the heavy hand of custom pressing down upon it.

So a new idea finds its way into the conceptual vocabulary of those who think about the human social order. What thinkers of the Age of Reason called *liberty,* thinkers of the middle of the 19th century were beginning to call *alienation* or *anomie* or something similar, for if liberty consists in being able to act independently from tradition and communality and an oppressive sense of duty, then alienation and anomie consist in being torn loose from precisely those same things—tradition, community, and, yes, a sense of duty. And the fact of the matter seemed to be that vast numbers of people were suffering from just that kind of separation. However much we respect the idea of personal liberty as an ideological and spiritual matter, we have no choice but to observe at the same time that human beings are social animals, bound to each other in ties of fellowship and dependent to some considerable extent on the force of custom. That, too, is built into our nature.

Now, one could respond to such a conclusion in a number of ways. A conservative like Edmund Burke might long for a return to the authority and the moral tidiness of times past. A radical like Karl Marx might long for a whole new order—a new form of human government, a new morality, a new set of social institutions. But either way, it is to be understood that people have a natural inclination to live in the embrace of society and do not fare well outside it.

It was with just such realizations that the Age of Reason began its slow fade and the age of sociology began to emerge.

Coming to Terms with Social Life:
Marx, Durkheim, Weber

IN THE LAST CHAPTER, we discussed the ways in which European thinkers came to recognize the importance of "the social." A new conceptual terrain had been opened up, and persons who cared about such matters began to wonder how they might best navigate that terrain, how they might best explore it. Years later, looking back, sociologists would ask who had been the most important of those pathfinders. "We stand on the shoulders of giants," Isaac Newton is credited with having said. But the naming of giants is no easy matter. It took a vast *procession* of persons to produce what we now call sociology or the study of social life more generally. Where to begin?

One of the shelves in my study has been set aside for books on the history of sociological thought, and every one of them seems to begin the procession with a different individual and at a different time. As we make our way along the shelf, in alphabetical order, we will note that Kenneth Allan begins his account with Karl Marx (as will I). Raymond Aron opens his with a brilliant French observer and jurist named Charles Louis de Montesquieu, who was born in 1689 and died in 1755. Harry Elmer Barnes—in the oldest book on the shelf—reached all the way back to Herodotus, who lived in Greece some twenty-five centuries ago. Randall Collins and Michael Makowsky open their account with Henri de Saint-Simon, who was born five years after the death of Montesquieu and lived through the first quarter of the 19th century. Lewis A. Coser, finally, starts off with Auguste Comte, who coined the term "sociology" and lived from 1798 to 1857. Quite a range, that.

But where one starts really does not matter. We are speaking of a continuous procession here, one without any obvious beginning, and no matter where we decide to enter it, no matter whom we nominate as founder of the tradition, the important thing is to get a sense of the direction of the flow itself.

Comte probably does deserve special mention here, partly because he taught us to name what we do "sociology" and partly because he made the first compelling argument for including the new discipline among the sciences. He was also the first to declare, in a voice others could not ignore, that the human social order is an entity unto itself, one that operates according to its own laws and logics, and is not just an extension of the human mind: "Society," he said, "is no more decomposable into individuals than a geometric surface is into lines, or a line into points." He deserves a special place in the procession for that line alone.

The three masters I am turning to now not only found new ways to convey in words—to come to turns with—what goes on out there in social life. They created a permanent shift in the way our eyes are focused, in the way we see.

The World According to Karl Marx

Marx was born in Trier, Germany, in 1818, and died in London in 1883. The details of his early life give us no reason to anticipate what we now know the rest of his life would be like aside from the fact that he was a person of special gifts and formidable intelligence. Both of his parents came from a long line of rabbis, but his father was almost exuberantly secular, a true son of the Enlightenment. He had even converted to Christianity as an adult in a move that everyone understood to have been a matter of professional convenience. Karl himself, so far as one can tell from this distance in time, had a comfortable and affectionate childhood.

At the age of 17, Marx entered the University of Bonn, and a short year later transferred to Berlin. Such a beginning was standard fare for those of his background and time, and he was known, or so the scanty records suggest, as a congenial companion in the taverns and beer halls that were so significant a part of university life then. He even fought a duel, as young men of the period often did, and he carried a scar on his face as a lasting emblem of that event. It is hard to see anything offering an indication of what was to be his future in those years, too.

Early in his time at Berlin, though, Marx seems to have closed himself off from the world around him to read, to study, to ponder, and then to re-read. He retreated into his own lodgings for months at a time and withdrew from the company of his fellows. He "repulses friendships," he wrote later, speaking of himself in the third person, "neglects nature, art, and society, sits up through many nights, fights through many battles, undergoes many agitations both from inward and outward causes."

During those long and lonely months, he became familiar with (and the master of) many of the philosophies of his time. On the one hand, he drew from them the outlines of a theory of history that owed a great deal to Georg Wilhelm Friedrich Hegel, who had died but a few years earlier. We will return to that shortly. But more important over the long term, he seems to have emerged from the experience with the first inklings of what was probably his main contribution to social thought—that the massive billow of words and utterances and abstract constructions that spill out into the world from the desks of philosophers and other commentators on the true state of things converge to form a thick cloud bank that has as its principal objective to obscure the hard realities of life for ordinary persons. We will return to that theme later too, but I will note now that Marx emerged from that period of study with a wary distrust of a large part of what was then understood to be human learning, and that was virtually to doom him to a career of professional loneliness. It was his destiny to view the social world from a place outside it—an isolated observation booth, as it were—from which to see things anew.

Marx was forced to leave his native Germany for his outspoken political views and found himself in Paris at the age of 25. That is where Comte lived at the age of 45, still a relatively young man. They never met or even knew of each other, probably, so there is no story to be told there. But they looked out at the same human landscape and saw quite different things. Comte thought he saw scientists and engineers hard at work with an earnest new class of industrialists to fine-tune the engines of progress and bring reason to bear on all human activities. It was that Enlightenment flame, still flickering. Marx, however, thought he saw a degree of misery lurking in the shadows that was not reflected at all in the plans of engineers, the theories of philosophers, or the debates of parliaments.

Marx drew a connection between the misery he sensed out there and the thick curtain of indifference that he thought was being drawn around it, and that has changed the way we think. For his insight was that humankind is not only blind to inconvenient truths but *systematically* so; that the ideas people arrive at, and especially people in positions of power, are designed so as to camouflage reality, to obscure it, to screen it from sight.

At some point during this period in Paris, Marx became acquainted with a like-minded spirit from England named Frederick Engels, who was then working on a book to be entitled *The Conditions of the Working Class in England,* published in 1848. The two would become close collaborators for the rest of Marx's life.

It would be foolish to try to convey the full range of Marx's thought in the space of a few pages, even supposing that I was up to the task. It is a rich, complicated, subtle weave, a mixture of strands from philosophy, history, economics, and all the other disciplines that would one day be considered members in good standing of the social sciences. Marx never used the term "sociology" so far as I know—certainly not to describe his own scholarly work—but there is a brilliant sociology to be found in that weaving nonetheless.

Marx the philosopher, as a student of Hegel, had been toughened in the heavy brine of German metaphysics. He drew from those beginnings a sense— reflected in all his work—that human history has a logic and a trajectory all its own. It is not just a record of things that have occurred in the past and are happening now, but the slow emergence of an established course of development, one that will bring us humans ever closer to a realization of our true nature. The eventual outcome of that course of events has been pre-determined, but the motive force that drives it forward is a process by which one set of social currents develops an aversion to another, creating a tension out of which a new and more advanced set of social currents emerges. Marx, then, viewed history as moving down an already fixed path, and he regarded conflict between class interests as the energy that that propels it.

So Marx the economic historian regarded the human record as a long, relentless chronicle of class struggle. History unfolds, step by step, as various forces collide and forge a new kind of social order in the fierce heat they have generated. The fundamental fact of human experience (up until the present, at least) is that people have always been divided into different classes and therefore have always varied enormously in wealth, power, and access to what Marx called "the means of production," and thus the principal actors in the scenes that have played out in the past and those that are yet to be played out in the future are not *people* but *social classes.*

Classes have been formed in many different ways throughout history, depending on the prevailing economic circumstances. But the critical line is always the one dividing those who hold property from those who do not. In ancient societies like Greece and Rome, for example, the principal antagonists were those who owned land or slaves and those who owned neither. In the feudal world, those roles were played by serfs and landlords, and in the modern world by those who own the means of production—land, machinery, capital, equipment, technique—and those who own nothing but their own labor power. No matter what the economic situation, then, and no matter how many other classes occupy the same social terrain at any particular time, the basic conflict has always been between a class of exploiters and a class of the exploited.

In every historical period, the clash between those two antagonistic classes is bound to lead to upheaval and pain. But it is a creative process as well as a destructive one, since a new order is gradually maturing "in the womb"—Marx's words—of the old. The present capitalist structure, he thought, is leading up to the point where it will produce one final convulsion, the victory of the proletariat. It will be expressed in the foreseeable future in a form of socialism, but, eventually, it will be expressed in the emergence of a truly human form of life that flows by itself, mirrors the real character of human nature, and becomes the governing force of everyday existence. This is the outcome toward which the trajectory of history has been aiming from the outset. It will mark the end of politics, the end of the state, the end of class distinction, and the end of that unrelenting cycle of old conflicts and new beginnings.

Marx the activist wanted to encourage this development, but Marx the historian felt that he could afford to be patient about it. For one thing, his reading of history assured him that the victory of the proletariat was inevitable sooner or later in any event. But he was also convinced that the new order could not emerge intact until it had gestated for a long enough period in the womb of the old. Premature revolution would risk the health of its offspring.

This brings us to Marx the sociologist and to two major themes that run throughout his work. The first has to do with the effects of the class struggle on the human spirit, a subject he dealt with under the general heading of *alienation*. The second has to do with the effects of the class struggle on human thought and human institutions, a topic he dealt with under the general headings of *class-consciousness* and *ideology*.

Alienation

We humans create many needs, Marx thought, and we satisfy those needs by reaching out into nature and appropriating its various bounties for ourselves. We do this by fashioning tools—implements for shaping stone or turning the soil or mining minerals or whatever. In a very real sense, these tools become an extension of our bodies. They are like a set of prosthetic devices by which we complete our existence. And to that extent we humans can be said to *create* ourselves—*become* ourselves—by the manner in which we relate to those tools and the objects we produce with them.

The flow of human history so far, however, has worked out in such a way as to gradually separate people from the products of their labor and to reduce their control over the process of production as well. When a hunter like Moke fashions a tool, it belongs to him. And, more than that, it becomes a part of him, a furnishing of his personal world. But when some slave tans a hide or fires a brick or plants a seedling at the behest of her master, she has no control over the product itself and frequently does not even know to what purpose it is going to be put. She has poured something of herself into the product, breathed life into it; but since it does not become a meaningful part of her existence, she has (and Marx meant this almost literally) given part of herself away. The same is true for serfs who tend someone else's crops on someone else's land, and for industrial workers who employ tools belonging to a corporation to make parts of larger objects they might never see or touch or know the use of. They, too, give a part of themselves away. Their very humanity is reduced.

So people have been increasingly fated to produce things that have no meaning to them, that do not bear their signature or enhance their sense of self-worth. Since they have nothing to offer in the market but their own labor, they are almost like commodities themselves, objects for sale. And for that reason they are not really full participants in a human community. They are partial persons, particles detached from a larger mass. They are alienated. Marx said that both workers and owners experience the same sense of alienation, but they experience it differently. Owners experience it as a sign of their own power, while workers see it as a sign of their own impotence and their failure to rank as truly human.

Class Consciousness and Ideology

Marx's most lasting contribution to sociological thought, in all likelihood, was his blunt declaration that the class structure of a society plays the dominant role in molding its moralities, its ideas, its beliefs, and its general cultural temper. As he put it:

> The mode of production in material life determines the general character of the social, political and spiritual processes of life. It is not the consciousness of men that determines their existence, but, on the contrary, their social existence determines their consciousness.

That is, the bedrock upon which every social order is built is its basic economic arrangement, its *mode of production;* and the thoughts that pass through people's minds, in turn, reflect the nature of that arrangement. The position people occupy in the class structure serves as a kind of screen, sifting out the ideas that occur to them, the creeds that appeal to them, the values that ring true to them, the philosophies and moralities and worldviews and even the scientific conclusions that make sense to them. If one wants to know the true character of a particular time or place, then, one does not ask persons who live there how they visualize it, for that is to stare straight into an opaque mist of rationalizations and distortions. One asks instead about the economic structure that has given form to those ideological mists. They are the reality that impel people to think as they do. How can that be?

Well, for one thing, the world is alive with ideas and beliefs and shards of this and that, all of them competing for human attention. And, Marx thought, it stands more or less to reason that people will consciously or unconsciously come to adopt those that seem to furnish the most convincing rationales for their own economic self-interest. In the same sense that people are apt to give conscious support to candidates or parties backing policies that work to their advantage, people give unconscious support to ideas or moralities that contribute the most to their comfort and well-being. Marx was not accusing you or me of cynicism or opportunism in making that observation; he was simply noting that human chemistry happens to work this way, that human beings, with all the good will in the world, drift as if by accident into moral arrangements that turn out to serve them well economically.

According to this reasoning, one might think, every class will have its own theories and doctrines, its own philosophies and moralities, reflecting the economic conditions under which it exists. Slaves should think differently from masters, serfs from landlords, workers from owners. And in one sense they do share what can be described as different "stocks of knowledge." Yet it is evident to anyone who studies the human record carefully that something else is going on as well. Oppressed classes can endure for centuries without being aware that they have different economic interests than their oppressors do and that they are able to develop ideological voices to represent their position in in the economic structure. The reason for this, Marx argued, is that members of the oppressed classes tend to accept the moral and even the cognitive views of their oppressors—adhering to religious doctrines, say, that keep them in bondage, or paying homage to leaders who do not have their interests even remotely at heart.

Raw coercion is one reason this can happen, of course, and Marx, of all people, did not shy away from that conclusion. Regimes often stay in power by repressing people who know perfectly well where their interests lie: the world has supplied a brilliant array of examples both in Marx's time and in our own. But Marx also recognized that no government can rule by brute force alone over the long term, and that persons who govern need to secure the consent of those who are governed and even to count on their active support every now and then. That particular species of statecraft is made all the easier by the fact that those who are in charge of the *means of production* are also in charge of the *cultural instruments* through which the stuff of the mind is processed—printing presses, classrooms, pulpits, parliaments, and the like. Oppressed classes simply lack the means to circulate or even to formulate ideological expressions of their own, and so it is understandable that they gradually absorb the outlooks of those who oppress them. The oppressors, in their turn—often without quite knowing what they are doing—employ specialists to aid in the process. When uncertainties enter a peasant's mind, for example, or when the child of a laborer begins to wonder about the fairness of the adult world, these doubts are quelled by a priest or teacher or philosophic elder who, without quite knowing it either, is paid to represent the views of those in power.

And so history offers the astonishing spectacle of peasants going off to war on behalf of landlords because they have been persuaded that a religious principle of some kind is at stake, workers going off to war to win new markets for a class that oppresses them because they have been persuaded that it is the patriotic thing to do, and, in general, men and women everywhere working until the joy has been drained from their lives and the vigor from their bodies because they have been told, and have come to believe, that hard toil—however poorly rewarded—is in itself a duty and an act of piety.

The class interests of individuals in power, then, can become the prevailing ideology of an entire age—one is tempted to add "culture" as well—because the viewpoints of the powerful are internalized even by those who suffer the most from that way of seeing things. And this grim fact can become the basis of a political movement, for the oppressed need devoted friends to help them develop a true class consciousness and to help them clear away all those ideological mists through which they have been groping for centuries. The working class, to be really free, would have to divest itself of all the beliefs and creeds, the laws and institutions, the literature and arts, that have been the bequest of the ruling class to civilization. It is to be quite a house cleaning!

The main point, however, at least for our purposes now, is that the noblest thoughts the mind is capable of—the purest doctrines, the sanest philosophies, the most radiant poetry—can issue from motives of a baser sort: the interests of the upper class formed into a universal set of values, beliefs, and practices. Marx saw this as an inevitability of the world he lived in but he was also persuaded that human thought can transcend those limitations of class at some point in the future. He took it for granted that his own writings had helped set that future into motion.

Among the intellectual gifts that Marx left us, though, is a permanent reminder that one should always look underneath the surface of things—underneath the rationales and certitudes that surround all human activities—to see what other motives, deliberate or otherwise, may be crouched out of sight.

We will soon encounter other sociologists, Émile Durkheim being a good example, who want us to notice that human institutions and human values can reflect an abiding communality reaching across the whole of a culture. But Marx wanted us to notice that even when we look at such forms, we may be seeing the ideology of a ruling class, symbols not of communion but of sheer power.

The Later Years

The first adjectives that come to mind for most readers of Marx's work as well as of his life story are apt to be intense, driven, wrathful, dogmatic, irascible. It is evident that a powerful engine was churning inside him day and night—"furnace" might be the better word—fueled in part by raw anger and generating tremendous heat. I am not speaking of that now because I think it matters how his personality was formed (he seems to have been a gentle and affectionate, if occasionally domineering, figure in his own household), but because his voice—so caustic and biting and indignant at times—dominated the tone and at times even the logic of his prose.

Contemporaries of Marx often remarked on the relentless ferocity with which he could attack others, many of them allies in both philosophical and political causes. Edmund Wilson, who knew of those remarks, thought that Marx's "opinions seemed always to have been arrived at through close criticisms of the opinions of others, as if the sharpness and force of his mind could only really exert themselves in attacks on the minds of others." It seemed as if the sheer abrasiveness of his assaults were the whetstone on which he honed his arguments, as if the heat of his wrath fired the forge in which his ideas were tempered and given a final shape.

Biographers have looked into both the early and later years of Marx's life for the source of what seems to have been a sustained anger. He lived on the margins for the whole of his adult life, unable to find a secure place for himself in the society of his times. He lived in the embrace of a loving family both as child and as adult, but he had few of what comforts come from being part of a religious tradition or nationality or community or other source of identity. He was born a Jew in a Christian country and became a Protestant in a Catholic part of it. He was a member of dissenting, vaguely rebellious student groups in Bonn and Berlin, but lost contact with both. He was expelled from two countries, including the one in which he had been born. He became a solitary force even within the socialist communities he had helped breathe life into because he could be so quarrelsome. And fate had handled him any number of other sharp rebuffs. So it is logical to suppose that the rage had its source in the circumstances of his personal life. That is how life stories are told, aren't they?

Wilson, who deserves to be listened to carefully, thought that:

> It is impossible to read *Das Kapital* in the light of Marx's life during this period without concluding that the emotional motivation—partly or totally unconscious, no doubt—behind Marx's excoriation of capitalists and his grim parading of the afflictions of the poor is at once his outraged conviction of the indignity and injustice of his own life.

Biographers are of course entitled to that way of relating any life story, but the same tale can be told in reverse. An individual of exceptional power looked out at the world in a way no one had before, and what he saw so aggravated him that it lodged down inside him and became part of his inner spirit. The narrative line here, then, is not that the state of mind produced the vision, but that the vision produced the state of mind. Both of those readings of the information available to us make a certain sense, but I lean toward the second of them, at least in part out of respect for the power of the vision itself. Marx thought he had seen something tremendous out there in the world of his time, and the wrath it generated in him became the tinder that fired his consuming internal furnace. That may be one of the signatures of genius.

Was Marx right? I think we should dismiss that as a poorly phrased question and let the matter lie. That may not be the point anyway.

It is probably fair to suggest that every great idea begins as an exaggeration, since new voices, no matter how wise they later prove to have been, need to be louder and more strident at first in order to obtain entrance into that hall of ideas where other voices have been echoing for ages. Once inside, the new voice often loses some of that sharpness, and it is no discredit to a great idea to count it as something other than an established truth. It is more than that. It is an insight of such extraordinary power, a vision of such clarity, that it forever changes the way we see and think.

The World According to Émile Durkheim

If Marx's great project was to identify the fault lines along which human societies split into classes and other warring segments, Durkheim's great project was to identify how human societies manage to cohere. In that sense, Marx can perhaps be described as more interested in and more sensitive to the *centripetal* forces in social life, the ones that drive wedges between groups of people; while Durkheim can be described as more interested in and sensitive to the *centrifugal* forces, the ones that draw people together.

The name *Durkheim* has a rather crisp German ring to it, but this Durkheim was French to the core. He was born in Epinol in the far northeast corner of France in 1858. He, too, came from a long line of rabbis and rabbinical scholars, and in fact he was preparing for the rabbinate himself in his early years of schooling.

He grew up in a close-knit, orthodox Jewish family, a circumstance he noted himself in later years because he traced his own outlook on social life back to "that tempering of character, that heightening of life which a strongly cohesive group communicates to its members." In an important work he simply entitled

Suicide—we will have occasion to discuss it again soon—he described the kind of small Jewish community he knew as a child as "a small society, compact and cohesive, with a very keen self-consciousness and sense of unity."

Durkheim soon gave up the idea of becoming a rabbi, but it became obvious quite early in his schooling that he was a person of very special promise. In 1879, at the age of 21, he was admitted to the *École Normale Supériere,* which was to France what the combination of Oxford and Cambridge was to England, although it was a far smaller and more concentrated center of learning. It was the traditional academy for those who would become the scholarly elite of the land.

Durkheim appears to have entered *L'École Normale* with a fairly clear sense of what he intended to do with his life, although he would not find the right words to express it for a number of years yet. It is far easier for us now, looking back, to understand the ideas that were forming in that remarkable mind of his because he did more than anyone not only to devise the language we use to give form to those thoughts but to fashion the lens through which we look at them.

The idea must have settled early into Durkheim's mind that human society is something like a being, an actual *thing* with its own inherent properties. It is a mass of living tissue, a field of force that is subject to the same laws of motion as any other physical matter, and it is available for investigation through normal scientific inquiry. It cannot be understood as the sum of all the individual existences that constitute it. Nor can it be understood by drawing on psychological or biological explanations. The words Durkheim used to convey all this came later, of course, but his sense of that *thing* was almost like part of the air he breathed. He called it an "effervescence" later, but what he appears to have meant was a deep inner feeling of fellowship and communality and togetherness that held the thing together.

Even in those early days, Durkheim was speaking the language of science, insisting that any social force one thinks one can *feel* out there in the world can only be confirmed by rigorous empirical research. But there were moments when his descriptions of those forces verged on the mystical, moments when he seemed to be referring to spiritual impulses that lie beyond the reach of the immediate senses. Those portions of his emerging argument were not lost on his fellow students at *L'École,* who called him "The Metaphysician." And, as we will see later, it was not lost on other persons who followed his teachings in France either.

Durkheim graduated from *L'École Normale* in 1882 at 24, and spent the next few years teaching in provincial schools. During that time, the concepts he had been weighing in his mind began to take clearer form. In 1887, at the exceptionally early age of 29, he was appointed to a chair at the University of Bordeaux, where he remained for a decade and a half. He was by that time calling himself a "sociologist," and he took it as his mission at Bordeaux to secure a stable place for himself and his chosen field of study in the university world.

His nephew, Marcel Mauss, who became a distinguished social scientist a few years later himself, wrote of his uncle in that period that "by a progressive analysis of his thought and the facts . . . he came to see that the solution to the problem belonged to a new science: sociology." So the task he assigned himself was to promote that new science and to give it "a method and a body."

First, a *method.* The term "sociology," he wrote about that time, "sums up and implies a whole new order of ideas; namely that social forces are indissolubly linked, and, above all, must be treated as natural phenomena governed by invariable laws." Sociology was, pure and simple, a science. He wanted us to study people in society in the same way we study celestial bodies in orbit or the movements of physical objects on the face of the earth. A Belgian statistician named Adolphe Quetelet had proposed close to fifty years earlier that the study of social life be called "social physics," and Comte, too, had used that expression. Durkheim did not use it, but what he had in mind fit it well. He once noted that social forces "determine our behavior from without, just like physico-chemical forces," and that those same forces can be measured "as one does the strength of electric currents." Amazing stuff for its time and place.

Second, a *body.* During one brief five-year period in Bordeaux, Durkheim was involved in what can only be called an explosion of brilliance. He wrote three of the four masterpieces that were his legacy in that time, and, in the process, defined and gave contour to the emerging field of sociology. We will discuss each of those titles (in a somewhat different order) soon, so I only want to note now the dates on which they appeared: *The Division of Labor,* 1893; *Rules of the Sociological Method,* 1895; and *Suicide,* 1897. If I were asked to identify one location, one concentration of work, and one span of time as the true crucible of modern sociology, that might well be it: the University of Bordeaux, those three books, and the years 1892 to 1897. At the close of that span of time, Durkheim had not yet turned 40.

A visitor to Durkheim's office toward the end of his time in Bordeaux offers this sketch. "His long, thin body was enveloped in a large dressing-gown . . . which concealed his bony and muscular frame, the fragile support for his thoughts. The face emerged, pale and ascetic, with its high forehead bare, a short beard, a thick moustache . . . but this austere and severe face was magnificently illuminated by two deep set eyes that had an intense and gentle power, so that he commanded respect." (The term "muscular" here was probably meant to suggest a body so spare that it was mainly skin, bone, and tough, lean sinews, not the bulk we generally associate with the word now.)

"The Metaphysician" was trying to present himself as a disciplined scientist engaged in the development of a new field of study, although he could not avoid hints of the mystical in the way he spoke of and wrote about it. That may say a good deal more about the vigor with which he pursued his ideas than about the ideas themselves. He was still speaking to a world in which "sociology," to the extent that the field had any currency at all, could still trace most of its basic premises to the thinking of the Age of Reason, and, like Marx, the urgency in his writing surely reflected the difficulties of being heard in such an intellectual climate. But if Durkheim's voice was insistent, his mind was that of a scientist, and he would have been the first to state: if you cannot apprehend it by the use of your senses or deduce it in the course of scientific study, then you have no warrant to assume that it exists.

Most social scientists of Durkheim's era, as we saw earlier, viewed society as an assembly of independent persons, connected to each other by an agreement to cooperate in the business of living. We should recognize this as the kind of social order envisioned by Thomas Hobbes and John Locke, and it had by now worked its way into the thinking of several generations of British economists like Adam Smith as well as that of "utilitarian" philosophers like John Stuart Mill and Jeremy Bentham. It had also worked its way into the thinking of another English scholar, Herbert Spencer, who was certainly the most celebrated person to call himself "sociologist" in the mid-19th century.

In Spencer's view, independent individuals occupy the core of the social world. Their minds, tutored by that old inner voice of natural reason, contained within them all the essential materials of which a society is composed. A social order emerges, then, when those individual persons contract with one another to engage in orderly forms of exchange, to live by a rule of law, and so on. The human beings depicted in this portrait were a calm and calculating lot who knew what was good for them and who ventured into everyday social life (as they ventured into markets) to exchange goods and to maximize their own self-interests. In that sense, a society is the same as an individual writ large. If you know the anatomy of the human spirit, that is, you know the anatomy of the social order.

This was the view that Durkheim went to such lengths to contest. The map of the social order, he said, cannot be contained in each individual mind, because the two are different orders of being entirely. Indeed, the individual is to society as a cell is to the organism of which it is a part—a scrap of raw material, without identity or function, that does not actualize itself or even *become* itself, until it is absorbed into the rest of the social whole. And that whole, he argued, is not only greater than the sum of its parts but different in kind. He agreed with Comte, who had written half a century earlier in a line you have already read but is well worth repeating: "Society is no more decomposable into individuals than a geometric surface is into lines, or a line into points." Durkheim went a step further: "Every time a social phenomenon is directly explained by a psychological phenomenon, we may be sure that the explanation is false."

As you look out at a world full of individuals scurrying this way and that on their own private errands, it is easy to assume that it is *they* who form society by reaching out and making contact with one another. But, Durkheim pointed out emphatically, it is obvious on reflection that society not only provides the theater in which all that activity takes place but choreographs it. He began with an argument that should be familiar to us by now because we have heard it before, but was quite new to Durkheim's audience. Consider contracts, he said. Agreements of the kind that figure so prominently in Spencer's vision of social life could only have taken place in a climate of trust and a shared universe of meaning, and those conditions, in turn, presuppose the existence of an established social order. That is why, Durkheim wrote, "we can be certain that in the entire course of social evolution there has not been a single time when individuals determined by careful deliberation whether or not they would enter the collective life or into one collective life rather than another." So much for *le contrat social!*

The true subject matter of sociology, then, is to be all those invisible fibers and linkages—that vast web of connective tissue—that bond individuals together. Durkheim wanted above all to demonstrate the existence of that web and to describe its character. It is a theme that runs like a brilliant thread through the whole of his published work, which includes the three titles I cited a moment ago, and the greatest of Durkheim's triumphs, *The Elementary Forms of the Religious Life,* that appeared fifteen years after the close of that explosive outburst in Bordeaux. My plan here is to trace that thread from book to book in an effort to describe Durkheim's vision for the field of sociology.

Durkheim's views on the nature of the social order and on the nature of sociology have been absorbed so deeply into the grain of modern social science thinking that it is easy to think, upon being exposed to Durkheim's expression of them for the first time, that you have heard all that before. If that occurs to you in what follows, take heart: you *have* heard traces of it before, at least once, because the introductory remarks with which this book opened are very indebted to Durkheim's spirit.

Division of Labor

Durkheim's first real effort to identify and study the sense of cohesion on which every social order rests was *The Division of Labor in Society.* By "division of labor" he was referring to the ways in which people in the more advanced industrial societies break up everyday work into a variety of specialized tasks, a subject that had been widely discussed in Europe since the appearance of *The Wealth of Nations* by Adam Smith in 1776, one hundred and twenty years earlier. This person specializes in the repairing of water pumps. This person specializes in the practice of law. This person specializes in the tending of geese. There are people whose job it is to read tea leaves and tend to the ill and hammer out the dents in pewter mugs and spay pets. The history of our times is one in which individuals in general become ever more specialized and the work that needs to be done is divided into ever narrower tasks.

Smith assumed that the division of labor in modern societies had been carefully worked out by thoughtful persons to increase productivity in a new age of industry. The social contract again. But Durkheim was sure that so elaborate a social structure as that must have had deeper roots. When a society is characterized by a complex division of labor, Durkheim wrote, people spread out over an ever widening social space and become increasingly unlike one another—not only occupationally, as the expression itself would suggest, but morally, temperamentally, even perceptually. In a modern division of labor, that is to say, people not only *do* different things as they go about their everyday rounds. They live different lives, think different thoughts, grow up in different ways, experience different realities.

The scene being sketched here is that of human particles scattered this way and that by the winds of modernity, and one might reasonably expect that scene to be one of chaos. But in fact an amazing degree of coordination prevails even there, and it seemed evident to Durkheim that people were attracted to that scheme of things not just because it was efficient and profitable but because they have some deep-seated need to draw on the distinctive qualities of others who are unlike themselves. The division of labor, then, is an intricate patchwork of reciprocity and complementarity with a symmetry all its own. It is not the consequence of a new human skill in calculation so much as an old human need for being together.

It had not always been that way. When the world was younger, Durkheim said, society was made up largely of individuals who scarcely varied from each other. They formed a gray, undifferentiated clump—a "horde," Durkheim put it—made up of human particles so alike that any one of them could replace any of the others. Durkheim called the manner in which these identical particles were linked together "mechanical solidarity," by which he meant a sense of fusion based on resemblance. The cells of this particular kind of social organism all look alike, think alike, see alike. They feel the same emotions, respect the same values, are moved by the same stimuli. They are the opposite, in short, of the highly differentiated creatures who make a complex division of labor possible.

People joined together in mechanical solidarity, said Durkheim, are so similar in temper and so identified with a common sense of morality that they share what he called "*la conscience collective.*" The term means more than one thing in French, and can be translated as "collective conscience"—thus reversing two words that have the same spelling and very close to the same meaning in English—or as "collective consciousness." Both translations are necessary to fully appreciate Durkheim's meaning, for he was speaking not only of shared moral sentiments—the stuff of the conscience—but to forms of awareness and ways of perceiving as well. He defined *conscience collective* as "the totality of beliefs and sentiments common to the average citizens of the same society." It is a shared worldview, an ethos, a culture. It is a shared sense of right and wrong that goes beyond codes, an agreement on basic principles that goes beyond saying. This body of "beliefs and sentiments" has a life of its own in the sense that it exists independently of the individual consciences (or individual consciousnesses) of the persons who participate in it. This is Durkheim at his most mystical, but he does not mean that *la conscience collective* is an actual presence that will continue to exist out in the ether when no one is left to be a participant in it. He means that it passes from generation to generation, and thus outlives the individual persons who have lived by it. It is a moral bridge connecting the people of one time with the people of another, and is, in that sense, timeless.

Durkheim's idea here is that all persons have an individual conscience, something more or less within them, while at the same time being a part of *la conscience collective,* something more or less outside them. In social orders where mechanical forms of solidarity dominate, the difference between the two is scarcely worth noting. Since every individual conscience is like every other, all are enveloped in the folds of the larger culture—"lost in the whole," is the way a fine French sociologist of a later generation, Raymond Aron, would put it.

Durkheim was never very specific about dates when he spoke of how things had been in the past. He was not tracing a historical line so much as wanting us to know that humankind had changed considerably from *then* to *now. Then* was the time of the horde, the time when people were similar in thought and action, when people related to one another in the fashion Durkheim called "mechanical."

Over time, though, for a variety of reasons, the gray clump began slowly to dissolve, and the cells that had been a part of it began to separate into the specialized niches that constitute a complex division of labor. Individual consciences began to withdraw, if only partly, from what had been a common consensus, drifting off into social spheres of their own—from which point of vantage they increasingly perceived the world differently, evaluated it differently, responded to it differently. The point Durkheim wanted us to appreciate is that a division of labor creates not only more specialized *work skills* but more specialized *moral reflexes.* The person whose job it is to tend geese lives in a different world of experience from the person whose job it is to sell stocks and bonds.

In advanced industrial societies, then, where one finds a more elaborate division of labor, *la conscience collective* has become more diffuse and less passionate. Mechanical solidarity has yielded to a very different way of linking individuals together into larger social gatherings that Durkheim called "organic solidarity."

Organic solidarity is based on *differentiation* rather than on *resemblance.* It involves the complementarity of diverse cells rather than the massing together of similar ones. Every person has a particular role to play in the larger whole, and, in order to do so, has developed a kind of individuality and autonomy that would be unimaginable in a society based on mechanical forms of solidarity. So the varied human beings who make up a society based on organic solidarity can be as unalike as is possible for creatures from a common species. But the networks of mutuality and interdependency that emerge from this arrangement are *themselves* a fundamental source of cohesion. Durkheim called this *organic* solidarity to indicate that the kinds of complementarity found in the modern division of labor are very like those found in a living organism: the parts of the overall system—kidney, colon, pancreas, liver—look and act very differently but are wholly dependent on the larger system of coordination. It is the way the differences are balanced and patterned that gives the whole its cohesion.

So the historical drift from mechanical to organic forms of solidarity means a decline in the sharpness and rigidity of *la conscience collective,* but it does not necessarily mean a decline in its ability to promote cohesiveness. The forces that bind us together are simply more abstract—structural rather than spiritual, perhaps. "Anomie," which is almost surely the best known of Durkheim's contributions to the vocabulary of sociology, is a collapse of organic solidarity that can take place when complementarity and mutuality fail and human particles wander off in their own directions. But that is not an inevitable outcome.

Whether its mood is fierce and consuming, as is the case when mechanical solidarity is the prevailing source of social integration, or whether it is calmer and more principled, as is the case when organic solidarity is the prevailing source, *la conscience collective* is a social fact, a palpable thing, a proper subject of scientific inquiry. You cannot see it? You cannot hear it or smell it or touch it? Well, said Durkheim, never mind: you cannot see the workings of gravity either, or the avenues in space along which things orbit. The "air is not less heavy because we do not detect its weight," he pointed out.

But how, then, do we know it is there? How can it be detected? Well, to begin with, you can see it for yourself—perhaps even feel it—if you watch people involved in ritual occasions of differing kinds. In patriotic ceremonies, civic celebrations, religious services, ethnic gatherings, persons share the moment with their fellows, become part of an emerging sense of communality. That emotion, Durkheim wanted us to understand, is *la conscience collective.* Do your eyes mist over a bit when you hear your national anthem? Do you feel a moment of elation or turn with a smile to the person sitting next to you when an athlete wearing the uniform of your home town or school does something well on the playing field? Do you experience a deep flash of anger when a countryman whom you have never met or even heard of is abused or humiliated by people of another country? There it is again, that unmistakable expression of group feeling.

Should that demonstration not impress you sufficiently, there are other tests to turn to as well. Look what happens in any community, for instance, when somebody commits a crime or trespasses group values in some other way. People wholly unaffected by the event feel a sense of outrage, and that fact alone needs explaining. It was not *their* house broken into, after all, or *their* children harmed; it was not *their* cemetery vandalized or *their* neighbors mistreated on the streets of a distant land. The indignation generated by the crime, however, can be very intense, sometimes taking the form of an anger so sharp that it moves otherwise decent people to acts of violence. These are the reflection of a common sense of morality, *la conscience collective.*

We are now persuaded, let's say, that this collective conscience actually exists, even in societies as fragmented and as complex as ours. It is a *thing.* We can feel it in the air or at least confirm that other people do. But that "thing" is of no real consequence until it can be shown to have an impact on human conduct, until it can be shown to be not just a feeling surging up from an inner well of communal sentiment but a force that constrains people, influences the way they behave, moves them in the way gravity moves other objects.

So Durkheim turned his energy to a beautifully crafted research report which he entitled, simply, *Suicide.* It is technically primitive by the criteria we observe now, but it can be viewed as the prototype, the natural grandparent, of every sociological study that has been undertaken since.

Suicide

What is the most personal act an individual can undertake—the most solitary, the most reclusive, the furthest removed from social influence? Suicide would certainly be high on most lists. It is a lonely and desperate thing, a cry of private anguish, as emphatic a withdrawal from communal life as can be imagined. It seems entirely logical to assert that acts of suicide can be understood only by looking at the unique circumstances in which they occur and the personal histories of those who engage in it. We need to know the emotional furnishings of their minds, that is, in order to get a true sense of the motives involved. Psycho-logic.

But consider this. If suicide is a profoundly private act, how might one explain the fact that suicide rates seem to follow social patterns the world over? Each individual suicide can be traced back to an inner moment of sorrow or despair, but at the same time all of those individual moments gather together and become submerged in a broader social force. Socio-logic.

No matter what allowances we make for the personal, Durkheim noted, we will still come up with the consistent finding that some groups in the social order experience far higher rates of suicide than others do, which is to say that they have a greater propensity to—a greater "aptitude for" was Durkheim's odd way of putting it—the act of suicide. Among Durkheim's findings were that Protestants committed suicide more often than Catholics in the Europe of the age, and Catholics committed suicide more often than Jews.

That seems like a strange conclusion. It cannot be accounted for on theological grounds, since Catholics observe stronger prohibitions against suicide than either Protestants or Jews. Nor can it be accounted for on economic grounds, since Protestants would scarcely have ranked as the most disadvantaged class of persons in the Europe of the time.

Where else might one look for explanation then? The answer, Durkheim proposed, is a matter of group integration. Jews have the closest spiritual ties as well as the strongest sense of communal identity of the groups in question, at least in part because the hostility of others has pressed in on them over past centuries and in that way molded them into a firmer collectivity. Protestants, on the other hand, are the most scattered and diffuse, the most alone and alienated, the least connected to some common spiritual core.

The lower the level of cohesion within a group, then, the higher the suicide rate. And, in general, the more separated one is from an integrated group—either because one is adrift in a sea without rules or values (as is the case with what Durkheim called "anomic" suicide) or because one is detached from the rest of society and going it alone ("egoistic" suicide), the less emotional insulation one has and the higher the odds that one will commit suicide.

Durkheim pursued his analysis of suicide rates far beyond the findings I have mentioned so far. Belonging to a family, for example, also seems to offer the kind of support that protects people from the urge to commit suicide, and so do popular wars and other social upheavals that promote national or tribal unity. But his main argument can be stated clearly without repeating all the evidence he originally gathered for the purpose: the more tightly people are enmeshed in a cohesive group—and the more securely they are located in a net of human linkages—the less likely they are to take their lives. Clean. Simple. Elegant. Social solidarity has demonstrable force in the social order. These findings would not cause so much as a ripple of surprise now, but in their day they were something of a revelation.

The Rules of Sociological Method

In 1895, Durkheim took leave from his other intellectual labors to write a thin volume entitled *The Rules of Sociological Method.* Marcel Mauss, remember, had noted that Durkheim had assigned himself the task of providing the new field of sociology both *body* and *method.* It was time for the latter. This was actually the second of Durkheim's books, appearing two years after the publication of *Division of Labor* and two years before the publication of *Suicide,* but the logic of our proceedings so far suggests that we deal with it in this order. *Rules* was meant as a kind of primer, a spelling out of the approaches and procedures that should govern sociological work, and for that reason what follows may also have a somewhat familiar ring.

The primary data of the new science are to be "social facts," said Durkheim, meaning:

> a category of facts with very distinctive characteristics . . . ways of acting, thinking, and feeling, external to the individual, and endowed with a power of coercion, by reason of which they control him.

Social facts constitute "a new variety of phenomena," and they include "every way of thinking which is general throughout society."

We know a good part of that by now: social currents that surround you, impinge on you, and in doing so influence the way you think and act. Examples? A custom held so firmly by the people among whom you live that your behavior is shaped by it. An anger so fierce or a dread so haunting that you and your kind are willing to slay other human beings and risk death yourselves on a distant battlefield. An enthusiasm shared so widely in the spaces you call home that you find yourself well in its grip. A movement of people from one corner of the world to another so contagious that you are caught up in it.

We may call them "currents" or something like that, but they are not to be understood as forces that engulf you and carry you along against your will, like a strong undertow or a heavy wind. Their strength is exactly that they exist *within* you as well as outside you, and in that sense the custom I just spoke of becomes so firm a part of your view of what is proper that you adhere to it without thinking about it at all and the enthusiasm becomes so compelling that you feel it in the very center of your being and experience it as if it had welled up from within you. And so on. The migrant stream flows like a body of water, tracing a course beyond your control or ken, but you joined it for reasons of your own making.

Social acts, then, are absorbed into our very being. They are experienced as inner urges as well as outer constraints. And their impact is so essential that that Durkheim instructs us: "The first and most fundamental rule is: *Consider social facts as things.*" The test of a social fact, the way one measures its quality of "thingness," is to see whether it has the "power to coerce," to reach inside, so to speak, and shape the outlook and behavior of those in its sway. One of the objectives of *Suicide,* of course, was to present such a demonstration.

When Durkheim described social facts as "new phenomena," he was not saying that he had discovered a new element in the life of society. They are a new way of *conceptualizing* the most familiar materials of everyday social life. Durkheim intended to provide us with a filter through which we can view things already known by other names. For example:

What does it mean to say "this is normal" or "that is pathological"? From an individual or a psychological standpoint, the answer seems obvious. Illness is pathological, we would say, both because it departs from the ordinary and is in that sense *abnormal,* and because it interrupts the state of health and is in that sense *dysfunctional* or *aberrant.* Who would argue with that?

But, says Durkheim, the logic of social inquiry invites us to think of it differently. As so often in his work, he used crime to illustrate his point. "If there is any fact whose pathological character appears incontestable," he began, "that fact is crime." It is noxious, morbid, baneful, and every right-thinking social order goes to considerable lengths to root it out. If you consider the subject sociologically for a moment, however, things do not look so simple. Crime is surely normal in the sense that it is found everywhere. It is impossible to locate (or even to imagine) a society without crime, and, in fact, the world has never produced one. In that respect, crime appears to be built into the very constitution of social life. Moreover, said Durkheim, crime can even be understood as "a factor in public health, an integral part of all societies." That startling argument had actually appeared first in *The Division of Labor,* though in a less emphatic form. Crime performs a needed service to society, Durkheim had written there, by drawing people together in a common posture of anger and indignation. The criminal violates rules of conduct that the rest of the community holds in high regard, and when people come together to express their outrage over the offense and to bear witness against the offender, they develop an even tighter bond of solidarity than had existed before. So crime has its positive functions, Durkheim had concluded then. But he was now ready to go a step further and declare flatly that crime "is bound up with the fundamental conditions of all social life" and is therefore "necessary" to it—which is to say, crime is healthy, normal, the very opposite of pathological. We thought we were marching in one direction, but with a few deft turns of phrase Durkheim has us marching in the other.

Behavior that looks abnormal to a psychiatrist or to a judge, that is to say, may not look abnormal through the differently ground lens of a sociologist. And behavior that looks normal in one social setting may appear differently in another. It depends upon one's point of vantage, the floor to which one climbs to look out at the social scene. If you were to hear that an individual named Myles Winthrop has begun to drink a good deal more whiskey than is good for him and his health is deteriorating as a result, you are likely to call that a pathological turn of events. But if you were also to hear that Myles's pathological behavior has so alarmed other members of his family as well as a number of neighbors that they have all foresworn liquor and other unhealthy substances and have become both happier and hardier as a result, what will you say then? That is Durkheim's point. Any individual who abuses his health in that way will seem pathological to us so long as we are focused on *him,* but when our focus shifts to the group as a whole and we recognize that others may be better off as a result of Myles's drinking, we realize that we need a different way of measuring what is normal and what is pathological.

Another example. A student named Mary walked out of a classroom one day without seeking permission when the rays of the sun slanting through the window made the day outside seem unavoidably welcome. There was no rule posted on the school bulletin board prohibiting that, after all. It was just taken for granted. But news of that delinquency was soon broadcast up and down the corridors of the school, and the rule was soon posted not only on bulletin boards but in the minds of every student there. Seen as a fleeting moment in Mary's life, then, it has to be counted as something pathological. But seen as a fleeting moment in the life of the school, it might even be counted as something beneficial.

Elementary Forms of the Religious Life

Durkheim moved to the Sorbonne in Paris in 1902, by now a famous if at the same time a somewhat controversial figure. He was still only 44, but he was treated as a distinguished elder in the sense that he was now a major force in

French academic circles. It was a recognition both of him as a dominant scholar and of sociology as a field of study.

He came to Paris, one of his biographers notes, "as a formidable intellectual armed with doctrine." That had something to do with his personality, of course—Durkheim was nothing if not dogmatic—but it also had something to do with a new theory he had come to town to speak of. It would eventuate a decade later in his fourth and most important book, entitled *Elementary Forms of the Religious Life*. Randall Collins and Michael Makowski, who have surveyed that territory as well as anyone, credit it with being "perhaps the greatest single book of the twentieth century." Not the greatest scholarly study or sociological treatise; the greatest book. Others would not know the subject of that writing until it appeared in 1912, but it served as lecture material from his early years in Paris. Durkheim was focusing his formidable gifts on the role of religion in human social life, and that, in turn, was focusing a good deal of attention on him. I propose to take a look at the argument the book would later enunciate and then return to Durkheim himself as we bring this sketch to a close.

In that book, Durkheim took careful note of the spiritual life of preliterate peoples and in particular those from inland Australia, but, as was the case with his study of suicide, he did so because it gave him an opportunity to make a larger and more general point. "If we have taken primitive religion as the subject of our research," wrote Durkheim (who used the pronoun *we* to refer to himself), "it is because it has seemed to us better adapted" to unearth "an essential and permanent aspect of humanity."

Durkheim begins by asking what all known religions share in common. One is tempted to say a belief in the existence of one or more deities or of a supernatural realm, but Durkheim stops us in the middle of that thought by pointing out that many religions in the past and several in the present—Buddhism being a well-known example—do not recognize supreme beings of any kind, while many others make no distinction at all between the natural and the supernatural. No, says Durkheim, the one attribute all religions share in common is a belief that some things are "sacred" and others "profane." (In using the term "profane," it should be added quickly, he was not suggesting that they are impure, which is one meaning of the word in English, but that they are secular, ordinary.) And that is the key. "The division of the world into two domains, the one containing everything that is sacred, the other all that is profane, is the distinctive trait of religious life."

Durkheim assumed, as did many social scientists of his time, that one can most readily grasp the true essence of a phenomenon, its inner character, by examining its most elementary forms. The reason he treated his readers to that long a journey—halfway around the world to Australia, with intermediate stops on the western plains of America and a few other locations—was to seek that "original essence." The native Australians Durkheim wrote about held group totems in special awe. A totem is a family of animate creatures that becomes the symbol of a particular clan or communal group—the fox or snake or kangaroo in Australia, for example, and the raven, bear, or beaver in North America.

Those ceremonial occasions on which members of a clan gather to honor their totem are extremely important to the community because they act to reinforce feelings of fellowship and solidarity—the collective conscience—that give the clan its life force. So far, of course, this is pure, vintage Durkheim. But he is now ready to go a step further and declare that the totem is not a representation of *something existing out there* in the supernatural world but a projection of something *existing within the group* and *within each of its members*. The qualities they admire in the totem, that is to say, are qualities they admire in their collective lives. The devotion they lavish on the totem is devotion they feel toward themselves as a group.

When we pay homage to sacred things, then, we are paying homage to the idea of social life. A deep and powerful feeling surges up from somewhere within us that has no name and no object to attach itself to. So people project it onto a totem or a deity or some other sacred thing *out there*. In doing so, however, they are in fact worshipping their own social selves *in here*. It is a way to give the feeling substance and a name.

Now that gets our attention. Durkheim is saying that a totemic image carved on the bow of a canoe, a venerated icon or chalice or relic displayed in a sacred place, or even some divinity known as Osiris or Zeus or Odin or Jehovah, is the projected image of a deep inner feeling that is the result of being part of a communal group. "In the last analysis," writes Raymond Aron, who always knew how to put such things, human beings "have never worshipped anything other than their own society."

It is certainly not difficult to appreciate why clerics of Durkheim's time (or any time, for that matter), would go pale at what would have sounded to them like an astonishing sacrilege: God is nothing but the projected image of group sentiments welling up from within! But in an odd way Durkheim was expressing more respect for religious faith than many other philosophers of the period because he was asserting that religious feelings had a firm foothold in reality. They were not "opiates" or "hallucinations" or the wild imaginings of priests, as many had suggested, but human emotions based on something solid and tangible. "The believer is not deceived" when he senses "a moral power" greater than himself, Durkheim said: "this power exists, it is society."

So Durkheim is not declaring that sacred spirits are a figment of the imagination (though he may well have thought so as a personal matter). He is declaring that feelings of reverence are the outcome of a deep inner respect for the social order, which, if one thinks that way at all, can be understood as a divine gift too.

There is a subsidiary argument in *Elementary Forms* that is often overshadowed by the sheer daring and brilliance of the idea I have been sketching here but may be more important in the long term—that *every* idea shared by persons who form a collectivity is a reflection of the social order they belong to, a manifestation of group feeling. The manner in which we see the natural world—the way we divide living matter into classes, the way we measure the passing of time, the way we perceive space or understand causality or make sense of any external reality—is a projection of the way the society of which we are a part is ordered. In other words, the way we live together and do things together forms the way we apprehend all things of the world.

There are clear parallels here with the thought of Karl Marx, though Durkheim showed no sign of being aware of it. Marx had argued, remember, that one's class position helps shape one's views of reality. But Durkheim was taking matters a full step further by proposing that human consciousness in general is a derivative of social life. He did not issue that thought as a grand announcement, ushered in with fanfare of trumpets, so it was never really broadcast as a compelling theory. But what would later be called "the sociology of knowledge," the study of where ideas come from, began here.

I will not pursue the idea further now or try to follow the argument Durkheim developed on his way to it. But what Durkheim really wanted to teach us is that social life forms the screen through which we humans look out at the world, and, thus, the screen through which the secrets of the world are filtered into our minds. The way we experience the things *out there* is at least in part a product of the way we experience things *in here*.

To return to Durkheim in Paris, then, it should be easy for us to appreciate that this was a stunning theory to be proposing to the crowds that were now attending his lectures: when we look to the heavens or some other remote domain as the source of the religious feelings that well up within us, we are really looking at ourselves, as if reflected in a mirror. We are worshipping "us."

There was an irony in this that Durkheim could never quite escape. What he had in mind initially was to demystify religious feelings by looking at them through the cool, rational, secular looking glass of science. But it is easy to understand why his listeners might come to feel that he was, instead, endowing the social order with sacred qualities. To declare, as he did regularly and with ever increasing confidence, that society is a palpable thing, governed by unwritten laws and set into motion by feelings from within, is to refer to it in terms very similar to the ones used by clerics in speaking of higher powers. The light actually glows down here, he was saying, not up there, and in making that point he seemed to be investing social life with powers once attributed to distant divinities. That may be the surest way to demystify the heavens above, but it is also the surest way to deify and glorify the social order below.

And there was something about Durkheim's manner that contributed to that feeling. He was dogmatic to a fault, as those who think they are in possession of a truth often are. We know from other sources that he was full of questions in private, which may, in its own perverse way, have contributed to the icy sureness with which he could write and speak. He did not present his views as interesting new hypotheses about human life. He presented them as well-established truths, as ancient and as certain as those in the Old Testament. Admiring students, without a hint of irony, often used terms like "prophet" or "oracle" or "apostle" when speaking of him, while others, who did not always share that admiration (and knew the uses of irony), were known to refer to him as "the priest" or "the pope."

Durkheim was certainly aware of the figure he cut. He must have been gratified to have made so clear an impression on his own generation and the one then moving into its place, but he must also have been aware of the mocking undertones it sometimes elicited among a number of his contemporaries. It is reported that he once walked by the cathedral of Notre Dame with one of his colleagues and said to him: "It is from a chair like that that I should have spoken." Of all the virtues that have been attributed to Durkheim, a sense of humor must rank near the bottom, but I would love to be able to report that he said that as a kind of wistful jest.

What adjectives, then, could be applied to that remarkable person? *Brilliant* goes without saying, as so do *austere* and *formidable* as well as something close to *imperious*. And why not? He took for granted that he had discovered some deep and critical verities, and he could hardly have persuaded so many others of the importance of those insights if he did not speak of them in bold and assured terms. I am venturing into unfamiliar territory now if I suggest that the rabbi Durkheim thought he would become when he was seven or eight years old was still a part of his makeup when he turned into his fifties. One young colleague who proved to be an understanding friend when Durkheim was alive and an understanding biographer after his death, Georges Davy, wrote about the *air terrible* that accompanied Durkheim in those later years and the forbidding aura that enveloped him then. But Davy was close enough to the older man to see and sense the softer edges that others knew to be there—describing him as "a mixture of severe authority and anxious affection."

Perhaps that should find a way onto Durkheim's gravestone too.

In many ways, Marx and Durkheim are located at opposite ends of the continuum along which most other sociological giants have positioned themselves. Marx's angry eye searched for evidence of friction, contradiction, and conflict, while Durkheim's cooler gaze sought evidence of cohesion and bonding.

They both offered brilliant arguments—all the more powerful because they were pursued with such unrelenting logic. Balance may not be a useful quality in persons of genius, but those of us who now look out at social life from the perspective those huge shoulders provide us might be tempted to offer the thought that Marx and Durkheim each suffered from indifference to what the other understood so well. Marx underestimated the degree to which religious beliefs, ethnic identities, national allegiances, and other sources of group cohesion can out-bid class interest as a governor of human conduct. This is what Durkheim knew. Durkheim greatly underestimated the degree to which some of the growing pains of Europe could be attributed to the exploitation of ordinary people by ruling classes. That is what Marx knew.

But if either of those outlooks had been moderated to accommodate the wisdom of the other, how much poorer each would have been! To that extent, it becomes our job, generations later, to draw from and make the most of those outlooks, and to make whatever allowances are necessary for the exaggerations that every great vision is almost sure to exhibit at first. It does not require any deep thought to convert a brilliant idea, with all its original exaggerations intact, into a form of orthodoxy, which is what happened, with different consequences, to the work of both Durkheim and Marx. But it takes a lot of serious thought to learn from such exaggerations as these what the possibilities of human life may be.

The World According to Max Weber

In some ways, both Marx and Durkheim could be described as simplifiers. I do not mean by this that they regarded social life as less complicated or less nuanced than other observers, but that they thought the task of the social analyst should be to peel away the levels of ambiguity and subjectivity that so complicate the human scene in order to reveal the patterns that lie at their base, and then, having accomplished that, to describe those patterns in as clear a way as possible. This may be exactly the right strategy for thinkers who view themselves as involved in lifelong arguments. In one sense, at least, they already *know* the answers, and their job is to portray their views in a few sharp and telling strokes. For Durkheim in particular, to seek underlying clarities and to state them plainly lay at the heart of scholarship.

Max Weber might have agreed with that intellectual strategy in principle, but everywhere he looked, especially in his own time, it seemed to him that the ambiguities and subjectivities of social life lay at the core of things. He was so overwhelmed by all those complexities, one might even say, that he went after them like an explorer charging into the thickest of underbrush to see if he can discover what is going on in there. His restless intelligence probed every facet of social life, both in his own time and in times past, and in order to fully measure his influence on social thought more generally, one would have to speak separately of his contributions to a wide range of the specialties into which the study of society is now compartmentalized. Pick up any volume on the nature of politics, on the philosophy or the history of religion, on social stratification, on the economy, on the sociologies of law, the city, or the state, and he is quite likely to be cited in the first few pages as one of the originator's of the field itself and as a continuing inspiration to scholars who continue to work in those precincts. We will come across Weber's name again and again in this book when we turn to topics as diverse as cities, divisions, and nationalism.

Weber was more instrumental than anyone else in locating and defining the center of the continuum that Marx and Durkheim had marked the outer edges of, and most sociologists of our time would probably agree that his spirit presides over that center even now. If Durkheim gets credit for having discovered a new continent in the world of knowledge, Weber should get credit for having done more than any of the masters to explore that intellectual territory and to chart its various dimensions.

Of the many adjectives one might use to describe Weber, then, *learned* would have to be one of the most prominent. Another might be *tormented.* You will hear more about that shortly, but I would note now that in Weber's case the two qualities may be related. Weber was forever seeking, pressing, questioning, investigating—driven by the need to *find out.* This took him into realms of knowledge that few others have even tried to enter, which is why the word *learned* is so apt. But it also took him to the very edge of human endurance, which is why *tormented* fits as well. Once, when asked why he studied so relentlessly, he replied: "I want to see how much I can stand." On another occasion, he described the fierce intensity of intellectual searchings like his own as "demonic." And on yet another occasion he wrote: "if one wants to settle with this devil, one must not take flight before him, as so many like to do nowadays. First of all, one has to see the devil's way to the end in order to realize his power and his limitations."

As was the case with Durkheim, Weber's career at first had the look of a steady journey down a conventional academic path. He was born in 1864 of a financially secure middle-class family in what was then Prussia. He studied at three of the most highly regarded universities in Germany, worked for a time in legal offices in Berlin, and then, at the remarkably early age of thirty, began what was scheduled to become a distinguished career as university professor, first at Freiburg and then shortly thereafter at Heidelberg. Weber was recognized early as one of the most promising young scholars of his time.

Theodor Mommsen, who was then the best known historian—and maybe the best known scholar—of that time is recorded as having said to the young Weber on the occasion of his Ph.D. thesis defense in 1889: "When I come to die, there is no one better to whom I would like to say this: Son, the spear is too heavy for my hand, carry it on."

In 1897, when he was 33, Weber suffered what was then called a "nervous collapse." He was only able to lecture intermittently and to work at his desk in short spurts. Those spurts could be intervals of intense creativity, but for the most part he saw himself, and was viewed by others, as a semi-invalid. Something profoundly troubling was going on in that rich mind of his, there can be no question about that, but it is also worth pointing out, as one of his biographers,

Donald MacRae, does, that "to be ill . . . was then an alternative vocation for the comfortably off." Six years would pass before Weber resumed the scholarly life, and almost twenty would pass before he returned to full-time teaching—a position at Vienna created expressly for him—and he was by then the giant we celebrate now. A brilliant mind and sensibility emerged from that illness—maybe even in part because of it. But it was a time of deep distress for Weber.

Like Marx, Durkheim, and most other social scientists of the late 19th and the early 20th centuries, Weber took as his principal project to understand the nature of the industrial order that was closing in on Europe like a fearsome new growth. Marx viewed it as a source of injustice on a massive scale, and as an aberration that history would one day correct. Durkheim was dubious about the approach of industrialism, too, but he saw it as an emerging social form that required careful study rather than the sounding of an alarm. Weber, though, found it disheartening to the very depths of his being. It might even be said that he was traumatized by it. He used to quote the German poet Friedrich Schiller, who had alluded to "the disenchantment of the world," and he himself wrote: "Not summer's bloom lies ahead of us, but rather a polar night of icy darkness and hardness."

Weber shared Marx's deep fascination with capitalism, but when he employed that term he had in mind the structure and temper of modern industrial society more generally. To Marx, capitalism was an economic arrangement. To Weber, it was not only that but something akin to a culture, a form of civilization—a "spirit," he called it in the title of his best known work—and he was interested above all in tracing its emergence over time.

That was no simple assignment for someone of Weber's scholarly temperament and huge capacity for learning. He felt obliged not only to survey vast stretches of historical time, a life's work for most, but to develop new conceptual and methodological approaches to the study of the social order as well. Weber was thoroughly familiar with methods then in use in his home fields of economics and history, but he found them inadequate to the purposes he had in mind. So he, too, set himself the task of charting a new discipline, a new way of looking at and gathering data about human society.

I plan here to follow three different threads that run though the rich tapestry of Weber's work to offer a sense of how his mind operated and how he helped formulate the sociology we now know. The first has to do with the nature of the modern world. The second has to do with the nature of sociology itself. The third has to do with the structure of the modern state.

On the Modern World

When Weber looked out at the Europe of his time, he thought he could see a new social form taking shape based on what he called the "rationalization" of everyday life. Everywhere, it seemed to him, life was becoming more orderly and more reasoned. Calculation was replacing spontaneity, efficiency was replacing a sense of craft, science was replacing faith, bureaucracy was replacing tradition. Specialists were taking over responsibilities once entrusted to people of broad cultivation and learning, and technicians were taking over work once entrusted to artisans. Something cool, measured, and mechanical was slowly replacing something warm and mystical and human.

On the one hand, Weber welcomed this development. The oldest hope of an earlier age, as we noted earlier, had been that reason would displace inspiration and tradition in the conduct of everyday life, and Weber shared with virtually everyone else of his generation an assumption that this trend was not only a good thing but irreversible in any case. Yet he was acutely aware of what was being lost in the process: a sense of wonder, of innocence, of the spiritual. To say that he was "acutely aware" of what was occurring, though, as we have already noted, does not begin to capture his mood. A more troubled vision would be hard to imagine.

Why, Weber wondered, did capitalism (by which term, to repeat, he was including what we would now call *industrialization* and *modernization*) come to flourish in the West but not in other parts of the world where conditions would otherwise appear to have been quite favorable for it? Why not in India or China? Why not in ancient Judea or Rome? That is two questions, actually, and Weber set to work on both of them. First, what was it about the West that favored the growth of capitalism? And, second, what was it about those other places that did not?

Weber addressed the first of those questions in what would turn out to be the best known of his writings, a remarkable essay entitled *The Protestant Ethic and the Spirit of Capitalism.* It seemed clear to Weber, as it had to many others, that there had always been a close connection between Protestantism and capitalism. They appeared on the European scene at more or less the same time, and each seemed to prosper in the presence of the other. Should this be viewed as a coincidence in timing? Or was some kind of complementarity at work here?

Weber moved into the archives to follow this relationship to its source in about the same frame of mind as another kind of explorer might take a deep breath and move into an uncharted landscape to follow the course of a river to its source.

Weber concluded from this inquiry that some of the early strains of Protestantism, and especially those that drew on the teachings of John Calvin and came to be known as Puritanism, may well have helped prepare the soil in which capitalism flourished. Puritanism was based on a highly disciplined approach to work and a willingness to defer the rewards of that work in the here and now. Industriousness, Calvin had taught, was a virtue of and by itself. It was a way to glorify the Lord, quite aside from anything else, and it may have been a way for the faithful to get some clue as to whether they had been selected for eternal life. To *enjoy* the fruits of that industry, however, was quite suspect. It hinted at sloth and avarice and a dozen other sins. So good Puritans were expected to labor mightily at whatever line of work they had been called to, and yet to remain contemptuous of the pleasures of this world. It is hard to imagine a spiritual cast of mind better suited to the needs of capitalism, since capital expansion relies exactly on individual persons being willing to exert themselves vigorously, to defer the benefits accruing from that exertion, to plough profits back into the market, and then to wait patiently for those investments to mature. The unworldly asceticism of the Puritan view of life, then, turned out to include mental habits that lent themselves almost perfectly to the worldly covetousness of the capitalist view of life.

And so, Weber concluded, a *spiritual ethos* had helped create the intellectual climate in which an *economic system* that had nothing in it of the spiritual could grow and thrive.

The Protestant Ethic and the Spirit of Capitalism has been widely honored from the day of its publication, and for many reasons. Among the most celebrated of those reasons is the fact that it seems to question the rock-hard materialism of Karl Marx. Marx had declared, you may remember, that the economic structure of a society shapes the values, ideas, and beliefs that the members of the society hold dear. The prevailing economic arrangements, that is to say, form the bedrock reality of social life, and the varying mental constructs that drift into our minds are like a vapor that emanates from it. Marx would have been compelled by the logic of his older argument to insist that a set of religious ideas—pure vapor, in his view—could only have come from an economic substratum.

Weber, of course, appeared to be proposing the exact reverse here. In his reading of the historical record, vapors had created bedrock.

It has been fashionable in some circles, then, to honor Weber for having turned Marx on his head. But Weber was careful to note that he was not making any kind of causal argument in *The Protestant Ethic and the Spirit of Capitalism* and was certainly not trying (in his words) "to substitute a one-sided materialistic" interpretation with "an equally one-sided spiritualistic" one. He was only proposing that the ethos of Protestantism and the spirit of capitalism have a certain "affinity," each serving to enhance the other. History shuttles back and forth from the material to the spiritual in an endless interaction, and which of the two seems to be acting as a precondition to the other at any given point in time depends on where we step into the flow of history, where we begin our frame-by-frame study of that continuing roll of film.

Marx might have said to Weber: "What you say might very well be true, but, if so, the Protestant ethic itself must have been preceded by some other underlying economic condition." Weber would then have been obliged by the logic of *his* argument to reply: "Now that is quite possible. I'll have to check into that." Whereupon it would have been back to the archives for Weber.

The second set of considerations Weber had to address in order to answer the question of why capitalism flourished in Europe had to do with the reasons it did not flourish elsewhere in the world. In order to satisfy his curiosity on that subject, Weber began a search for the source of a number of other rivers as well. This was a serious explorer. His studies took him to such ancient territories as the aforementioned India, China, Judea, and Rome, and into such disparate worldviews as Taoism, Confucianism, Judaism, Buddhism, Hinduism, and, as he neared the end of his time on earth, Islam. He tried to show in each of these cases what it was in the cultural atmosphere that discouraged the emergence of an activity like capitalism—dependent as it is on calculation and rational decision-making.

The findings of those studies need not concern us now, but it is quite important to note that Weber's explorations into the past required new ways of conceptualizing the social world and new methods for inquiring into it. His book on *Protestantism and the Spirit of Capitalism* may have been his best-known work, but his essays on method are the real source of his lasting influence on sociology and the rest of the social sciences generally.

On the Nature of Sociology

Like Durkheim before him, Weber was determined to impose the same standards of rigor on the social sciences as were known in the physical and natural sciences. But it seemed obvious to Weber that the workings of the human mind are so different in kind from the workings of the physical universe that social investigators would need to develop their own ways of approaching reality and their own ways of framing questions about it.

Social acts. Durkheim was entirely comfortable talking about the currents and drifts and pulls that he sensed were operating like forces of gravity in human life. Weber was not. He was gifted in the art of generalization himself, but he insisted that a true social scientist should begin with the most elementary particles of which human social life is composed and work outward from there. These particles are the *social acts* in which individual persons engage. The adjective "social" was very important here. He was not speaking of isolated scraps of behavior that have no social content at all, like blowing one's nose in the privacy of one's home or staring absently through a shop window on a sidewalk. He was speaking of acts that have an impact on how other people behave or feel. Acts with a purpose. *Social* acts.

Society, Weber thought, was the sum of all those purposive acts, and in his view the task of the social scientist is to determine how patterns form and institutional structures emerge from that immense wash of detail.

These social acts, Weber said, are of four kinds. A "rational" act is one motivated by *calculation,* as when I decide to vote for a candidate because she backs programs that are likely to increase my income. A "value-rational" act is one guided by *moral* (or sometimes *aesthetic*) considerations, as when I decide to vote for a candidate because of the stand he takes on prayers in school or on abortion rights. A "traditional" act is one prompted by *custom,* as when I offer my support to a particular party or person because my family has always done so. An "affectual" act, finally, is one that follows from *emotion,* as when I back a candidate because I have been so moved by something she said or did.

These may not seem like important distinctions to keep in mind now, a century or more after they were first devised. But they played a significant part in Weber's analysis of his own times, because he felt that the emotional tone of the world he lived in was changing before his eyes. When he wrote of the "rationalization" of modern life he was describing a shift in the center of social gravity from "traditional" and "affectual" forms of behavior to more "rational" ones. Whether he would have selected different adjectives if he was looking at the landscape you and I face now is something we cannot know.

Weber was aware that the four categories of social act he had identified, no matter how easily defined in the abstract, lost a good deal of their conceptual crispness the minute they were applied to actual human conduct. In real life, of course, I am likely to vote for a combination of reasons. The fact that the policies of a particular candidate look as though they might enrich my purse may impress me, but at the same time the fact that I approve of the way he lives his life or feel a sense of kinship with him because he, too, is Irish, are part of the mix—and so is the fact that at some deep subliminal level I may be drawn to him because he reminds me of my mother. We are not talking about computers or calculators here but of human minds—elusive chambers full of ambivalence, enigma, confusion, ambiguity.

Ideal types. How, then, can we distinguish between varying kinds of social acts such as "rational" and "traditional" if actual behavior is almost never that clearly differentiated? Weber proposed that we learn to think in terms of what he called "ideal types"—a concept so simple in the telling that its importance is easily misunderstood.

An "ideal type" is an exaggerated portrait of something, almost a caricature. It does not try to capture what the eye actually sees out there in everyday social life, but the essence of it, its pure form. The term "ideal" might not serve Weber's purpose that well in English, where it means "perfect" and "utopian" as well as what Weber had in mind, "archetypical." When he drew a distinction between "rational" and "traditional," he knew that he was not differentiating one kind of social act from another so much as he was identifying the contrasting poles toward which those acts seem to lean. An act described as "traditional" tends toward one pole. An act described as "rational" tends toward another. As was often the case, Weber did not really help matters very much when he offered his own definition:

> An ideal type is formed by the one-sided accentuation of one or more points of view and by the synthesis of a great many diffuse, discrete, more or less present and occasionally absent individual phenomena, which are arranged according to those one-sidedly emphasized viewpoints into a unified analytical construct.

That could slow one down! But his meaning seems clear enough once we work our way through that thicket of words. An "ideal type" is a model, a template that one holds up to reality in an effort to fix something in the mind—an event, say, or a category of events—that might otherwise be lost in the swirling eddy of sound and color and movement that is society.

Weber had confidence in the concept in part because it is a mental strategy people use all the time in everyday life without knowing that they are doing so. If you were to ask me "what is a Protestant, anyway?"—a sensible question under the circumstances—I would have to reply that it is somebody who believes in this or that article of faith or who worships in this or that manner. You will recognize even as I speak that I am not listing qualities shared by everyone who can be called Protestant, or even by most of them. I was brought up Protestant, but the states of mind or the ways of behaving I will be relating to you may or may not have any bearing on my own circumstances. Nor does it matter, because both you and I will know that I was offering an abstract representation of Protestantism when I answered your query. A model. An ideal type.

Verstehen. I noted earlier that the fundamental particles of social life—and, thus, the subject matter of sociology—are individual acts and the patterns they form. The particles that make up the *natural* world can be treated for the most part as discrete specks of matter. But the particles that make up the *social* world are of a different kind altogether. They are shifty, liable to human whim. They seem to dance in front of one's eyes, drifting out of focus whenever one tries to fix a steady gaze on them.

The reasons for this, Weber thought, are two. First, the subjective values of those who perform social acts are always working their way into the texture of things, influencing behavior like erratic gusts of wind. Those gusts of wind even out over time, so there is predictability and pattern in the social order. But at any given point in time, the manner in which people behave does not appear to be governed by any obvious form or design. When we study human society, moreover, we are actually studying ourselves—using our own minds and imaginations to inquire into the minds and imaginations of other people just like ourselves. In that sense, what we social scientists learn about the social world comes to us filtered through screens of our own making. So the behavior we look at is ruled by subjective impulses, but so are the eyes through which we see.

One would suppose, then, that we social scientists operate at a real disadvantage when compared to colleagues in the natural and physical sciences. The information we gather is full of subjectivities, and so are the instruments with which we gather them. Our work is subject to all the distortions that human flesh is heir to. And yet, Weber pointed out, exactly because we study *ourselves* we have an asset that no one in the older sciences can even begin to enjoy. Since we, too, are human, we can *think* our way into the minds of the people we are trying to fathom and in that way gain a special level of insight into why they act as they do. *Verstehen,* Weber called this ability—"understanding," "comprehending."

This is one of the most important and yet most easily misunderstood of Weber's many contributions to sociological thinking. *Verstehen* refers to the process of imagining oneself in the position of someone else, using the tunings of one's own mind to reach into and get a sense of the tunings of another's mind. It is a deliberate effort to put one's powers of empathy and intuition to work. "One does not need to be Julius Caesar in order to understand him," Weber wrote. One need only work one's way into Caesar's mind and study it from within.

On its face, this looks like an invitation to suppose that you and I, thinking as intently and as sympathetically as we are able, can have access to the inner workings of minds from worlds wholly different from our own. Understanding the mind of Julius Caesar? Of Moke? Of the unnamed artist who painted a bison on the wall of a cave thirteen or fourteen thousand years ago? Really?

But that is not what Weber meant. When he referred to *Verstehen* he was only trying to point out that acts of empathy are a natural activity of the human mind in any event. He was not suggesting that you or I could truly *understand* a person like Caesar who died 2,000 years before either of us were born and spoke a language that I do not know and you probably do not either. Nor did he mean that *I* could understand *you* if I put my mind to it—or you me. His point was that most of us have at least a general idea of how it must feel to win an election or lose a friend or (as in Caesar's case) return home in triumph after a military campaign in distant lands. We obviously have no way of knowing whether Caesar reacted to the things that occurred to him in the same way we think we would have had we been in his position, but our common humanity should give us a hint as to how he might have felt.

Verstehen, moreover, is not to be understood as a procedure for *finding out* the truth of things, as other scientific methods often are. We cannot learn anything definitive about social reality by projecting ourselves into the lives of others or by using all our powers of empathy to imagine what is going on in their minds. We turn to *Verstehen* to get an inkling of things, to become more sensitive to the way others live. What we learn from such a procedure does not really become *knowledge* until it is verified by some other kind of empirical test. It is a way of developing hunches, a way of framing hypotheses.

Value neutrality. How is it possible for anyone to construct a legitimate science from subject matter as elusive as social acts turn out to be? We just noted that every scrap of human behavior reflects the subjective feelings of the individual who enacted it, and that by the time those scraps come to scientific attention they are subject to further distortions by the subjective values of the person undertaking the study. This problem is simply inescapable, and there have been any number of commentators in Weber's time and even more in our own who have argued that this is the fatal flaw in the very idea of an objective social science.

Weber was quite adamant, however, that it is possible to reduce the amount of bias that seeps into scholarly work by a careful application of what he called "value free analysis" and "ethical neutrality" in the classroom, the laboratory, and out in the field. He seems to have had nothing more complicated in mind than an earnest effort on the part of scholars to sublimate whatever ideological or ethical urgings threaten to drift into the research they undertake and to exercise a healthy measure of self-restraint in the teaching they do.

One hundred years later, this pronouncement sounds rather naïve—a hopeful recipe for objectivity. Give it your best shot! It is important to keep in mind that Weber was addressing audiences for whom that message resonated quite differently than it would to most of us today. But even so, Weber's voice remains the prominent one in sociological discussions of the topic. He did not resolve the problem of objectivity in the social sciences, of course, but he phrased it in such a way that the issue itself is very clearly joined. On the one hand, the primary materials of sociological analysis will always be value-laden, and the process of studying them will always be subject to bias. Yet social scientists must press on—never sure that they are not projecting their own values onto the scenes they are depicting, but always alert to that possibility.

In some respects, then, it is the *sound of Weber's voice* as much as the *meaning of his words* that constitute his legacy to us on the topic of objectivity in scholarly work. The burden of sociological analysis, the voice tells us, is to never forget that human life is played out on a plane of subjective values, but to always act professionally as if those subjective values can be neutralized at least in part by being aware of the difficulty they pose. This may be little more than what I called a hopeful recipe a moment ago, but most sociologists think it is a wise one and try to live by it.

Weber's voice continues to help locate the center of what seems to be an ever-widening space in social thought, marked on the one side by scholars so eager to emulate the positivism of the older sciences that they simply ignore the subjectivities of everyday human life, and on the other hand by scholars who have abandoned the very notion of objectivity in social research and come to the conclusion that they might just as well rely on their own inner leanings than on the unreliable evidence the world is ready to offer up. Weber knew what that species of mindless positivism was like, having encountered it in his own time, and he was profoundly troubled by it. But the retreat from value-free analysis that has characterized much of modern social thought took place after his death, although he knew earlier variants of it himself. I think that it would have troubled him even more.

On Forms of Political Authority

Weber saw the world of his time as increasingly characterized by the bureaucratization and routinization of the marketplace, of the workplace, of the conduct of everyday life, and of the state. He defined the state as a political entity "that successfully claims the monopoly of the legitimate use of violence within a given territory." That has since become a well-known and off-cited definition, but it sometimes lends itself to meanings that Weber clearly did not intend because of the stress it seems to place on "violence." "Force" is closer to what Weber had in mind here, as he made clear in other contexts, or perhaps "the *means* of violence." He clearly did not have in mind that modern states rule largely by the exercise of violence and terror, but that they claim the exclusive right to maintain armies and police forces within a given domain.

Weber took it for granted, as did Marx and most other observers of the political process before and since, that no government is likely to remain in power over the long term unless a considerable number of those being governed think that it is *entitled* to do so—unless, that is, it is widely seen as *legitimate.*

Weber, as you will have discovered by now, had a mind that lent itself to the formulation of typologies. One of his most celebrated is an account of the three bases of political legitimacy: rational-legal, traditional, and charismatic. If the purpose of this chapter was to offer an account of Weber's principal contributions to social science thinking, we would have to pause here for a longer time than we can afford. So I will just note as we bring this discussion to a close that in the political realm, as in so many others, Weber sensed that rational thinking was driving out the customary and mystical and transcendent—and maybe even the human—in political life. This, too, is part of the disenchantment of which Weber wrote with such sorrow.

Weber had worked his way back from a crippling disability to chart the field of sociology in such brilliant detail. He became ill at the age of 33, and recovered to the point of being able to function as an independent scholar by 40 or so. *The Protestant Ethic and the Spirit of Capitalism* was published about then, and so were many of the methodological essays I have been drawing on in this sketch. As the years passed, he gradually returned to the eminence that had once been predicted for him, becoming, finally, one of the most renowned lecturers in the university world. In 1918, he resumed a full-time academic position at the University of Vienna and then transferred to one in Munich one year later. He was tall, dignified, sturdy, even commanding in appearance, and he had clearly recovered his voice literally and figuratively. In both Vienna and Munich it proved difficult to find lecture halls large enough to accommodate the audiences that hoped to hear him. We have no way of knowing what residual hurts still lingered inside that huge spirit, but we do know that his return was a true triumph.

It was not to last. For two years he pursued old projects and began new ones, and all of those materials were piled on his desk in anticipation of the fifteen or twenty years he had every reason to suppose lay before him. But he died without warning one summer afternoon when he was 56. He had fought off an invisible demon crouched down inside him, but he succumbed to an invisible virus that attacked from the outside. He had no defenses against that.

In Conclusion

Durkheim and Weber were contemporaries, but they set different goals for themselves. Durkheim, obviously, devoted the bulk of his career to creating a secure place for sociology in the world of knowledge. But Weber, only six years younger, could look upon sociology as an established field, allowing him to turn his attention to the subject matter it should focus on and the methods it should adopt. The six years that separated them in age may have had something to do with it, since Weber stepped into that historical stream that much later. And the miles that separated Paris and Berlin may have played a role here too, since the German academy turned out to be less resistant to the new discipline than the French one.

The biggest difference, though, may have been the fact that Durkheim wrote three of his four recognized classics before he reached the age of 40, while many of Weber's most seminal contributions came later in his life. Indeed, his influence on the field of sociology was not fully felt until after his death. That scatter of half-finished manuscripts and outlines and other notes that were on his desk at the time of his death—together with the lecture notes of students—were posthumous collections gathered by others, and our intellectual portrait of Weber relies heavily on them. His legacy, then, was less a set of conclusions than intellectual exercises in his way of thinking and seeing. It is not obvious that Weber would have come to conclusions in any case. The restlessness of his searchings was built into him.

Even though those two masters were born within six years of one another, then, and died within three, it makes a certain sense to suggest that they really belonged to different centuries—Durkheim to the 19th and Weber to the 20th. If we do look at things that way, it may help explain what to me is the astonishing fact that neither of them paid any attention to the other. Durkheim never mentioned Weber anywhere in his work, so far as I know, and Weber, who seems to have been aware of Durkheim, must have thought him of no special account. Marcel Mauss, whose memory of his uncle we called on earlier, once told Raymond Aron that he had seen a complete set of *L'Annee Sociologique,* the journal Durkheim had edited and regularly contributed to, on the shelves of Weber's study. Still, Weber never referred to him.

The two masters were very different anyway. Weber held out no hope whatever that a science of society might one day discover laws like those being formulated in chemistry or physics or develop causal explanations of the kind common to those other sciences. He would not have had much patience for Durkheim's assurance that sociology could be as systematic a science as any other. Durkheim often called on a fairly mechanistic vocabulary to frame his observations on the workings of the social order: "social facts," he said, should be regarded as "things"—*les choses*—and human life should be seen as organized into "systems" and subject to "laws." But there were no "things" in Weber's vision of society, and no stable patterns of the sort Durkheim urged us all to be on the lookout for.

So the two most original voices in what by that time was called "sociology" were being sounded at the same time to very large and appreciative audiences no more than a few hundred miles apart, and neither could hear the other.

Few sociologists in our time think that their discipline will ever uncover the degree of orderliness that Durkheim wrote about so insistently. I sometimes wonder whether Durkheim thought so either, but I am probably in a minority here. He encouraged us to proceed *as if* the social world is made up of things and *as if* it is governed by laws, and he did so because that is the way of science. But there is quite a difference between declaring that we should "*consider* social facts as things" and declaring flatly that they *are* things in the same tangible, concrete way as physical matter. If I am right in this, then Durkheim's confident and dogmatic view of human society may have been a bit closer to Weber's darker, richer, more nuanced and more troubled one.

Durkheim, in turn, may not have had much patience for Weber's remarkable attraction to complexity and his endless definitions and qualifications. Donald MacRae complained in his biography of Weber that he appeared to enjoy carrying his readers with him down into that vast and bewildering labyrinth called social life, and then just leaving us there without instructions as to how we might extricate ourselves from it, how we might get back again. Weber might have smiled grimly at that reproach. He wanted to acquaint us with the perplexities and ambivalences of social life, and it is entirely reasonable for us to suspect that he would not have minded if we were forced to spend a period of time tangled up in them ourselves. He might even have added in one of his more reflective moods that he did not know how to get out of the labyrinth either, an admission that Durkheim would probably have had a hard time understanding.

So they were different, to be sure, but together they were voices of such wisdom that a new field of study issued from them.

The Journey of Piotr and Kasia Walkowiak

BETWEEN 1820 AND 1920, WHEN THE WORLD was considerably less crowded than it is today, thirty-five million people came from Europe to the United States. The stream of migrants was scarcely more than a steady trickle at first, but it became a heavy flow in the years following the Civil War, and by the first decades of the 20th century it had cascaded into a real torrent. They began their journey in many parts of the old world, those immigrants—Ireland, Lithuania, Norway, Sicily, Greece. But in one particularly important respect, a considerable majority of them were from the same place. They were peasants, swept by the sharpest of winds off lands their ancestors had occupied for hundreds of years.

This visit to the field will trace the paths of two of them, a couple I will call Piotr and Kasia Walkowiak. The words I am going to attribute to them were taken from the hundreds of letters and diaries gathered in the 1910s by two sociologists from the University of Chicago, W. I. Thomas and Florian Znaniecki, for their remarkable study *The Polish Peasant in Europe and America,* published in five volumes between 1918 and 1920. So the words spoken and events recalled here are all real, even if "Piotr" and "Kasia" are composites and in that sense a kind of invention.

But who were they? What populations are they being asked to represent here? In the first place, obviously, they are migrants from Poland, and that places them in the company of millions of other Poles who came to this country somewhere between 1890 and 1920. In the second place, though, they were for the most part from the rural heart of Europe, tuned to the ways of the village and the seasons and the fields, and that places them in the company of millions of other peasants who moved from the old world to the new. Their story would have sounded much the same if it had been told of individuals whose names were Italian or Serbian or Greek or Scandinavian. But even more than that, Piotr and Kasia Walkowiak represent the many millions of people who were transported in the space of a generation or two from the contained world of the village to all the complexities and fluidities of modern life—a transition we will discuss in more detail later in the book. So Piotr and Kasia carry a heavy burden here. They are being asked to stand in for a large portion of humankind.

They are important figures in the history of the United States as well. A representative cross-section of one hundred Americans would break down (roughly) as follows: one person whose ancestors walked to this continent when there was still a land bridge connecting Alaska and Siberia; five or six persons whose ancestors came from England and Scotland before the American Revolution on the decks of proud merchant vessels; eleven or twelve persons whose ancestors came from Africa in the 18th and 19th centuries, chained in the holds of the most shameful vessels the world has ever known; and one or two persons whose ancestors moved across a border yet to be charted into lands that would eventually be named Texas and New Mexico. That's about twenty out of one hundred. These are the old-stock Americans—to use the expression correctly for once— Native Americans, Anglos, African-Americans, original Hispanics. Together they constitute a fifth or so of the population. Most of the rest of us are descended from people like Piotr and Kasia.

As we will see in a subsequent chapter, the names of migrants to the United States in more recent years now are far more likely to have a Hispanic or Asian ring than an Irish or a Polish or an Italian one, but the story of their settling here will have a lot in common with that of the Walkowiaks, and they are settling into a world the Walkowiaks, in their turn, helped shape.

A few dates, then, to locate the story. Piotr and Kasia, we might as well suppose, were born in one of the poorer regions of Poland, in 1875 and 1880, respectively. They were married in the final year of the 19th century and gave birth to four children in the decade that followed. Piotr migrated to the United States in 1911, working for five years at a foundry in Pittsburgh and then at a steel mill in Chicago before being able to send for the rest of his family. He died in 1940 at the age of 65, about average for a man of his time and place. She, tough and resilient, lasted another twenty-five years. Piotr had a brother named Jan, who will enter the story soon. Other names will appear in the narrative from time to time, too, but those three are the ones you need to keep track of now.

The Old Country

Piotr and Kasia were born in a time of real change, but they came from a part of the world that had remained largely the same for as many years into the past as village history could reach. The people of the village, as Émile Zola wrote of French peasants at roughly the same time, "had been born and bred here for centuries, like a tough and hardy plant." We will review some of the more significant features of that world when we discuss "Villages," so I only want to note now that the world Kasia and Piotr were leaving rested on three bedrocks: *family, village, land.*

Family

People like Piotr and Kasia grew up in the grip of a family whose members were linked almost like the atoms in a molecule. We may of course assume about those peasants that they were held together by feelings of fondness and loyalty, but we have to add as we do so that they were also held together by elaborate networks of obligation that had every bit as much force. Every individual in the family felt responsible for—and was held responsible for—everybody else. This could be a mixed blessing, of course. On the one hand, the linkages of family could feel like an embrace, forming a warm pocket of caring in a cruel world. On the other hand, they could tighten like a coil, binding persons to one another, harnessing them, fixing them in place. Family members could be surly or harsh to one another but they were nonetheless connected, part of an organic whole. There was sometimes an irony here, as old tales relate: members of your family would not allow anyone else in the world to abuse you as much as they felt entitled to themselves.

The family shared virtually everything in common. The land, though managed by the father in a legal sense, was understood to be held in trust for children born and yet to be born—so it was not really disposable property in any useful sense of the term. The wages earned by grown family members, too, were assumed to belong to the household in general. When Piotr's younger brother—I named him Jan earlier—went off to work the farmlands of Prussia around the turn of the century, for example, the money he earned was counted as a family resource, and even when he emigrated to Pittsburgh a year or two later, he saw himself at least in part as an extension of the family working far from home for the benefit of those who still lived there.

Everyone had a more or less defined role in the family constellation. A visitor from afar might well have concluded that the husband took as his sphere of responsibility the family fields, scattered here and there across the area, and whatever marketing the family was involved in, while the wife took as her sphere of responsibility the household, the garden, the livestock, and the younger children. Other members of the family—young and old—had tasks appropriate to their gender or condition. To that extent, it would probably look to the visitor as though people were drifting through life's rounds in a kind of orbit, drifting in circles that were fixed, mandated by custom, and understood by everyone.

The visitor may also have noted that the family structure was sternly patriarchal, with the father occupying a position of ultimate authority. That would have been an accurate observation so far as it went, but it would have provided no more than a partial insight into family life. The father could sound imperious and unrelenting as he pronounced the voice of tradition to those around him, but the voice of tradition spoke just as sternly to him. It was he who told members of the family where to sit at the dinner table, for example, and it was he who called for silence and offered a blessing. That is certainly the look of authority. But he was as bound by the dictates of tradition as anyone else, and it is difficult to make the case that his will was any freer than that of other family members. At one point Jan wrote Piotr from abroad berating him for not being assertive enough. "I inform you, dear brother, that you manage your household badly. It is your wife who walks in the breeches, not you. Your wife governs. Things are bad in a household where the cow shows the way to the ox." We have no idea what provoked Jan to so sharp a rebuke, but we may presume that he and Piotr and everyone else in the village must have known that this was a kind of posturing and that the forces of custom and circumstance bound the husband and father as tightly as they did everyone else who lived in that confined space.

Village

People like Piotr and Kasia were held in the grip of a village, too—a cluster of families that must have seemed as though they had been rooted there like trees for hundreds of years like those "tough and sturdy plants" that Zola spoke of. To most of us, those settlements would have looked monotonously alike: a spare wooden church, a central square (as often a mire of mud as anything that could have been called a green or a common), a gathering of twenty or thirty thatched cottages, and, just outside that inner circle, a patchwork of fields. But the residents had a clear sense of the difference between their own village and a neighboring one. That is where they are "from." That is where they belong. That is their place, their niche. That is where, to recall my encounter with the Haitian migrant farm workers, they are "persons."

Older villagers had never known of a time when things were different. Seasons followed one another and generations replaced one another in looping cycles, time turning in on itself. For centuries—or so it seemed to them—people had been living by the same precepts, moving to the same rhythms, marveling at the same mysteries, and working the fields as they had been worked for generations. They did not calculate the most efficient uses of land or labor or materials, as was becoming the way of the cities. They relied on the fitness of ancient wisdoms and listened to the voices of nature.

In Piotr and Kasia's time, Poland was entirely dominated by three neighboring powers: Austria, Prussia, and Russia. But to most villagers, abstractions like states and empires were not entirely real. They knew that such entities existed, of course, and that small slights as well as large arguments could cause armies to meet in combat. But those were not realities that helped locate them or identify them. Monarchs came and went; the village outlasted them. Armies swept through, the village endured. Borders were drawn and redrawn as treaties were signed and royal marriages arranged; the village remained.

And they knew, too, that the state could reach into the village and make a hard life harder yet—collecting taxes, conscripting young men for service in wars that villagers knew nothing of and cared nothing about. Those things touched the villagers' existence, of course. But the state was something that happened *to* them, a force that originated in another universe. "To the peasant," wrote a man named Carlo Levi, speaking of a peasant village in southern Italy in the 1930s.

> the State is more distant than heaven and far more of a scourge, because it is always against them. Its political tags and platforms and, indeed, the whole structure of it do not matter. The peasants do not understand them because they are couched in a different language from their own, and there is no reason why they should ever care to understand them.

A word should be said about peasant spirituality before we leave this discussion of the village, since the parish formed the core of village life and piety was its prevailing mood. To deal with religion under a separate heading, however, is almost to miss the point. The idea that God governed the whole of the universe was so self-evident to villagers that the words we now use to describe that feeling of reverence would have made no sense to them. The question "do you believe in God?" would have about the same standing with them as the question "do you believe in gravity?" would have with us. Religion was not one of the departments into which life was partitioned. It was the whole of it. "And in the peasant's world," wrote Carlo Levi, speaking again of that village in Italy many years ago, "there is no room for religion, because to them everything participates in divinity, everything is actually, not merely symbolically, divine . . . the heavens above, and the beasts of the field below."

Land

Piotr and Kasia and their fellow peasants shared a deep attachment to the land they lived on and worked. One can hardly overestimate the importance of this tie, as we shall see in more detail later. It is a familiar habit of speech when talking of country people to say that they live *on* the land, which is true enough, but they think of themselves as rooted *in* the land, part *of* it. Its seasons are their seasons, its rhythms their rhythms. The land and the people who work it are of a piece.

This sense of identity with the land may not have been the kind of thing peasants spoke of often or easily, but the need to converse in writing, as happens when people are separated by long distances, requires a search for words to express what otherwise is taken for granted. That is one of the priceless virtues of the materials Thomas and Znaniecki collected. Sometimes the words seem as flat and direct as the land itself. A young man from a village like Piotr's, conscripted into the Tsar's army, wrote to his family from the vastness of Siberia: "I am very accustomed to the earth and I know how to manage it. Just for that I am so awfully homesick in the army, for I am away from the soil, I cannot work in it." There are times, though, when the words take off. Jan must have been astonished when Piotr, thick of hand and slow of speech, wrote him in Pittsburgh:

Probably you are longing there, dear brother, and sometimes sorrowful. I anticipate that although some great distance of land and sea separates you, still in your thought you visit your country, your relatives, and friends. . . . Your native country-house with its straw-roof and its dear inhabitants seems lovely to you; perhaps even the curved ridge between the fields or a naked stone upon the stripped soil reminds you sweetly of some mystery of the past.

The composition of that letter may owe something to a local priest or school-teacher enlisted to help Piotr with this task, for putting words to paper was an awkward business for him. Still, the thoughts reflected in them were his. They were a product of the village.

The End of an Age

That was the world into which Piotr and Kasia were born. Its ways were stable, and its people were thought to be massively stubborn and massively tough. And so it had been for a long time. That world, though, had already begun to change. It had endured the savageries of nature and of invading armies, but it could not survive two shifts in fortune that made a vast difference. For one thing, the population experienced a large, abrupt spurt of growth, and for another, the Industrial Revolution that had been moving like a slow and relentless tide across the continent from west to east throughout the 19th century crossed the border into Poland in the 1870s and 1880s. This meant that urban centers like Warsaw and Łódź and Kraków were beginning to industrialize and to expand in size, and it also meant that the land itself came under a good deal of pressure because the demand for food in Poland and in the rest of Europe was growing with the times. Poland was becoming a hinterland of the industrializing west.

The death rate dropped sharply throughout the 19th century as well, first in one part of Europe and then in another. A blessing, one has to say. But it was a bleak blessing at best, for the peasant world continued to produce children as it always had and the swelling population could no longer be absorbed into the rural economy. The logic of this situation was both harsh and simple. For a time, at least, the population increase could be contained by tightening belts, subdividing already overcrowded parcels of land into smaller units yet, and supplementing the yield of the land with the wages of family members who left home for periods of time to work on the holdings of others. At first, this meant walking to a nearby village to assist in seasonal tasks like plowing, sowing, harvesting, threshing. But once that migratory pattern had been established, its reach grew: into the richer farmlands of Austria, Slovakia, the Ukraine, Prussia—which is where Jan was when we first learned of him—and then into the growing cities like Warsaw or Łódź.

In the midst of this new ebb and flow, one's home village continued to be the center of one's world. Those who worked the harvest in Prussia or labored for a time in the factories of Warsaw or Kraków returned home at the end of the season, their pockets emitting the unusual sound of coins jangling together. But the time soon came when sons without land to work or trades to follow, and daughters without dowries or prospects, had no choice but to cut their ties with the land and drift away, some to nearby countries with a need for farm labor, others to the rapidly expanding cities, and still others to places as far removed as the United States. It was as if the earth had shuddered for a moment like some great beast and shaken people loose from the moorages that had held them in place on its flanks.

The drain of people out of the countryside took pressure off the land in one sense, but it only increased it in another, for the new migrants to the city, even though no longer on the land itself, nonetheless had to be fed by it; and the same harsh logic applied there as well. The only way to feed all those surplus people, clearly, was to make the land itself more productive. That required the elimination of a number of familiar old routines in the practice of agriculture and their replacement by efficient new methods. It meant the consolidation of fields and as a result the abandonment of customary ways of reckoning land ownership. It meant the selling off of common fields, and with it the disappearance of a time-honored basis for communality. Robert Redfield said of peasants everywhere that "their agriculture is a livelihood and a way of life, not a business for profit," so the shift from older forms of cultivation to more efficient ones meant the dilution of an old social order and an old cultural ethos as well as the modernization of an industry.

That is how things stood when Piotr and Kasia were young. Piotr's father, unable to see how he could subdivide his already meager holdings any further, knew that some if not most of his children would have to leave the lands that had sheltered his lineage for generations. Jan had moved to America a few years earlier, remember, as had quite a number of younger people. The time for vast waves of migration had come to the village. For those who went to distant places like America for long stretches of time, or even to neighboring regions for a season or two, the experience opened up new worlds of promise and possibility. It extended one's range geographically, clearly, but it also extended the reach of one's imagination and the scope of what one dared to hope.

Most of those who ventured across the Atlantic, however, did so on the assumption that they would return one day with savings enough to improve their prospects at home. When Jan first left Mazowsze, for example, his plan had been to earn a stake in America and then return, find a wife and a workable plot of land, and live out his time in the familiar surroundings of the village. Late at night in his Pittsburgh boardinghouse, with his "inner eyes" (as Ewa Morawska suggests about a different immigrant) Jan "saw himself returning to his native village dressed in a city suit and flashing a golden watch, in a high celluloid collar and a ribbon-trimmed gentleman's hat." Pinned in his clothing is a bank check for money enough to buy a few acres of land, a few cows, and a serviceable house.

"You cannot imagine how many people go to America," wrote a friend of Kasia's to her daughter in America. "So very few will remain in our country." And Piotr's father wrote to Jan in Pittsburgh at about the same time:

> Dear son, your mother would be glad to see you before she dies, but it is difficult, because here in our country it gets worse and worse. Now many people get separated, although they have land. Many husbands leave their wives and go in search of work, some of them go to America, others to Prussia . . . because misery creeps into the houses and drives people away into the world.

In 1910, Piotr was 35 and Kasia was 30. They already knew that they would not inherit enough of the Walkowiak holdings to draw a living from them, certainly not enough to provide for their four children. And as they watched their neighbors drift off, they began to make plans themselves. When Jan first reached America, Piotr had written him to see what he could learn about the lay of that distant land:

> Meanwhile please answer me whether it is easy to find a job, what are the conditions—lodging, boarding, work, pay, journey. Please tell me this, for in our shriveled and impotent Europe a somewhat more energetic man has nothing to do. In order to live, one must have the mind of a goose, the patience of a stone, and be an ox—devout, obedient, polite.

But that was before the children. And since he had exhausted all his resources by the time the fateful day arrived, Piotr wrote to an agency he had heard about called the Emigrant Protective Association in Warsaw for help in financing his passage:

I want to go to America, but I have no means at all because I am poor and have nothing but the ten fingers of my hands, a wife and four children. I have no work at all, although I am strong and healthy and only thirty-five years old. I cannot earn for my family. . . . I have no land of my own. I am not a craftsman and it is very difficult for me to live here. I rent some [two acres] of land, and now I cannot pay the rent to the proprietor; therefore I must soon leave this place. . . . I wish to work, not easily only but even hard work, but what can I do? I will not go to steal and I have no work.

So Piotr, too, who had never ventured more than a few miles from his home, began an extraordinary journey, leaving Kasia and the children in the village. What little money the two of them had been able to scrape together would certainly not take a family of six to America, and, of course, their main hope was that Piotr would be able to earn enough during his stay in the new world to buy land in the old. Piotr had lived the whole of his life in the ordered niche of the village, but he now joined a procession of people he had always been taught to be wary of. He was a migrant, walking the roads like a common wayfarer. Piotr did not complain in letters to Kasia, since he knew her life was hard enough, but he wrote to other friends as he made his way across Europe. "I am an exile and a pilgrim, far away from you, from my father's land and my family," he wrote to one old comrade, and to another he said: "I am a wanderer in a strange land for the sake of my children. . . . If God grants me work and help I will soon be back in our country."

The Journey

The "miseries that crept into" Piotr's house and drove him out into the world, as we will see more fully later, had been spreading across Europe for years, so the procession Piotr joined had been long under way. It was a flow made up of commingling national streams, but one in which people from different parts of the continent took turns dominating the mixture. In the 1820s and 1830s, four million Scots and English. In the 1840s and 1850s, five million Irish. In the 1860s and the 1870s, eight million Germans and Scandinavians. In the 1880s and 1890s, five million Italians and three million Greeks, Syrians, and Armenians. And, following hard upon them as the world shifted into a new century, eight million Poles, Slovaks, Ukrainians, East European Jews, with many more yet to come. Thirty-five million immigrants in all, with the stream at its heaviest when Piotr stepped into it in 1910.

Piotr had high hopes of the country to which he was making his way. Everyone in the village knew of younger men who had sought their fortunes in America and who spoke warmly of their experiences in letters home. "I am getting along well, very well," wrote one of them. "We eat here every day what we get only for Easter in our country." "I do very well," another announced:

In the beginning I was a little homesick, but now I have already forgotten about it. I have good and easy work. . . . Time goes on very quickly in America, you don't notice when the week is past, and of money we have our pockets full. We have music every day.

But more ominous messages had been circulating, too, and Piotr had seen his share of them. In the first place, there had been gloomy reports about the availability of work. "And I inform you," a neighbor's son had written home, "that in America things are very bad. Work is bad and living is very dear." Another young neighbor had written to his sister: "As to work, I haven't worked for four weeks. There is no work. Brother still works but he is not doing well, because all factories are closed. Things are so good in America that people are going begging!" Moreover, terrible rumors had swept across the village from time to time, sending parents to whatever served as their writing desks in search of reassurances. Their children had moved to a world so far outside the accustomed frames of reference of the village that nothing seemed implausible:

We ask you now, dear son, to inform us how long you intend in America, for about America bad rumors are spreading, that it is about to sink in, and even priests order us to pray for those who are in America.

Everybody dissuades me from going to America saying that I shall have to work hard and still to die from hunger, and that I shall be killed, for there are so many robbers.

Here papers write that there is war in New York, that houses are destroyed with bombs.

Even if all such rumors could be discounted, however, the road from rural Poland to urban America was alive with perils and uncertainties. It took Piotr months to negotiate the trip, in fact. He traveled across borders guarded by watchful patrols, through lands where strange languages were spoken and strange ways observed, along roads where furtive eyes appeared to mean him harm, and at every step of the way he encountered customs offices and check-points and border posts, inspections and interviews and examinations, and an unending avalanche of forms.

Piotr, like many of his fellow wayfarers, had the advantage of a brother in America and other friends who could share their travel experiences with him. "Be careful in every place about money," Jan had written, "and," he added, sounding as though he may have a story to tell, "don't talk to girls on the water." The advice was welcome even when it was not consistent:

> If you have any baggage, I mean any large trunk or large bag, you can give it up, but don't give it into anybody's hands without a receipt. Without an iron receipt don't give up your baggage, because it would be lost.

> On the way to Illowo [a border town] wear clothes which you can throw away when they disinfect them, and take good clothes in a valise, because they do not disinfect clean clothes. To live on, take some smoked meat and dry cheese.

> Take fifteen rubles with you, it will be enough, and change them at once for Prussian money. As to the clothes, take the worst which you have, some three shirts, that you may have a change on the water. And when you come across the water happily, then throw away all these rags. Bring nothing with you except what you have upon yourself. And don't bring any good shoes either . . . but don't take any cheese.

The journey was difficult and dangerous. I noted earlier that thirty-five million people entered the United States through embarkation centers like Castle Garden and Ellis Island, thus leaving a record of their passing on the official ledger. But it is clear that many more than this set out from their homes in rural Europe. Many died on the trip across the continent, during the long wait in crowded ports, or aboard ships taking them across the ocean. And that is only to speak of mortality, for many others were stranded along the way, succumbing to exhaustion or illness or despair, and sinking from sight into the farm labor pool or the urban masses in cities along the way or in ports like Bremen, Hamburg, and Antwerp.

Piotr, whose cast of mind had been formed in the village world, had some aptitudes that served him well during the long journey. He was determined, strong, and distrustful enough to remain on the alert. The sad fact was, however, that most of the qualities that had given him a secure place at home were of little value now. Though tuned to the ways of communal life, to shared decisions and common responsibilities, he now traveled alone. Though raised in a place where no one was a stranger, he now passed through lands where everyone was. Though reliant upon custom to help regulate the pace and substance of everyday life, he now had to negotiate a path among people who organized their lives very differently. Though wise in the ways of the land and the seasons, he had little experience with the unfamiliar circumstances and unfamiliar people he encountered on the way.

So Piotr Walkowiak, like so many of his kind, arrived in the new world disoriented and out of breath. He felt a bit like a child again, if only in the sense that he had a new culture to try to come to terms with, a new language to learn, new habits of mind to acquire, and new sources of confidence and self-respect to discover.

History will record that Piotr—and the millions of other persons he is representing in this account—reached his destination. But in one important respect, he did not. His original plan had been to earn enough of a stake there to buy land upon his return to Poland: "If God grants me work and health I will soon be back in our country," he had written. But the tides of history were flowing in a reverse direction, and Piotr, like so many others, was caught in their undertow. He never saw Poland again. By the time he could send for Kasia and the rest of the family, he had become a creature of the city, living in tenements and absorbed into the industrial work force. There was a true irony in this, because it meant that some of the most rural people to be found in the old world had become some of the most urban people in the new.

About a third of Jan's and Piotr's fellow voyageurs did return home, as it happened, and we might as well include Jan among them. We do not know how fine a figure he cut when he reappeared on the village green with his celluloid collar and gold watch, but we do know that things did not work out for him. The village may not have had a place for him, and he may have learned that he was no longer as well suited to life there as he had once been. Life in America had been hard, but there was something about Pittsburgh that generated hope. As a fellow migrant of Jan's said to Ewa Morawska some time later: "It was terribly hard work, coal mine—back-breaking, dirty, awful. But I still preferred it here. Thought it was better. I saw here some future. At home there was none."

The New World

Piotr entered the United States in 1911 and went to Pittsburgh, where Jan worked in a foundry. But by the time Kasia and the children were able to join him eight years later he had moved to Chicago and was working in the steel mills. Conditions of life in the two locations were much the same.

For one thing, the cities into which Piotr and so many of his fellow immigrants flowed were immensely overcrowded. People found themselves pressed into dark, narrow tenements, often several to a room, where the air was rank, the water foul, the smell of rotting garbage stifling, and the war with insects and vermin never-ending. And Piotr, a great man in his own terrain, had few skills to offer in this new labor market. He knew nothing of iron foundries and steel mills, of coal mines and tanneries, of machine shops and packinghouses. So work for him was not only difficult to find but difficult to keep, and the jobs open to him often full of danger.

Kasia knew that things were difficult. Piotr would write her from time to time about his difficulties—explaining, perhaps, why the amount of money he could send home was so meager or why the family reunion was being delayed again. "I came to this massive golden whore, but I feel terribly sad," Piotr wrote at a bad moment. "I am without work and I don't know what will happen, whether things will get better or not. . . . Thus have I improved my lot in this America which our immigrants love!" We can assume that there were good reports, too, since Piotr was, after all, making it, but it was very hard going.

Among the problems Piotr had to face during his early years in America was one he had no words for. He knew he would have to learn a new language and new habits and new trades. But he had no way of knowing how difficult it would be for him to become oriented to his new surroundings. It was a long distance from the fields of Poland to the streets of Pittsburgh, from thatched cottages to tenements, not only in miles but in cultural tone and feeling. Here he was separated from nature and, thus, from an important part of himself. Everywhere a thick crust of pavement cut him off from the soil. Everywhere buildings soared upward and blocked him off from the sun and the wind. The city is a thing of straight lines and sharp right angles, of level surfaces and sudden verticals, of squares and perpendiculars—and that was a strange geometry for someone like Piotr, who grew up in a landscape where pathways circled the base of a hill or followed the bends of a river, and where the horizon was an unending line of curves.

Social space was a problem too. When Kasia joined Piotr in Chicago with the children, they both knew, as did most of their fellows, that old country habits and customs might be of limited use in this new life. But the ways of the American city proved even more difficult for them to fathom than they had anticipated. For one thing, immigrants in places like Pittsburgh and Chicago often found that their family roles had been almost entirely reversed without their quite noticing that it was taking place. Piotr reported every morning to a steel mill where the signs were in Polish as well as in English, and he paused at a tavern or coffeehouse on his way home from work where everyone had come from his part of the old country. So, more often than not, it now was Kasia who negotiated with the larger world, learned from the gossip at the market, and brought home the food served at the dinner table. She may have been the first person in the family to learn some of the new language, to develop a feel for the tempos of the city, to make contact with school teachers, shopkeepers, and civil officials. And she may have been the first to master the mysteries of money and savings and interest and credit, unfamiliar concepts to immigrants from the rural reaches of Europe.

It would be the same with their children. Kasia and Piotr had fed them, sheltered them, and given them life. The older ones had memories of their lives in Poland, of course, but those memories grew fainter as the family accommodated to the new land, and the younger ones, in common with those born in the United States, remembered little or nothing of those times. They grew up for the most part in immigrant neighborhoods, learned something about the old village ways around the dinner table with their parents, and probably read or heard letters from Poland of the kind Thomas and Znaniecki were then collecting. But to some extent, at least, family roles were beginning to reverse in this situation as well. Most of the knowledge Piotr and Kasia had spent half a lifetime acquiring had little immediate application to children trying to make a place for themselves here. Specialists from outside the family took on much of the task of teaching them how to act, how to talk, how to prepare for the workplace—how to be Americans, in short. No matter how much they loved and respected their parents, the children knew that they would have to turn elsewhere for useful advice about the ways of the new land. When the specialists they turned to were teachers or priests or social workers from a local settlement house, then a parent might feel content, but when those specialists were comrades from the streets, as Thomas and Znaniecki feared was becoming the case, there was reason indeed to worry. For sidewalks and street corners could be dangerous places for unsure young minds to negotiate during the second and third decades of the 20th century.

Both Piotr and Kasia felt less than whole in yet another way. Piotr was not growing or reaping or husbanding, as men in his realm were born to do. He stood at his appointed place of work, day after day, shoveling coal into a furnace, handling pieces of red-hot steel, or working a lever as half-finished objects passed by him on a conveyer belt. And Kasia, trying to come to terms with tenement rooms that would never be clean, unable to afford the kind of wholesome foods she once grew in her own garden, must have wondered at times whether she was less than a true woman or a true mother.

Although Piotr and Kasia had dreams over the long years he worked in Pittsburgh and she bided her time in Poland, it was clear to both when they took up residence in Chicago that they were never going home. But it was equally apparent to them that they would never be fully absorbed into this new cultural landscape either, for the roads that carried one to "success" in this sprawling land seemed to rely on qualities of mind and temper that were alien to the peasant experience. They knew how to work, they knew how to endure, they knew how to bend to the inevitable. But it would have been almost impossible for them to "get ahead" in the way most Americans did without undergoing a major shift in outlook. In that respect, as in so many others, Piotr and Kasia lived out their days suspended between the peasant world they had left behind but could not withdraw from and a new urban world they did not know how to be a part of.

Sidewalks and Street Corners

In some ways, the story of Piotr and Kasia Walkowiak can be read as a sad one. History sometimes takes the least prepared of people, picks them up from the lands in which they have been rooted for generations, and casts them onto alien shores. Piotr and Kasia had moved from a 19th-century village to a 20th-century city in a short span of time, and the costs of the journey had been considerable.

And yet there is another side to the story, for the chemistries of human life can work in such a way as to take a number of different elements and combine them into an altogether new compound. The tenements saw more than their fair share of sorrow and disorder, but something new was emerging from that unlikely terrain at the same time.

The immigrant drama was played out on the city streets. That is perfectly sensible, for people could only escape from the smothering closeness of their living quarters by gathering on the front stoops and street corners, in the candy stores and saloons, of their neighborhoods. On the one hand, it was there that the most dispirited and confused of the adults drifted into mental illness and alcoholism, vagrancy and crime, and where the most dispirited and confused of the children drifted into delinquency, truancy, and the lure of territorial gangs. Many sociologists of the time—particularly in Chicago, where the lives of Piotr and Kasia Walkowiak intersected with the careers of W. I. Thomas and Florian Znaniecki—were drawn to that part of the story.

As it happened, however—and this may be the most improbable reversal of all—these streets turned out to supply a fertile soil for the transplantation of old village ways. The inner cities of America—which in those days meant the industrial cities of the East and the Midwest—were in some ways becoming more peasant in manner and outlook than the rural countryside.

We noted earlier that many peasant immigrants brought with them from the old world a sturdiness and durability that served them well in the American labor market, even though they had limited industrial skills to offer. But they also brought with them a readiness to join with others in communal undertakings of one kind or other, to fold their individualities into a larger whole, and this proved to be an even more important aptitude in the long run. Piotr had written to Kasia in one of his lonely first years in Pittsburgh:

> Here in America it is very difficult for a peasant, because as long as he is well then he always works like a mule and therefore he has something, but if he becomes sick, then it is trouble, because everyone is looking only for money in order to get some of it. And during the sickness most of it will be spent, and in old age, when one has not health or money, then there is trouble again.

The peasant knew how to work, he was saying, and could do well enough when his back was strong. But there was nothing to fall back on—no family, no village, no parish—in times of adversity.

Piotr was to learn, though, as his eyes adjusted to the hard light of urban America, that the inner city was beginning to fill up with associations that had something of the look and feel of village institutions—mutual aid societies that served as a kind of substitute for the extended family networks of the village, neighborhood improvement groups to supply the kind of order once mandated by custom, savings and loan banks that catered to particular nationalities, social clubs to sponsor the important rituals and ceremonies of everyday life. The inner city, in fact, had become home to a whole array of lodges, orders, fraternities, clubs, and other groups that had as their main purpose the nurturing of fellowship and the provision of communal services. Some of these associations were church-related, others were sponsored by local businesses, and still others seemed to emerge unaided out of the soul of the neighborhood. They had a distinctive urban edge to them, of course, but they were also a product of the village temper in at least the sense that they drew on the familiar cadences of village life and depended on a peasant way of looking at things.

Before long, the ethnic neighborhoods of the city were alive with activity— citizenship schools and foreign-language newspapers, bands and theatrical troupes, bowling leagues and baseball teams, singing groups and sewing circles. Those associations had a relatively short life as history measures such things, although traces of them can be found in any urban community now. They meant a great deal to the first generation of European immigrants and often to the second, although they usually did not have the same meaning to the third and almost certainly to the fourth. Piotr's and Kasia's grandchildren grew up speaking English, attending American schools, reading metropolitan newspapers, sometimes feeling more at home in suburbs than in ethnic neighborhoods, going to Hollywood films more often than to local theatricals, and becoming more and more accustomed to the general manners of working-class and middle-class America. But in their days of glory, those associations had two lasting impacts on the American cultural landscape.

First, while ethnic associations provided fellowship for persons who were otherwise in danger of being isolated, it also introduced them, often for the first time, to their own national heritages. Piotr and Kasia knew that they were "Polish," of course, in the sense that they spoke the language and knew where they came from. But they were villagers from a distant land, and it was in Pittsburgh and then later in Chicago that they came to think of Polish history as their history, Polish literature as their literature, Polish figures as their national heroes. That was also true for many other fellow immigrants with whom they shared the city. It took a while for neighbors from Bohemia to think of themselves as Czech or their neighbors from Apulia to think of themselves as Italian. And the same could be said of those who came from Andalusia or Slavonia or Ruthenia. National borders, remember, were hardly any more to them than lines drawn across the surfaces of the world by rulers anxious to mark the edges of their domains or by congresses that met in order to redraw the political map. They had little relevance to those who worked the land. But in Pittsburgh, Chicago, Buffalo, and Cleveland, people who would never have imagined themselves fellow countrymen under any other circumstances gathered together in national groupings at meetings of the Sons of Italy or the Polish Falcons. And after a time, they found themselves celebrating national holidays that they were not even aware of in the old world and expressing a kind of national pride that may have astonished their kinsfolk in the village.

Second and maybe more important, peasants from Italy, Germany, Greece, Poland, and other parts of Europe had never participated in what the rest of the world called politics. Why should they care who set state policy in Warsaw or what political party occupied the most seats in a parliament that met somewhere else? When had anyone in a position of power ever asked them what they wanted or what they thought anyway? So another irony to add to what is now a fairly impressive list is that these European immigrants, without really knowing what they were up to, helped fashion a new political form that changed the urban face of America.

This is a long and complex matter, and we will only touch on it briefly here. Piotr and Kasia, like endless waves of immigrants before them, turned to local associations for fellowship and assistance. But their introduction to the political character of the new country began there too, at least in part because those social clubs and lodges often wrote charters, elected officers, conducted business according to established rules of order, and, in short, acted like miniature states. It was a form of apprenticeship in political processes. One day Kazimierz Kalinowicz, who lived in a nearby tenement building, solicited Piotr's support for a seat on the council of a local society. And Piotr, who was beginning to feel more comfortable in such settings, rose to his feet one evening to ask whether a measure being considered by the club was contrary to its constitution. Heady stuff, that.

Moreover, when you have that many people gathered into established groups, most of them on the verge of acquiring citizenship and the vote, you create an irresistible prospect to politicians. Soon Piotr and Kasia and their neighbors found that they were being courted and treated with elaborate respect by individuals seeking elective office and the power it conferred. They were becoming a constituency.

Peasants like Piotr and Kasia were usually quite comfortable accepting the authority of those in positions of leadership. It was an old habit of mind, centuries in the making. And once they sensed their importance as a constituency, they cast their lot with a new breed of politician making an appearance on the urban scene—men (they were almost all men) who were frankly ethnic in their appeal and who knew how to influence the machineries of government without forgetting their own immigrant roots. Their power came from the ability to deliver the votes of people like Piotr; their financial support came from easy alliances with local businesses and local rackets. They acted a lot like village elders, in short, and indeed the new ethnic politics was in many respects a species of village politics. It was tribal. It was familial. It was well-suited to a people who felt at home embedded in the structures of family life, who respected the authority of parents and priests and elders, and sensed the importance of territorial units the size of parishes, communities—and, in time, wards and precincts.

This kind of politics, as one can easily imagine, was quite unlike anything envisioned by James Madison or Thomas Jefferson or the other original theorists of American democracy. It was not concerned with tariffs or antitrust legislation or military ventures into Nicaragua or the Philippines. It was concerned with garbage collection in the seventh ward, the need for a public bathhouse in the fifth ward, a building project in the third ward. It was concerned with helping people get papers filed, having bureaucratic problems solved, finding ways to help the widow Callahan or the orphaned children of the Piotrowskis. The main figure in this politics was the ward boss. No distant, mannered lord he, with long fingernails and fresh collars, but a rough, accessible, shrewd chieftain. He was a member of the community and seldom missed a festival or baptism or funeral, and if politicians of another stripe sometimes used words like "graft" in talking of him, he was nonetheless fiercely loyal to his people, knew them by their first names, and gave them a way to participate in the governance of their new land.

When the Walkowiaks' fifth child was born in Chicago, the baptism was attended by the ward boss. When word came from Poland that Kasia's sister had died, flowers appeared in their flat. When Piotr was laid off by an Italian foreman, the boss put in a good word; and when Piotr died, the boss attended the funeral, sitting in a pew right behind the family, and he saw to it that Kasia was provided a ham the next Christmas. In return the Walkowiaks offered their loyalty and their vote.

From Generation to Generation

At this point we lose sight of Piotr and Kasia. They lived out their lives in the shelter of an ethnic neighborhood, and at the time of their deaths, separated by a quarter of a century, they were content enough. Their children and grandchildren had found places in the new land, and that is what they had hoped for from the beginning. That was their gift—the dowries they gave their daughters and the portions they settled on their sons. Sometimes, however, the gift was more expensive than they had guessed, all the more so because the children and grandchildren did not always understand its terms.

One of the sharpest fears of peasants everywhere in the world is to lose their children. They are a couple's insurance policy in old age. They are a symbol of family continuity. They are the new generation for whom the present is being held in trust by the older one. And in one important respect, it has to be said that Piotr and Kasia and other people like them were almost sure to distance themselves from their children. This was not because members of the younger generation turned hard-hearted and forgot their family obligations (although that occurred often enough) but because they gradually drifted off into social universes their parents could neither fully understand nor fully enter. In a peasant village, the cycle of generations is clear. Children inherit their parents' customs, their parents' land, their parents' standing in the community, and their parents' outlook on life. Who knows more than parents about the life the children will one day have to live? So sons and daughters began their schooling at home. The lore gathered by their parents over a lifetime became their curricula. That, clearly, was not to be the case in America. No one had less of a feel for the intricacies of American culture than immigrant parents, and no one was a less adequate role model for young people seeking a secure niche in the new country.

So, some of those children began to move away, emotionally if not geographically, and their children were caught up in the same momentum. The process was sometimes resisted by parents who felt the pain of what was happening, but for the most part the Piotrs and Kasias contributed to that process and have to be counted as collaborators in it. They may not have understood right away that when the grandchildren moved into the American institutional landscape, its schools in particular, they were moving into a new cultural and spiritual landscape as well.

The Walkowiak family settled into the Immaculate Conception parish in South Chicago. In the early years, the children enrolled in a parochial school run by the church where the priests and nuns were for the most part of Polish extraction and most of the other activities of the week were organized and supervised by members of the parish. Many of the children took jobs in the local mills, remained in the neighborhood, and married within the parish. For them, continuity was maintained. Others, though, went on to public high school and began to live in a world of broader horizons. But those who stayed and those who moved were all Americans now, who spoke English without the old world accents of their parents and were increasingly comfortable with American ways. And when they became parents in their turn, they sent their offspring to public schools. Piotr and Kasia knew at some level that American schools, even the parochial ones, were taking over what had once been their province, but they said little even when their children and grand-children became a part of that world in tacit admission that their own values and attitudes, their own stores of knowledge, were for the most part now obsolete.

It is clear from the letters Thomas and Znaniecki collected that those who remained in Poland were deeply concerned about what might happen when young persons left the land and were exposed to what must have seemed to them the dangerous air of a distant world. "We are both away from the native home," wrote a young man who had left his home village for another part of Poland to his brother in America:

> but I am at least among my own people while you are far away beyond the ocean, surrounded by people who speak to you in a strange language, and often pray to a different God. So don't wonder, brother, if I feel often anxious lest you forget that you are a Pole and a Catholic. . . . And God preserve you from the idea that you might remain in America forever! . . . It is a sad fact, for in this way hundreds of Polish men and women are lost, settling forever in America, or—what is worst— getting morally lost there.

Those old fears were echoed again and again in letters written home by persons who settled, at least for the time being, in the United States. "Marta works in a tailor-shop," one young man wrote to his parents about a fellow villager who might have been his cousin,

> but she refuses to listen to me, else she would have been married long ago. So I inform you that I loved her as my own sister, but now I won't talk to her anymore,

for she refuses to listen. Family remains family only in the first time after coming from home, and later they forget and don't wish anymore to acknowledge the familial relations. The American meat inflates them.

A mother in America, meantime, to her sister in Poland:

> Dear sister, I write as to a sister and I complain as to a sister about my children from the old country. They will not listen to their mother. If they would listen, they would do well with me. But no, they wish only to run everywhere about the world, and I am ashamed before people that they are so bad. They were good in the beginning but now they know how to speak English, and their goodness is lost.

Znaniecki, who was himself Polish, received a number of letters addressed to him personally in the course of the monumental study he did with Thomas. "I don't like the American education of children," wrote one distressed father: "Here the child is not morally educated, it knows no respect for its elders. It knows only how to throw snow or stones at the passers by." Another man registered his own disappointment:

> You want to know, respected sir, my opinion, how America influences the Polish girls. You may be sure, not positively, but a hundred times negatively. I have not yet had the luck to meet in America a girl who would be even an imitation of those girls whom I knew in the old country. They find at once companions who impart to them information which will have a very bad influence on their future, and they soon become tools of demoralization, and so on. I have not yet met in America a single girl to be compared with those in the old country.

The behavior being complained of here probably consisted of minor misde-meanors when compared to the high rates of crime, mental illness, and alco-holism that we know to have been common in some of those immigrant neighborhoods. But these lapses, light as we would judge them now, had their own special cruelty because they were evidence that the young people were withdrawing from the moral center of village life. Most immigrants knew that something of the sort had to happen, but the pain it induced was no less sharp for all that. Children might come home from the rough camaraderie of the school yard with nicknames like "Spike" or "Fats" or "Red," were caught in what they judged to be harmless trespasses, wore clothing never seen or even dreamt of on a village green, and permitted themselves to imagine, even if they did not act on it for another generation or so, that they could find a life outside the parish and marry people who were alien by every standard their parents knew and respected. And the parents, in turn, misunderstanding, would look at the new clothes and the new manners with a mixture of anger and sorrow and contempt, and reach into their new vocabularies for words they scarcely knew the true meaning of: "slut," "bum," "thug."

So distances sometimes widened between generations not only within particular family groups but throughout the community more generally. It must have been a wrenching pain for the older people, but many of them understood, if only dimly, that this is what the change from old to new worlds feels like. Piotr died in 1940. He had attended the christenings of a dozen grandchildren by then, and watched a number of them grow into adulthood. But none of them grew up speaking Polish, and he had not learned enough English to converse with them.

When I was a first-year graduate student, trying to follow what I thought was the advice of Everett Hughes, I spent several months wandering around a Polish parish in South Chicago (it was in fact named Immaculate Conception). I read a letter in a local neighborhood newspaper from a woman who wanted her neighbors to know how disgusted she sometimes felt at what she could not help but see from the window of her apartment. I asked her over the phone whether she would show me what things looked like out her window. She invited me for tea, served in glasses with wire handles. Her face tightened as she pointed out the window at a pair of teen-age girls walking along the sidewalk in denim jeans, a gathering of younger boys near the corner pitching pennies, and a young woman smoking a cigarette as she strolled along holding hands with someone who could have been a husband or boyfriend. My new friend was looking out at a scene so new to her that she thought it bewildering if not unwholesome. I was looking out at a scene so familiar to me that that it took me a moment to realize what she was talking about.

That was 1954, decades before I invented Piotr and Kasia and knew something of the history they shared with so many others. But the episode came back to me then, and it occurred to me that the person I visited that day could have been Kasia—widowed for fourteen years by then and about to celebrate her seventy-fourth birthday. She was looking out the window at a generation that included her own grandchildren, in some ways strangers to her now.

But, for all of that, it was clear that she would not have changed a thing. Her journey had been a blessed success.

PLACES

In this section we will turn to different *locations* in which people have spent their lives, paying particular attention to the ways of life that have emerged there.

We know from the chapter on *Origins* that our ancestors were in continuous motion for something like 99 percent of the human career on earth. And we know, too, that the age of agriculture began ten thousand years ago or so and began its gradual reach out into the rest of the world. Most of our immediate ancestors, then, lived in village clusters for millennia, earning their living by working the soil, and we can consider that form of settlement a basic template of human experience. And we know from that same reading that the Industrial Revolution moved steadily across Europe during the 19th and the early 20th centuries like a relentless tide and that vast torrents of people drained out of the rural countryside and into the growing urban centers. It was an immense shift of population, and in the process the city has become—or is on the verge of becoming—the prevailing habitat of the human animal. For those caught up in that current, it meant not only a change in location but a change in the very texture of everyday life—in the way people thought about themselves and in the way they related to one another.

The first two chapters in this section, then—logically enough—are *Village* and *City,* those being the two essential forms of human settlement to have appeared in what I will just call historic times. But it is the *transformation* from the one to the other—from the village world to the urban world—that has had a special fascination in sociological thinking, all the more so when discussion turns to those changes in the texture of social life I just alluded to. So we will pause for a moment there.

Most of the early sociologists who sensed that transformation taking place thought it was proceeding with the inevitability of a natural force. It was a shift from simpler forms of social order to more complex ones, from relationships based on communality to ones based on individuality. Virtually every social theorist of the time had something to say about that turn of events, although they used different terms to describe it and varied considerably in the degree to which they welcomed it. Émile Durkheim spoke of a shift from *mechanical* to *organic* forms of solidarity and Max Weber of *traditional* and *rational* forms of authority, as we have seen, and Herbert Spencer had seen a shift from *homogeneity* to *heterogeneity.* In the United States, where sociology was even newer than in Europe, Charles Horton Cooley saw a movement from *primary* to *secondary* groups, Robert McIver one from *communal* to *associational* relations, and Robert Redfield one from *folk* to *urban* ways of life. Edward A. Ross, writing in 1901 when Durkheim and Weber were in mid-career and largely unknown on the other side of the ocean, put it with a crisp elegance: "powerful forces" he noted, are "transforming *community* into *society,* replacing living tissue with structures held together by rivets and screws." Weber, who does not seem to have read much that made him smile, might have if he had encountered that line.

This familiar chord was struck in its most memorable form by a German sociologist named Ferdinand Toennies in a work entitled *Gemeinschaft und Gesellschaft,* published in 1887. When that title is translated into literal English, it usually comes out "community and society," which may be as accurate a rendering as we can manage. But those terms do not really convey what Toennies meant very well, so many English-speaking sociologists have come to the conclusion that the original German can serve the purpose quite well. Since "gemeinschaft" and "gesellschaft" have been taken from another language intact, no other demands have been placed on them in English, and so they can serve as working concepts without confusion. They have a nice ring to them, too, a Teutonic bite and timbre. Say them aloud and you are almost sure to get the feeling that you are dealing with matters of substance. *Gemeinschaft! Gesellschaft!*

But that can pose a problem of its own, since those imposing nouns— capitalized in German—almost seem to be pointing to tangible *things,* established elements out there in the social world, when the subject at hand is subtle differences in sensibility and behavior, matters of tone and accent. So two things should be noted before we move ahead.

First, the purpose of concepts like gemeinschaft and gesellschaft or any of the other pairings above is not to give an identifying name to the phenomena under consideration but to help us get a clearer sense of things out there in the blur of ongoing human activity. And second, those concepts have as their real object to mark the outer poles of a continuum along which actual behavior is arrayed—a familiar narrative strategy in the social sciences, as we now know. Think of them as "ideal types."

In the discussion to follow, then, I will be drawing on terms like "village ethos" and "city ways," "gemeinschaft" and "gesellschaft," and a pairing I feel particularly comfortable with, Robert Redfield's "folk" and "urban." The important thing to remember, though, no matter what pair of terms is being used at any given time to mark the outer edges of social space, is that the subject being focused on here is not a *state* or a *condition* but a *movement* across a plane—the ways in which the competing pulls of village ways and city ways create a continuing tension. In any given setting, that is, one finds traces of both. And when we portray a particular social scene as having a "folk" or an "urban" character, we are saying that one or the other of those pulls appears to have a prominent place among the mixture that gives the setting its distinctive character.

The first two chapters to follow, then, are *Village* and *City*. The third chapter, *Worlds Beyond,* is for all practical purposes an extended footnote to the other two. It takes a glance at three new formations—"places" in at least a sense—that have exerted an especially telling impact on our times: the emergence of the national state, the colonization of a large portion of the world, and the process we have come to call *globalization.* The field visit that brings the section to a close, *It Seemed like the Whole Bay Died,* deals with what happened to the Native people of Alaska after and before what has come to be called The *Exxon Valdez* Oil Spill, one of the most devastating disasters of its time.

The matter discussed in *Village* is bound to cover some of the same territory as the early pages of the journey undertaken by Kasia and Piotr Walkowiak. They came from a peasant hamlet in Eastern Europe at the turn of the last century—a *village* if there ever was one. But we will be dealing here with villages the world over, and in that sense the place Piotr and Kasia came from is a local specimen of a far more extensive genus.

Village

WHAT WE HAVE BEEN CALLING "THE VILLAGE ethos" or "gemeinschaft" or just "folk" is the way of life of the fishing village, the mountain hollow, the island community, as well as the kind of rural hamlet in which Kasia and Piotr grew up. It dominates the life of the peasant everywhere. It can be considered a universal of human experience at least in the sense that it is part of our shared heritage and served as the milieu in which our kind became seasoned as a social species. It is found in every corner of the world, and it is entirely sensible for us to presume that it looks and feels much the same in Spain, Indonesia, Mexico, China, Egypt, Ireland, Greece, Pakistan, and . . . We have to say such things with respect and caution. Any traveler will encounter a good deal of contrast and variety in the settings that can reasonably be called "folk," so we cannot assume a simple uniformity there. Yet a number of common themes appear in village life everywhere, and those similarities will be our topic now.

Researchers who work in and around folk communities, in fact, are often struck by the uncanny aptness with which an observation made half a world away seems to fit a local circumstance. For example, a sociologist I knew some years ago was studying a Hispanic village in New Mexico, where the ground underneath has been baked as hard as concrete by the sun and the prevailing worldview is profoundly Catholic. She was surprised to learn one day while doing some idle reading that the community profile that proved richest in insight for her purposes had been written about a mountain community in Appalachia near Buffalo Creek, where the ground can be soft and moist from rainfall and the worldview is distinctly Protestant. The writer of that Appalachian profile was a minister named Jack Weller, and he noted in the introduction to his book that he had learned a lot about the mountain people he was trying to understand when he came across the study of a social reality that appeared to be wholly unlike it on the surface—a study of Italian-Americans in the West End of Boston by Herbert Gans. Weller wrote:

> On reading Gans's descriptions of the patterns of life, the organization, and motivations of those second- and third-generation people from southern Italy, I felt my excitement rise. . . . Illustrations from my own work flooded into my mind. Vaguely understood incidents that had happened in the mountains began to make sense. . . . [The West Enders] are so much like the people of Southern Appalachia.

And that is not the end of it, because Gans, in his turn, had drawn inspiration from a study of a people who lived ten thousand miles from Boston in a setting completely unlike it. "My view of the West Ender's self," Gans said in his intro-duction, "bears considerable similarity to the findings of a study made by Daniel Lerner and his associates among Middle Eastern peasants." Now that is a stretch. From the high deserts of New Mexico to the mountains of West Virginia to an urban neighborhood in West Boston to peasant hamlets in the Mideast. And Lerner? He did not speak of the matter in his book, but it would be interesting to learn what social science works were on his mind as he went about his research errands in Syria and Iraq and Turkey.

I plan in the next few pages to call on voices from parts of the world where a sense of community once remained strong to help illustrate the nature of the village ethos. These places include Alcalá de la Sierra, a mountain village in Andalusia, Spain, visited by Julian Pitt-Rivers in the 1950s; Colonsay, a small island off the coast of Scotland visited by John McPhee in the 1960s; Akenfield, a farming community in East Anglia, England, visited by Ronald Blythe also in the 1960s; New Burlington, a village in Ohio visited by John Baskin in the 1970s; and Buffalo Creek at about the same time. The people whose voices I will be calling on here are not really "representative" of people from all over the world in any useful sense of the word. They are all from the West, and all but the people of Alcalá de la Sierra speak English. It is a reasonable assump-tion, though, that together they reflect a temper and an outlook that, until quite recently, was familiar to most of humankind.

One critical proviso before we continue: I am going to be speaking in what follows about life *within* the village circle and the sense of fellowship and even equality that often obtains there. So it is essential to make clear that these are qualities of the *contained village* and not of the *larger world* that surrounds it on all sides. Raymond Williams once made a striking observation when writing about the great country houses of England:

> It is fashionable to admire those extraordinary houses: the extended manors, the neo-classical mansions, that lie so close to rural Britain. People still pass from village to village, guidebook in hand, to see the next and yet the next example, to look at the stones and the furniture. But stand at any point and look at that land. Look at what those fields, those streams, those woods even today produce. Think it through as labour and see how long and systematic the exploitation and seizure must have been, to rear that many houses, on that scale. . . . It isn't only that you know, looking at the land and then at the house, how much robbery and fraud there must have been, for so long, to produce that degree of disparity, that barbarous disproportion of scale. . . . To stand in that shadow, even today, is to know what many generations of countrymen bitterly learned and were consciously taught: that these were the families, this the shape of the society. And will you then think of community?

A very good question, to which the answer can only be "yes" and "no." It is no, of course, if one's sociological gaze reaches across the whole of the countryside and includes the lords of the manors, the money lenders, the absentee landlords, the members of the royal household, the brothers of the monasteries, and all of the other people who lived off the peasants' labor and enjoyed positions of special privilege. We are talking about exploitation and cruelty on a grand scale here. The answer is yes, though, when one's sociological gaze is confined, if only for a time, to those hundreds of thousands of little encirclements—those communities, villages, neighborhoods, parishes, in which the common folk lived.

Some of the people whose voices I will be calling on here can be called peasants and others cannot. But if you look at them in that larger context, most share in common the fact that they or their predecessors have been exploited by any decent meaning of the word and rank in the lower registers of whatever class structure prevails in the societies they are a part of. But within the precincts of the village itself, which is our subject here, a different order prevails.

Kindred

Above all else, the village ethos is characterized by an overarching sense of *unity,* a feeling of being fused into some whole larger than the individual selves that make it up. It is a communal tissue *in* which one is embedded, *to* which one is committed, *of* which one is a firmly connected and firmly attached part. The same Robert A. Nisbet we heard from earlier put the case with conviction:

> Community is a fusion of feeling and thought, of tradition and commitment, of membership and volition. It may be found in, or be given symbolic expression by, locality, religion, nation, race, occupation, or crusade. Its archetype, both histori-cally and symbolically, is the family, and in almost every type of genuine commu-nity the nomenclature of family is prominent.

That is probably a more extravagant statement than most social scientists would feel comfortable making, but the comment on family has a special ring of truth. Observers from a variety of contexts testify that the imagery of family is virtually inescapable when people search for ways to convey what the bonds of community feel like. There are times when the expressions people use to make the point sound so conventional and habitual that they take on something of the cadence of ritual. The following words (and thousands like them) were spoken by Appalachian mountaineers on Buffalo Creek, but they will have a familiar sound to anybody who knows rural communities. The first speaker is Wilbur, whose thoughts on the matter you heard earlier:

> We all just seemed, in that vicinity, like one big family. We raised our children with our neighbors' children, they was all raised up together, and if your children wasn't at my house on a weekend from Friday to Sunday, mine was at your house with your children. And that's the way we raised our children. We raised them together, more or less like brothers and sisters. The whole community was that way.

The second is a woman who lived nearby:

> In a coal-mining town, it's like we're all one big family. When my husband died, I went someplace, to the store maybe, and when I came back home there was a pile of money that covered the table. And when I went out again and came back, the place was full of groceries, boxes sitting everywhere. So they really did take care of their own, the miners did.

In the folk ethos, then, the sense of family reaches beyond linkages of kin to include a wider circle of people, and the attachments one is expected to feel toward the persons in that wider circle are similar in *kind,* and sometimes even in *intensity,* to the attachments one is expected to feel toward one's own family. This parallel has its limits, of course: taboos are observed within blood lines that do not extend out into the community, for example, and in moments of emergency (as Wilbur and his neighbors on Buffalo Creek have good reason to know) the bonds of family generally prove stronger than the bonds of community. But the point to be made here is that the obligations of communal life are of the same *sort* as the obligations of family life. They are drawn from the same human well.

Niche

We discussed the importance of attachment to the land in Piotr's and Kasia's time. And, indeed, it is difficult to imagine applying the term "village" to any gathering of folk that does not involve a deep sense of connection with specific parcels of place. The village ethos, then, is grounded. It has location. It occupies a given niche. Richard Critchfield, whose travels have taken him to a variety of rural spaces, says of villagers the world over:

> Most villagers have a love of their native land, a desire to own land, an intense attachment to their ancestral soil, a personal bond to the land, a reverence for nature and toward habitat and ancestral ways; there can be an almost organic relationship between a man and a woman, their labor, and the land.

That language would seem to suggest that villagers have an active passion for their land, a lively devotion, when the actual feelings involved might be better described as a tenacious, unreflective, maybe even passive sense of connection. But it has been noted over and over again that the niche occupied by a community is a place residents have mapped out in their minds and know as intimately as their own households, a place they have felt and handled and know the grain of. John McPhee, writing of Colonsay, an island just off the coast of Scotland:

> Almost every rise of ground, every beach, field, cliff, gully, cave, and skerry has a name. There are a hundred and thirty-eight people on Colonsay, and nearly sixteen hundred place names. . . . All of these names are preserved in the memories of the people.

Imagine being able to recite the names and know the locations of 1,600 streets or 1,600 towns or 1,600 anythings, and you will sense the size of this feat. An old man from a small farming village in Ohio called New Burlington, who had left the region decades before John Baskin asked him about it, nonetheless knew exactly what McPhee meant:

> I identify with that dirty hole in the ground. I belong there. From the age of two on I heard nothing but: "This is where we came to, came from. We know every inch of this place." My aunt could name everyone within twenty miles.

Robert Coles, speaking of the mountain folk of Appalachia:

> They are unmistakably poor children . . . but they love the land near their cabin, and they know that land almost inch by inch. Indeed, from the first days of life many of the Appalachian children I have observed are almost symbolically or ritualistically given over to the land. One morning I watched Mrs. Allen come out from the cabin in order, presumably, to enjoy the sun and warm, clear air of a May day. Her boy had just been breast-fed and was in her arms. Suddenly the mother put the child down on the ground, and gently fondled him and moved him a bit with her feet . . . and spoke very gravely to her child: "This is your land, and it's about time you started getting to know it."
>
> Mrs. Allen's attitude toward the land is by no means rare among the families I have worked with in the Appalachian mountains. In fact, an observer can make some generalizations about how children are brought up in, say, western North Carolina or eastern Kentucky and West Virginia if he looks at the land as a sort of unifying theme. From the first months of childhood to later years, the land and the woods and the hills figure prominently in the lives of mountain children, not to mention their parents. As a result, the tasks and struggles that confront all children take on a particular and characteristic quality among Appalachian children, a quality that has to do with learning one's roots, one's place, one's territory, as a central fact, perhaps *the* central fact of existence.

Irish country people sometimes say "their name is on the land" when describing the relationship of a family and the property they live on. This does not mean that people have written their signature on the land to indicate their ownership of it. It means that the land derives its identity from those who live on it and work it, and those who live on it and work it derive their identity from the land.

Heritage

So the village ethos involves a deep sense of fusion and of place. And, I will now add, it involves a deep sense of shared destiny. "We" are part of a common past; "we" will be part of a common future; and, meanwhile, "we" are bound together in the present by the fact that we share a common moment in time and a common niche in space. This is one reason why the oral tradition is so important to the village spirit. The stories a people relate about themselves are the sum of their own history, the sum of what makes them distinctive. John McPhee says about the tales told on Colonsay that they "include a high proportion of factual incorrectness, but truth and fiction often seem to be riding the same sentence in such a way that the one would be lonely without the other." That is beautifully said, but stories like these have to be measured by a different set of standards than the one we generally use to distinguish truth from fiction. These stories contain the *traditions* of Colonsay, the *lore* of Colonsay, the *history* of Colonsay; and, like most of the histories people tell, certainly about themselves and their own kind, accuracy in the narrow sense cannot be counted as anything more than a minor virtue.

Village history is not meant as chronicle anyway. It does not involve a linear sense of time, for events from the past fold back in on themselves like repetitive cycles, like the seasons, like the rhythms of nature. Another oldtimer from New Burlington put it:

> The village people brought things up in conversations as if they were momentary. But they occurred one hundred years ago! All history was collapsed in on itself. Into that tiny space were all events.

In that sense, the village is bounded both in space and in time. It is an encirclement that contains "us" and those who came before us. It does not necessarily stand out from other enclosures except that it is "Ours" rather than "Theirs."

Surveillance and Tolerance

The boundaries of a community encircle a territory in which surveillance can be both fierce and unrelenting. A 92-year-old schoolteacher, speaking of the New Burlington of his younger years, noted: "One of the conditions of a village, of course, is adjacency. Everyone is adjacent to everyone else. Therefore the villagers watch each other closely because they didn't have much of a choice, living so close together." That feature of village life has been the subject of a good deal of comment over the years. The space between people is narrow and pinched, the need for a degree of orthodoxy is great; so it makes excellent sense that the image of the village in the Western literary tradition is one of austerity, watchfulness, and a kind of sullen oppression. All of this is quite true.

And yet it is another of the odd chemistries of social life that the mood of vigilance, no matter how vindictive or how cranky it can become, has as its counterpart a form of local clemency. Another old man from New Burlington, whose memory was both long and clear, explained:

> New Burlington was like a medieval society. You were so close. Thrust together. Everybody watched everybody else. How could you possibly get out of line? One of the villagers saw a couple of little girls wading in Anderson's Fork. Two inches of water. "I saw their ankles," he said. "Indecent!" But that life causes certain tolerances, too. If you know all you forgive all. You met these people every day, face to face.

So one trains a wary eye on people who live within the communal circle and deals harshly with them if they behave improperly. The things that take place within the circle, however, are known quantities, familiar quantities, while the things that take place outside the circle can be strange and mysterious and hint vaguely of evil. Thus allowances are made for the local and the familiar, not necessarily out of any generosity of spirit but because the things of home are easier to understand than the things of elsewhere. I went to visit an old man at his cabin on Buffalo Creek one morning and could see as I approached the door that it was marked with several bullet holes. When I asked what had happened, he said calmly that one of his neighbors had been drunk the night before and had gone on a rampage. "So what are you going to do about it," I asked. "Oh, nothing," he said, "that's just the way Billy is." I have no trouble imagining what his reaction would have been if those bullet holes had been the work of a stranger!

Our seminar from New Burlington continues with a woman of middle years:

> In New Burlington, everyone had a place. Everyone was accepted. Outside, there was no place. Outside were things they didn't know about. But there were no mysterious corners in New Burlington. Even going to Xenia or Wilmington scared them. There was an aroma of sin about those places.

The 92-year-old schoolteacher, looking back on a long life of listening to village gossip and swapping village tales, put the matter wisely and gently:

> We had all these things, all manner of pride and gluttony, and sins real and imagined. But the village life caused a tolerance among us. It had to. Everyone came face to face every day. . . . Like a family, the village shifted, arbitrated, accommodated, and came to terms with its own life. I have witnessed these tolerances in otherwise intolerant people and I have marveled at it.

Craft

Toennies wrote in his 1887 essay:

> The Gemeinschaft, to the extent that it is capable of doing so, transforms all repulsive labor into a kind of art, giving it style, dignity, and charm, and a rank in its order, denoted as a calling and an honor.

That thought, obviously, is more rhapsody than actuality. How many peasants, gnarled and leathery and bent to the hoe after decades in the fields, knew of that charm and honor? Yet scores of observers over the years have suggested that there is something about village life that can lead to an almost compulsive cleanness of line and symmetry of pattern in everyday labor. It is as if work had a ceremonial aspect to it. It is as if work were almost a form of worship in which people of the village both signal their presence in life and express their devotion to it by the precision of the marks they cut in the ground or the shapes they give to the objects they make.

The ritual character of work may have something to do with the comforts that come from an orderly life (our seminar right now is being conducted by the people of Akenfield, courtesy of Ronald Blythe):

> My mother died in 1945. She was like all the old folk, she did everything in strict rotation. That is how they all thought and lived. It was always washing on a Monday and baking on a Wednesday. It could be raining cats and dogs on Monday, but she'd still wash—sheets, flannel shirts and all. Like as not, Tuesday would be hot and she would have burnt half the coal up Monday night getting it dry. I've heard her say time and time again, "if I get out of my routine I'm finished."

But a simple respect for orderliness is clearly not the whole of it, for the exact-ness of the routine and the pattern, the perfection of the ritual, is itself a source of something akin to a sense of art, and, eventually, a sense of self. A seasoned old thatcher notes: "We all have our own pattern. It is our signature, you might say. A thatcher can look at a roof and tell you who thatched it by the pattern." Does it make sense to use the word "art" here? That surface is not a canvas on which the thatcher is free to express whatever creative urges happen to occur to him, any more than the quilts and harnesses fashioned by other members of his family provide an opportunity for them to improvise. We are talking about obedi-ence to custom here: it takes another thatcher even to *see* those variations within the traditional pattern. But the care with which those old forms are observed as well as the "signature" the craftsperson weaves into it lends a real measure of dignity and purpose to the most routine of chores. "The old men will tell you what an interest they took in their tasks," a veteran of Akenfield ways said: "You could call this their main argument. They were brought up on quality work."

The point can be illustrated further by three other persons from Akenfield, the last two of whom disapprove vigorously of the whole thing. The first is an old farmer who said of his neighbors in an age now long past: "The men . . . worked perfectly because it was *their* work. It belonged to them. It was theirs." The second is a local pastor.

> I have sometimes dared to question the incredible perfection attached to certain tasks. . . . Take ploughing or ricking, why should these jobs have had such a tremendous finesse attached to them? The harvest would not have been less if the furrows wavered a little. But, of course, a straight furrow was all that a man was left with. It was his signature, not only on the field but on life. Yet it seems wrong to me that a man's achievements should be reduced to this. It was a form of bondage, if he did but know it.

And third, a young farm worker speaking of the ways of his elders:

> They'll talk all day about what they did years ago. . . . They'll fiddle about with some ditch or other miles away, making such a rare fuss of it. It is all quite unnec-essary, but nobody dare say so, of course. They are quite slow. They have to touch everything with their hands—they dislike the idea of not touching things. They must handle, touch. . . . Of course we know that the old men had art—because they had damn-all else! It kept them from despairing.

Leveling

Let me note, too, on this wild dash across the topic, that a particular kind of leveling is characteristic of the traditional folk village, a certain democracy of the spirit. This is not because the people of the village are egalitarian in any ideological respect. It is because they presume each other to be not only equal in status but largely identical in temperament and outlook. They are of the same kind. So the issue is not one of *equality* so much as it is one of *equivalency.* Pitt-Rivers speaks of the mountain people of Andalusia in a way that can apply to villagers everywhere:

> Here . . . we touch upon one of the essential values of the pueblo, which is the equality, in the sense of the identity of nature, of all those who are born in the same place. Whatever they do . . . they remain by nature the same.

Class distinctions are observed within the village itself, to be sure. Those who have title to the land they work have a higher social standing than those who till someone else's land, and both enjoy more status than farm laborers who toil for wages. Those distinctions shrink to almost nothing, though, when compared to the immense class fissures that separate villagers from the better off of the gentry. This is easy to understand as a practical matter. People do the same kind of work as their neighbors, whether they own the land or not, and they command domestic territories of roughly the same size and quality. They rarely excel or stand out in any other way. Their children go to the same schools and apprentice for the same futures. Some peasants may be more successful than their neighbors in the sense that they bring home more goods. But even then the leveling tendency persists, because members of a community generally do not want to feel different from their fellows and tend to regard status distinctions as divisive, as fissures on the surface of village life. Good fences might make good neighbors in the New Hampshire of Robert Frost, where relationships are based on cleanly demarcated parcels of individual land, but they are seen as lines of division in most folk communities.

Spirituality

A form of spirituality that is hard to see and harder to name is general to village life, where people are drawn to the land by ancient pulls and are governed by the seasons and the whims of an erratic nature. This is often the kind of thing a wise and sympathetic outsider can see more clearly than the persons involved, so, before we turn to other matters, we will hear from three witnesses on peasant spirituality who were not *of* the village but nonetheless lived near its center. The minister from Akenfield:

> They are a hard people. They live their lives at the higher level—and make no mistake, there *is* a higher level: I have seen it, a fugitive glimpse into a country where I cannot belong—present and imponderable. It is the only word I have for it. Fatalism is the real controlling force, this and the nature gods, the spirits of the trees and water and sky and plants. These beliefs have no language, but they rule.

The minister from New Burlington:

> Most of these villages, of course, are made up of farmers, and their outlook is rural. . . . The rural people are involved in life from its beginning to its end. They depend so much on nature, you see. The storekeeper does not worry particularly in drought because his trade goes on. Because of this I think the farmer may be a more devout person.

And, finally, the distinguished Italian we heard from earlier who was exiled to a village in southern Italy in the 1930s. This deserves to be read slowly, carefully, and more than once:

> The deities of the State and the city can find no worshippers here on the land, where the wolf and the ancient black boar reign supreme, where there is no wall between the world of men and the world of animals and land spirits, between the leaves of the trees above and the roots below. They cannot even have an awareness of themselves as individuals, here where all things are held together by acting upon one another and each one is a power unto itself, working imperceptibly, where there is no barrier that cannot be broken down by magic. They live submerged in a world that rolls on independent of their will, where man is in no way separate from his sun, his beast, his malaria, where there can be neither happiness, as literary devotees of the land conceive it, nor hope, because these two are adjuncts of personality and here there is only the grim passivity of a sorrowful Nature. But they have a lively human feeling for the common fate of mankind. . . . They do not express it in words but they carry it with them at every moment and in every motion of their lives, through all the unbroken days that pass over these wastes.

We of the cities and the academies are good at drawing distinctions, as noted earlier. We differentiate religion from science, fact from fiction, reality from dreaming, natural from manmade, human from animal, and so on. But those boundary lines do not always have the same meaning to people who live *on* the land and are absorbed into its rhythms. Life around them is a seamless whole. Politics is not separate from economics. The laws of God and the findings of science are not different: they are both descriptions of what *is*. Knowing and believing are sometimes the same thing. A stone wall built by human hands one thousand years ago is not less natural than a bird's nest or a beaver dam built the day before yesterday; nor for that matter are the creature who built the wall and the creature who built the dam that different in the larger scale of things. The folklore of traditional villages is alive with tales in which people turn into other creatures for a time, passing through membranes that are not so impermeable as we of the cities would have it. And what is the difference between things of religion and things of science to those who truly count both as factual? As given?

The Dark Underside of Village Life

One difficulty in speaking realistically about "village" and "community" is that the vocabulary we use for the purpose seems so often to reflect a longing for ancient securities, warm human bonds, and a slower, calmer, simpler way of life. These nostalgias lie deep in the Western grain, and it is important that they not be mistaken for social reality. Raymond Williams, whose work we consulted earlier, noted that "community" is the only term in the sociological vocabulary that "seems never to be used unfavorably, and never to be given any positive opposing or distinguishing term."

So let it be repeated that the costs of the village way of life can be very high. They include an iron code of obligation and duty as well as an inhibiting of whatever strains of originality or individuality threaten to break through the crust of tradition. Villages are not places where individual freedom is celebrated or the imagination is invited to soar. Rare the new thought published there. Rare the new tool fashioned there. Rare the sonnet composed there.

Peasants who work small holdings of land barely make it even in the best of times, and they have a tendency of long standing to assume that change is more likely to do them harm than to help them. That is a wholly rational calculation when you consider that even a small turn for the worse can have lethal results for them: why would anyone who lives that close to the edge be willing to take a chance? That being so, villagers the world over have earned a reputation for being numbingly stubborn in the face of what people elsewhere call "progress"—displaying a narrowness of mind and vision that follows from what looks like an almost instinctive aversion to risk and anything that might evoke change.

Exactly because the village is so narrow and confined a place, moreover, emotional charges that pass back and forth between persons tend to be more personal, more volatile, more electric. That will result in a particularly warm brand of affection and caring at times, but the spaces that separate one person from another are so cramped that those charges can erupt suddenly into a sharp and crackling hostility that remains a part of the village climate for generations. This can take the form of active feuds between families—elders who will not talk to or forgive or even allow children born long after the event to live in peace with one another. It can take the form of ripples of gossip and slander and vilification so fierce that members of the community are sometimes shunned and treated as if invisible. And in many parts of the world it can take the form of acts of witchcraft—harmless invocations at their mildest, a dark and lethal business at their worst.

Add all that together and it is easier to see why two of the shrewdest observers of village life—both of them named Marx, as it happens and neither of a village background—took so dim a view of community life. Karl Marx, who wrote at one point of "the idiocy of rural life," warned us all not to forget "that these idyllic village communities, inoffensive though they may appear," have always

> restrained the human mind within the smallest possible compass, making it the unresisting tool of superstition, enslaving it beneath traditional rules, depriving it of all grandeur and historical energies.

Now that's an indictment! But the other Marx, Groucho—quicker off the mark and a good deal less solemn—simply revised the then-familiar World War I lyric: "How're you gonna keep 'em down on the farm once they've seen Paree," with a version of his own: "How're you going to keep 'em down on the farm once they've seen—the farm."

The Village Ethos in Modern American Life

Villages of the kind we have been dealing with are disappearing. Remnants can be found here and there, but they are now scarce in the United States and other developed parts of the world, and they are becoming scarcer elsewhere as well. In an age of modern communication, of television and internet, the village settings I have been talking of sound like echoes of a long-distant past.

Even when we see a dot on the map marking the location of a small group of homes in some remote part of Nevada or Minnesota—Lake Wobegon, say—the chances are good that the people who reside there are tuned to the ways of the city and live on much the same plane of reality as their urban compatriots. They listen to the same music, watch the same television programs, and learn about the rest of the world through the same news broadcasts. On Thanksgiving day they make long-distance telephone calls to relatives hundreds of miles away who, in an earlier time, would have been sitting with them at the same table.

In a sense, then, we have been visiting the past so far in this chapter. John McPhee's Colonsay, Ronald Blythe's Akenfield, John Baskin's New Burlington, Carlo Levi's Italian village, Julian Pitt-River's Alcalá de la Sierra, and even the Buffalo Creek I visited for the first time several decades ago are now part of history. Yet I think it is reasonable to suggest that most of us human beings are villagers in some measure, and I suspect, without knowing quite how to make a case for it, that the spirit of the village is deep in our bones somewhere.

We have been speaking of places on the map known as villages, but our true subject from the beginning has not really been a kind of *structure* or *form* so much as a kind of *temper* or *spirit*—a way of feeling, thinking, relating, and seeing. That human experience is still quite common, even if the places from which it originally derived are disappearing, and we will close this discussion by asking where traces of it can yet be found on the contemporary social scene that continue to have some of the same look and feel of the village ethos even in this age of modern communication. If we were gathering material for a booklet to be entitled *The Village Ethos in Modern American Life,* what entries would we include?

The first entry in our booklet might focus on places in the rural countryside where what Toennies called "gemeinschaft" can still be said to survive if only in part—places that have been occupied for generations by the same lineages of people and where a deep sense of community was formed and tempered by the passing of years. A writer named Sherwood Anderson remembered the feel of such places in the midwestern towns where he had grown up before the turn of the 20th century:

In all that great Mississippi Valley each town came to have a character of its own, and the people who lived in the towns were to each other like members of a great family. . . . A kind of invisible roof beneath which everyone lived spread itself over each town. . . . Within this invisible circle and under the great roof everyone knew his neighbor and was known to him. . . . For the moment mankind seemed about to take time to try to understand itself.

But a wave of industrialization was sweeping across that land by the time Anderson became a celebrated novelist, and the "invisible roof" he had written about with such nostalgia was on the verge of disappearing. We would not find many traces of the village ethos there now. Yet we may be looking in the wrong places. In my generation, at least, if American students had been asked to name the oldest continuously occupied town in their nation, a substantial majority would have mentioned Jamestown, Virginia, or Plymouth, Massachusetts. That is what most of us were taught then. But there were established Native communities in the southwest centuries before the first Europeans set foot on this continent and took credit for "discovering" it. Some of them are still there, and provide a good place to look. There are Hispanic villages not far from those native pueblos in New Mexico and elsewhere that still can remind one of Alcalá de la Sierra or New Burlington. There are mountain hollows in Appalachia that continue to have the look and feel of the village ethos, and other settings elsewhere that do the same.

The second entry in the booklet could also deal with survivals from an ever-receding past, this time with communal enclaves in the modern city of the kind Herbert Gans called *urban villages*. This was the book that so impressed Jack Weller, you may remember. That entry could open with a passage from the journal that Alexis de Tocqueville kept during his celebrated visit to the United States in 1830. Tocqueville was at a real loss during the early stages of his visit here because he had not come across any Americans who *looked* or *acted* like peasants. He was a well-traveled European and had met peasants in every other corner of the world. Why not the United States? He thought he had come close a number of times:

You quit the large roads, you penetrate paths scarcely cleared, you perceive finally a cleared field, a cabin composed of half-squared logs, into which daylight enters only through one narrow window, you believe yourself at last come to the dwelling of an American peasant. *Erreur.* You enter this cabin which seems the asylum of all the miseries, but the owner wears the same clothes as you, he speaks the language of the cities. On his rude table are books and newspapers; he himself hastens to take you aside to learn just what is going on in old Europe and to ask you what has most struck you in his own country. He will trace out for you on paper a plan of campaign for the Belgians, will gravely inform you what remains to be done for the prosperity of France. One would believe oneself seeing a rich proprietor who has momentarily come to live for several nights in his hunting lodge.

Tocqueville was deep in the Michigan wilderness when this encounter took place, but we can say now, with the wisdom that time confers on everyone, that America's most observant visitor may have simply missed the chance he sought. The peasant heart of this country, to the extent that it makes sense to talk about such a thing at all, was beginning to form a few city blocks from the New York hotel in which Tocqueville spent his first nights in America, for it was there that the early Irish immigrants, most of them of rural origin, were beginning to gather and to build a new life in the urban slums. As we now know, they would soon be followed by wave upon wave of others, almost all of them of peasant stock, and the new industrial city was becoming in part an assembly of urban villages full of civic institutions like parishes, lodges, union halls, taverns, and other gathering places to which people turn for fellowship. Today, many of those parishes and clubs and orders will have a Vietnamese or Colombian character rather than an Italian or Irish or Polish one, but the basic forms will be similar.

A third entry in our booklet might deal with a species of social order that historians of the United States have described as uniquely American—the utopian community. There is a sense in which the urban ethos, gesellschaft, drives out the village ethos, gemeinschaft. That is what Toennies, Durkheim, Weber, and most social theorists of the time had in mind when they wrote about what was happening to their Europe. Modernity moves in like an irreversible surge and swamps the village way of life, converting it into something rational, instrumental, bureaucratic, without any soul. We are certainly familiar with that concept by now. But there is also a sense in which gesellschaft *creates* gemeinschaft, or at least an imitation of it. This is because the city and its urban ways can provoke a longing for the warmth and security of the village, and that longing—even if it is based on a false memory of what life was actually like—can result in a deliberate effort to produce social forms that reflect at least some of those qualities. The movement of people to the American suburbs, for example, was for many an attempt to recapture the sense of neighborliness that people assume to have a feature of the village past. And the same is true for many of the countercultural movements that have sprung up periodically in this country, and for many of the communal experiments that have marked the American experience from the very beginning. They have had as their explicit purpose to re-establish something of the *mood* of the village ethos by deliberate acts of sharing and simplicity and good will. The ghost of Toennies may implore us to come up with another term for this phenomenon—"pseudo-gemeinschaft" was one sociologist's proposal, thereby making a long word longer yet—but it surely belongs in the booklet.

The fourth entry in our booklet might turn to what we have already heard Edmund Burke describe as the "inns and resting places of the human soul"—those niches, enclaves, pockets, islands, where individuals find refuge from the modernity that presses in on them. Families and households lead that list. It probably ranks as a universal of human experience that families reflect the true essence of gemeinschaft. People everywhere use terms of kinship to convey what they mean by *community,* as we saw in the case of Buffalo Creek and other village settings we visited subsequently. Homes provide a contained, protected space in the midst of the most harried sectors of modern life: a sense of hearth. "Haven in a heartless world," Christopher Lasch called them. In other ways, as well, the most industrialized and urbane of social settings are full of those "snug recesses" that Edmund Burke spoke of. We spend a good part of our lives in such enclaves no matter how specialized or how tightly organized our daily rounds become. Each one of us may draw a different list of the niches we tend to take refuge in, but most will refer to the kinds of bonds that connect members of the same schools, congregations, neighborhoods, and so on. And some will refer to street gangs that defend turfs and fashion a life form that is somewhat village-like in the process.

When I spoke of these matters at Yale and other academic settings, students often commented that the social circles they had become a part of—athletic teams, choruses, clubs, study groups, residential units—not to mention the campus as a whole—had something of a village feel for them. A campus is, by definition, a temporary haven at best, but it can last a lifetime for some. I do not know whether this kind of *fellow-ing* (to coin a term for one sentence) will fade with the advent of online teaching, but whether it turns out to be a relic of times past or a continuing feature of the future, it deserves at least a footnote in the booklet.

The final entry in our booklet moves us into a darker conceptual terrain. Modern life can leave people so detached from familiar and secure surroundings that they turn from the present to more tribal forms of national feeling and more fundamentalist forms of religious observance. We will turn to that subject later, so I only want to note now that "nationalism" in its starkest form is in many ways a form of the village ethos. It gathers persons together on the ground that they share a sense of place (homeland), a sense of kind (peoplehood), a sense of destiny (national history), and all the other identifying features of folkhood noted at the beginning of the chapter.

Perhaps new forms of human social life are now being generated down there in the still warm ashes of what Toennies called gemeinschaft, some of them volatile and dangerous. One of the most influential reflections on contemporary nationalism to appear in our time describes nations as "imagined communities." So we come full circle. *Le village est mort. Vive le village!*

City

THE HUNTING AND GATHERING LIFE WAS GOVERNED by a simple arithmetic. Food supplies were so widely dispersed that only a few individuals could be fed by the yield of one square mile, and for that reason the bands had to be small in size and mobile enough to cover large territories. Someone looking down on that scene from a great height—a stranger in orbit, let us say—might have found it hard to distinguish the human animals who lived down there from other creatures who roamed the world in packs, each band a small cluster of foragers moving across the countryside and leaving few traces of its passing.

The agricultural life, too, was governed by a simple arithmetic. In the early years of agriculture, the yield of one square mile could feed something like twenty persons, varying with the fertility of local soils; and since the fields being cultivated had to be within walking distance of every residence, a farming village could not easily absorb more than two or three hundred people. Villagers are a stationary lot. They fan out into the countryside by light of day to work small patches of land, and then return to the shelter of the village as night falls.

Our orbiting stranger, looking down on *that* scene, would probably have noticed that human life had shifted into a rather different configuration. But he might not have been very impressed, since those early village communities were not much larger than the temporary encampments they had replaced—fixed in place, to be sure, but still tiny clusters spread out across an immense landscape. Nothing there to suggest that humankind was slowly and quietly undergoing a major transformation.

The world is now moving into an age when the vast majority of our kind will live in (or around) cities. This is already the case in Europe and the United States. It is becoming the case in Latin America. And it will soon be the case in Asia and Africa unless something truly miraculous happens to reverse what now appears to be an inevitability.

We have already looked at some of the causes of that transformation, so it need only be repeated now that the most essential of them were advances in agricultural technology so extensive that they came close to emptying out the countryside. Up until the time of that transformation—still under way in many parts of the world—as many as 98 persons had to be working the soil at any given time to grow enough food to sustain 100. Only 2 percent of the population, that is, could turn their energies to other pursuits. Even during the most celebrated urban civilizations of antiquity—Mesopotamia, Egypt, China, Greece, Rome—an absolute minimum of 90 percent of the population was bound to the land. We are now moving into an age when those percentages are almost completely reversed. Two persons can now produce calories enough to nourish one hundred. Transformation indeed! That is the surplus we spoke of earlier. It is the stuff on which the cities feed.

At the same time as those millions of people were cut loose from their ancient ties to the land and drifted into urban places, new industrial plants—themselves an outgrowth of the surge of innovation that had brought about those changes in agricultural production—began to take form near sources of power. A new labor force, made up of migrants from the rural hinterland, began to gather within walking distance of the plants or transportation hubs set up to handle the goods produced by them. In the United States, for example, an almost empty island where the Hudson River and the East River flow into New York Bay, a triangle of land where the Allegheny and the Monongahela meet to form the Ohio, and a flat plain where the Chicago River enters Lake Michigan all attract vast waves of growth.

That way of life is governed by a very different arithmetic. Thousands of people can mass within a single square mile, even when they are all confined to ground level, and when builders learn how to place one layer of living space on top of another until the stack seems to reach the skies, that number can climb into the tens and even the hundreds of thousands. The orbiting stranger, finally, is impressed. What is going on down there at ground level is a rearrangement of the world's growing population, a huge implosion as the flows of human traffic are drawn inward toward a few powerful magnetic poles.

Thomas De Quincey, an English essayist who wrote in the early decades of the 19th century, looked upon that process as an amazing new human experience. One can sense his astonishment even now, two centuries after he wrote the following:

> It was a most heavenly day in May when I first beheld and first entered this mighty wilderness, the city—no, not the city, the nation—of London. Often since then, at distances of two or three hundred miles or more . . . have I felt the expression of her enormous magnitude . . . in the vast droves of cattle . . . all with their heads directed to London, expanding the size of that attracting body. A suction so powerful, felt along radii so vast . . . operating night and day, summer and winter . . . by land and by sea . . . and hurrying forever into one centre the infinite means needed for her infinite purposes.

He then goes on to speak of

> the whirl and the uproar, the tumult and the agitation, which continually thicken through the last dozen miles before you reach London. Launched upon this final stage, you soon begin to feel yourself entering the stream as if it were a Norwegian maelstrom, and the stream at length becomes a cataract.

An excitable man, this De Quincey, but he was on to something important.

Early Cities

People had been gathering in assemblies known as "cities" long before the coming of the Industrial Revolution, of course. The first of them appeared in the great river valleys of antiquity—the Tigris and Euphrates, the Indus, the Nile, and the Hwang Ho in China. Little is known of them. They were submerged under the silt of centuries before the age of written records began, but it is possible to reconstruct a general outline of what happened from the fragments that remain nonetheless.

If we were following those thousands of years on a speeded-up roll of film, we would notice a shift in the way people drew a living from the soil beginning about 5,000 years ago. Farmers who had been scratching away at the ground with wooden implements for millennia were devising new ways to improve their productivity. These were modest advances, when measured on the scale of what was later to happen, but they made a crucial difference. Draft animals and plows were replacing the hoe. Humans were learning the uses of metal and of systems of irrigation. The skills of the potter were developing, and with them new methods for storing goods. As a result of these and related developments, the agricultural surplus had increased to the point where more people could leave the land and take on other livelihoods.

The flow of people from the rural countryside into those early urban settlements was little more than a barely perceptible trickle this early in the history of things, but a breed of person new to the human scene was now making an appearance. Merchants with wares to sell and specialists with skills to offer were taking to the road, thus opening up the first trade routes, and market towns began to emerge where those routes intersected. Individuals who had been recognized as chieftains because of their prowess in the hunt or the quickness of their mind or the circumstances of their birth or the ability to convince others of their unique qualities began to move into the towns, and, as time passed, to gather useful people around them—warriors, accountants, artisans, scribes, priests, servants. These new townspeople were all nourished by the agricultural surplus, which chieftains managed to extract from the countryside in the form of voluntary or involuntary tributes—measures of grain or heads of cattle, for example—and then redistributed for their own purposes. Thus the first towns were formed around a core made up of buildings to lodge the chieftain and his household, shrines to formalize and give focus to worship of the gods, granaries and cisterns and other facilities to store the surplus, and, because things of value were now accumulating in central places, walls or ramparts to protect it from inevitable attack. A fine urban historian named V. Gordon Childe described the city as "an instrument" for "the extraction and concentration of the surplus." And so it was.

In time, the towns grew into something we would recognize as cities. The range of the chieftain's domain increased, and the day came when he let it be known that he should now be known as *lord* or *baron* or maybe even *king*. His lodgings become a great house, and then eventually a palace. The shrine became a temple, and then, over time, a cathedral. The granary became a vast storehouse, and then a treasury. The walled stronghold became a citadel, and then a fortress. The town was now a true urban center, a place through which goods flowed and in which wealth was accumulated and records were kept. Payments from the surrounding villages, once written down as gifts or tributes, were now written down as taxes or tithes or rents—a permanent and regular cost to the people of the countryside.

Thus the origins of the city, sketched so broadly here that, once again, they approach caricature. It is important to add to this brief sketch, though, that the early towns and cities initiated a kind of feedback loop that has characterized the relationship of the urban center to its hinterland from that time to this. The toil of villagers nourished the city. That much is obvious on its face. The city drained the countryside of whatever scrap of surplus it could—not just tangible goods like crops and livestock, but hours of labor from hard-pressed peasants on projects of benefit to the city. But at the same time the city sent engineers to the villages to supervise the building of irrigation systems, metal smiths to teach the shaping of plows and other useful implements, and skilled craftspersons of many other kinds to teach the uses of looms and potter's wheels and forges and the like.

One can call this a form of complementarity if one wants to put a benign face on it—the city and its hinterland engaged in an exchange of profit to them both. The countryside supplies the city with food and raw materials; the city supplies the countryside with military protection, the administration of justice, education, places of worship, markets, and the like. But the city received so much more proportionally from that exchange that the relationship almost has to be depicted as a form of exploitation. The services provided by the city were a mixed blessing at best. The way justice was administered rarely worked to the advantage of the peasantry. Whatever solace the people of the village drew from the awesome religious edifices of the city and the well-fed clergy who presided over them, it had all been a product of their labor and their sacrifice in the first place. And the people of the countryside needed protection primarily because military projects launched by the city endangered everyone.

The early market centers and the cities that followed them marked the first time in human history when raiding and other forms of armed assault became a profitable pursuit. Our hunting and gathering ancestors faced one another in fairly ritualized forms of combat, but they did not go to war over territories or possessions as our kind learned later to. It was the kings and pharaohs and warlords—and the ever growing networks of people gathering around them—who went off to war to enrich their treasuries and to add to their dominions. And as often as not it was the tillers of the soil who were sent into battle for those purposes. Exploitation may be too gentle a word to cover that. This all came about because of the agricultural surplus. It is in part what I had in mind earlier when I spoke of "original sin."

Meantime, the city gathered people, goods, and materials within its narrow precincts, and in doing so created a new and distinctly urban problem. Things move into a city easily, that being the natural flow of civic life, but they are removed from the city only as the result of considerable effort. So the city became a kind of compost heap, made up of layer upon layer of rubbish, until it quite literally gained elevation, each age regrouping, as it were, on the packed refuse of the age preceding it. Waste disposal is a major problem even in our technologically advanced period, of course, but it was far worse then. No one knew how to flush away human or animal excrement, how to remove the bodies of the dead, human and animal, or how to cart off the enormous mounds of garbage that accumulated in the city center. Nor did anyone see it as a problem. The countryside may have offered a soil well suited to the growing of crops, but the city offered a soil ideally suited to the growing of insects and vermin, bacteria and viruses, with the result that the city became a place where diseases as well as people and goods converged.

Cities, then, had been known in various parts of the world for 3,000 years before the arrival of the Industrial Revolution, when Thomas De Quincey saw all those people being drawn into London by a force he likened to suction and sensed that he was witnessing the beginning of something new. But the great cities of antiquity—Babylon, Nippur, Nineveh, Ur, Thebes—were sorry affairs by comparison. The urban centers of Mesopotamia or Egypt rarely contained more than 5,000 or 10,000 people, the size of a small town in our age, and Ur, the largest of them, does not seem to have ever reached 25,000. Athens in the time of Pericles, a towering metropolis by comparison, occupied less than a single square mile and had a population that hovered around 120,000 persons, the size of Ann Arbor, Michigan, or for that matter, Athens, Georgia, now. Rome in the time of Caesar Augustus had 500,000 inhabitants and may have reached 1,000,000, but that was a very special case, a striking historical anomaly, no matter what count we accept. With the collapse of the Roman Empire in the 4th century, Europe went into that long decline known as the Dark Ages, and Rome itself shrunk into a town of 20,000—a few ragged survivors crouched within the ruins of what had once been a magnificent city. The Romans had begun to build cities in sites that would one day have names like Paris, Vienna, Cologne, London. But those places, too, fell into disrepair when they were no longer held together by Roman skills in administration and engineering.

Five hundred years would pass before something we might reasonably call a "town" appeared on the scene. Settlements that came close to that modest standard began to emerge here and there by the 11th century, but by the 15th century only a handful of them—Venice, Florence, Milan, Paris—had even approached the size of Athens two thousand years earlier. And those few settlements were exceptions to what had almost become an iron law of scale elsewhere. For one thing, an urban citizenry had to be pressed together within the walls of the city for protection in time of conflict, and those encircling ramparts had become so massive as a result of advances in the power of artillery that the costs of moving them further out to accommodate a growing population had simply become prohibitive. The city's walls had become a barrier to further expansion.

Medieval cities were confined to relatively narrow spaces for other reasons as well. Plato had argued many centuries earlier that the ideal city should be limited to the number of persons who could gather within the range of a single voice, and that view of the nature of civic space was very alive even then. The idea here was that the natural size for an organic, true city was one in which citizens lived within walking distance of the market, the temple, and other civic places, and within hailing distance of the city bells. In fact, the scale of the medieval city had more to do with the logistics of water supply and of food distribution and of military defense than with ancient philosophy—arithmetic governed here, too—but the upshot of both was that urban spaces rarely reached farther out than half a mile from their centers, and rarely had populations of more than a few thousand.

When De Quincey saw a London that was about to reach the one million mark, then, he was certainly right to suppose that he had happened onto something truly remarkable. He was in fact witnessing the early phases of an altogether new form of human settlement. But the tide had only just begun. It would still be many decades before Paris or Vienna reached a million. No city in the United States would reach it for almost another century. And the swollen giants of our day—Mexico City, Seoul, São Paulo, Mumbai, Jakarta—were hardly more than lazy market towns.

Cities in the United States

There comes a moment in any discussion of the sociology of cities when the subject, like urban places themselves, becomes too large to be considered in a single chapter. Cities in Europe, Latin America, Asia, Africa, and the United States grew in different ways and at different paces, and since it would take many volumes to cover all that even in a glancing way, we must narrow our focus. So I will turn now to the American urban experience, not because it is representative of what happened elsewhere on earth—it is not—but because it comes closest to home for most persons who will read these pages. As the chapter comes to an end I will say more about the emergence of cities in other parts of the world.

Industrial cities emerged in the United States at a far slower pace than was the case for England and for the Continent more generally. As the 18th century turned into the 19th and the republic was learning to govern itself, Philadelphia had a population of 60,000, New York 50,000, and Boston 25,000. Human traffic in and out of those stately towns would not have made much of an impression on Thomas De Quincey. Thomas Jefferson became President in 1801, a time when 95 persons were needed to work the land in order to produce food enough for 100. He assumed that the new country was destined to be a land of small farms and rural villages. He had written earlier that cities are by nature "pestilential to the morals, the health, and the liberties of man," and he took it altogether for granted that they would never flourish in these climes. On that subject, as on so few others, he could not have been more wrong. In the century and a half that followed his presidency, the United States became the scene of continuing flows of population moving into urban cores—an immense convergence of people drawn inward by that same force of suction that had so impressed De Quincy.

Immigration

When Jefferson died in 1826, shiploads of Irish immigrants were landing in places like Boston and New York, and the genteel American towns he had wanted to protect from the "corrupting" influences of large-scale urbanization were soon to be stocked by as diverse a gathering of persons as the world had yet seen. Within a few years, as we now know, the cities of America were alive with newcomers, most of them recent arrivals from Old Europe. When Piotr and Kasia arrived in Chicago, not long after the beginning of the new century, the population of the city was 90 percent foreign-born—a staggering figure— and most of the other industrializing cities of the new world such as Pittsburgh, Cleveland, and Buffalo were not far below that mark. Chicago had more Poles than Kraków, New York more Italians than Naples and almost twice as many Irish as Dublin. They were all participants in the largest mass migration the world had ever known.

The Statue of Liberty was dedicated in 1880, the year Kasia was born in Poland, with lines by Emma Lazarus carved on its pedestal:

Give me your tired, your poor, your huddled masses yearning to breathe free, the refuse from your teeming shore—send these, the homeless, tempest-tost to me.

That was as open an invitation as could have been imagined. It had been acted upon for several decades up to then, and would continue to be acted on for another forty years or so. The huddled masses poured into the new land in waves. There was pattern to that, as we already know: the earlier waves were made up largely of Irish countryfolk, following hard on the English and Scots who had been making their way into the new land for generations. And then, in wide arcs radiating eastward and southward from the British Isles, additional waves of people in which Germans and Scandinavians dominated, followed by waves that included large numbers of Poles and Italians, followed by yet other waves made up in large part of Russians, Armenians, Serbs, and Greeks. Once again, it would be a mistake to speak too precisely about the composition of those waves, since we are concerned with general tendencies here. But that pattern of succession had a decisive influence on what happened to the immigrants as they arrived. The social geometry of the situation, if one can speak of such a thing, was that new arrivals to the city tended to move into the worst of the housing and to take on the worst of the jobs—almost as if some law of motion was involved. When new waves moved in, that is, the waves that had preceded them moved *out* residentially into more desirable parts of the city and *up* occupationally into more desirable jobs.

It needs to be said one last time that the pattern I have been describing was not clean or crisp. There were always a number of people from other lands on ships full of Irish in the 1840s, and a number of Irish and Scots on ships full of Poles and Italians in the 1900s, so the waves were far from homogeneous. And, too, on this side of the ocean, there were always clusters of Irish and Poles and Italians holding onto ethnic enclaves in the midst of the city even as large numbers of their fellow countrymen moved upward and outward with the shifts that had been set into motion.

Still, one can see the general outlines of that pattern if one looks in the right places. Were we to consult lists of people being served by a local post office over the period of time I have been dealing with here, for example, in places like

Pittsburgh or South Chicago, we would probably discover that English names tended in the mass to yield to Irish ones, Irish to German, German to Polish and Italian, and so on as we worked our way step by step up the escalator of time. Moreover, it is easy to imagine urban scenes in which the pattern of succession is reflected more or less in passing. Stories could be told or films produced of a police officer with a distinctly Italian name who is patrolling a black neighborhood in East Harlem, the very spot in which he had been born forty years earlier, and reporting at the end of his tour of duty to a German sergeant in a precinct headed by an Irish captain. Or of a Hispanic communicant confessing to a Polish priest who reports to an Austrian bishop in a city presided over by an Irish cardinal. This kind of thing lends itself to caricature as easily as it does to sociological analysis, but it is *there* nevertheless—a tendency, a probability, a social fact. Émile Durkheim would have appreciated that.

Migration

The flow of European newcomers into the United States began to slow appreciably in the 1920s when Congress decided to revoke the welcome carved on the Statue of Liberty and enacted a series of sharply restrictive immigrant laws. But the flow of people into the *city* continued without pause as migrants from the American South and elsewhere took their place. These new arrivals were every bit as rural as the European peasants who had preceded them, for this was a movement from countryside to city as well as one from South to North. A very considerable number of them were black—a demographic shift so immense that it changed the American landscape starkly.

In 1920, there were about ten million blacks in the United States making up 10 percent of the total populace. Roughly 90 percent of them lived in the South, mostly in the rural countryside. That's an easy demographic so far. By the end of the century, however, there were closer to twenty-five million blacks in the United States, making up something like 12 percent of the total population. Of these, more than half lived in the North, and fully 85 percent of them had become city dwellers. These are just sums, of course, and it is becoming more and more difficult in this age of prodigious numbers to be impressed by that way of expressing the magnitude of things. But pause for a moment and try to see it as the orbiting stranger might: that's a lot of people on the move.

The first surge of internal migration into the cities took place in the 1920s. The flow was interrupted during the worst years of the Great Depression in the

1930s, but it picked up again during World War II and the decades to follow. At first, the old pattern of succession looked as though it was reasserting itself. The early waves of Southern migrants replaced the waves of European settlers that had preceded them by stepping into the lowest rungs of the employment ladder and into the innermost ring of tenement housing. And when still newer waves of migrants arrived from the South, their predecessors fell into the familiar sequence by moving up a step occupationally and out a step residentially. So far so good.

But the pattern did not hold. For reasons we will turn to shortly, a majority of the industrial plants that had been built near the urban core either closed, moved out to the edges of the city, or left the region altogether; and as subsequent waves of migrants arrived to take their rightful place on the escalator, it had slowed to a virtual stop. By the 1970s and 1980s, manufacturing jobs had in large part left the central city.

This was a striking shift, with the consequence that many of the inner cities of the United States began to look like vast wastelands into which new waves of huddled masses, many of them tired, poor, and tempest-tost, were now gathering. African-Americans and landless whites from the South arrived first, but they have been joined in recent decades by native Americans, Puerto Ricans, Mexicans, migrants from other Latin American lands, Asians, and a number of others.

I would like to emphasize two points as we conclude this part of the discussion. The first is how immense and how rapid the population shift was from the rural countrysides of Europe and the United States to the central city in the late 19th and particularly in the first half of the 20th centuries. The second is how abruptly the old pattern of succession that had characterized the industrial cities of the country for the better part of a century came to a halt in the second half of the 20th century, leaving the newest arrivals marooned in a barren place that was full of people but largely empty of promise.

Sociology and the Emerging City

I noted earlier that sociology can be said to have reached its maturity as a discipline in the early years of the Industrial Revolution, when millions of persons were spilling out of the countryside and into the city, and when all the other developments we have been dealing with so far in this chapter were beginning to take place. It will be no surprise, then, if I add that sociologists in

Europe and the United States took an early interest in the structure of the modern city and have been preoccupied with the topic ever since.

Sociological research into the nature of the American city began at the University of Chicago in the early decades of the 20th century, where the first important group of American scholars who called themselves sociologists were gathering. It was there that Thomas and Znaniecki collected data for *The Polish Peasant in Europe and America.*

The main working assumption of the Chicago sociologists, as that huge, frightening, exhilarating metropolis formed around them, was that the modern city had to be understood as something new to human experience. It was not the ancient city swollen to a thousand times its original size, and thus a familiar arrangement of parts cast onto a far greater screen. It was a new life form altogether, a new kind of social structure. It was like a newly evolved creature with its own anatomy, its own metabolism, its own personality, and its own rhythms of growth and decline.

Because the city is a different kind of social order, they assumed, it produces its own cultural ethos and its own psychological temper. Robert Ezra Park, the dean of the Chicago School, wrote that "the city is a state of mind, a body of customs and traditions." People of the city, then, are likely to be more individualistic, freer from tradition, more creative. And—this is the other side of that coin—they are likely to be more frazzled, more irritable, more alienated. Georg Simmel, a brilliant German sociologist of the early 20th century, whose ideas the Chicago sociologists had at least a glancing familiarity with, argued that the human nervous system was bombarded by so many different stimuli in the modern city that people who lived there ran the risk of developing a thick layer of psychic scar tissue and becoming ever more distanced from each other. City life makes one anxious, wary, calculating, ill at ease. Louis Wirth, a prominent member of the Chicago group, who coined the expression "psychic overload" to convey exactly that point, went a long step further by arguing that the modern city was not just a strain on the human nervous system but quite literally a source of pathology in the sense that its ways could drive people to crime, mental illness, alcoholism, and a host of other deviancies that Wirth and his colleagues (Florian Znaniecki among them) often lumped together under the general heading "social disorganization."

The modern city, in that view—like so much else in human life—has to be counted a mixed blessing. On the one hand, city ways free the imagination, excite the intellect, and offer the mind a broad canvas to paint on. On the other hand, city ways can do real damage to the human spirit, which is why urban places contain so many persons who are unhinged, wander through life in an alcoholic fog, or make a living preying on their fellow citizens. A whole generation of Chicago sociologists, notebooks in hand, fanned out across the city to get the measure of street corners, boarding houses, union halls, brothels, pool rooms, ethnic neighborhoods, skid rows, and slums, and to study the new species of human drawn to such habitats—hoboes, bohemians, loners, drifters, and hustlers of many different stripes. They saw the city as an easy place to lose one's footing, and they thought they saw evidence all around them that urban life created a good deal more than its share of deviant behavior.

In many ways, then, the modern city was viewed as a form of settlement lying near the *gesellschaft* end of the continuum, and the same would have been so if Durkheim's *mechanical* and *organic,* Redfield's *folk* and *urban*—or any other of the contrasting pairs I alluded to earlier—had been used to describe the character of the city.

It has since become apparent as sociologists continue to study urban life that a good deal is wrong with that old Chicago portrait. For one thing, Wirth and his colleagues wrote as if urban dwellers were exposed to the city as a whole once they took up residence there and thus experienced the same conditions of life. Since they were sharing the same stretch of land and were pressed so closely together, the theory seemed to be suggesting—breathing the same air, sharing the same climate—they must have been subject to the same social and cultural atmosphere as well. But that turned out not to be the case for many urban dwellers, and those early Chicago studies, in their own way, helped explain why. The modern city is an amazingly heterogeneous place when viewed as a continuous social fabric, and observers might well wonder how ordinary individuals can cope with so much diversity. But the fact is that many residents inhabit smaller enclaves within the larger cityscape—households, parishes, neighborhoods, places of work, taverns, clubs, and groupings of a number of kinds that help insulate people from the harsher edges of city life as a whole. I wrote earlier about the role played by ethnic associations in the lives of immigrant newcomers to the American urban scene, but the same is true for many others as well. The city is an endless mosaic of bowling leagues, occupational societies, alumni associations, fraternal organizations, athletic clubs, book groups. Of groups who gather to sing chorales or follow the same sports teams or watch their weight or help one another recover from drug or alcohol abuse. The list is as long as this whole chapter. The point to be made here is an arithmetical one too. Groups of these kinds can only gather in settings where there is a large and diverse population pool to draw from. It takes a city, that is, to assemble a large enough variety of individuals for those who share a particular interest to form a critical mass. How many lute players or collectors of rare coins or recovering drug users or devotees of Marcel Proust can one find in Alcalá de la Sierra or New Burlington or Buffalo Creek? But in Chicago?

This has been one way in which the cityscape has formed. What the internet is now doing to rearrange those forms of gathering will have to be another topic for another time.

A New Urban Configuration Appears

So the converging industrial cities of America attracted wave after wave of people from the rural countryside throughout the 19th and 20th centuries. That is exactly what took place in every part of the industrializing world. No sooner had that magnetic pull finished its work in the United States, however, when things took an unusual turn: a backflow was set into motion that carried a considerable part of what was then the urban population away from the core of the city and out to its furthest edges, those perimeter regions that would soon be called "suburbs." A strong centripetal force had drawn people into the central city from hundreds and even thousands of miles away in the second half of the 19th century and the first half of the 20th, but it was followed in the second half of the 20th century, right after the ending of World War II, by a kind of reverse tide, a centrifugal force that sent a number of them—largely white—out a few miles from the center to its outskirts.

Suburb was an old word about to take on new import. It means "outside the city" in Latin, and it had been used in medieval times to refer to a ring of settlement beyond the city walls where the poor, the indigent, and the disreputable clustered. These were, both literally and figuratively, *outsiders*. In early 19th-century American cities, zones just outside the city limits were reserved in part for both commercial establishments and public institutions that were thought too unsavory for the downtown—slaughterhouses, brick yards, and tanneries in the first instance; poorhouses, orphanages, and asylums for the insane in the second. In poorer parts of the world even now, peasants streaming in from the countryside have to survive as best they can in shantytowns and squatter huts that rim the city. So suburbs have always been reserved for people beyond the pale. The *sub* in suburbs had roughly the same implication as the *sub* in "substandard." In many parts of Europe now, suburbs are for the working poor and more recent waves of immigrants.

But a very different urban configuration was taking form in the United States. The industrial city seemed to be turning inside-out, with people and activities that had once been massed near the core of the city moving out to its fringes, and people who had once been too poor or unattached to find a place in the urban core now being drawn there in almost the same way particles are drawn into a vacuum. It was an extraordinary repositioning of the urban population.

Moving out to the neighboring countryside has always been an option for families that could afford it, so the suburban idea was clearly not new in either Europe or the United States. But the vast reconfiguration I alluded to above was. It began tentatively in the 1920s just as immigration from Europe was tapering off, grew slowly but perceptibly during the economic depression of the 1930s and the world war of the early 1940s, and then exploded into being in the late 1940s. Millions upon millions of new homes were constructed in the decades following World War II, and almost all of them were built on vacant farmlands beyond the city limits. Nothing even remotely like it took place anywhere else in the world.

Why here? Well, for one thing, historians of American culture have been suggesting for quite some time that there is a longing found deep in the American spirit to move from what we heard Jefferson call the "pestilential" city to arcadian glades somewhere outside it where the land is green, the air is fresh, and residents are insulated by a comforting cushion of space from the alien ways and alien people of the city. And, too, that longing may reflect a nostalgia for the village communities from which so many city dwellers originally came.

But far more to the present point, an immense advertising and lobbying campaign to develop suburban areas took place in the years following World War II. The campaign was launched in large part by bankers, home builders, land speculators, real estate brokers, insurance agents, suppliers of building materials, and many others who sensed an enormous profit in the opening of suburbia. But it was clear from the start that the circulation system of this new urban growth—the means by which people and goods would be moved to, from, and between its various parts—would be provided by automobiles and trucks. It is certainly no coincidence, then, that one of the most prominent advocates of suburban growth was the automotive industry, the stated ambition of which was to put the entire population in cars and to eliminate other forms of transport as decisively as possible. That goal was shared, quite understandably, by manufacturers of tires, refiners of gasoline, and builders of roads.

It makes good sense to assume that the campaign to develop the suburbs appealed to those old American yearnings for the wholesome country life, then, but it makes even better sense to assume that the campaign helped *create* those yearnings. However historians sort that out, the combination of old longings and new promotions changed the shape of the geographic as well as the social and cultural landscape in profound ways.

So market forces were clearly at work here, but the decision to invest that heavily in the development of the suburbs was a matter of federal policy as well. To encourage home buying in the new suburbs, the government offered low-cost mortgages, tax benefits, home insurance policies, and a number of other incentives. To encourage the use of automobiles and trucks, it constructed roadways that connected not only suburbs with their urban hubs but suburbs with suburbs and cities with cities in a vast web that stretched across the whole country. And to encourage other forms of investment in suburbia, it offered depreciation allowances and other tax breaks that made a profound difference.

It is important to remember that when a government elects to subsidize one form of development rather than another, it is making a fateful choice. This was a decision to invest in *single-family homes outside the city limits* rather than in *the housing stock of the central city.* It was a decision to invest in *roadways* and *private automobiles* rather than in *railways and other forms of public transit.* It was, in effect, a decision to isolate the inner city.

The American suburb and the American inner city, then, are closely related subjects, and I will turn to each—the suburb first because it did so much to shape the rest of the city.

Suburbia

That shift of people and priorities in the years immediately following World War II must have seemed to the orbiting stranger like a strange new growth of some kind. He was looking down at a landscape he had never seen the like of in all his millennia in the skies.

As the sun rose in the morning, streams of vehicles flowed into the city center from all points of the compass—buses, trains, and increasingly automobiles. And as the sun set in the afternoon, they flowed back out again along those same transportation routes, splayed outward like the spokes of a gigantic wheel. It must have looked at that elevation as though the city were breathing, inhaling deeply as all those particles were drawn inward toward its inner core, and exhaling with the same vigor as they were expelled again. One historian of suburbia described the motion as "that great tidal wash in and out."

Not long after that exodus of urban dwellers to the outer edges of the city, however, many of the plants and offices they worked for in the city center—as well as the stores they shopped in—moved out to boot. People were no longer anchored to the central city because the automobile had so lengthened their range, and it was soon the case that manufacturing firms were no longer anchored to the central city either because electrification meant that they did not need to depend on centrally located sources of power to produce goods or on centrally located transportation networks to ship them afterward. Trucks were becoming for industry what automobiles had become for the people of suburbia.

By the 1980s in many parts of the land, the suburbs had become an endless sprawl not only of housing tracts but of shopping malls, industrial parks, office complexes, research centers, and a scattering of schools, hospitals, places of worship, movie theaters, municipal buildings, and so on. By that time suburbia was not so much an extension of the city as a new form of settlement altogether. Urban spaces in other parts of the world grow out from their centers in gradual increments, cells added onto cells until the whole reaches its natural limits. That is how most cities of Europe grew and how most American cities did initially. But the American suburbs are something else entirely. Most of the structures one finds out there were built by developers on much the same prin- ciple employed in line assembly, using methods of mass production and taking advantage of economies of scale. The logic at work here is the kind of cold rationality and efficiency that kept Weber awake at night—human habitats shaped not by a sense of communality or tradition but by sheer calculation.

Efficiency argues that those elements of an urban area that use space in the same way should be grouped together. Retail establishments should be clus- tered in a common setting, as should residential housing, and a similar pattern of spacing should be used to govern the placement of industries, offices, medical facilities, and everything else. When you are free to construct urban spaces from the ground up, you can actually think that way, since there are no town greens or historic structures that have to be taken into account and no local landmarks—cemeteries or parks, for example—that have reached their present shape through the slow workings of time rather than the designs of planners. Land use can become specialized in towns and central cities too, of course, but it is not the *fact* of it so much as the *scale* of it that matters here.

So a new metropolitan map begins to emerge. From the air we look down on large housing tracts that can appear like an endless spread of equally sized and similarly designed homes, spaced at intervals across a neatly shaved land surface covered largely by lawns. Then scores if not hundreds of retail stores, gathered into a single place and sometimes under a single roof—an expanse more easily measured by the acre than by the square foot. And other clusters of buildings reserved for offices or industrial plants or automobile showrooms or something of the sort. No one would mistake it for a village community.

Street corner delicatessens are hard to find in that sprawl. So are street corners, for all of that, or front stoops or newsstands or pocket playgrounds. Few sidewalks for strolling down Main Street. Moving from one place to place to another is accomplished largely if not entirely by automobile, which means that vast portions of urban space must be set aside for roadways and parking lots. A shopping mall can look from the air like a flat, rectangular island in a sea of pavement. An industrial park or office complex may be surrounded on all sides by parking areas, taking up more space than the buildings they serve. Automobiles are the connection, the lifelines.

What one cannot see from the air, moreover, is that a large portion of each home (a quarter of the total square footage is not uncommon) is set aside for sheltering automobiles. Most of us have learned to take that for granted, but it would have stunned Kasia and Piotr, who raised five children in a space smaller than many suburban garages, and it would have stopped Moke dead in his tracks. A shrewd, thoughtful man, he might have concluded that automobiles must be the most sacred objects in America if they are assigned larger sleeping quarters than any member of the family! Imagine what a three-car garage, taking up that part of the house fronting on the street, would seem like to a Polish peasant or a hunter from the Ituri Rain Forest or, for that matter, a city dweller almost anywhere in the world.

* * *

It should be clear from what I have been saying thus far that the American land-scape was profoundly changed by the shift to suburbanization. Those changes were geographic in the sense that an important relocation of population had been involved. But they were also social and economic and even cultural in the sense that the American social order as a whole had been reshaped in telling ways.

First, it is widely presumed that the shift of population from the central city to the suburbs was intended in part to separate urban whites even further from urban blacks than was already the case. I say "intended" because it is well known that many of the people who made the move had just that object in mind, and it is also well known that it was one of the reasons the federal government supported it. The suburbs have attracted large numbers of African-American families over the past several decades and recent immigrant waves from Asia, Latin America, and the Caribbean have moved into the suburbs without pausing elsewhere because so many jobs are now located there. But the long-term effect of suburbanization in the United States has been to create sharper lines of racial segregation across the surface of the land than were ever drawn by local ordi-nances or regional customs. One of the most important studies of the urban ghetto, by Douglas Massey and Nancy Denton, is entitled *American Apartheid,* a term that not only anticipates the main argument of the book well but is an accurate description of that urban scene in general. Centuries ago, the word *ghetto* was used in parts of Europe to refer to sections of the city set aside for Jews, but it is widely used in our time to refer to neighborhoods occupied by other minorities. No one is *obligated* to live there as a matter of law, but people drift there in the hundreds of thousands and even millions as a consequence of invisible market forces that press in on them and government policies that act to support those market forces. No public ordinances or private covenants could have achieved so neat a separation. Why mark a water fountain "colored" in a location where no one but African-Americans and other minorities gather? Why mark a water fountain "white" in a suburban shopping mall where virtu-ally everyone fits that description? The modern ghetto has walls, but they are not visible to the eye or written into law.

Second, those persons in a position to take advantage of the federally subsi-dized move to the suburbs were the recipients of a tremendous asset, one that has grown over the years to the point where it has acted to widen the already considerable gulf between the haves and the have-nots in American society. Up until recently, at least, home owners have known and counted on the fact that their financial prospects improve the instant they enter the housing market and begin to gather equity. It is a way to move onto a more secure financial plane. It is a way to become a stakeholder in the larger economy. Families in the tens of millions were able to shift onto that plane as a result of the subsidies they received, and the benefits available to them then have matured into a permanent advantage in the American economy. The net effect of the preferential treatment given those home buyers was not just a modest jump start but the formation of a propertied class of persons, large numbers of whom have grown relatively more comfortable in the years since. By now, the difference in wealth between those who own homes and those who do not—which is one way of distinguishing families that live in the inner city from those that live in the suburbs—is a dividing line across which it is ever more difficult for the poor to pass. To attribute that widening gulf wholly to the emergence of the suburbs would be to oversimplify, but any historian who traces that development back in time will have to spend a good deal of time looking at and thinking about the years immediately following World War II. During the abrupt and painful bursting of the housing bubble a few years ago, quite a number of people who thought they had joined the propertied class learned to their sorrow that things were not as simple as that. But the line is still there and remains an important marker in American life.

Finally, I referred earlier to "that great tidal wash in and out" that characterized the movement of traffic to and from the city center as suburbanization began to take hold in the 1950s and 1960s. The inner city, though, huddled against the commercial downtown, was not a part of that rhythm. It was a zone *through* which that swarm of people passed, or, as the highway network became larger and more complex, a zone *over* which or *under* which they passed. When the country turned its energies to suburban development, the urban ghetto was to a large extent left to its own devices, and in that sense, the problems that now beset the slums of the American industrial city are a cost the country has elected to pay for the development of suburbia.

The orbiting stranger, who we have been calling on here to supply a different angle of vision on our world, has been watching all these ebbs and flows from a distant place. He will probably have noticed by now that the central sections of many of the industrial cities are experiencing something of a revival now—a matter we will turn to briefly later. But he will also have noticed that the tidal wash in and out of the central city that characterized the early years of suburbanization is no longer the powerful current it once was, since the suburbs have become a separate and distinct urban formation unto itself. Most people who live in suburbia and work regularly have jobs there now, and most of the rest of their daily rounds—including shopping—is conducted there as well. So suburban traffic now tends to move in rings around the perimeter of the city. Beltways that encircle the metropolis are likely to be busier now than highways reaching into and out from the central city, and suburban centers are frequently more congested now than the cities they were designed to provide an escape from.

Think of this paragraph as a kind of footnote, but it is important to be clear that we are not speaking here of townships with civic histories of their own that encircle growing cities and have been absorbed economically and culturally into their orbit. Those towns often have village greens, observe civil celebrations, and have a clear neighborhood feel to them even though a majority of their residents commute into the urban center to make a living and to connect in other ways. Such places qualify as "suburbs" in its dictionary meaning of "a district lying immediately outside a city," but they are nothing like the new developments we have been calling "suburbia" here.

The Inner City

Let me pause for a moment to note that "inner city" is the term social scientists and many others find themselves using when referring to what might just as accurately be called "the homes of the urban poor," or "the urban ghetto," or simply "the slums." It does not mean the inner core of urban space, as the term itself seems to be suggesting, but neighborhoods where the disadvantaged, largely African-American, are drawn by forces well beyond their control. All those terms are in common use. They all mean the same thing for our purposes.

The people of the urban slums reside near the very heart of the urban landscape I have been sketching, but they are not truly a part of it. They have little or no connection with the downtown commercial district they live at the edges of, and little or no connection with the suburban perimeter that lies just beyond their horizon.

We noted a few pages back that manufacturing plants that had once drawn people by the millions into the core of American industrial cities had in large part disappeared. Some were no longer there because the goods they produced had become obsolete. Others were no longer there because they had been moved to parts of the world where the costs of labor were considerably less. And quite a number, of course, were no longer there because they had been relocated to the suburbs, where land was cheaper, parking plentiful, highways easy to reach, and the problems of the inner city a reassuring distance away. So rewarding jobs in manufacturing had become a good deal more scarce.

In 1954, as the shift began in earnest, Chicago had 10,000 manufacturing firms that employed 650,000 persons. Many of those employees were supporting families, so we can assume that those firms were a source of livelihood for two million persons or so. Thirty years later, the number of firms had been reduced by half, and the number of jobs by two-thirds, and both numbers have since become smaller, even though the community has grown in size.

White people have left the inner city in large part, and a considerable proportion of the better-off black people who once lived there—professionals, shopkeepers, tradespeople—have moved off as well. In consequence, it has become more segregated by *class* as well as by *race*. People who continue to live there are a good deal poorer on the average than those who preceded them, and they are farther removed from a sense of membership in the larger society. The people of the inner city often feel that they have been set apart, marooned, as if quarantined. They live in another universe.

Piotr and Kasia, early residents of the urban slums, might not recognize the city blocks in which they once raised their children. A number of the old tenements have been demolished and replaced by housing developments, for one thing, and street traffic looks nothing like it once did. But the main difference, according to observers who know the setting well, is that whole sections of the ghetto have become regions where everyday life is a matter of survival and prospects for the future in the usual American meaning of the expression are dim. I do not mean by this that the life one encounters on those streets is drab or colorless or that the prevailing mood is one of depression or apathy. A strong case can be made, in fact, that feelings of community and kinship are warmer there than in many other parts of the urban world because that life requires a banding together. Yet many of those who live there have skidded so far down the class structure that they can almost be thought of as having dropped out the bottom of it altogether, and for that reason are often characterized as belonging to an "underclass." That term has to be used with caution, as I will note shortly, but it can be an instructive one even so—for it suggests that some persons can be contained within the physical space of a social order but feel so detached from its everyday workings and from its basic spiritual and moral tissue that they do not see themselves as belonging to it in any meaningful sense at all.

Life in the inner city, like life everywhere, ranges across a fairly broad spectrum, so it is important to appreciate that when observers of that scene focus on particular features of it, they are sampling, not covering the whole. But a number of things should be pointed out.

The urban ghetto is a world in which drugs play an important part. I am not speaking of widespread use: no more than a small minority of inner city residents take drugs, and fewer yet deal them. But they have nonetheless worked their way into the texture of life as a result of their place in the informal economy, and it is a particular source of tension in the way the area relates to the larger society.

The inner city is also a world in which the everyday routines of life are punctuated by explosive bursts of violence. African-Americans constitute roughly 12 percent of the population of the United States, but, by some measures, they make up close to 50 percent of those arrested for murder or manslaughter or other violent crimes, and 60 percent of those arrested for armed robbery. This stunning disproportion, it has to be stated immediately and emphatically, has nothing at all to do with racial or ethnic differences, since it is a clearly established fact that crime rates for blacks, whites, and everybody else who lives in comparable residential areas are essentially the same. Violence is a property of the ghetto, of the space set aside for the urban poor, and not of the individual persons who are fated to live there at any given point in time.

One has to be wary about figures like these anyway because they represent the total number of *arrests* and of *convictions* rather than the total number of *offenses,* and those are altogether different matters. There is a considerable body of evidence to suggest that blacks are far more likely to be arrested in the United States even when their conduct is not different in any discernible way from that of whites. Moke, you may remember, wondered about that. Still, no matter what allowance we make for the character of those arrest figures, the rate of violent crime in the inner city can only be described as alarming—all the more so because the victims of that violence tend to be other people caught up in the same web.

And the inner city is a world in which people know—really know—what prisons are and what they do. The roadways connecting the inner city with the downtown core, located but a short distance away, have hardly any traffic. The roads connecting the inner city with the suburbs have virtually none at all. But the roads connecting the inner city with places of confinement are very well traveled, not only because so many young persons are transported along them on their way to and from incarceration but because so many other members of the community use them to visit relatives and loved ones being held there. This thought will require a moment's detour.

As a general matter, the rate at which people are being imprisoned in this country has risen sharply over the past several decades. The prison population passed the million mark a number of years ago, and the construction of new prison facilities to make space for yet more is still under way.

The main reason for this sharp rise in the rate of imprisonment has been tougher drug laws, aimed not at more affluent parts of the American scene, where the recreational use of drugs is certainly not unknown, but to the inner cities. The idea here (to the extent that there really is one) has been to take as many dealers and heavy users away from the streets of the ghetto as possible in the hope of bringing that form of street commerce to an end. This may seem logical in a heavy-handed sort of way, but the available evidence suggests that it will not work. It makes little sense when one thinks about it sociologically anyway.

For one thing, sending young men to prison (those convicted are for the most part young and male) is unlikely to reduce the number of dealers or discourage the use of drugs in other ways. So long as there are potential customers out there, others will volunteer to act as suppliers. This is the way markets work, after all. Dealers taken off the streets for a stretch in prison, meantime, tend to regard this outcome as one of the costs of conducting business, almost a tax that is owed fate, and so long as that continues to be the case, putting dealers in prison only enlarges the number of individuals who enter the trade. We need a different calculation here. If we commit one hundred dealers to prison, it is only reasonable to expect that one hundred more persons will volunteer to fill those vacancies, and when the original hundred are released, as almost all of them will be sooner or later, there will now be double the number of seasoned hands available for duty on the streets. Things do not usually work as simply as that, of course, but the point to be made here is that incarceration normally adds to, rather than subtracts from, the dealer ranks. It is easy to understand the frustration felt by policy-makers when they contemplate the human costs of drugs and feel that they should do something about it, but simple logic should compel us to realize that we have to address the reasons why drugs are in *demand* rather than the way in which that demand is *supplied.*

Even more to the point, imprisoning that many young people is a tremendous blow to the larger community. As things now stand, something like one of ten inner city youths is in prison at any given time, and according to some estimates, the percentage of those who have spent a stretch in prison is close to a third and in some places even close to a half. Putting persons behind bars, clearly, punishes them for their misdoings. That is why we do it. But putting persons behind bars can punish other members of the community even more sharply, and most of them have never been convicted of anything.

Every time someone is taken to prison, at least one household, and sometimes more than one, loses an important source of support both financially and emotionally. Every time someone returns from a prison term, it threatens to increase by one the already large number of individuals in the community who have been hardened by prison life, and it threatens to increase by one the already large number of individuals in the community who have a hard time finding work, either because imprisonment has eroded their occupational or even their social skills, or because employers are reluctant to take chances on applicants with prison records. Criminologists have known for two hundred years or more that incarceration can have these effects on those who experience it, but we are only beginning to appreciate now that incarceration does equally grievous harm to the communities from which the inmates come. In some ways, at least, the wrong people are being asked to suffer. This observation is perfectly reflected in the title of the best study I know on the topic: *Doing Time on the Outside* by Donald Braman.

It should be noted that the inner city is a world where unemployment is so common, particularly among the young, that it has almost become a community norm. Those who *do* have work, furthermore, and thus appear in the official records as "employed," often find themselves in dead-end jobs with very little in the way of security, benefits, or realistic opportunities for advancement.

One housing development in Chicago had a population that averaged around 24,000 in the mid-1990s. The median income *per family* was $5,500 a year, meaning that virtually every person in the neighborhood lived below the official poverty line. That income figure would be higher now as a result of inflation, but so would the official poverty line, meaning that the proportion itself would still hold. The unemployment rate was 50 percent, but even that grim statistic was worse than one might suppose at first because it only took into account people who were actively looking for work. It did not include those who had settled for the low-paying jobs I spoke of a moment ago, nor did it include those who had simply given up hope of entering the employment picture entirely. Individuals without jobs, we might add parenthetically, are often called "idle" in official employment figures. But that term borders on the ironic here, since the ranks of the "idle" include any number of young people who move with spectacular vigor through the complex networks of the underground economy, involved in pursuits known locally as "hustling," "ripping," or, "the action."

It should be noted, finally, that the inner city is a world in which a high proportion of households with children are headed by a single parent, almost always a woman. This is a troubling observation for many people who live in other parts of the American countryside because it suggests to them not only that the inner city is a place of immoral goings on but that the immorality is a *cause* of that poverty. Wanton young women being impregnated by irresponsible young men down there in the ghetto—"illegitimate" is the name used for the birth that ensues—which dooms everyone involved to a life of poverty and draws upon the resources of the larger society unfairly.

Most people reading that paragraph will know, if only from the promptings of their hearts, that this conclusion is much too simple. Single parent families do not create poverty. Poverty creates single parent families. Young women in the ghetto give birth at about the same rate as they always have, and at about the same rate as women in other regions of the country. They tend to begin the process somewhat earlier than those who go to college or who apprentice for a trade. But the difference that really matters here is that they are less likely to marry and form a nuclear family either as a precondition to becoming pregnant or as a consequence of it, and the reason for that is very clearly that that the available men are so much more likely to be unemployed, without prospects for the future, and in no position to support a family.

To describe someone in this circumstance as a "single parent" is to draw on a term that derives from a very different reality in any case. The family circle into which the newborn is welcomed is often a warm, secure, caring enclosure, made up of two or sometimes even three generations of mothers as well as an inner ring of caring men. The family of the inner city does not always have the same shape as the suburban family.

Culture of Poverty?

It has been a common habit of mind in recent years to refer to the people of the inner city as an "underclass," living in what Oscar Lewis called a "culture of poverty." Some of the best-informed sociologists on the subject no longer use the term because it appears to suggest that the urban poor live in a different kind of social space where people are so damaged, so wounded, that nothing much can be done for them. Charles Dickens wrote of a street urchin named Jo in his novel *Bleak House:*

> Homely filth begrimes him, homely parasites devour him, homely sores are in him, homely rags are on him. . . . He is not of the same order of things, not of the same place in creation. He is of no order and no place; neither of the beasts nor of humanity.

When one speaks too emphatically about the miseries of the ghetto in an effort to get others to at least *see* the place in their minds' eyes, one runs the risk of making the people who live there seem a little like Dickens's Jo—a species apart, occupying a new kind of social space. It is crucially important, then, to find a point of balance between two truths of equal force. First, nothing in the inner city is beyond repair. Things need not be this way. Second, sustained poverty *does* cut to the emotional and spiritual bone, exposing people to life conditions that can easily be damaging to the human spirit.

The climate there—I am trying to step nimbly around the term "culture"—can be so disheartening that lives shaped there take on a different cast than is the case for those of us who live in other portions of the same society. The moods that can dominate everyday life in the inner city—a sense of fatalism, a lowering of what comfortable people like to call "self-esteem," a feeling that the world is a desolate and uncaring place—pose a problem that few individuals in positions of authority know what to do about, or, for all of that, show much evidence of caring about.

Physical assaults are common enough in those neighborhoods, but the soundless, intangible assaults that African-Americans frequently encounter in what Elijah Anderson calls the "white spaces" of the world around them–streets, public places, not to mention the criminal justice system–are sometimes far more damaging and painful. All of this is reflected in statistics of life expectancy, too. Dying young in the inner city as a consequence of outright violence is easier to come to terms with, but dying young as a consequence of sheer, unrelenting stress and anxiety from living conditions provided by the larger social world is not.

The reciting of fact, as I have suggested before, has a way of numbing both head and spirit. If I tell you (having learned these facts from William Julius Wilson's very important book *When Work Disappears)* that there were neighborhoods in Chicago where only one eligible adult out of three—and in some places only one out of four—had a job of *any* kind in a typical week, will you be impressed? If I add that a large proportion of those jobs were part-time, dead-end, and miserably paid, will you be impressed? And if I report to you that one of those neighborhoods lost 75 percent of its business establishments in the decade from 1976 to 1986—and moreover that the 25 percent remaining consisted of one bank, one supermarket, 48 lottery agents, 50 currency exchanges, and 99 licensed bars and liquor stores—will you be impressed?

Perhaps. But sometimes the weight of such figures presses down so heavily on the mind that it is unable to convert the grim array of detail into a recognizable human portrait. When that happens, a simple street scene can sometimes add a certain depth and dimension. Here is a passage from Wilson's book that caught my eye because it spoke of a street corner not far from where I lived in my graduate student days where I listened to music from time to time and drank an occasional beer. It was mostly black then, as it is now, but it seemed to me to be lively and welcoming and without the brooding sense of emptiness that it has now.

> The once-lively streets—residents remember a time, not so long ago, when crowds were so dense at rush hour that one had to elbow one's way to the train station— now have the appearance of an empty, bombed-out war zone. The commercial strip has been reduced to a long tunnel of charred stores, vacant lots littered with broken glass and garbage, and dilapidated buildings left to rot in the shadow of the elevated train line. At the corner of Sixty-third Street and Cottage Grove Avenue, the handful of remaining establishments that struggle to survive are huddled behind wrought iron bars. . . . The only enterprises that seem to be thriving are liquor stores and currency exchanges, those "banks of the poor" where one can cash checks, pay bills, and buy money orders for a fee.

That report was of a time long past, of course, and will seem even more so for younger readers of these pages. But the conditions it describes continue to exist.

The urban ghetto has much in common with Buffalo Creek after the flood. The disaster that visited Buffalo Creek was a sudden thunderclap that seemed to come from nowhere and destroyed almost everything it encountered in a few minutes. The devastation that visited the inner cities of America has been a slow, grinding force that has done its grim work over many years. But it is a disaster nonetheless, and it has been responsible for many of the same kinds of traumatic wounds as we find in the wake of earthquakes, tornadoes, and other catastrophes that damage in a single sharp blow.

There are no urban places elsewhere in the industrialized world quite like our urban slums, and for that reason it is doubly important to keep three things in mind.

For one thing, it should go without saying that no one who lives there did anything to invite the troubles that have visited them, and no one, by any standard of fairness, can be regarded as *deserving* it. But that needs to be repeated frequently because a cruel circularity is often set into motion in public discussions about the matter which can blur that otherwise obvious point. When most social scientists look at what happens in the inner city, they see a natural and even predictable human response to extremely difficult social conditions. But when observers of a different kind take a brief and unthinking glance at the same scene, they often think they see a tendency toward crime, drug use, sexual irresponsibility, and a lack of what people who live in relative ease call "the work ethic," and they view the people there as suffering from a lack of virtue rather than a lack of opportunity. One reviewer of Wilson's book *When Work Disappears* put that view as bluntly as language allows by entitling his commentary "When Decency Disappears." That can be a comforting way of looking at those places because it invites us to think that we need not do anything about the pain of our fellow human beings: they brought it upon themselves, you see; they are what the well-off of another age called "the undeserving poor." The available evidence, though, requires other conclusions. Unemployment is widespread there because there are so few worthwhile jobs to be found. Young women bear children out of wedlock there because marriage is more apt to damage their prospects than to improve them. Violence is common there because people there live in a precarious world not of their making. The inner city is the place to which the rest of the society has consigned poverty. It was not produced there.

Moreover, conditions of social life in the inner city are not inevitable. They are not a natural outcome of the way markets work or of the way the social order functions. They are a by-product of the way the leaders of our society have chosen to apportion the nation's resources.

And, finally, for all the misfortunes pressing down on the folk of the inner city, one of its most striking features is the sheer amount of warmth and humanity to be found there—the tenderness reflected in so much of its parenting, the devotion reflected in so many of its family relations, the loyalty reflected in so many of its informal groupings, the generosity reflected in so many of its spiritual gatherings. Jonathan Kozol was so taken by the kindness he witnessed in Mott Haven, one of the most devastated combat zones to be found in the universe, that he entitled his account of the neighborhood *Amazing Grace.*

What Now?

Our objective so far has been to focus on the formation of the urban world we are looking out at now. In that sense, clearly, we have been dealing with events of the past. Any account of how a particular gathering of people came about is almost bound to have that character: in our case, a surge of immigration from eastern and southern Europe, a surge of migration from south to north and from hinterland to urban center in the United States, and then a vast redistribution of urban dwellers from the center to the outer edges of the cityscape. All of this has shaped the urban scene we live in now. It has been a history.

But new developments are shaping what may well be the urban landscape of the future. That discussion deserves every bit as much attention as the one we have been engaged in, but time and space will not permit that now. And maybe as much to the point, our inability to predict very accurately in this ever-changing world makes that a slippery project. In turn, then, we will take a look at (a) what is happening in the new downtowns of many American cities, (b) more recent waves of immigration, "recent" meaning in the past two decades or so, and (c) shifts in population to what is often called "the sunbelt." Each of these topics deserves its own chapter, but we will have to settle here for glances.

The New Downtowns

We have already seen that a major shift in the urban center of gravity, beginning in the years following World War II, drew millions of people away from the central city out into the surrounding suburbs, and then, almost like an undertow, brought along with them many of the manufacturing firms and retail stores that had once formed the city core. Steel mills, automobile plants, chemical firms, packing houses, factories of every imaginable kind either moved out to the suburban ring or drifted off to other parts of the country if not other parts of the world. It looked for a time in the 1960s and 1970s as if many of the downtowns were about to be abandoned, leaving a wasteland of decaying plants, warehouses, and other commercial buildings behind. Indeed, that is what did happen in a number of urban places. Flint, Michigan, is an oft-mentioned example.

In the 1980s and 1990s, however, things began to shift again in a number of respects. Among the reasons why industrial firms welcomed a move to the suburbs when the chance first presented itself was that they are better served when they can expand outward at ground level rather than upward in rising buildings. It is a real convenience when the shop floor on which goods are produced, the loading dock from which they are shipped, the warehousing facilities in which they are stored, and all the other cells of that complex system are located on the ground floor. So industries that process palpable goods tend to like horizontal space.

But industries that process weightless abstractions like ideas and information are completely comfortable with vertical space and compact work stations. The new downtowns, then, tend to be places where *money* is managed rather than *material,* where *data* is processed rather than *goods.* The tenants of downtown office space specialize in research and development, management and finance. They offer services for corporate needs: accounting, designing, legal advice, consultation of a thousand different varieties. They handle the manufacturing of things even though the production process itself may be taking place half a world away. They advertise things and insure them, negotiate their price and arrange for their shipping. Most of this work can be done by people who occupy no more space than that required for a desk, telephone, computer screen—and maybe access to a copier, an overnight courier service, and (to get down to the essentials) a water cooler.

The new downtowns, then, are places where great streams of information converge, interact, and flow back out again in modified form. The poet Carl Sandburg once described Chicago of a century ago as the "city of big shoulders," and other industrial cities of the time were often characterized as places that owed their vitality to strong backs, sturdy arms, and sound constitutions. But poets looking into the human anatomy now for metaphors to help them describe Chicago or any other modern city are not likely to think of muscles or sinews. What flows into and out of the central city now are electronic impulses that move without effort and almost without cost, and in that sense the new downtowns most closely resemble nervous systems.

The commercial climate of the new downtowns has also attracted medical facilities, educational institutions, and government offices that use space in largely the same way, and it has inevitably attracted hotels, restaurants, convention centers, cultural facilities, and the like to provide services for the human traffic that circulates in and around the city. All this has created new employment opportunities, for both skilled operatives who know what to make of the images appearing on those computer screens and unskilled workers who clean up the offices, drive the taxis, make the beds, wash the dishes, and take care of all the other menial tasks that make the downtowns work.

In some ways, at least, the modern downtown is more closely connected to other central cities all over the world than it is to the metropolitan region it sits at the center of. It has its location in a global network rather than a particular space, and in that sense is part of an altogether new geography in human history.

The New Immigration

As we have already seen, the flow of immigration from Europe to the United States in the years from 1860 or so until 1920 was a profoundly important event in the history of the country, changing the contours of the American social and cultural scene in decisive ways. That flow slowed appreciably in the 1920s when laws were enacted to restrict it, and by the 1930s it appeared as though the age of immigration had come to a close.

In 1965, however, a new age of immigration began with the adoption of a measure that removed many of the earlier restrictions. A scattering of immigrants from Europe took advantage of the opportunity, but most of those who made their way into the United States through those newly opened gates in the years that followed were from Asia, Latin America, and the Caribbean. Unlike the earlier arrivals who came by ship across the Atlantic Ocean and entered the country through Ellis Island, the recent arrivals entered through a variety of portals—by airport, by seaport, and by both charted and uncharted paths across the border of Mexico and the United States, large numbers of them drawn across the border for opporunities in farm labor.

Most of the new immigrants have been drawn by the same gravitational force as the one that carried their predecessors into the central cities. Roughly

40 percent of them have ended up in either New York or Los Angeles, and another 40 percent have ended up in a relatively small handful of other American downtowns: Chicago, San Francisco, and Miami are high on the roster of host cities, and not far behind are Washington, Houston, Anaheim, San Diego, and Boston. These arrivals are a significant part of the new urban workforce, serving the information age in largely the same way their predecessors served the industrial age. A substantial number have special skills to offer: close to a quarter of those who settle into New York City, for example, have some professional or managerial experience. But most do not have those qualifications, and have been drawn into the downtowns to tend to service needs.

The current rate of immigration is difficult to pin down precisely, since the numbers shift frequently and since a fair number of newcomers are undocumented, either in the sense that they crossed a border into the country illegally or in the sense that they have overstayed their official welcome. The prevailing estimate among specialists who pay attention to the matter is that somewhere between 500,000 and 600,000 immigrants enter the country every year, and while some of them return to the places from which they came, most elect to stay. The world in general and the United States in particular were experiencing a new wariness of "outsiders" as this book was being prepared for press, and time will tell how that plays out.

Cities of the Sunbelt

Three clear shifts of population and economic activity took place during the second half of the 20th century in the American urban world. The first, which we have discussed in some detail, was the emptying out of the central city and the dispersal of its contents, both human and industrial, into the surrounding hinterlands. The second was the revival of the downtowns of a fair number of those cities. We discussed that as well. The third has been a shift of both persons and activities from the Northeast and Midwest to the Southeast and Southwest, a topic we will touch on now briefly.

In the last few decades, the growth of urban places in Florida, Texas, and Southern California has greatly outstripped that of the older industrial cities. The four largest cities in the United States now are two giants of considerable standing, New York and Chicago, and two relative newcomers, Houston and Los Angeles. Other cities that have grown rapidly of late are Miami, Atlanta, Dallas–Fort Worth, San Antonio, Phoenix, and San Diego.

It was widely assumed in the early phases of this new development that people were leaving the industrial heartlands of America and relocating in what was soon to be called the "sunbelt," but that does not really seem to have been the case for the most part. The currents along which migrants drift from place to place in this land continue to be a movement from countryside to city, as they have for more than one hundred years, but those currents now flow in a southerly and western direction. It is something like a change in wind currents. The older industrial cities like Pittsburgh and Cleveland are holding their own, if only barely in some instances, but the overflow from the countryside is now draining into the sunbelt.

These migrants are not being attracted by heavy manufacturing or other smokestack industries, obviously, but by a wholly different economic playing field in which electronics, highly skilled manufacturing, oil and gas production, defense industries, and a number of other high-tech industries dominate. The sunbelt has also attracted many more visitors and retirees than it used to, so much so that tourism and the construction of new homes are now major industries themselves.

It should be noted, too, that federal subsidies have been responsible for a share of that growth, since those parts of the country have been heavily favored in the locating of military facilities and other federal activities. And the fact that the South and Southwest do not have a tradition of trade unions is clearly one of the more impressive advantages of those climes for many business concerns.

It is hard to guess what will happen next. Part of the appeal of the sunbelt has been its very newness. Most sunbelt cities had never developed an industrial base in the first place or invested in heavy manufacturing, so there was less old debris to scrape away when the post-industrial age arrived. They had never been subject to the centripetal forces that drew persons and buildings inward toward an urban core, as the older industrial cities had. They were more likely to be located on open spaces on all sides, too—no lakes or oceans or mountain ridges—and could grow outward rather than upward. For a while, at least, this meant the promise of more open spaces and fresher air and water. And it meant fewer taxes.

But an old dilemma is expressing itself here too. The larger the number of people who seek open spaces, clean air, and fresh water, the less there will be of it. The larger the number of people who want to get out from under the burden of paying for public services, the greater the need for them will be.

Growth, then, almost by definition, eventually means congestion as well as higher taxes, increasing levels of pollution, depletion of groundwater reserves, and other environmental difficulties. Either the costs of living there go up or the comforts of living there go down. Or both.

Coda

The social sciences of a generation or two ago did not do a particularly good job of forecasting what would be happening to the American city at the turn of the century, even though the early indications of what did emerge look rather obvious now in hindsight. So I will not take the risk of making any predictions, but we might talk about possibilities built into the present that may have an impact on the future.

It is increasingly the case in the United States—and in other parts of the world—that the way we represent geographical space on maps is no longer the most accurate way to portray what is "urban" and what "rural," what is "city" and what "countryside." It is, for most of us, a fairly familiar habit of thought to draw a borderline around the outer edges of the central city that marks where it ends and the suburbs begin, and then to draw another borderline that marks where the suburbs, in their turn, give way to farmlands and prairie. That is what maps do for us.

That has always been an awkward way of charting urban space. The lines we see on maps are drawn for jurisdictional purposes and bear little relationship to population densities or land uses or any other measure of city-ness.

But it would be even more difficult now. The city has always asserted a centripetal pull on the people and the activities caught up in its vortex. The strength of the pull, as we noted earlier, has varied with the technological profile of the time. One hundred years ago, city industries had to cluster near the sources of steam power, and the persons who worked in those industries had no choice but to reside within a walking distance of them. That's a very strong pull. With the development of street cars and tramways, the effective limits of the city grew outward by a matter of miles. And when automobiles and other new forms of transit opened up the suburbs, those edges expanded further yet. But there was always an outer limit, always a line on the other side of which things were no longer in contact with the city in any useful way. In order to remain a functioning part of the city, that is, one had to be in touch with persons located there, have access to information stored there, do business with offices maintained there.

That is less and less the case. The centripetal force, to the extent that it continues to exist at all, has become a good deal fainter. Information is now stored in cyberspace rather than in file cabinets, and is available on the instant to anyone with a working computer and a password, and person-to-person contact is also available on the instant from anywhere on earth, even up in the skies and out to sea. Vast industries can now conduct business with participants spread out as far as lines of contact remain open by computer, telephone, and overnight courier services. If the city can be seen as a kind of huge nervous system, its impulses now reach over the globe. There will always be good reasons for concentrating activities of one kind or another in central places, which helps explain the continued growth of global cities like New York and Tokyo, but the fact is that the city in general has become less a form of human settlement with a defined center and a ring of outer boundaries—less the matrix it once was.

The ways of the city, too, now reach into the hinterlands of even distant cultures by way of radio, television, films, internet, and the kinds of personal contact that travel makes possible. "The city," Robert E. Park remarked in a passage cited earlier, "is a state of mind, a body of customs and traditions." That observation may never have been as accurate as Park assumed, but to the extent that the city can be said to have created a new cultural form, its ways are increasingly familiar to people who live in places that were once thought very remote— mountain hollows, the camps of migrant farm workers, fishing villages, and so on.

The social sciences may soon need new vocabularies to talk about all this because the country is in many ways becoming a vast, interconnected metropolitan region. Indeed, as we will suggest in the next chapter, it may not be long before we have no choice but to see the whole world in that way—a vast, interconnected metropolitan region—since globalization *is* a species of urbanization. The same will be true for sturdy old concepts like "immigration" and "migration" and so on. When being in motion becomes a way of life, these terms lose much of their usefulness.

So the landscape has changed considerably. But it is important to keep in mind that to understand the social order we are a part of now we need to turn back to the origins of the momentum that has brought us to our present state— the roots of its poverty, the nature of its class structure, and the human moods that trace back to an earlier time. Understanding the present is always a reach into the past.

Lands of the Poor

As the world turned the corner into a new millennium, urban growth in what we have learned to call the "less developed" countries or the "Third World" was creating a new form of human settlement and in many ways a new form of human life.

Three stark facts will shape the human future:

The population of the world is now growing at a rate of 100 million persons *every year:* the population of the whole globe was that size at the time of the French Revolution.

Something like 90 percent of that growth will occur within the less developed countries.

Most of that overflow (we can say "all of it" without stretching the facts very far) will find its way into the crowded cities of that world.

This means that if current trends continue, the population explosion we have heard so much about recently will be absorbed *in its entirety* by the poorest urban places on earth.

Those places are already so swollen in size that we may soon need new terms to refer to them. They bear very little resemblance to the New Yorks and Tokyos and Londons and Berlins that have supplied the world's models for what a true "city" is. A number of terms are now being auditioned by commentators on the subject: megacity, hypercity, supercity, megalopolis, and conurbation are just a few of the ones now in fairly common use. Others will surely work their way into the language soon.

Emptying the Countryside

The immense surge of people now moving into the already crowded urban places of the poorer land is the outcome of two developments.

The first, obviously, is that villagers in Africa and Asia and Latin America continue to bring children into the world at far too rapid a rate. Even in places where the idea of birth control comes to be better understood and better appreciated, knowledge about it and access to it remains a serious problem.

So the world is becoming overpopulated. That, surely, no longer qualifies as news. But even if that were not the case, the countryside would still be emptying at a drastic rate because the land can no longer absorb the numbers of people it once did, never mind all the newcomers who pour in like rainfall.

For one thing, modernization is gradually reaching the most remote of hinterlands: agricultural production is becoming more and more mechanized; small holdings are being consolidated into larger ones for the sake of efficiency. This has reduced the need for farm labor greatly and has left millions of people without places in the countryside—not even quiet niches in which to go hungry. These efficiencies have been widely encouraged by the more developed world in the hope that they would prove a boon to the poor of the earth, and that may indeed turn out to be the case over the long haul. But working the land, as we noted earlier, is a way of life as well as an occupation to those who engage in it, and the problem with this form of "rationalization," as Weber understood so well, is that the calculations involved so rarely factor in the human costs. Those costs go beyond the brute fact that people become homeless when they leave whatever shelter they had in their home villages, and include the more subtle fact that they also had to leave a cultural context that was important to their sense of the fitness of things, a cultural context in which they are "a person."

The countryside in many parts of the Third World has become less hospitable for a number of other reasons as well. Natural disasters like drought, many of them the result of environmental excesses, have sent millions of people off the land, and human disasters like civil wars and ethnic slaughters and all the other bloody stirrings that now mark our times play a role as well. Changes in the use of land, though, rank first among the reasons people are being expelled in such immense numbers from the rural countryside.

So whatever terms come into general use to refer to those huge urban concentrations, they are becoming the catch-basins of surplus humanity. Shanghai, Jakarta, Seoul, Mumbai, Beijing, Lagos, Dhaka, Karachi, Mexico City, São Paulo, and maybe one or two others have exceeded the 20 million population mark or will do so soon. Manila, Belhi, Kolkata, Cairo, Khartoum, Lima, and Rio de Janeiro are in the 10 million population range. So are New York and Los Angeles, for that matter, but the comparison means little because the cities of poorer lands are expanding by the moment and the cities of the more developed world have either grown as large as they are likely to or are growing at a far slower rate. All of the population numbers I cited above are almost sure to have grown by the time you read them here.

It may not be long, moreover, before those newly coined terms like "hyper-city" and "megalopolis" will themselves become obsolete because in many parts of the world pools of people are beginning to spread out over vast urban corridors that reach from city to city and fill in the spaces that once separated them. The wide swath of developed space that reaches from New York to Philadelphia is approaching that point now, and so is the urban landscape that connects Tokyo and Osaka as well as the one that stretches along the lower Rhine. New candidates for whatever this new human form is eventually called are appearing elsewhere: the Pearl River and Yangtze River deltas in China, as well as the heavily developed corridor emerging between Beijing and Tianjin, are good cases in point, and so is the unruly sprawl that reaches from Abidjan to Ibadan in West Africa and includes Lagos.

What makes these patterns of settlement new to human experience is that people are moving into urban places not because they have been lured there by economic opportunity but because they have been driven out of the country-side. The history of urbanization until very recently, of course, has followed the now familiar trajectory: industrialization creates a set of migratory currents that draw surplus farm labor into the city, where jobs are available and prospects for the future are promising. We have also seen that this momentum, once in motion, can continue to draw people into the city long after the need for their services has diminished, but the momentum itself was activated by a source of pull from within the city. The anomaly here is that the urban economies of the poorer countries are shrinking while the flows of migrants into them are growing. That is not how markets are supposed to work, of course, but it is becoming the norm in most of Africa below the Sahara, most of the Middle East, and large portions of Asia—the principal exceptions being found in urban China and North Korea. In effect, the paths along which migrants move from the rural countryside to the city are formed in their entirety by a push from the hinterlands rather than by a pull from the urban center. The cities of the Third World are in danger of becoming enormous dumps into which human waste is washed.

Conditions of Life

The vast overflow of persons pouring into urban places, many of them migrating in family groups, press into whatever empty corners they can find. Some try to find a place in the already crowded lodgings of relatives or of fellow villagers who preceded them. Others stake out claims along public sidewalks or crouch into niches underneath or on top of or in between existing buildings. But most move out to the ever widening outer ring of slums and shantytowns and squatter camps— the *favelos, kampongs, bidonvilles, villas miseries*—that encircle the city.

The following is from a novel written by Michael Thelwell entitled *The Harder They Come,* describing the moment when a boy named Ivan from the rural countryside of Jamaica first approaches the capital city of Kingston by bus:

> They were now on the outskirts of the city. The canefields and pastures had given way to scattered houses, then shops and bars behind crowded side-walks. Then, off in the middle of a field so flat, so dusty, and so desolate that it seemed to have lost any ability to nurture even the most miserable weed, they passed something for which nothing in Ivan's experience or his wildest imaginings had prepared him. He was first attracted to a cloud of black smoke in the dusty air; as they drew closer, he saw that what was burning was huge, sprawling, and shapeless piles and small mountains of what? The air in the bus began to smell like burning rubber. Then he could see broken boards, dirty newspapers, rags, bottles, tin cans, bloated corpses of animals, the rusting and rotting shells of cars, and worn tires all thrown together in a chaotic jumble.
>
> Ragged people were digging in the rubble, pulling and tugging, while over their heads squadrons of vultures wheeled in the smoky air. The mountain of trash seemed to stretch very far, then gradually without perceptible demarcation or boundary it became something else. But what? A jumbled and path-less collection of structures. Cardboard cartons, plywood and rotting boards, the rusting and glassless shells of cars, had been thrown together to form habitations. These shanties crowded each other in an incoherent jumble of broken shapes without road or order. Out of the detritus of urban life, they made a dense mass, menacing in its ugliness and carrying in its massed sprawling squalor a meanness and malevolence that assaulted Ivan's spirit. Looking at it, he felt joy and excitement shrivel within him, and he began to be afraid. Most of the people on the bus were looking straight ahead, sullen shamed expressions on their faces, though some, like Ivan, couldn't take their eyes away.
>
> The man nearby was looking at him again. "Is the firs' you seein' it, young bwai?" he asked quietly. Ivan swallowed and nodded. "Das whe' dem call de Dungle," the man said as if that explained everything.

We turn to another scene:

> Fed by methane from the decomposing garbage, the fires never go out on Smokey Mountain, Manila's vast garbage dump. The smoke envelopes the hills of refuse like a thick fog. But Smokey Mountain is more than a dump, it is a neighborhood that is home to thousands of people. The residents of Smokey Mountain are

the poorest of the poor, and one is hard pressed to imagine a setting more hostile to human life. Amidst the smoke and the squalor, men and women walk deliberately about doing what they can to survive, picking plastic bags from the garbage and washing them in the river, stacking flat cardboard boxes up the side of a family's plywood shack. And all over Smokey Mountain are children—children!—kids who must already sense the enormous odds against them. . . . What chance do they have, living in families that earn scarcely a few hundred dollars a year? With barely any opportunity for schooling? Year after year, breathing this air?

These are extreme cases, obviously, as the authors intended. The world's shantytowns vary from the kinds of desolation depicted here to amazingly inventive gatherings of hand-built dwellings. But they share in common the fact that they cluster at the edges of the city without really being a part of its life. The city has little of value to offer them. There are few jobs worth having there because unemployment is already high and on the increase. The real wages of those who do have work, moreover, have been dropping, with the result that the once steady urban middle classes are themselves sinking into near poverty. Prices are soaring, and public services, to the extent that they can be said to have ever existed at all, are shrinking. Public transportation is virtually unknown. So is welfare of any kind. The migrants who form a rim around the city, then, rarely have access to health care or sanitary facilities or garbage disposal. Few of them hold title to the land they are settled on, which means that they can be removed on little or no notice, and the tiny plots of land they occupy are often located on precarious grounds—in swamps, on the sides of hills, along the edges of rivers, as well as near toxic dumps and chemical plants and tanneries that poison the air and threaten water supplies. These are not only difficult terrains, then, but dangerous ones.

They also share in common the fact that they have been largely abandoned by their own countries. This is partly a matter of resources: where on earth would the governments of Nigeria or Indonesia, say, find the funds to house and feed and care for the poor of Lagos or Jakarta? But it is also a matter of pressure from the developed world, which, for reasons easy to sympathize with and reasons not so easy to sympathize with, have generally made it a condition of aid that loans and other forms of financial assistance be devoted primarily to the modernization of the countryside. What makes this easy to sympathize with is that poor countries everywhere will clearly have to increase agricultural productivity before they can feed the children born to them. What makes this harder to sympathize with is that so much of the increased productivity is siphoned out of the less developed countries to the more developed ones. A sensitive and wise observer of such matters named Mike Davis (upon whom I have drawn shamelessly in this section) wrote: "at the end of the day, a majority of urban slum-dwellers are truly and radically homeless in the contemporary international economy." He did not mean simply that they are without adequate shelter or nourishment, but that they are without the protection of a state or of the international community more generally. They are a population for whom the world no longer has any use.

The news I have been able to provide on this subject so far has been uniformly sad. The slums now gathering in rings around the world's poorer cities are places of numbing poverty and limited promise. But humankind has proven to be an amazingly adaptive creature from the beginning, and ways of life are now emerging in those *villas miserios,* those dark and dismal neighborhoods, that compel respect and wonder.

The urban slums are forgotten land so far as most state governments are concerned and empty space so far as most multinational corporations are concerned. In that sense, they are essentially isolated from whatever forces can be said to give shape to the modern world.

But a new influence has moved into that vacuum—call it a movement or impulse or source of energy—that is religious in its language and ethos but quite unlike the churches of the developed world in its organization. These movements have taken on activities provided by public agencies in other parts of the world, and they have become, to quote Mike Davis one more time, "the real governments of the slums." One of those movements issues from Islam and has reached the urban poor in North Africa and Asia; the other issues from Pentecostal Christianity and has found a place in Latin America and in Africa south of the Sahara. They offer religious services, of course, but they also provide schooling and health services, help of many other kinds, some protection from abuses of the state, and ceremonies that mark vital moments in the flow of everyday life: baptisms, marriages, funerals, festivals, and the like.

This should be a familiar pattern to us because it bears resemblance to the parishes that played so crucial a role in the urban villages of Piotr and Kasia's time and continue to play so crucial a role in the inner cities of our time. But these religious organizations are a good deal more: they are not only parishes but ward headquarters, union halls, emergency rooms, and ethnic societies. They are nerve centers of what might otherwise be forsaken communities.

Worlds Beyond

IN THE EARLY YEARS OF WHAT I earlier called the "age of sociology," as we have seen, a considerable amount of scholarly attention was focused on villages, cities, and other places where people gathered together in clusters. Most of those scholars, understandably—Marx, Durkheim, and Weber among them—were primarily concerned with the social worlds they lived in—the Europe of their time.

In the decade after the end of World War II, however, the world seemed to become a good deal more interconnected, and sociologists in Europe and the United States became far more involved in the study of lands that anthropologists had been visiting for decades: Africa, South America, Southeast Asia.

In this chapter, then, we will turn—far too briefly—to three social formations of broader compass than the ones we have been dealing with so far. First, the modern state and the sometimes tense relationship that can develop between *peoplehood* and *statehood*. Second, the age of European colonialism and its effect on the shaping of our times. And third, the global networks that now stretch across the surfaces of the earth like an immense web.

States and Peoples

The View from the Map Room

Most of the maps we turn to in an effort to better understand the profile of the world portray it as a mosaic of oddly-shaped realms, nested together like the pieces of a puzzle. If I open the atlas on my desk to a map of Central Europe, for instance, I note that a parcel of land known as "Hungary" lies flush up against another parcel of land known as "Austria" on its western border, and that, as we circle around it clockwise, it is flanked by yet other parcels identified as "Slovakia," "Ukraine," "Romania," "Serbia," "Croatia," and "Slovenia." Each parcel has a distinct shape. Each is edged by clearly drawn borderlines and is usually tinted its own color, and each shares borders with yet other parcels reaching out in all directions to fill the land mass of three continents. You will not find a single acre of land in all three of those continents—or anywhere else in the world, for that matter—that does not fall within the boundaries of one or another of those parcels.

In the same way, if I open my atlas to a map of Africa I can see that a land known as "Chad" near the center of the continent is surrounded neatly by places named Niger, Libya, Sudan, The Central African Republic, Cameroon, and Nigeria.

These are all sovereign states. Cartographers tend to outline them as if they were the natural segments into which the surface of the earth is divided. That is not what the orbiting stranger sees, of course. We have a better sense now than we once did what the world looks like from that altitude because we know how to launch cameras into space to take photos of ourselves, and the view from up there only confirms what was already obvious: the lines we draw to indicate the outer edges of states may sometimes be affected by natural features—a river, a mountain range, a coastline—but otherwise they have little to do with the world's topography. We chart the world in the way we do because we view the administrative units into which it is divided as territories in which different peoples live, different governments preside, different languages are spoken, different cultural styles are recognized, different currencies are used, and different histories are told. There are something like 150 units of that kind on the surface of the world, each represented by a location on the map and a seat in the United Nations.

That way of visualizing the land masses of the planet is quite new. The notion that every acre of land and every living human being belongs to an identifiable country is hardly two centuries old in the West and still ranks as a novelty elsewhere. There have been human settlements with established names and holdings for thousands of years, of course: Babylon, Egypt, Greece, Rome. But ancient cartographers could not have mapped those settlements as modern ones do even if the idea of doing so had occurred to them. They would obviously have known how to mark the location of fertile valleys and flood plains where people spread out across the land as well as the location of urban centers where they concentrated in tighter knots. But they could not have charted the outer edges of those territories. They knew that there were frontiers out there beyond which the sway of a sovereign power could no longer reach, but those distant territories were empty space, terra incognito. Egypt and Greece and Rome had capitals and ports and other centers of commerce, but they did not have borders. Maps of the kind I consult in my desktop atlas could only have been drawn in recent times.

Moreover—and far more important for our purposes here—even in later times when governments exerted sway over huge territories and envisioned land the way cartographers do now, it was a long time before the peoples who lived within those bounded spaces came to regard states as relevant facts of *their* existence. When Piotr and Kasia were young, their country could be located on official maps readily enough. But what did it mean to villagers like them that they inhabited a region known as "Greater Poland" or "Congress Poland"? What would it have meant to Moke to discover that the Ituri Rain Forest was a part of the Belgian Congo when he was young and became a part of Zaire when he was older? What does it mean to an Inuit hunter even now if his sled moves silently over that invisible line separating Alaska from Yukon, and thus the United States from Canada? States are often formed years before the people who live there recognize that they are citizens of them, derive a sense of national identity from them, or even become aware of them. There are persons alive even now who have been residents of several countries over the course of their lives without moving one foot from the place in which they were born. They remained where they were, as stationary as oak trees, but the borders that cut across the land around them were drawn and redrawn as armies they never saw or monarchs they never heard of divided up the land.

I taught briefly in a town near the eastern border of Austria that had once been part of Hungary. I was told that not long before my arrival a visitor like myself had walked up to an older man passing the time of day in the town square and asked him the kind of question a social scientist might: "Where are you from?" That's the same question I was asking those migrant farm workers from Haiti, you may remember. The visitor wanted to know whether the old man considered himself Austrian or Hungarian. The man hesitated, uncomfortable and puzzled, and then replied hesitantly: "I . . . I'm from *here*." That was a wiser and more accurate response than the visitor deserved. "I'm from here."

Where else? Even if the man in the square had understood perfectly well what the visitor had in mind and had answered "Austria" or "Hungary," the visitor would not have learned anything useful about the man's true sense of nationality. He was not from a *state*. He was from here, a *place*.

So the maps we consult now may look as though they portray stable realms on fixed land surfaces, but it is clear that the borders separating them—drawn with such crisp finality—would nonetheless look like flickering images if seen on a speeded-up film of the world's crust. If the atlas I was studying when my eye fell on Hungary had been published twenty years earlier, I would have been looking at an entirely different portrait. Five of the seven countries that bordered Hungary when I first studied the map were not independent states at all two decades earlier. If the map had been drawn seventy years before that, it would have been very different from either of those two later versions. And if the map I was looking at when my eye fell on Chad had been seventy years older, I would have found that Chad did not exist at all, being then a part of French Equatorial Africa, and that Libya was an Italian possession, Sudan British, Zaire Belgian, Cameroon and Niger French, and Nigeria British.

The *idea* of states, then, has been around for a long time, but the map of the world as it has been envisioned over that span of time has been in a constant state of flux. There are many reasons for that, but we need not consider them now; they are the stuff of history. As illustrations of what can happen anywhere in this state of flux, though, we will return for a moment to our earlier readings of the maps of Hungary and Chad.

Increasingly in our times, an eruption of some kind among the peoples of an established state create fault lines along which the state divides into smaller fragments. That is why five of Hungary's seven neighbors have only become recognized states in the last two or three decades. Both Czechoslovakia and Yugoslavia splintered into separate independent countries, creating Slovakia, Serbia, Croatia, and Slovenia, and Ukraine separated from the Soviet Union.

A foreign power that has exercised dominion over a distant colony for some time withdraws, either because it was driven out by the people whose land it is or because it elects to leave for other reasons or some combination of the two. That is why Chad did not exist at all seventy years ago and why every single one of its current neighbors are new states.

The details do not matter here, but the result is that the face of Eastern Europe, much of Asia, and virtually all of Africa has changed dramatically within the space of a generation or so. A map is a slice out of time. It has a look of permanency, but it should be seen as one frame taken from yards of rolling film—or, to shift metaphors abruptly, one page taken from a vast ledger that changes by the year.

What, Then, Is a State?

Hundreds of definitions have found a way onto the pages of social science accounts, but most are variations on the following theme: a state is a bounded territory presided over by a government with the ability to impose its policies on those who live within it.

The assumption is widely made that a *state* is the homeland of a *people* with its own distinct language and history and way of life. France is the land of the French, Denmark of the Danes, Sudan of the Sudanese. That is how most of us learned about the matter in grade school, in any case, and it makes a kind of rough sense at least a good part of the time.

The fact of the matter is, though, that the boundaries of many—it is probably fair to say most—states have been drawn to fit the geopolitical designs of persons in positions of power who have little concern with *peoplehood* and may not even understand the concept. That is how the modern map came into being. So it is not at all uncommon for the borders of a state to encircle more than one population grouping that views itself at least a part of the time as a distinct *people*. And, conversely, it is not at all uncommon for the boundaries of a state to cut right through the heart of spaces that a *people* is known to view as its traditional homeland, thus locating them in two or sometimes more jurisdictions. To illustrate the first instance, what we now call Spain contains several population groups that once regarded themselves separate peoples and still do at least a part of the time. To illustrate the second, Kurdish people now live within the boundaries of several states with international standing.

When either of those things happen, two competing strains can be set into motion—one of them tending toward a partitioning of the state into smaller parcels to accommodate the sense of peoplehood of those who live within it, and the other tending toward a fusion of differing peoples into a larger whole.

The first set of strains appears because a minority people living within the territory of a state is almost always aware that it has a kind of moral claim to a homeland of its own. That minority may be fairly content with its present political circumstances, but the idea of breaking away and forming an independent state is an invitation that hovers in the air, as it were—an option out there in the realm of the possible. That is the situation of the Catalans of Spain, for example, as it is of the Québécois of Canada, the Flemish of Belgium, and the Scots of Great Britain—to draw on illustrations only from the West. This is important for a number of reasons, far from the least of them being that opportunistic leaders often emerge in unsettled times to provoke a minority's sense of *peoplehood* in the hope of creating new constituencies for themselves. We will see that process at work in the final field visit entitled *War Comes to Pakrac,* where we will also learn that feelings of peoplehood can be far more plastic and mutable than is sometimes supposed. That one is a "Serb" or "Québécois" or "Scot" or "Igbo" may be a historical fact of some standing, but it can lie dormant for generations and even for centuries, so much so that its reappearance as a source of personal or group identity should be regarded as a reinvention. More on that later.

The second set of strains appears because a state, once in charge, will as a matter of course seek to create a sense of nationality and peoplehood among the population it intends to control. The state has a territory to administer, and that task is made a good deal simpler if the persons who live within it speak the same language, feel as though they are a product of the same national history, derive a sense of identity from viewing themselves as French or Danish or Malaysian or whatever, and share feelings of loyalty to the state. In that sense, it is in the interest of a state to take possession of *human minds* as well as of *physical terrain,* and it tries to do so by establishing a common system of education, encouraging the use of a common language, creating a common set of national symbols, and seeing to it that people employ standard ways of measuring things, telling time, counting assets, and even judging what is right and what wrong.

The history of many countries is one in which persons from different backgrounds and outlooks found themselves gathered together within the boundaries of a particular state and gradually coalesced into a *people.* One of the most celebrated consequences of the French Revolution was that the people of France were now "citizens" rather than "subjects." But the vast majority of them did not know they were French and did not speak the national language. The time for that was yet to come. When the disparate regions of what is now Italy were forged into a new state by force of arms, a shrewd participant in the process is credited with having said: "We have made Italy. Now it is time to make Italians."

Developing a sense of nationality, then, obviously makes governing easier. But we can go a step further and say that it also makes governing *possible* over the long term. Most definitions of "state," like the one I offered a few paragraphs ago, draw attention to the role of coercion in political life. Max Weber, you remember, defined the state as an entity "that successfully claims the monopoly of the legitimate use of violence within a given territory." He meant that a state must have a sufficient police force to compel its will over the people who live within its jurisdiction.

But Weber, like most sociologists then and since, assumed that a state rarely stays in power long for that reason alone. Sooner or later a state has to depend on a general feeling among its citizens that it has a legitimate right to exercise authority within that domain. We discussed that in the chapter on Marx, Durkheim, and Weber. If we view "legitimacy" as a matter of lived experience, however, and ask why it is that persons who live down there at ground level accept the authority of a government that taxes them, conscripts their children, and regulates their everyday lives, the answer will be far more prosaic. Ask that question of a goat herder in Spain, a seamstress in Pakistan, a midwife in Guatemala, a miner in South Africa, a sharecropper in the Philippines, a weaver in Iceland, and you are likely to learn that they accept the government that rules over them in largely the same way that they accept the changing of the seasons or the circling of the moon. It is a fact of the world they live in. It is very like all the other inevitabilities of their existence: the family they were born into, the religion they were brought up in, the countryside they try to extract a living from.

I certainly do not mean by this that resistance is out of the question. The history of our species is full of protests and rebellions. But resistance is far more likely to occur when a government is seen as violating the *terms* of its legitimacy—not when it levies taxes but when it raises them beyond the level that has become customary, not when it regulates trade but when it imposes restrictions that go well beyond the norms it has itself established.

Legitimacy, then, can refer to passive acceptance as well as to active approval of the state as a raw fact of existence, and once the state can count on that sway, the appearance of common ways of speaking and acting and counting and seeing has its own inevitability.

My intent here has been to locate the modern state on our map of "places" in human social life. We will be returning to that subject matter in later chapters on nationality, what I am calling "social speciation," and the final pages on *War Comes to Pakrac.*

Colonies

Back to the map room. If we were to study a map of the 16th century world drawn as modern practitioners of the art do, it may seem to us that Europe then looked largely as it does now. The parcels were quite different, of course. Most of the borderlines that divided the continent into separate national territories were in different places. Most of the states those lines marked off had different shapes and even different names. What are now called Germany and Italy were then elaborate mosaics of independent kingdoms and principalities. Spain controlled the Netherlands. The Ottoman Empire had moved into the Balkans with the sureness of a glacier and had become master of domains reaching from the southern tip of Greece into Hungary. Some of the lands with places on that map no longer exist at all, having been absorbed into larger national entities since then: Saxony, Münster, Bohemia, East Pomerania, Piedmont, Lombardy. But the details are not what matter here. The map would have had a familiar look because the persons who drafted it were able to draw clear borders around national territories and mark the capitals that served as their nerve centers. Europe had become an assembly of states.

The maps drawn of most other areas of the world, though, would be quite different. The outer *contours* of Southeast Asia and Africa and the Americas were fairly well known, since seafarers had been bringing back sightings from their journeys for many years, but the land masses themselves would appear as immense empty spaces. Some cartographers may have been able to identify regions where peoples known as Berber or Hausa, Inca or Aztec, could be found. But these were not bounded domains. They did not constitute states in any European sense of the term.

Our orbiting stranger, who has the wonderful capacity not only to see things from a vast distance but to visualize the passing of time as if it had been recorded on a speeded-up film, might have begun to notice as the 15th century turned into the 16th that hundreds and then thousands of ships were venturing out from the seaports of Europe to distant coasts in America, Africa, and Asia. The stranger would not have been able to make out what was in the holds of those vessels, of course, or what was in the minds of the men and women who sent them out to sea, but the pattern of that traffic was clear enough: Europe was reaching out in all directions. The stranger's eyes might even have been sharp enough to see that the ships were far more heavily laden on their return trip to Europe than they had been when they first set out.

This period is often called the Age of Exploration or the Age of Discovery. It was certainly that. A deep and compelling urge to know what lay out there beyond the horizon was growing throughout Europe. That may have been the principal motive of some of the seagoing captains who undertook the voyages and some of the persons who followed their progress in Europe. But it was certainly not the principal motive of the ruling houses that sponsored those adventures. They had in mind expanding their dominions by laying claim to far-off lands and enlarging their treasuries by plundering those lands of whatever might be of value on or in them.

Three or even four centuries will be collapsed in the telling of this grim story, but it is the outcome, not the sequence of events leading to it, that interests us now.

The seafaring countries were the first to venture out. In the 16th century Spain laid claim to Mexico, Central America, portions of the Caribbean, and most of South America, while Portugal took over Brazil. In the 17th century, England established colonies on the shores of North America. By the 18th century England had extended its holdings to New Zealand and Australia on the other side of the world, and the Netherlands had taken a hold in parts of Southeast Asia. When the 19th century began, England had moved into India, Burma, and parts of Africa, and by the second half of that century almost all of Africa had been partitioned into territories controlled by Germany, France, Italy, Belgium, Spain, Portugal, and, for good measure, the Ottoman Empire.

The upshot is that maps drawn at different times throughout the years of European colonization would increasingly portray those blank spaces in Asia and Africa as defined blocks of land, but those domains owed their shape and their name not to the fact that they were the homelands of particular peoples but to the fact that they were the administrative units into which those occupying powers had divided up the continent. The lands that the English named Nigeria, for example, after the Niger River running through it, included the homelands of three distinct peoples who had lived there, essentially, forever—the Igbo, the Yoruba, and the Hausa.

A number of different impulses provided the thrust for that reach outward.

First and most obvious, if in the long run not always the most critical, was a craving for wealth. The crowned heads of Europe simply planted their flags wherever they thought they could get away with it and began to raid the land of its valuables—gold, silver, coffee, tobacco, timber, furs, sugar, silk, spices, amber, and foodstuffs of all kinds. Sometimes the riches were simply appropriated without ceremony; sometimes a form of trade was involved. But the terms of exchange were set by the visiting Europeans and affirmed by a display of arms. The value of the goods offered by the visitors and the value of the goods they sailed home with were usually so entirely out of proportion that what the Europeans called "trade" should really be called another form of plunder.

The sheer audacity and ruthlessness of those raids make them hard to come to terms with when seen through a modern lens. But the audacity and ruthlessness of the slave trade belong on a scale all its own. Fifteen million fellow human beings were chained together and transported in the holds of merchant vessels to distant lands, where they were sold in auction like all the other cargo that arrived in port: bolts of silk, kegs of nails, casks of wine. It is simply impossible to come to terms with that. When we turn to the topic of "speciation," we will discuss the process by which one group of people can come to regard another as so unlike themselves that they can be treated as a different kind, even a different species. That process surely figures here. But an important chapter of this dreadful story is that the human cargo loaded into those holds was for the most part rounded up and offered for sale by fellow Africans to begin with.

Second, the population of Europe grew sharply during the years of this brief telling, so the hunger for wealth was soon joined by a hunger for new sources of food and new lands to cultivate. Before the age of colonization came to its close, large numbers of people had moved from Britain to North America and southern Africa, a larger number yet moved from Spain and Portugal to various parts of Latin America, and other Europeans occupied land in Southeast Asia, Africa, and elsewhere.

Those of us who look out at the world from a secure location in the West tend to see that form of colonization as a process by which people from overcrowded parts of the globe moved into "empty" lands in less crowded parts of the globe and "settled" them. Those new arrivals were breaking the sod of what they took to be unused, vacant farmland. It is evident to us now, looking back, that the land was neither unused nor vacant. It had been occupied for centuries if not millennia by people who hunted the game moving across it, gathered the plant matter growing on it, and cultivated it intermittently by allowing open stretches of land to remain fallow for a time while it slowly regained its nutrient strength. To the Europeans of the time, though, agricultural to the core, untilled land was empty land, and they took it over as if they were moving into a vacuum.

That could serve as a brief history of North America. A continent was invaded by migrants in search of new lands to cultivate. "Planters," they called themselves, by which term they meant not only that they intended to plant crops but to plant villages and towns and even commonwealths. They called the forests along the Eastern seaboard "wilderness," even though they were aware that other people lived there, because it was not being put to the plow, and to them, that was the elementary qualification for calling something civilized. So they "tamed" that wilderness by converting it into farmland. And years later, when they spread out across the vast open plains to the West, they called that land "unused" because it was not being put to the plow either, and they called it "vacant" at least in part because they did not view the people whose homeland they knew it to be as fully human. The land was barren, not only because it did not produce crops but because it was not occupied by beings whose humanity had to be respected.

Third, cheap labor was always an important part of the colonial venture. In the early years, colonizers counted on native labor to help them extract resources from the land. After all, it was not the *colonizers* who harvested the tea and silk and coffee. It was not *they* who trapped or brought down the animals that brought them furs and ivory. It was not they who mined the silver and gold and amber. It was not they who shaped the pottery and wove the fabrics and carved the figurines sold in the markets of Europe. And, as we noted a moment ago, it was not they who rounded up the unsuspecting natives who found themselves bound for slave auctions in the New World. And later, as the Industrial Revolution reached a more advanced stage, colonizers realized the benefit to them of using labor from the poorer lands to replace the increasingly less docile and increasingly more expensive workers at home. In many parts of the colonized world, in fact, hard labor was often done by natives who had for all practical purposes became slaves without even leaving their homelands. In those cases, the cost of labor could amount to little more than the expense of housing and feeding those unwilling hands.

Fourth, and most important in the long term, coupled with those economic impulses was a feeling, running deep in the Western consciousness, that the "advanced" nations had an obligation to bring the benefits of their ways of life to peoples out in the dark continents who were less well-off and not yet—a word worth thinking about—"civilized." This, too, is a topic difficult to discuss sensibly now, since it is so obvious, looking back, that the *greed* which motivated some Westerners to exploit the land and enslave its people, and the *sense of moral superiority* that motivated other Westerners to impose their own values on the rest of the world, are natural partners. It often happens in human affairs that impulses issuing from very different chambers of the heart fuse for a moment in what later looks like a strange if not unholy alliance.

The Stern Benefits of Civilization

The stark exploitation of colonized lands was accompanied by a strong feeling that the moral, spiritual, intellectual, and scientific disposition of the West was the human spirit at its most elevated. It was God's work reaching perfection. It was the goal toward which the evolution of human society had been pointing all along. Europeans saw themselves as representing an advanced version of what the immature peoples of the world would one day become.

This view came to be called "Manifest Destiny" in the United States, but the idea it expressed was far older. It really meant two things: first, that the *natural wealth* of the rest of the world should be entrusted to the West because only those who lived there really knew to what use it should be put, and second that the *minds* and *moralities* of the rest of the world should be entrusted to the West because only those who lived there really knew what the forces of history had in store for humankind. It was the destiny of the people of Europe and the West, mature members of the human species, to take the immature peoples from the rest of the world and take them in hand.

Thus missionaries went out into the far corners of the world in organized battalions to instruct natives how they should conceptualize as well as to worship, absolutely sure that they were inspired by the true faith and had been divinely appointed to undertake the work they were doing. They were followed by teachers who also thought they were in possession of great truths and were willing to share them with natives by instructing them in hygiene, manners, modesty, decency, and the uses of a truly civilized language. This was (and is) an incredible conceit, especially when seen in a modern light, but it is worth noting that in some respects it was also a brave and a generous one. Those who ventured out into that darkness often endured immense discomforts and sometimes lived in serious peril as well. People who think that they alone know what is true and good can perhaps be forgiven for not understanding how much harm they can do when others come to believe them. But the record has to show that on balance they mostly inflicted harm, and of a grievous kind.

The upshot was that peoples whose countries had been taken over lost not only the bounty of their own lands, condemning them to a grinding poverty, but many of the cultural frameworks that had given shape to their lives—their languages, their systems of meaning, their religious viewpoints, their ways of making sense of the universe around them.

Those of us who live in the West should try to imagine what it must have been like then (and is still the case in many places now) to live in a region under the colonial sway of a foreign power. One is welcome to take comfort from thinking that the experience will be good for natives in the long run if that helps. But it is important at the same time to realize that the persons on whom we impose our goodness can be damaged by the process in ways that are not easy to anticipate. It is well known that visitors from other climes often bring with them to new lands viruses and other infectious agents for which natives have no built-in immunity. But it is not as well understood that visitors from afar also bring with them ideas and beliefs that natives have no immunity from either, and the result is often a devaluation of the languages they speak and think in, the philosophies that order their lives, the customs that orient them, and the ways in which they perceive reality. Relatively few persons have written about that experience, but those who have (a brilliant and spirited physician named Franz Fanon being one of them) describe it as a sense of being submerged under a relentless, incoming tide, and being made to feel smaller, less important, less relevant in the process.

(I spent a week in Oaxaca, Mexico, as I was writing this chapter, and paid particular attention when my wife pointed out on a walk through town that many of the manikins in the local shops had blond, curly hair, eyes as blue as azure, and figures that would strike many New York models as anorexic. And yet the customers being appealed to were in large part Zapotec, a strong and handsome people with sturdy builds, dark complexions, straight black hair, and deep brown eyes. The Spanish left Mexico 150 years ago, so those manikins may owe their look more to television broadcasts from the United States than to *conquistadores* from the past. But it began then, and we have to appreciate what it must be like to measure one's own beauty by the standards of another people who came into the world looking very differently than we do. Some readers of these lines will know that feeling all too well. The rest of us owe them as well as ourselves the effort to try.)

All of these things we have been discussing were called *colonization* or *settlement* or *bringing the benefits of civilization to primitive lands* in their time, but the nouns we need to draw on now to relate that tale come from a harsher vocabulary. Whatever rationalizations make it possible for an otherwise good people to engage in those pursuits, the most accurate name for entering the land of others without invitation is *invasion,* the most accurate name for stripping the land of its resources is *pillage,* and the most accurate name for forcing other persons to work against their will is *slavery.* When Spanish soldiers raided the treasures of Mexico and Peru, they knew they were stealing. When English and French traders ventured deep into the forests of Canada to exchange glass beads and flasks of rum for furs worth a hundred times more, they knew they were taking advantage. But as colonization spread out over the world and became the practice of most nations of the West, the impulse to plunder and the impulse to convert became intertwined, with the result that they fused into a moral crusade. If ever we need a demonstration that humankind is very skilled at rearranging its moral priorities to fit its economic interests, here is a case in point. It would have been an occasion for Karl Marx to point out how prescient he had been on that point, but his smile would not have been one of satisfaction.

And Then?

The colonial empires had seasons of one, two, or three hundred years, and then they disappeared. After World War II, European powers withdrew the military garrisons and administrative offices they had installed in the lands they once colonized, and simply left. The reasons for this were varied. Rebellions in some of those lands had increased the costs of staying there, and shifts in moral feelings back home made the whole project seem harder to justify. And in any case it was becoming increasingly evident that the same result could be accomplished by taking over distant *markets* as by occupying distant *territories.* Trading companies and large corporations could do the same work more efficiently. What mattered was the way the flow of money and goods was managed, the way manufacturing firms were established overseas, the way investments were made in the poorer countries, the way local people were put to work, and so on. An American named Ludwell Denny put it neatly: "We will not make Britain's mistake. Too wise to govern the world, we will simply own it." His point was that the rate at which natural resources and manufactured products make their way to the core countries of the world has not diminished in any significant way as a result of the close of the colonial era, and the costs of labor in the Third World are so much lower than those in the First World that it is possible to *use* another people without occupying their land. The age of colonialism may be over, but the siphoning continues in a different form.

That, of course, has something to do with the shrinking of the globe, which is the topic to which we will now turn.

Globalization

We began this chapter by looking at modern maps and how the land surfaces of the world are portrayed on them. We noted that this way of visualizing things is relatively new to human experience. Central Europe could not have been represented as a vast patchwork of bounded states until four hundred years ago, accurate maps of Latin America could not have been drawn for another two hundred years or so, and of Africa not until more recent times. That way of visualizing the face of the world, though, may be on the verge of becoming less and less relevant. This is not because nation states are likely to disappear anytime soon. They will continue to maintain armies, impose taxes, post sentries along their borders, and send delegates to the United Nations. But we are now entering an age in which traffic across those borders in the form of information and goods and persons has become so fluid that we have to wonder whether social and cultural differences among the peoples of the earth are now dissolving.

For one thing, the rise of the digital era has meant that ideas and data, images and sounds, now pass through space as indifferent to boundaries staked out on the ground as migrating birds. And even on the ground, where national borders are still drawn as sharply and as decisively as ever they were, the mass of persons moving across them on their way to new homes or new places of work, temporary or permanent, and the mass of goods moving across them on their way to new markets, has reached a new high. It is a time of dislocation and relocation, altering our world—even if we set aside for one moment the insistent flow of migrants seeking new places to call home as a result of political unrest and changes in global climate.

A full discussion of globalization would require us to deal at some length with flows of money, changes in the political structure of the state, shifts in the nature of markets, the development of new technologies, revisions in the organization of modern corporations, and so on. But the main point I want to make here is that these shifts are drawing the things of this world closer together, compressing them into ever narrower spaces. The migration of *persons* and *goods* across national borders creates a migration of *customs* and *outlooks* and *points of reference* and all the rest of the cultural luggage that individuals on the move bring along with them. In the same way that states seek to create national cultures in order to help them take control of bounded territories, the economic forces that drive globalization seek a global culture in order to help facilitate the flow of money, goods, images, information, and the like. Amin Malouf, whose sensitivity to these matters I have taken advantage of before, writes:

> We might say that everything human societies have done through the ages to mark differences and establish frontiers between them is due to come under pressures aimed at reducing those differences and abolishing those frontiers.

In many ways, then, the peoples of the earth are beginning to close in on each other and to share a more common outlook. Distance does not matter in the same way it once did, nor do differences in language or custom or taste. Some commentators expect that a kind of global culture will emerge from this, and that may well turn out to be the case over the long term. But it probably makes better sense in the meantime to call it a *sensibility* rather than a *culture*. It has more to do with impulses and sensations, with moods and atmospheres, than it does with basic values and worldviews that run deep in the human grain and fit what social scientists generally mean by "culture." But that sensibility might have the capacity to dilute cultural differences at least some of the time, and in the process to establish something like universals in behavior and thought.

Billions of people react to the same advertisements, for example, and it is assumed by those who produce them that they have the power to develop common tastes and desires all over the world. Billions of people stare at the same images that flutter across television screens, too, and in doing so learn to see in similar ways. Thus a mass protest in Beijing, the meltdown of a nuclear reactor in Japan, and a terrorist attack on New York become a part of everyone's consciousness, a moment in everyone's history, a datum in everyone's store of knowledge. It is almost as though these events happened *to* everyone who was old enough at the time to be a distant witness of them.

So in many ways the whole globe has become a vast interconnected and interactive system politically, economically, and socially. People are in touch by telephone and internet over huge distances, and, perhaps more to the point, are now observers of, and in that sense participants in the same events, and caught up in the same cultural currents whether they are aware of it or not.

A Note on the Nature of Capital

Globalization is made possible by new technologies, but the driving force behind it is modern capitalism. It is in the very nature of capitalism to seek wider markets for the goods it produces and to reduce the costs of producing those goods to a minimum. The structures that accomplish those goals, in these times, are a new class of transnational institution, some of them more powerful than the sovereign states they normally do business in: international banks, trade associations, multinational corporations, and other organizations that can reach across local boundaries. Mills, factories, and corporate offices are usually located within the borders of a particular state, but the activities they engage in are not. Information, currency, even palpable products flow effortlessly across space. And even when corporations have stable addresses that can be reached by surface mail, they often reside less in *places* than in *sets of shifting connections.* The officers of a given corporation may be in almost constant motion, its records stored on microchips, its assets deposited in banks all over the world, its products manufactured in a variety of locales and sold in a variety of markets, the meetings of its sales representatives and board members conducted by telephone or Skype, and so on. In such cases, information does not flow from office to office or from floor to floor of an established center, but via satellite links, overseas cables, telephone linkages, and other telecommunication devices. An office does not need to have a location in physical space.

Two things are worth noting in this connection.

First, the classical vision of a market is that of an arena in which consumers let it be known by the way they behave in the marketplace what it is they want and are ready to pay for, and producers are quick to oblige by supplying the desired goods. Demand and supply, in that order. But in this age of images and sensations, producers create not only the goods being asked for but the demand for them. "Advertising" is the word in general use to refer to that process. In classical theory, advertising is the means by which a producer informs a buying public that this object or that service is available for sale. Supply meeting demand. But advertising has increasingly become a process by which producers try to reach into the minds of buyers to generate demands that did not exist before. Sometimes, advertisements have as their object to convince buyers already on the market that a Nissan will serve them better than a Subaru or that this brand of mayonnaise tastes better than that one. But a very substantial part of the advertising created for overseas markets, especially in the poorer countries of the world, has as its object to create a longing for products that potential buyers had never really given a minute's thought to before. It is easy to see how the producers of cigarettes, carbonated beverages, deodorants, and designer accessories profit from reaching new markets in Indonesia and Ecuador, but it is far harder to see how the quality of life in Indonesia or Ecuador will be improved as a consequence. A good case in point is provided by growing sales of infant formula in poorer countries, a product that is designed to replace a natural resource that is readily available and essentially without cost: breast feeding. The point of this kind of advertising is to *manufacture* needs, to *establish* the habit of buying, to *promote* a style of life based on consumption.

Second, I noted earlier that information and images flow from one part of the world to another on the instant, and in doing so create a vast interconnected web. But those flows are not random. They have their own direction and logic. "The Internet," writes Maalouf, who is himself from the Middle East, can be viewed from the perspective of less developed lands as "an ectoplasmic monster enabling the powers that be to spread their tentacles over the whole planet." A wise and widely respected American sociologist named Immanuel Wallerstein, whom we shall hear from again soon, has been saying the same thing for years, though in a calmer tone of voice. The globe is now connected by an interactive system of great complexity, he notes, that serves to reduce cultural dissonances of one kind or another. But the flows of information originate in what he calls the "core" countries of the world—the United States and Europe in particular— and stream with purpose toward outlying countries. The *lingua franca* of the new sensibility is English, the images being broadcast are in large measure fashioned in the United States or Europe, and the products being shipped across the world's borders, although many are manufactured in outlying countries, are nonetheless controlled by American or European (and, increasingly now, Japanese or Chinese) interests.

Many observers have stories to tell of times when they were startled by what felt to them like an odd counterbalancing of cultural traces. I have three stories to share by way of example:

I was once in one of the most remote of the Marshall Islands at the time of a village feast. The island was a small coral atoll out in the middle of the Pacific with no electricity or plumbing or any other kind of modern convenience. When the poi and rice and roast pig had been served in baskets made of coconut fronds, a dark liquid that turned out to be Coca-Cola was poured slowly into plastic cups and passed around as though it was a rare vintage wine. It had been flown in that day on the same once-a-week packet plane I had arrived on. I grew up in the land of Coca-Cola, but I found the sight deeply distressing. No television set or radio can be found on the island, and only a few persons speak any English. How in the world did Coca-Cola get there?

I recall with a similar shudder the day my wife and I entered a record store in Sofia, the capital of Bulgaria, soon after the communist regime there collapsed in 1989. Bulgaria has a long and celebrated tradition of ecclesiastical choral work as well as folk music, and we had hoped to buy recordings of both. The walls of the shop were covered with posters of Madonna, Michael Jackson, and Western rock stars we had never heard of, and the clerks we turned to at first (with the help of our Bulgarian host) had no idea what we were talking about. Finally one of them found what we were seeking in a drawer at the rear of the shop.

Both of those encounters were disheartening, but my blood ran cold for a moment during a visit to a temporarily quiet zone in the Yugoslav civil war of the early 1990s. I was driving past a group of young militiamen carrying automatic weapons and dressed in oddly familiar costumes—bandannas wrapped around their heads, the sleeves of their shirts cut off at the shoulder, and bandoleers draped across their chests. My idea how to maneuver through that scene was to slink slowly along, becoming as small as I could manage behind the steering wheel. But my passenger, a young Croat who was serving as my interpreter, rolled down the car window and yelled "Rambo!" "Yo!" came the cheerful response, as my heart almost stopped entirely. The young men, many of them in their middle and late teens, had been in fierce combat not long before, firing at other young men just like themselves, and both sets of combatants were dressed to resemble a character in an American film. If it was not for the menace that hung in the air, at least for me, one could have mistaken it for a movie set. And in a way it was that.

Global Corporations and Sovereign States

All of this suggests a shift in consciousness that reaches across the entire globe. We will soon have to find ways to depict social formations that connect people together but have no obvious location on the earth's surface. Global corporations may lead that list, but, as we shall note shortly, religious movements and similar assemblies of people now extend over terrains larger than any country or any combination of countries. These formations have no centers and no edges. They involve overlapping dimensions of power, and the way they are linked in space simply cannot be represented by modern conventions of mapmaking. It has been estimated that of the hundred largest economic units to be found on earth, one-half are states and one-half are corporations. How would you chart a terrain looking like that?

For all these reasons, the global corporation and the sovereign state have an uneasy relationship. On the one hand, multinational corporations depend on the governments of the countries in which they do business to supply particular services. States have police forces and armies that can provide security within the home country and stabilize markets overseas. They maintain educational establishments that train skilled persons for corporate positions. They can build essential roads and railways, seaports and airports. They can impose tariffs when that serves corporate interests well or deregulate trade when it does not. And in general they have a deep influence on the larger cultural climate in which business is conducted. In that sense, the corporation needs the state.

On the other hand, though, these huge, body-less corporations would profit the most if they could conduct business in a world that spoke a single language, shared a common set of consumer tastes, and moved to the same larger cultural rhythms. The corporation, then, is a natural *enemy* of the state, if only in the sense that it works best when it is not hemmed in by national borders and is not constrained by national interests. Thomas Jefferson once remarked that merchants have no country, and Benjamin R. Barber, two hundred years later, put it: "Markets abhor frontiers as nature abhors a vacuum." Multinational corporations, at least some of the time, would be glad to see sovereign states back away from the regulation of commerce altogether.

In many respects, that is what is happening. I noted earlier that it is easier for a state to conduct its business if it can count on a shared national culture, and in the same way it would be easier for an international corporation to conduct its business if variations in national culture were somehow to dissolve in the great solvent of modernity. The flows of information from what Wallerstein calls the core countries to the peripheral ones are doing precisely that, and it suggests a parallel. Missionaries from the West once sailed out into the world with a faith to promote, recognizing that the principal obstacles to achieving their goal were differences in language, worldview, taste, and sensibility. And now capitalist operatives from the West venture out into the world with goods to promote, recognizing that the principal obstacles to achieving their goal are exactly the same—differences in language, worldview, taste, and sensibility.

Among the things core countries have exported to peripheral ones over the past few decades, as we noted in our review of cities of the underdeveloped world, is the theory that local governments should abandon efforts to protect local economies and instead leave them to the ways of the open market, this in the assumption that it is the most effective way to bring growth to poor regions. It was the stated policy of global financial institutions like the International Monetary Fund and the World Bank, in fact, to invest only in countries willing to accept that theory. The result has been a widespread withdrawal of various state agencies from playing any role in the economies of their own countries. Like many other imports from the West, the theory may have issued from an impulse to help. But what the policies have really accomplished, in the opinion of a number of experts, is to make it easier yet for wealthy countries to take advantage of poorer ones. The theory itself is sometimes known as the "Washington Consensus," and its longer-range objectives have been to reduce the costs of government services, privatize state enterprises, encourage foreign investment, reduce taxes on businesses, encourage a less costly labor force, and in general to promote the notion that local economies need to take their chances in the choppy seas of the open market.

By some measures, these policies have improved the quality of life elsewhere. At the time of this writing, however, 1.2 billion people throughout the world live on less than $1 a day, including 640 million in Africa (nearly half the population of the continent) and another 300 million in each of South Asia and China. In the world's poorest lands, incomes have declined and poverty has risen. The open market—whatever its long-term potential—has not yet behaved as classical economists promised it would.

The withdrawal of the state from the economic scene, particularly in the poorer parts of the world, has posed yet another problem. In national economies left to the mercies of the open market, what agencies are responsible for aiding the poor, protecting the environment, and in other ways acting on behalf of the common weal? What agencies are assigned the job of dealing with the welfare of the young, the aging, the sick, and those yet to be born? As inadequate as many governments have proven to be in that respect, agencies assigned those responsibilities at least recognize that they have been charged with that trust and given the power to do something about it. But markets and the multinational corporations that operate in them do not even *pretend* to have those responsibilities or obligations. Those who hold positions of authority in global corporations may be as compassionate and caring as the most blessed of parish priests at heart, so I am not talking about individual virtue here. But the institutions they represent are not in the business of charity and, more to the point, are organized in such a way as to extract as much wealth as possible from the poor to profit the already well-off.

This gives new meaning to the term "stratification," a topic we will be turning to in an upcoming chapter. We will note there that disproportions in wealth between the richest and the poorest citizens of a country like the United States are now staggering, but the gap that stands between the wealthiest of the developed world and the poorest of the less developed world, as Immanuel Wallerstein points out, can only be called stupefying. Ponder this. The total wealth of the 358 richest people on earth is said to equal that of the 2,300,000,000 poorest. Divide 2.3 billion by 358. By my arithmetic, each of those wealthy persons has a fortune equal to that of 6,500,000 of his or her fellow human beings—six and a half million! Or ponder this. Some 22 percent of the world's total wealth belongs in the Third World, which contains 80 percent of the world's population. And in the few seconds it took you to read that sentence, the disproportion increased.

The Folk Ethos Reappears

One of the most important things to say about the process of globalization, however, from a social, cultural, and even psychological perspective, is that the homogenizing effects of the new age are also creating their own counterbalances. Out in the peripheral regions of the world, where modernization feels like an encroachment of Western and particularly of American sensibilities, the impulse to resist is also growing. To quote Amin Maalouf a last time: "Never have men had so many things in common—knowledge, points of reference, images, words, instruments, tools of all kinds. But this only increases their desire to assert their differences." This is because one of the results of the encroachment has been a dilution of local culture, a flooding out of old and sustaining social forms, which has meant for a significant number of the world's peoples a loss of local language, a loss of both local and national memory, a loss of group history, a loss of communal ritual, a loss of a sense of homeland—a loss, in short, of selfhood. Michael Jackson and Madonna, whatever their other virtues, will never be able to represent the national soul of Bulgaria. The result is that people from many parts of the world are withdrawing into ethnic enclaves and joining nationalistic political movements or religious crusades that offer them a feeling of security as well as a sense of belonging and identity. The irony of those young paramilitary troops in Croatia and Bosnia is that they are wearing uniforms that have become universal while killing one another in the name of ever narrowing ethnic groupings. Jonathan Friedman notes: "one thing that is not happening" in this globalized world "is that boundaries are disappearing. Rather, they seem to be erected on every new street corner in the declining neighborhoods of our world."

No review of "globalization," then, can be complete without pointing out that when old differentiations begin to dissolve, new differentiations have a way of appearing in their stead. That may not be a law of social science, but it is certainly a widely remarked occurrence. On the one hand, globalization asserts a centripetal pull that threatens to convert the surface of the earth into a continuous, open space, on which people are liable to feel exposed and alone and vulnerable. But on the other hand, perhaps as a reaction, people everywhere are withdrawing into communal enclosures where they feel at home and among their own kind, and where, to recall my Creole-speaking colleague, they "are a person." These can be profoundly sensitive and yet at the same time profoundly volatile gatherings. Erik H. Erikson, about whom you will hear more soon, wrote that "people and peoples would rather murder than take chances with their identity." He did not see the explosions that occurred in Yugoslavia or Rwanda or other of the killing fields that have darkened our time, but he would have understood them.

Cultural activities often take place on a broad plain across which the contrary pulls of a number of different tendencies work their way out. That may be a good way to look at the larger map of modernity. Globalization has as its natural contrary a kind of localization that springs up as if in reaction. Where we find a tendency toward homogenization we also find new forms of differentiation. Where we think we see uniformities and harmonies and a tendency toward standardization, we would be wise to look for evidence of diversity and dissonance and fragmentation. The social world is a complex creature.

One last point. Readers of this book have another vocabulary to draw on when the subject being raised here comes up. Nothing could be more *gesellschaft* than the notion of a global economy and a global culture. Globalization is the name of a process by which the earth becomes more and more like a single, interactive system, the organizing principle of which is capitalist efficiency on a grand scale. It is a final stage on the long drift from the world of the village to the world of global rationalization, and it is the clearest realization of that "polar night of icy darkness" which Weber so feared. At the same time, however, when we move down to ground level and make contact with the local people and the local places caught in that web of efficiency, we see efforts to create something communal, something village-like, in the very midst of modernity. One can sense it in the growth of ethnic and national movements, a return to a feeling of kind, a feeling of kin. One can sense it in the religious revivals that bring new hope and communality to the *bidonvilles* and *villas miserios* of this world. One can see it in countercultural movements of a number of kinds. These are all forms of fundamentalism in both the religious and the ideological sense of the term, an attempt to reduce a world of relativities and ambiguities and uncertainties to a few elementary understandings that offer firm grounding underfoot. That, of course, is the very spirit of *gemeinschaft*. And, as we shall see when we turn to nationalities, social speciation, and the war that convulsed Yugoslavia, it has a mean and dangerous edge.

There are many indications as this book goes to press that a return to nationhood and to the closing of national borders are much in the air. If so, that may very well be a reflection of the same set of urges and urgencies described here.

It Seemed Like the Whole Bay Died

ON THE EVENING OF MARCH 23, 1989, a huge, lumbering supertanker named the *Exxon Valdez* cleared the dock at its home port of Valdez, Alaska, and began what was intended to be a 3,000-mile voyage down the coast to Los Angeles with 53 million gallons of crude oil on board. Shortly after midnight, the vessel ran aground on a well-charted and well-marked reef in Prince William Sound. It may rank among life's minor ironies that the reef on which the *Exxon Valdez* came to an abrupt halt was named for Captain William Bligh, who had sailed these waters in the 1770s and 1780s before earning a different kind of fame in the celebrated mutiny aboard the HMS *Bounty* in 1789.

Half an hour after the accident, the ship's captain radioed a brief and rather laconic message to the Coast Guard: "We've fetched up hard aground off Bligh Reef, and evidently we're leaking some oil. . . . It looks like we'll be here a while." He was certainly right about that. At least eleven million gallons of crude oil—other reports suggest that the total was considerably higher than that—spurted through the gashes in the ship's hull over the next five hours, and before the hemorrhaging could be brought to a stop, it had blackened more than a thousand miles of Alaskan coastline. This was not only the largest oil spill in the history of North America up until then but far and away the most damaging, spreading rapidly across what the official report to the President called "one of the nation's most sensitive ecosystems."

One well-positioned observer wrote as he watched the spreading oil slick reach a stretch of shoreline some twenty miles from the place where the hull of the *Exxon Valdez* lay damaged on Bligh Reef: "A thick layer of black crude oil covered the water as far as the eye could see and had just coated the entire inter-tidal zone. Every living being—seals, otters, birds—was either dead or dying in agony." In the days that followed, one way to take a measure of the damage that had been done to the natural environment was to count those casualties: a number of reports were issued shortly after the oil spill to the effect that whales, seals, and eagles had perished in the hundreds, sea otters in the thousands, seabirds in the hundreds of thousands, and fish like herring and salmon in the many millions. That kind of accounting, however, can offer no more than a start, for it takes several generations for that thinned a population to be restored to its earlier size and level of health even when things go well, and it takes a good deal longer to find out whether the fragile equilibrium on which an ecosystem like that relies has been thrown out of balance in some other way.

The most immediate question, of course, had to do with the amount of damage done to the people caught up in that immense spread of oil. It was alto-gether obvious that the accident had been a profound blow to the fishing industry, critical to the Alaskan economy, and that a considerable number of individuals who made their living working the sea and its shoreline were suffering from injuries of a personal as well as an economic kind.

A number of legal actions were filed in the months following what everyone agreed had been an avoidable accident, among them one devoted specifically to the impacts of the oil spill on the Native peoples involved. It seemed clear to experts on such matters that the disaster tended to have had a quite different *meaning* for Natives than it did for other residents. They *saw* it differently, *felt* it differently, were *harmed* by it in different ways, and suffered from it more grievously. I was invited to play a role in those proceedings. I was not an expert on the Native peoples of Alaska by any stretch of the imagination, although I had encountered a number of similar peoples elsewhere on my research travels. But I did have a fair amount of experience by then on what disasters in general can do to the persons and the communities exposed to them, and that was the basis for my being asked to participate in the proceedings and to offer testi-mony. Two different issues were at stake here: First, and most obvious, what harm did the accident do to the Native individuals exposed to it? And second, what damage did it do to the texture of their customary ways of life? In that sense, the disaster had been a different category of event for the local Natives than it had been for a majority of their white fellow citizens, and the nature of that difference deserved attention.

But the presiding judge ruled that he would only hear testimony on the "economic consequences" of the spill. He felt bound by a judicial decision that had been rendered in a maritime case on the eastern seaboard of the United States more than eighty years earlier, when Woodrow Wilson was President and Alaska was a vast and largely unexplored wilderness. The judge meant that he would not hear testimony on *cultural traditions* or *ways of life* or anything of the sort. The court would focus exclusively on that one segment of human life. The attorneys who represented the Natives appealed the ruling, but the judge declared in a written statement that the testimony I was planning to present, like that of several others, was "non-economic" and therefore inadmissible. That was the end of that.

And it posed a particular problem for those preparing to participate not only in the legal hearings but in general conversations about the meaning of the disaster. In the white, English-speaking world, it makes a certain sense to separate social life into partitions like "economic," "religious," or "political," but it makes very little sense in the Native world. Even when modern Natives converse easily in English, it does not mean that they *experience* reality in the same way their white fellow citizens do.

The Subsistence Life

I am going to quote Alaska Natives fairly extensively in what follows, so it is worth knowing that most of the comments below were offered at public hearings into the impacts of the spill. They are not quiet reflections made to a visiting social scientist in an interview setting, then, but careful statements, almost like testimony offered in courtrooms. But they have largely the same objective: to explain to others what the spill meant to them and their kind. They are teachings. (Each separate paragraph of testimony below, as throughout the book, contains the comments of a different speaker.)

The Natives who live along Prince William Sound, where the oil spill took place, are generally called "Alutiiq." The term refers to individuals who are descended from a number of different local strains, but live similar lives. Those strains have become so intermingled over time that we can now speak of them as a distinct "people."

The Alutiiq have traditionally been what is often known as a "subsistence" people—a term used by observers looking in from the outside, by white neighbors, and by Natives themselves. This means, first, that they derive nourishment and whatever else they need to survive from their immediate surroundings—in this instance from fishing, hunting, trapping, and gathering foods from along the seashore as well as plant life from further inland. And it means, second, that they adhere to a mode of living that is consistent with and attuned to that base. To "subsist" means to make it—often without much to spare. It can be a precarious existence.

It is important to be careful here. Native communities in our times are a mixture of the traditional subsistence economy and the familiar cash economy found throughout the rest of Alaska. At times, Alutiiq villagers take their boats out to sea and follow trap lines on the land in order to sell what they harvest in the market—fish, furs, and so on—as well as to consume it themselves, and they employ snowmobiles, outboard motors, firearms, and any other contrivances that make them more proficient in the process. Once the day's work is over, furthermore, they return in all-terrain vehicles to homes equipped with refrigerators, television sets, and other conveniences.

So when we speak loosely of "Native" and "white" outlooks, we are not dividing the populace into two distinct categories so much as noting that the people of Alaska come from different social and cultural roots and that the milieu they share contains elements of both. Many white persons who migrated to Alaska from elsewhere did so at least in part because they share the Natives' respect for the environment and the way of life that naturally issues from it. And it is increasingly the case that persons who come from Native origins have accepted the invitation to enter into at least a portion of what I will call the "white culture" here, for lack of a better term.

The best way to phrase this may be that a considerable number of Natives live in a kind of suspension between those two worlds but are regarded both by themselves and by fellow Alaskans as "Native" even when they become adjusted to white ways. In that sense, the traditional round of life has always been an elementary part of the Alutiiq definition of self. "This is a way of life for us," said one Native fisher. "It's not just 'subsistence' for us. It's *part* of us. We are part of the earth." Other voices you will hear in what follows—like the one just heard—are from persons speaking in English to largely white audiences in an earnest effort to make them understand better. But a reverence for the Native way of life is unmistakable in them.

Most of us who come from what I will continue to call the "white world" tend to view the land, the waters, the forms of life to be found out there, and all the other elements that make up the natural world as a kind of backdrop. We think of them as existing outside the window, beyond the fence, on the other side of whatever it is that marks the outer edges of human living space. For Natives the world over, though, we humans and the rest of the natural environment are a continuous whole. People do not live *on* the land or draw their sustenance *off* the land—usages that imply separate entities. They are *of* the land, absorbed into its very grain. Those of us who have derived our sensibilities of such things from an agricultural past tend to view tilled fields, gardens, and orchards as of a different *kind* than open plains and forests; animals raised in herds of a different kind than animals found out in the wild. Those distinctions, however, have far less meaning to a subsistence people. All nature is a garden for those who gather food from the land around them; all animals are part of a great natural herd for those who hunt. "That is why Native people so often refer to their lands, seashores, and waters as their bank, their table, or their garden," as one wise observer of Alutiiq ways, himself Native, put it. Another Native elder noted: "We always say 'when the tide goes out, the table is set.'"

And because that is so, the befouling of tidal pools or sea grass or any of the other natural sites visited by the *Exxon Valdez* oil spill tended to be experienced by local Natives as a befouling of their own home turfs. It is important to keep that in mind when we learn that a large part of the natural envelope in which Alutiiq villagers lived out their days was contaminated. Everything was covered by a thick layer of oil in the weeks following the spill—"all you could see was black," said one person, "I just cried"—but in the weeks and months and even years that followed, dark traces of oil were cast upon the shores by shifting waters or seeped upward through gravel or sand onto nearby beaches. Far worse, streaks of oil continued to appear in every form of wildlife. As one expert noted:

> Native people harvested seals that had oil coming out of their mouths, birds whose internal organs smelled rotten, salmon that were "all dark inside," sea bass with sores and infused gills, oily clams, and many other signs of damage from the oil spill.

One white official, counting on the few blessings he could find in the days after the spill, announced: "Well, at least there was no loss of life." He meant human life, of course, but that was an unfortunate turn of phrase for Alaska Natives listening in. No loss of life? To them, the universe is bursting with life, and people who feel as close as they do to their fellow creatures of other species are not likely to take much comfort from such a thought. Listen:

> We walk the beaches, but instead of gathering life we gather death: dead birds, dead otters, dead seaweed.

> Seeing the dead animals day after day really got to me. I found myself standing in the middle of Main Street crying.

> Those days were horrible. Dying animals were floating around. Dead animals. People would come up and say, "We can't catch any more birds" [in order to help save them], and they'd break out sobbing. It's beyond imagination. Oil everywhere. . . . Dead otters. Dead deer. Dead birds.

> When you pick up those dead carcasses day after day, you go through a mourning process. It's not only death in your environment, but, in a sense, it's a death of yourself. Because you're part of the environment.

Assaults on the environment, then, are not experienced as doing harm to something vaguely *out there* but reaching to the very core of existence. That is why it is more than a casual figure of speech when local villagers, in an effort to find the right words to explain such things to their white neighbors—and maybe to one another—say things like:

> They killed something vital in me when they spilled that oil. You see, there's a rapport, a kind of kinship you sometimes develop with a particular place. It becomes sacred to you. That connection has been severed for me.

> People around here are closely related to the land and the ocean, so the death of birds and animals and seeing so much oil in the water has a deep impact on their lives. This is their home, and it's been violated.

> I was born of this land, these waters. . . . I'm as infected as Mother Nature is—suffocating and gasping for breath. As the environment deteriorates, we, too, deteriorate.

In other ways, too, the Alutiiq sense of what was at stake in the disaster and how its effects should be assessed was different from that of most whites. Natives tended to see the amount of damage done as considerably greater than was the case for most of their fellow citizens, for example, because they were far more likely to regard the land and the water as forms of living matter that can suffer wounds or even die. "Last year it seemed like the whole bay died," said one, and many others shared that view:

> The beach was sick. The water was sick. We couldn't give it medicine to make it well. It was sick, and there was nothing I could do to fix it.

> The excitement of the season had just begun, and then we hear the news: oil in the water, lots of oil killing lots of water. It is too shocking to understand. Never in the millennium of our tradition have we thought it possible for the water to die. But it's true.

Moreover, if the surrounding environment, of which one is a natural part, has been severely damaged by the spill, how should human victims think about their own well-being? "If the water is dead," one elder speculated, then "maybe we are dead." Others added:

> It's not only death in your environment, but in a sense it's a death of yourself, because you're part of that environment.

> The Sound isn't dead, but it's very, very sick. My heart is sick, too. Along with the countless birds, otters, and other casualties of the spill, a part of me has died.

The Native Way of Being

So the spill had a devastating impact on the states of mind of a considerable number of individual Natives who came into contact with it, but it also had a devastating impact on their way of life, their way of *being*. Damage to the tissues of the human body and even of the human mind can be diagnosed and measured by clinical tests that are accepted in most modern forms of medicine and in most modern courtrooms. But damage to the tissues of a cultural ethos—a quite different form of trauma—are a good deal harder to understand or even to describe. There are no tests. The task of the social scientist here—as was the case on Buffalo Creek—is to make out the nature of those damages and then to describe them in a language that fits the logic that governs the American judicial system.

"Economic," in the courtroom, is an easily defined element of life in a modern social order. But *everything* is economic in traditional Alutiiq thinking in one sense or another. Everyday life for the Native people of the south central coast of Alaska, as we have seen, is organized around fishing, hunting, gathering, and other ways of extracting calories from the immediate surround, an "economic" activity by any definition. But it was also a traditional activity, a form of religious observance, a school for the young. It is one of the definitions of *being* Alutiiq, and, thus, of being human. It is not a separable unit of reality.

The way Alaska Natives gather food, as well as the way they distribute it, prepare it, and consume it, becomes a form of *communion* in the sense that it acts to strengthen kinship and other social ties. "In the past," one man from Port Graham noted, "whole families would go out and collect food off the beach. People met one another and talked. It was like a coffee shop." A man from Chenega Bay added: "We used to gather [food] together all the time; it was like a big party." Expressions like "coffee shop" and "party" sound as though they were borrowed from another vocabulary to make a point, but these are occasions for persons to share information, to express feelings, to teach the young, and to *be* Alutiiq. More than that, the collective gathering of foodstuffs can almost be thought of as a form of worship, since it gives people an opportunity to express their gratitude to the forces of nature responsible for their good luck in the first place. To the Native way of thinking, the things acquired in a hunt or a gathering expedition are not simply caught unawares—although great skill may be required in tracking them down. They offer themselves as gifts to their human sisters and brothers, so the shellfish or deer or roots being harvested on any given day should be thanked for their generosity and fellowship.

In that sense, too, fishing and hunting and gathering are the cultural theater in which the Alutiiq way of life is articulated and given form. When young people join their elders in acquiring foodstuffs, they are attending an Alutiiq school. When they rejoice in a good haul, they are celebrating their heritage. When they help distribute the food they have taken part in bringing back, they are learning the ways of their people and becoming ever more deeply enmeshed in their community. It is in the *doing* of it that Alutiiq people express their thanks to the spirits of nature and their reverence for the world around them.

The sharing of food—the sharing of life—is affirmation of the ties that draw people together in kinship groups and in village communities. It is the native equivalent of sitting down at the same table, of gathering around the same hearth. It is an expression of the cultural ethos that gives Alutiiq social life its meaning.

The men would be gone hunting and the women would gather snails and seaweed, and we would all get very close. . . . It was always a great chance to talk, to renew old ties, and to teach your children about the tide pools.

In the summertime, that's when a lot of the elderly and a lot of the women are left behind to tend to their families, tend to their children. This is a time to share, a time to gather. This is how you show them how you survive in a village. You go down to the reef and you pick up bidarkies. You pick seaweed, you eat snails, you teach their kids the way life used to be.

And since the oil spill?

Our elders feel helpless. They cannot do all the activities of gathering food and preparing for winter. And most of all they cannot teach the young ones the native way. How will the children learn the values and the ways if the water is dead?

The point being made here is that when people derive a sense of who they are from a traditional round of life, they are apt to feel as though they have lost their mooring in reality when that round is disturbed. "I feel homeless in a strange country," said one. "Subsistence is our last tie with who we are." Others echoed much the same thought:

Subsistence is the way of life of the Native people. We all feel great pain. [The oil spill] affected our lives because we live off the ocean and it is a [source of] fellowship among our people. We live to gather and think of others and help them when they cannot help themselves. We want to teach the next generation to gather, hunt, and share. It is an art, an identity, a being. . . . We are cut off from our way of life.

When we worry about losing our subsistence way of life, we worry about losing our identity. . . . It's that spirit that makes you who you are, makes you think the way you do and act the way you do, and [affects] how you perceive the world and relate to the land.

In summary, then: the *Exxon Valdez* oil spill did a terrible amount of damage to the natural environment in which the Natives lived, and in doing so it harmed both the persons exposed to it and the nature of their social order. Native culture had been shaped over time to the needs of a subsistence economy, but when that way of life was compromised by the spill, the cultural logic that gave it substance and meaning lost a good part of its force. We speak of the disaster in the past tense now, and it is reasonable for us to hope that a good many of its impacts have been reduced in the years since. Most of the oil has disappeared from the surfaces of the earth, although a considerable residue may now be crouched out of sight in remote corners of the ecosystem—caught in rock crevasses, curled into coagulated tar balls on the ocean floor, or lodged somewhere in the bodies of living organisms. And much the same can be said for the Native communities damaged in that dark season. The troubles we have been speaking of here are less visible now than they were in the months following the spill.

But it seems clear that the Native sense of order remains vulnerable in ways that time may not be able to correct anytime soon. Some Natives trace this back to the day the water died, and they have a good point. "You can deal with the dead salmon and the dead otters," said a thoughtful village chief, "but you can't deal with the damage done to the fabric of the community."

There is a compelling wisdom in those words, and I am going to suggest that the chief would also attribute a considerable amount of that damage to the sheer insensitivity to the Native worldview as reflected in the administrative procedures brought to bear on the issue of recovery. This has been a disadvantage experienced by native peoples all over the earth, and it will take us back for a moment to a matter discussed in the chapter preceding this one: colonialism. So, herein a tale.

Once Upon a Time

The Native peoples of Alaska came across what was once a land bridge connecting Siberia to the Alaskan mainland at the time of the last ice age. The best guess that can be made now is that they were following migrating herds of mammoths, mastodons, and other large herbivores—hunters keeping track of their main sources of food. We can speak of this now in a brief sentence or two, but in doing so we are covering glacially slow drifts of people over thousands of years. The animals eventually disappeared, their time on earth having expired, but the human beings who followed them kept right on going, inch by inch, to settle that empty continent. In the fullness of time, they moved eastward as far as the Atlantic coast of North America, and southward as far as Tierra del Fuego, the southern-most tip of dry land on earth.

No one knew of all this until recent times, of course, so the Natives who remained in what is now Alaska quite naturally regard themselves as having been rooted there since the beginning of time. This is *their* land, and it has always been so.

It is reasonable to assume that the people who traveled across the land bridge over those many thousands of years came from different locations, were gathered into separate bands, and had their own customary ways of doing things. It may have been too early in human time to speak of different "cultures" in the way we do now, but it is likely that those clusters of migrants looked upon themselves as distinct units, something apart. It is also reasonable to assume that the people who spread out across the vast wilderness of Alaska continued to adhere to their own patterns of life and to build on them. That is how it is with our species.

When anthropologists first came upon those assemblages of people in modern times, they saw distinct tribal groupings with their own traditions and their own sense of being "a people." They had their own tribal names, too: Tlingit, Athapaskan, Inupiat, Aleut, Eyak, and a number of others.

But when one views that wide cultural canvas from even a modest distance away, the variations seem to merge into a single portrait. Those tribes may have differed in the way their members spoke or the way they explained the mysteries of the universe to one another, but they had to adjust to the same natural habitat, confront the same circumstances, and live the same life—hunting, fishing, gathering. They were, in that sense, of a *kind,* sharing similar views of how to relate to the world around them and how to relate to their fellow beings. That is why it is entirely logical to refer to a "Native ethos" or a "Native way of life" while at the same time recognizing the tribal variations that remain.

But nothing can make those commonalities stand out more vividly to the persons who live them than the sudden, rude appearance of intruders from a wholly different world who—sometimes without quite knowing what they are doing—impose their alien ways on the people whose land they have ventured into.

The first outsiders to enter the territory were Russian fur traders who came by boat in the mid-18th century across the strait once occupied by the land bridge. They may have been adept in the art of trading, but they knew little of the arts of hunting and trapping and were not about to do that strenuous work themselves in any case. So they did exactly what their European counterparts were doing in Africa and Asia and elsewhere: they compelled Natives to do it.

That was the fate of no more than a minority of Alaska Natives, and nothing even remotely resembling an armed intrusion had taken place. But over time, and in slow stages, Alaska became an occupied territory, a possession. That is certainly how the rest of the world viewed it when Russia simply sold Alaska—a "possession," after all—to the United States in 1867 without a word of notice to the people who lived there.

The American occupation, like the Russian one that preceded it, may not have had that much effect on Natives living inland or along the more remote western and northern stretches of the coast, but colonialism has its more subtle effects as well. It is not just that those unwelcome visitors invade the land but that their sheer presence eventually becomes an invasion of the lifeways— the minds and spirits—of the people who live on it. Taking over means establishing new institutional forms that mirror the cultural perspectives and sensibilities of the newcomers: the definitions of *knowledge* that will rule the classroom, the forms of *reasoning* that will preside over the courtroom, the *logics* that will govern the marketplace, the *moralities* that will be heard in places of worship, the *philosophies* that will be debated in the political arena, and, as we move into more recent times, the sense of what is *real* and *actual* that will be offered in newsprint, radio, television, and, when the time comes, the internet.

Even when those new institutional forms were established to help bring order and coherence to the places the newcomers were settling into rather than to dominate the Native population, the understandings of *reality* they reflected reached out into the Native hinterland and became a part of the larger cultural landscape—where they conflicted with and cast shadows of doubt over Native understandings of what is real and what is true.

And the official language of the land became English. To the Natives who had to take that new language into account at least a part of the time, it meant a different set of meanings than the ones they lived by, a different screen to look through in order to make out the contours of the white world—what is real and what is unreal, what is natural and what is of human invention, what is moral and what is sinful, what is living matter and what is not. It meant a different logic for sorting the things of the world into separate elements or parts. That is one of the things that languages do.

The word for this is *colonialism,* even when it does not remind one of the barbarities of King Leopold's Belgian Congo or the Algeria of which Frantz Fanon wrote so brilliantly. The identifying feature of colonialism is not just the taking over of territory by force of arms but the gradual imposition of the outlooks and perspectives and way of life of the intruders on the natives who live there. And that, surely, happened in Alaska.

Feeling Homeless

A moment ago, we heard an Alaska Native say: "I feel homeless in a strange country," and we then heard from another Native who spoke of "losing our identity," which she described as "that spirit that makes you who you are, makes you think the way you do" and shapes "how you perceive the world and relate to the land."

I want to return to that thought as we end this inquiry by suggesting that fate has visited two quite different but related traumatic blows upon the Native people of Alaska and contributed to their vulnerability.

The first, of course, was that horrifying oil spill that endangered the very "fabric" of Native life. It did a good deal more harm to Native people on the whole than it did to their white compatriots. A carefully executed clinical study reported in the *American Journal of Psychiatry* several years after the event concluded:

> When the *Exxon Valdez* ran aground in Prince William Sound, it spilled oil into a social as well as a natural environment. . . . Alaska Natives were particularly vulnerable to depressive symptoms after the spill.

And that outcome, clearly, was because they envisioned the natural habitat surrounding them—the lands and waters and the things living on and in them—as a part of themselves, as an extension of their own being. The person who spoke of feeling "homeless" was looking out at a spoiled landscape that she no longer recognized.

The disaster itself was a sudden burst coming across the horizon from nowhere, but we can add from what we know of the Alaskan past that this acute shock had been preceded by another and much more gradual shock—one many generations in the making—that had left the fabric of Native life far less resilient and more fragile than it had been before. That trauma was brought about by those intruders from a distant world who imposed their own visions of what constitutes reality and morality upon the Natives who lived there. In doing so—again, without fully recognizing it themselves as often as not—they dismissed and discounted and even ridiculed the Native way of life and the understandings that were a part of it. So the Native ethos retreated into ever smaller settings—villages and other recesses on the larger landscape—where it became the lifeway of a scatter of contained communities rather than the governing logic of the countryside generally. Alaska Natives, then, had very compelling reasons to feel "homeless" in yet another sense: they were not fully at home even in their own land. So one reason for telling the story of the *Exxon Valdez* is that it was so important a moment in the history of Alaska.

But another reason for doing so is that it can serve as a kind of parable, providing a neatly concentrated example of what colonialism could be like and what it often brought in its wake—the manner in which Native peoples were subjected to new and alien conceptions of how the world is ordered, often without a shot being fired or a loud word being uttered.

One can take that parable a step further and note that what happened in Alaska has clear parallels to what is happening elsewhere in the world where people who remain in touch with the rhythms of nature—that would include growers and herders as well as hunters and fishers and gatherers—find that their ways are disappearing under what often feels like the relentless momentum of globalization. People everywhere are losing their connection with the land, either because they are being uprooted from it or because they are losing the sense of belonging to it.

There is a deep irony here in that the Native way of relating to the natural world that we seem to be letting slip away may offer exactly the forms of wisdom we most need to cope with climate change and related threats that lurk in the near future.

Few hunters would voluntarily endanger the animals of the land, knowing that to do so would make life more difficult for their children or their children's children. Nor would a fisher or grower or gatherer or trapper. That is the key provision in the unwritten contract that such people have with life. They are trustees of the land and of the living waters rather than owners of it. Their pledge is to renew the land itself and tend the life on it rather than strip it bare. It is a deep feeling of obligation to generations yet to come, and it is a feeling we modern people would do well to retain.

It might have been a valuable strategy if white intruders from the West had learned this wise teaching from the Alutiiq and other subsistence peoples whose lands we invaded and whose minds we imposed our ways of thinking on. We call other peoples and lands "underdeveloped" because they did not follow the same trajectory we did and become a modern, industrialized economy. But it is becoming ever more important for us to appreciate that those "underdeveloped" peoples developed a far saner and far more realistic philosophy of relating to the natural world than we have managed to.

PROCESSES

In the previous section, *Places,* we dealt with locations on the surface of the earth where people live out their days and develop ways of life suited to those settings. In this section we turn to three *processes,* ongoing activities that we humans have been engaged in over the course of our career on earth.

The first is the process by which the newly born of our species become *persons,* which is to say *social beings*—the way they become aware of the social world they are a part of and learn to participate in it. That process is widely called "socialization" in social science literature. But we will also consider what happens to persons who find later in their lives that they need to adapt to a very different set of social circumstances than the ones they grew up in. It is a starting over, almost a rebirth, and it is often called "secondary socialization" or "resocialization" in the social science vocabulary.

The second is the process by which every society we know of finds ways to divide itself into a vast tracery of classes, ranks, orders, estates, stations, and so on, including races and genders. This process is widely known as "stratification" or "differentiation" in social science usage.

The third is the process by which we come to view other persons who we know to be fellow human beings as if they were so unlike us in form or thought or spirit that they can be treated as though they are of a different order of being altogether. A psychoanalyst named Erik H. Erikson (whose last name bears an almost uncanny resemblance to my own) called this *pseudospeciation.* My plan here is to suggest a few minor changes to that concept and to offer it as a contribution to sociology and anthropology as well as to psychoanalysis.

Becoming a Person

I NOTED EARLIER THAT WE HUMANS ARE born relatively early in our developmental cycle compared to other creatures with whom we share the earth. Our bodies and brains have a lot of maturing to do before we appear on the scene as fully functioning components of human society. The process of maturation begins in the warm pocket of caring adults that I earlier likened to an extension of the womb—that contained space into which infants are born and where they are originally nurtured. But the process continues well into life.

Learning the Score

To say that the newly born of our species evolve into social (and thus human) beings is to say that they become ever more attuned to the flows of social life swirling around them and learn to act in concert with others. Expressions like "becoming attuned" and "acting in concert" might suggest too musical a metaphor over the long term, but they offer a place to begin. The cultural rhythms by which a people live, Émile Durkheim might have suggested, is something like an orchestral score: every player has a somewhat different contribution to make to the overall effect. There has to be enough leeway in that arrangement for individual expression and improvisation, since we are learning who *we* are as individual presences at the same time we are learning how to collaborate with others in the wider social context. But the larger ensemble is coordinated at least to the extent that those of us who are part of it come to share understandings on such matters as key, tempo, pitch, and the like. Everybody in the ensemble has to *know the score* even if—as we shall see later—he or she devotes a lot of time and energy to withdrawing from it, deviating from it, or actively resisting it. And, as we always have to remember, the score itself will vary from location to location and from class to class.

Storytellers of many lands tell of occasions when abandoned infants were raised by wolves or bears or other warm-hearted beasts and were then returned to the societies from which they came. These are wondrous tales, full of another kind of wisdom, but, alas, they have no basis in fact. There have been several cases on record, however, of human infants who managed to survive into childhood without experiencing any meaningful contact with parents or other adults, locked away in attics or closets or basements and kept alive without word or ceremony. Those children were unable to talk or communicate in any other way, which is certainly not surprising, but, more than that, they appeared at first to be unable to see or hear. They were initially thought to be deaf and dumb, in fact, and sometimes even blind. But their problem lay elsewhere. Their eyes could record images perfectly well, but their minds did not know what to make of them. Their ears could register sounds, but their minds could not figure out what they signified. Those sad creatures simply did not know how to process or make use of the information their sensory organs were supplying to them because human beings must become participating members of a social order to make sense of the world around them.

This process is an essential part of the human story, then. But what is it? How does it work? Many specialists in the social and behavioral sciences have tried to visualize that process. I will not try to do justice to any of those theories in what follows, but one can get some sense of their range if I describe two variants that lie at opposing ends of a continuum.

At one extreme is the classical Freudian vision, exaggerated somewhat here to make a point. The human infant bursts hungrily into the world, bristling with instinctual needs. It is greedy, impulsive, and full of libidinal urges. The social order, in turn, goes to work with the very first breath the infant draws to curb those impulses and to inhibit those needs. In that view, becoming a social being is the process by which the requirements of social life are imposed upon that aggressive bundle of energy, and the human career that follows is marked by a life-long struggle between an assertive individual and an imperious society. These are the pains Freud was referring to in his important book *Civilization and Its Discontents*.

At the other extreme (again with more than a trace of exaggeration) is a vision shared by sociologists and psychologists in the early years of the 20th century such as William James, George Herbert Mead, and Charles Horton Cooley. It is found in the work of Émile Durkheim as well. An infant slips gently into the world, a genial lump of protoplasm, eager to know the ways of its elders. Its mind is an empty vessel into which the stuff of society is poured.

Most American sociologists would now take a position somewhere in the mid-range of that continuum, recognizing that neither of these exaggerated visions can reflect what we have learned about child development. It is fair to say that the human animal does not come into the world with many programmed drives, the inborn instructional manuals that other animals do. But that certainly does not mean that the vessel is empty. Human infants begin life with a number of built-in tendencies and attributes that need not detain us now, and they become active participants in the process that follows rather than passive recipients.

Becoming a social being, then, has to be seen in part as a negotiation between child and society. From birth, the child observes and studies and explores the world that opens up in ever wider arcs around it. The instruments it uses for that probing are eyes, hands, mouth, ears; and the lessons being learned have to do with the shape of things, the texture of things, the color and movement and sound and tone of things. And at the same time, of course, the widening world—a surrounding made up at first of parents and other members of the family but later to include playmates, classmates, teachers, figures appearing on television screens—is flooding the child with urgings of a hundred other kinds.

Sociologists on the whole can be said to lean toward the James-Mead-Cooley end of that continuum. This is partly because the weight of evidence tilts in that direction, but it is also partly because our contribution to an understanding of child development is to consider the ways the social order works its way into a child's self. In the end, becoming a person is the process by which the innate tendencies of the child and the looming presence of society are brought into a kind of synchrony, and it is the latter that sociologists generally take to be their natural subject matter.

The Lessons of Early Childhood

In our society (in all societies, probably) childhood is seen as a period during which young people play in a rather aimless fashion until they are old enough to get involved in the real business of learning. Their apprenticeship in the ways of the adult world begins early when they go off to school to begin their exposure to reading and writing and arithmetic, or when they go off with adult relatives to learn the ways of cooking, harvesting, curing hides, tending cattle, laying traps, or the steps of important ceremonies. Serious stuff, that.

The fact is, though, that infancy and early childhood may well be the most intense years of learning in the human life cycle. Indeed, children have learned a good part of what they are ever going to before the formal age of instruction even begins. They have already absorbed a rudimentary map of the family structure and their place on it, and have begun to absorb what will be revealed in time as an elaborate moral code. They have learned a language, far and away the most complex skill they will ever be asked to master. This all adds up to an amazing accomplishment. In some ways, the schooling and tutoring yet to come is little more than a refinement of knowledge the child has been introduced to by the age of three or four.

The most important psychological question to be asked in this connection, of course, has to do with the workings of the mind. How is all this learned? How can an organism that is by any definition still developing take in and retain so much information?

The basic sociological question, though, has to do with *what* the lessons are that one learns so early in life. Sooner or later a child will learn to tie shoelaces, feed livestock, conjugate verbs, or act properly in important rituals. Sooner or later a child will learn a few elementary things one should and should not do. Do not put your finger in the light socket. Do not stare at the medicine man. Here's the proper way to pick up a baby or start a fire or skin a muskrat. A good part of that content is conveyed through well-studied mechanisms like reward, punishment, and other deliberate attempts to instruct. But much of it does not involve any active tutoring at all. It is a process almost like osmosis, in which the teachers do not know they are teaching and the students do not know they are learning.

An infant begins life with few immediate needs. It must have nourishment. It must be separated from its own wastes. It must be in contact with adults, upon whom it is wholly dependent. It must have some form of stimulation. Infants "know" how to inform adults who make up their immediate surround about those needs. A gnawing feeling in the pit of the stomach or a discomfort of some other source triggers a cry loud enough to attract adult attention. For the infant, this is simply a reflex action, at least to begin with. Those adults, however, respond to those alarms in a number of different ways, reflecting both their own personalities and the cultural ethos in which they live. These can be the first lessons of life. I am speaking here of hints, inklings, intimations—the opening moments of what will be a long and intricate process through which infants learn something about the prevailing tone of the world they are entering. Its emotional temperature, let's say.

We do not know much about such matters, but we do know that those early lessons can be so well learned that they actually affect the body's chemistry. Children everywhere feel pangs of hunger at times of day appointed by the culture they are learning the ways of, and in a similar way children everywhere have been known to gag at the sight or smell of edibles their elders view with disgust, or salivate at the sight or smell of edibles their elders view as unusually tasty. Nor are we speaking of states of mind here. These are measurable physiological reactions. Whether one's mouth waters when looking at a serving of roasted beetles depends on the cultural setting in which one grows up. Whether one is struck by the beauty of someone whose forehead is a mass of self-induced scars also depends on cultural contexts. These are among the things a child learns in the early years without ever having been taught.

Let us turn now to two other bodies of knowledge that we are all exposed to early in life and remain a part of our basic social repertory for the rest of our time on earth. None of it is taught. Unless we stop to think about it, none of us even know that we know it.

On Learning a Language

One of those bodies of knowledge a child acquires early in life is language. Learning a first language is not like learning a second, as was evident in the case of those abandoned children, because the act of acquiring language is one of the ways children learn to perceive the world around them and to sort out information about it supplied them by the senses. The great psychologist William James, whom I have already mentioned more than once, wrote a century ago that the world children see when they first look out at it is a "blooming, buzzing confusion"—a swirl of commotion, a wash of colors, a blur of sounds. The young, he noted, have to learn how to pick individual details out of all that confusion. James of course knew that human infants who have not yet mastered language can nonetheless *see* and *hear* and *touch* things: they can make out shape and pattern, color and motion, texture and grain, and they can discriminate sounds of differing pitch and timbre. So can other animals that know nothing at all of the nature of language. But the young mind does not yet know how to order those varying sights and sounds into a coherent landscape, and it learns to do so at least in part by dividing the blur into discrete objects by creating concepts about them, by naming them. When we assign a name to something, we bracket it, set it apart from its background. In effect, we instruct our senses to freeze the moving scenery for a moment so that we can see or hear or smell or in some other way get a fix on a part of it. Walter Lippmann, a thoughtful commentator on the American political scene as well as on American culture more generally, put the matter flatly several decades ago: "For the most part we do not see and then define, we define and then see."

One of the most remarkable persons of our time was a woman named Helen Keller, who became both blind and deaf in infancy, a terrible combination. When still a child, she was placed in the care of another remarkable woman named Anne Sullivan who had been brought into the Keller household to see if she could find a way to reach through the wall of silence that surrounded the young Helen. Sullivan tried everything she could think of, and then one day, as Keller later remembered it:

> We walked down the path to the well-house, attracted by the fragrance of the honeysuckle with which it was covered. Someone was drawing water and my teacher placed my hand under the spout. As the cool stream splashed over one hand she spelled into the other the word *water,* first slowly, then rapidly. I stood still, my whole attention fixed upon the motion of her fingers. Suddenly I felt a misty consciousness as of something forgotten—the thrill of returning thought; and somehow the mystery of language was revealed to me. I knew then that "w-a-t-e-r" meant the wonderful cool something flowing over my hand. That living word awakened my soul, gave it light, hope, joy, set it free!...
>
> I left the well-house eager to learn. Everything had a name, and each name gave birth to a new thought. As we returned to the house every object which I touched seemed to quiver with life. That was because I saw everything with the strange new sight that had come to me.

This is a rare insight, for Keller was experiencing something that is normally known only to infants who are far too young to understand the process or to remember it. "Everything had a name, and each name gave birth to a new thought."

Adults are sometimes allowed a glimpse at that process. I can remember the day in a high-school biology class when I first *saw* the tiny organisms our teacher was pointing out in the blur of movement visible through a microscope. My vision had not been made sharper by that exercise, but my powers of discrimination had. I *saw* things that I simply could not make out but a moment earlier. Many persons reading this paragraph will remember, as I do, how difficult it was at first to make out particular words in the continuous flow of utterances that make up an unfamiliar language. Native speakers of a language do not produce words or sentences. They issue streams of sound, and it is the task of the listener to insert the pauses and the punctuations that break the stream into sentences and the sentences into words. The ear can only hear a flow. And once we have learned to make those discriminations—to see the organism, to recognize that "mamereesttresjolie" has to be re-heard as "ma mere est tres jolie"—we wonder why it took us so long in the first place.

That is how things are with children at first. They organize the world around them cognitively in the process of developing a vocabulary and learning a language. So language is not simply a means of communication. It is a way of sorting out the things of the world, of giving order to reality. Every human society, every language, accomplishes that task in a somewhat different way, and to that extent, organizes reality in a somewhat different way. It should be noted in passing, moreover, that most languages vary in usage, if only slightly, from one social class to another or from one region to another, and that those differences, too, will be reflected in the way speakers make sense of the world around them.

A fairly simple example, by now famous enough to rank as a stereotype, has to do with the manner in which the continuous materials of nature, spread across an unbroken vista, are divided into pieces of reality. There is a form of precipitation common to lands of the north that speakers of English know by a single term, "snow." Some English speakers (skiers, for instance) take into account that "snow" can have a number of different qualities, so they coin adjectives to mark the differences between them. People who live north of the Arctic Circle, however, use a number of different nouns to refer to the range of substances we gather into that broad designation "snow." These are not just variations on a common theme. They refer to realities as different in the experience of the people who live in those lands as grizzly bears and timber wolves are in ours, and their welfare depends on such discriminations. Hugh Brody, a wise and seasoned anthropologist, spent many years among the northern Inuit, and he notes that there are a number of terms in Inuktitut for what English speakers know simply as "snow."

> These include snow that is falling, fine snow in good weather, freshly fallen snow, snow cover, soft snow that makes walking difficult, soft snowbank, hard and crystalline snow, snow that has thawed and refrozen, snow that has been rained on, powdery snow, windblown snow, fine snow with which the wind has covered an object, hard snow that yields to the weight of footsteps, snow that is being melted to make drinking water, a mix of snow and water for glazing sledge runners, wet snow that is falling, snow that is drifting and snow that is right for snow house building.

This does not mean that speakers of English are forever destined to know a different reality than speakers of Inuktitut. You and I can presumably be taught the difference between one form of snow and another, as Hugh Brody himself was, and, moreover, we would not even have been able to make out the meaning of the comment above if we were not capable of making similar distinctions. Still, the language we speak does not equip us at first to "see" the northern landscape as the Inuit do. Our words do not parcel out the things of nature in that way. Speakers of English can journey across Europe translating "apple" into "pomme" and then into "apfel" or "manzana" or "mela" whenever they cross a national border without shifting into another mode of perceiving things, but that is not the case when they cross over an invisible border into the land of the Inuit, where there is no root word for "snow" and the white cover one can walk on easily has a different name than the white cover that makes walking more difficult. Brody also notes:

> The same principle applies to the words for fish in Inuktitut. There are terms to mean arctic char, arctic char that are running upstream, arctic char that are moving down to the sea, and arctic char that remain all year in the lake, as well as words for lake trout, salmon, and so on. There is no word that means "fish." Similarly, there are Inuktitut words for ringed seal, one-year-old ringed seal, adult mail ringed seal, harp seal, bearded seal, and so on. There is no word that means "seal."

That is the sense in which language helps us apprehend what the world out there looks like and feels like as well as the way it is spoken of.

Here is another example. If you take a child of four or five to see a giant redwood, stretching to the very skies, she will know it as a tree. If you show her a Japanese bonsai in a flower pot smaller than she is, she will also know it as a tree. That is a remarkable feat of abstraction. What features do those two growths share in common? How can a child know that they belong to the same category of being? Here is another child of four or five. Show him a Chihuahua—a scrawny, hairless creature, looking vaguely like a shaved rodent—and he will call it "doggy." Show him a Saint Bernard, a huge, shaggy, lumbering creature— to him the size of an adult buffalo—and he will call it "doggy." These children have no idea in the world why it makes botanical sense to place a redwood and a bonsai in the same class of living matter, or what anatomical similarities place a Chihuahua and a Saint Bernard in the same species. To be able to see across those enormous differences in size and shape and to recognize the kinship of such pairs as these is quite something. It is accomplished, at least in part, through the use of language, and at a very young age.

"Do you see yonder cloud that's almost in shape of a camel?" asks Hamlet. "By the mass, and 'tis like a camel indeed," Polonius replies. Hamlet: "Methinks it is like a weasel." Polonius: "It is backed like a weasel." Hamlet: "Or like a whale?" Polonius: "Very like a whale." Well, Hamlet is playing with Polonius here, and Polonius, in his turn, is trying to be agreeable. But something similar happens in real life as well. A cloud is but a cloud, a puff of mist, a bit of concentrated moisture. Many of the things of nature, though, are like clouds to the untutored eye, and it is the task of culture, the task of language, to give them identity and shape. And why? So that those who participate in a social order can experience them alike and coordinate their activities in respect to them.

The Pygmies of the Ituri Rain Forest offer another example of what we are dealing with here. The same Kenge who roused Moke from a deep sleep in the middle of the night once drove to the edge of the forest with Colin Turnbull, the anthropologist from whom we learned the story in the first place. Kenge had never been out in the open countryside, where the eye beholds an almost endless vista, because he had spent the whole of his life in the shelter of trees where it is rare to be able to see further than a few feet ahead. Turnbull pointed to a group of water buffalo grazing a mile or more away, and Kenge broke into laughter because he could only see a cluster of miniature creatures looking like ants a few yards from where he was. Kenge may have had the sharpest eyes in Africa, but they had never been trained to see things at a distance and to make the necessary allowances for assessing the true size of things. Objects that take up no more than a tiny fraction of one's field of vision are bound to seem tiny when one has no experience of horizons that extend any further than a clearing in the forest. The lens through which he was looking, then, was shaped by social and cultural criteria as well as by optical ones, and the same would be true if we were asked to see the shapes of the Ituri Rain Forest in the way Kenge did.

All this makes it easier to understand why those children raised in closets and attics were unable to see what we "sighted" people can. Their optic equipment was presumably in good working order, but it is the image in the mind and not the image on the retina that sees a Chihuahua and a Saint Bernard as creatures of the same kind or char moving upstream and char moving downstream as creatures of a different kind.

Mind you, I have drawn my examples of the process I am dealing with here from the simplest level possible—the way language helps us shape our perceptions of objects in the natural world. I do not even know how to speak of the way language helps us arrange the experiences of life into *moral* categories or into *aesthetic* ones. But I do assume that in the same way that language plays an important role in instructing the senses how to see objects out in the surrounding landscape, language plays an important role in helping us distinguish right from wrong, beautiful from ugly, tasteful from crass. This is not to say that the moral sense is a product *of* language, but to note that its forms have linguistic contour. Children have an understanding of much of this long before their first day of formal instruction. It is a mighty thing.

George Herbert Mead on Childhood Learning

Theorists who have thought about the nature of human development often divide the years of childhood into distinct developmental stages. Those schemes are quite different in their points of emphasis, but they share in common an interest in the inner life of children as they mature over time. A number of sociologists would add the name of George Herbert Mead (1863–1931) to that list. He was a philosopher and social psychologist who taught at the University of Chicago during the same years as the pioneer sociologists we met earlier. What made his approach distinct was that he was less interested in the way the young mind develops over time than in the way the social world out there works its way into the child's awareness. In that sense, the questions he raised lent themselves to the study of the social order more than to the study of the individual mind. Like many important theories, this one should be appreciated not for the technical accuracy of its observations but for its ability to open up new conceptual territory.

Mead suggested that children work their way through a sequence of phases as they grow. He did not see them as developmental stages in the child, as other theorists like Jean Piaget did, but he spoke of them as general periods through which young people pass.

The first is a time of *imitation*. Human toddlers are endowed with endless curiosity, as all young creatures appear to be, and as they develop better motor skills and learn more about the world around them, they not only watch carefully what others are doing but try to imitate it, either in imagination or in actual conduct. As often than not, they do not really know what the activities they are copying are meant to accomplish, so it is the shape and the rhythm of those activities rather than their formal content that the children are attracted to. A mother, deep in thought, hand cupped under her chin, looks over at her child and notices that he has assumed the same posture. He is not really *thinking* that intently. The time for deep reflection has not yet come for him. He is rehearsing, getting a feel for adult life. A father opens his newspaper, looks over at his child, and notices that she is staring at the real estate section. She is not *reading*. She might not even know what that is. She is practicing an adult activity. And much the same thing happens, we may assume, when children are first exposed to the gestures and mannerisms appropriate to the culture or class or gender they are a part of—the spacing of an encounter, for example, or how loudly one is invited to talk.

The second is a time of *play*. I pointed out earlier that play may be the most serious work an individual is ever asked to do, and an important part of that work is to act out the roles of other people one encounters in the course of everyday life—parents, teachers, mail carriers, physicians—or characters of an altogether different kind one meets on television screens, in books, or on the shelves of a toy store. In one sense, playing the part of somebody else or something else is scarcely more than an advanced form of imitation, developing a feel for social life by copying the mechanics of adult behavior. In another sense, however, it can be a great deal more. Mead called this "taking the role of the other," and he meant by the term that children are not only learning the outer contours of the behavior of others but trying to enter the minds of those others in an effort to imagine what life must be like for them. In doing so, Mead added, they are also imagining what *they* must look like to the people whose roles they are playing.

This is a very abstract activity. We are speaking of small children here, quite early in the process of becoming social, who see themselves as objects in someone else's line of vision. When children, talking about themselves, announce solemnly that "Sammy is tired" or "Mary wants a glass of water," they are looking at themselves in the way they sense that others are looking at them. Those expressions can take on moral overtones, too. "Mary is a b-a-d girl," she says of herself in a disapproving tone of voice, perhaps wagging her finger for emphasis. "No, Sammy mustn't do that," says he, slapping himself slightly on the wrist. The voice is borrowed from someone else, but the subject is oneself. The child is learning who she is or how he should act by looking at the image they see reflected in the eyes of other persons. Charles Horton Cooley, a contemporary of Mead's, called this "the looking glass self."

The third is a time of *games*. In play, Mead suggested, children act out the ways of other people, and in doing so see a reflection of themselves. But games are a good deal more complicated and involve a different form of rehearsal for life in society. Play is improvisation. Games, on the other hand, involve sets of rules that have to be observed by all the participants if the activity is to work at all. Mead thought that games were perfect miniatures of society, the master metaphors of social life. In his view, a game can only be played successfully— the social life can only be conducted successfully—when everyone involved plays the roles of everyone else in that social scene simultaneously. Mead found baseball to be an especially compelling example of what he had in mind, but readers more familiar with cricket or soccer or some other complex game can transpose as necessary. A ground ball is hit toward the shortstop, whose name, we will say, is Tinker. Tinker must keep his eye on the ball in order to field it, but, even so, he can "see" what everyone else on the field of play is doing. The first baseman—Chance, say—is moving in one direction, while the second baseman—Evers—is moving in another. And if there are runners from the other team on base as all this is going on, Tinker senses what they are up to as well. This is a very intricate choreography. Mead supposed that Tinker is able to keep track of all this movement not just because he understands the flow of the game so well intellectually but because he is playing everyone else's position in his own mind even as he plays his own. He knows what Evers is doing because he knows what *he* would be doing if he were in Evers's shoes. He knows what the runner coming down the base path is doing because he has been there himself. In other words, said Mead, Tinker is mentally playing every position in the field—taking the role of all those other players—as he focuses on the task before him. And when he picks up the ball hit in his direction, he turns toward the spot where his teammates are expecting it to be thrown even before he directs his gaze there because he can count on them to act as he would have if he had been in their position. Even though he was looking the whole time at the ball coming his way, the play had taken shape, as it were, before his eyes. And the same thing has been happening, meantime, to everyone else involved as well. This may sound a bit mystical, but it is a relatively simple—and a very human—process.

The baseball game, Mead suggested, serves as an excellent analogy for the workings of social life everywhere. We know the roles of all the other players in our immediate world because we identify with them, can imagine ourselves in their places, and thus have an idea how they will behave in the social arena. That does not mean that we can take their places, of course, or even do a plausible job of impersonating them. It only means that each of us has a sense of who the people around us are and where they stand in the social order. And that is how *we* know who we are and where we stand in the social order as well. Robert Burns once wrote a famous couplet:

> O wad some Pow'r the giftie gie us
> To see oursels as others see us!

Burns was musing about a mental process quite different than the one we are dealing with here—he was watching a louse making its way up the back of a woman's bonnet as he sat behind her in a church pew—but Mead would suggest not only that we *do* have that power but that the workings of the social order depend on it. Since we are able to imagine what the world looks like from the vantage point of others, we have at least a basic understanding of how we look to them. That, Mead thought, is how we develop a sense of self, how we learn to situate ourselves in the dance of life. It works somewhat like radar (although Mead, who developed these thoughts a century ago or more, knew nothing of that invention). We humans send exploratory probes out into the social world around us, and we learn from the signals that bounce back both where we stand in relation to everyone else and what we look like to them. We learn to see ourselves as others see us (if not always accurately).

So children have mastered a considerable body of knowledge before their formal education even begins. The process of socialization continues into the years of schooling and all the other experiences that contribute to the shaping of the young. But we will pause for a moment to raise three last-minute thoughts before we move ahead.

First, I suggested a few pages ago that Mead should be understood as a philosopher offering us an abstract metaphor on social life rather than as an ethnographer offering us a report on child play. It seems quite unlikely that he spent very many afternoons observing children like those of Kasia and Piotr in playgrounds not far from his university office in South Chicago. That was not what inspired him to write about the shape of child play or about carefully choreographed baseball games. But he was a colleague of Thomas, Znaniecki, and other Chicago sociologists who were then studying the nature of contemporary social life, and he was surely aware that the rules of "the game" were different in the black ghettos that were already beginning to take form near the center of the city, or in the affluent suburbs like Lake Forest that were then appearing at the outer edges of the city. And, of course, the same would have been the case if we added Boston's West End, the mountain hollows of Appalachia, Ohio's New Burlington, or any of the communities we have encountered in the book so far.

Second, even in places where the rules seem to be widely shared, there are always those who want to conform but find that a difficult course to follow—who drift off into worlds of their own, who never quite know how to shift into the same gears as others, who can never quite understand how Tinkers and Evers and Chance were able to pull it off. They tend to be few in number, and in our society they are likely to be diagnosed as suffering from a form of mental disorder.

But many persons who can be said to deviate from the score do so as a matter of choice, and they tend to be every bit as familiar with the score as their compliant fellows—if not more so. She who quietly opposes or actively resists a set of rules is likely to have a clear sense of what they are. He who dissents from the ways of his community or his society knows them particularly well. Those who rebel or withdraw usually know the lay of the land they want to leave behind, the ways of the society they want to replace. Conflict, too, takes place within a network of rules and expectations. Among those who develop a particularly keen sense of the "role of the other" are antagonists in other forms of engagement, or anyone else trying to anticipate the moves of an adversary. Joseph Conrad put the point beautifully in his 1916 novel *The Secret Agent*. His two adversaries were a knowledgeable police officer and an experienced criminal, and he portrays them as "making countermoves in the same game." "Products of the same machine, the one classified as useful and the other as noxious, they take the machine for granted in different ways, but with a seriousness essentially the same." To comply and to dissent, to conform and to rebel, to accept and to reject, to be an ally or an adversary, all take place within an arena that is itself at least somewhat scripted.

Third, and more important by far for our purposes: Mead drew his conclusions from the realm of abstract reasoning rather than from the realm of actual observation, as we noted a few moments ago, and we can say now that he vastly underestimated the degree to which both the play of early childhood and the games of later childhood involve a considerable amount of testing and experimenting with the teachings of the adult world. That was true even in Mead's day, long before the age of television and other mass media—never mind video games, cell phones, and all the other forms of social networking available now. What happens in the playgrounds of our time, we learn from William Corsaro and others, is even more unlike what Mead imagined. Children of an early age come together in playgrounds and other gathering places with a shared sense of how things are and how things ought to be—the basic score, we can say—and they act it out, develop a feel for it, in play and in games. It is a form of rehearsal, in one sense—a way of coming to terms with that script. But this is not a docile acceptance of those lessons from the adult world, a dutiful recital of them. It is a time of improvisation and innovation and even invention at the same time, an adaptation that draws on both the teachings of the elders and the learning that comes from being a part of what Cordero calls the "peer culture."

Becoming a Person Yet Again

Learning the score is a life-long process. It begins the day of one's birth and is at its most intense in the early years of childhood. The human career in modern times, however, often presents situations in which persons have to become adjusted to radically different life circumstances—so much so that the experience looks and feels like becoming a person all over again. This process is known in the social sciences as "resocialization" or "secondary socialization" or "adult socialization," and it refers to the urgent need, usually in adulthood, to learn to move to an altogether different set of social rhythms. Throughout human history, individuals have had to weather abrupt transitions as they move through a familiar round of life from its beginning to its end— graduating from childhood to adulthood, for example, and from a single state to a married one. But these transitions are part of a predictable sequence, and they are celebrated by rites of passage that mark their location in the procession of the life cycle. The forest people whom Moke and Kenge lived among or the farming people of Kasia and Piotr's time knew lives of such continuity that the very thought of becoming a person all over again would rarely if ever come to mind.

This process can take a number of different forms. It will be useful for our purposes here to distinguish two. The first is when persons move across cultural or national borders and have to come to terms with new customs, new ways of life, and, often, new languages. We saw a fairly extended example of this when we traced Piotr and Kasia's journey from a village in Poland to a neighborhood in South Chicago. The second is when persons remain within the same social and cultural universe but find themselves in the position of having to move, often on short notice, from familiar surroundings to unfamiliar ones—either because they elect to or because they have to. I am not just speaking here of shifts in occupation or in residence, but of being wrenched out of familiar social niches into spheres in which one feels alone and alien. One hears stories every day of families that have lived for generations on farmlands that now need to be abandoned, of individuals from every walk of life who fall out of the bottom of things and find themselves homeless or abandoned or without any real sense of belonging to the world they grew up in. Such changes can be profoundly traumatic for those who experience them, naturally, but the shock and the disorientation that follows is made all the more complicated by the fact that the persons involved now have to find their way across a largely unfamiliar social terrain.

The reverse trip can require wrenching readjustments too. To move out of the ranks of the homeless into the ranks of the steadily employed can be a joyous thing, but it is easily forgotten that offices and industrial plants and wheat fields and construction sites are social worlds with their own customs and codes that have to be learned like any other.

Lost in Translation

Eva Hoffman was born in Kraków, Poland, in 1946, and emigrated to North America at the age of 13. She became a remarkably perceptive writer in her new language, English, and so has found a way to pass on to us telling insights into the process by which somebody with a distinctly Polish sensibility, expressed in a distinctly Polish cadence, shifted over into a new reality as she learned a different language and a different way of seeing things. It was not easy, as we learn from a memoir entitled *Lost in Translation: A Life in a New Language.*

Unlike Kasia and Piotr Walkowiak, who arrived in the new world from Poland half a century earlier, Eva's family settled into what was for them the unfamiliar cultural milieu of Western Canada. Her landing was not cushioned, as the Walkowiaks' had been, by living in a Polish-speaking neighborhood as she began to learn the rhythms of the new world. It is reasonable to guess that the Hoffmans spoke Polish at mealtimes and in moments of family leisure during the early years of their time in Vancouver, but Eva had to relate to everybody else in her immediate surrounding by the use of English words. She had no trouble learning the dictionary meaning of what to her were unfamiliar, lifeless words. Indeed, she may have known their meaning far better than most native speakers who absorb them thoughtlessly in childhood. But the use of those terms resulted in what she later called a sharp "disconnect" with "the forms of the world" in the "here and now." She felt as though she was in "exile," by which she did not mean separation from homeland—which is of course what emigration had done to her—but being separated from reality, from the human community altogether.

At first, she thought in Polish, which is to say visualized in Polish, sensed in Polish, but the words that made up her reality were not easily translated into other terms. Learning that the English word for the piece of furniture on which one eats breakfast is "table" does not do it. Those words are not replaceable labels—we shall henceforth call this "a table"—but sounds, expressions, that give the object its life and its true nature.

Let's say that we are walking with her to the edge of a body of water flowing in easy curves along a valley floor. "What is that?" we may ask by way of testing her knowledge of English. "River," she says without a trace of hesitation. And what do they call it in Polish? we ask, and she provides what is for us an unpronounceable sound. But we are missing the point. For her, "the words I learn now don't stand for things in the same unquestioned way they did in my native tongue." The word for river in her Polish

> was a vital sound, energized with the essence of riverhood, of my rivers, of my being immersed in rivers. "River" in English is cold—a word without an aura. . . . It does not evoke.

The new term cannot substitute for the old. It cannot reflect the same reality that the old one did. And for that very reason, the old words simply disappear—"atrophy," "shrivel" are the English words she selects when trying to convey to us later what that experience was like. When she looks at "a river," she is looking through a lens formed by the new word: "it is not shaped, it remains a thing, absolutely other, absolutely unbending to the grasp of my mind." And she later adds, "this radical disjoining between word and thing drains the world not only of significance but of its colors, striations, nuances—its very existence. It is the loss of a living connection." The "problem is that the signifier has become severed from the signified."

In Vancouver still, the Hoffman family has a brief visit with a neighboring family. Vocabulary, again, is not the problem. Eva knows what words mean. Afterwards, though, "my mind gropes for some description" of the people she just visited,

> but nothing fits. They're a distant species from anyone I've met in Poland, and Polish words slip off them without sticking. English words do not stick onto anything. Kindly or silly? The words float in an uncertain space. They come from a part of my brain in which labels may be manufactured but which has no connections to my instincts, quick reactions, knowledge. . . . A verbal blur covers these people's faces, their gestures, with a sort of fog. I can't translate them in my mind's eye.

There is the language of spacing to learn as well, and Hoffman remembers: "I learn my reserve from people who take a step back when we talk, because I'm standing too close, crowding them. Cultural distances are different, I later learn in a sociology class, but I know that already."

Looking back at her experiences in Vancouver, she recalls that "it was here that I fell out of the net of meaning into the weightlessness of chaos . . . an infuriating beating against wordlessness, against the incapacity to make oneself understood, seen." Speaking later of a time then long past, she remembers realizing: "This language is beginning to invent another me." She was becoming a person yet again.

> How does one stop reading the exterior signs of a foreign tribe and step into the inwardness, the viscera of their meanings? Every anthropologist understands the difficulty of such a feat, and so does every immigrant.

It should go without saying that we have been listening to a remarkably gifted informant here, sensitive to the *feel* of words in a way that most persons who share the experience she is describing are not. So this is a rare look into an important matter, and if she expresses a stronger sense of urgency than most of us would, that makes the message all the clearer and sharper.

Total Institutions

Among the most difficult transitions from one social circumstance to another in our society are those that occur when persons are removed from accustomed places in the social order and transferred into establishments that require a marked shift in patterns of life from them. One of the most remarkable sociologists of the past century, Erving Goffman, called these "total institutions." They are *total* because they separate individuals from the rest of society and because they provide a setting in which most of the activities of everyday life take place. People eat and sleep and work there; they play and worship there; they carry on all the other undertakings of life there. Prominent examples in our society would include prisons, mental hospitals, and religious retreats such as convents and monasteries. Some of these institutions—prisons, for example—are involuntary. Others, like religious orders, are not only voluntary but sometimes eagerly sought. The movement of individuals into and out of these places provides a sharply-etched portrayal of the process of becoming a person once again, and I will discuss it in some detail now not only because it is an important and telling aspect of social life but because it can serve—here comes that word again—as a parable, a defining instance of less drastic versions of the process.

Total institutions operate by different assumptions and rules than is the case for other establishments in the social world around them, and to that extent they are like enclosures within a larger countryside. When newcomers enter those enclosures the gates seem to close behind them—literally in the case of prison inmates, symbolically in the case of individuals taking religious orders. They are about to pass through a kind of decompression chamber in which they will be divested of old habits and ways, old roles and identities, and issued new ones better suited to the reality they are about to enter. The purpose of the decompression chamber is not simply to transform the newcomer from one kind of social being to another—from citizen to convict, from schoolgirl to nun, or, to add another example, from civilian to soldier—but to effect a major change in the way the newcomer thinks and behaves.

During that period, the newcomer is dispossessed ("stripped" was the term Goffman used) of most of the outward markers of self—clothes, hair styles, jewelry, and sometimes even names. They are given standard haircuts and issued standard clothing so that they will begin life in the new setting looking as alike as possible in at least those respects. In some religious orders, initiates are given new names altogether, but even in prisons and military posts, where new arrivals retain their civilian names, they are issued identification numbers that serve as designations every bit as important as names.

Goffman called this "mortification," and like so many of the terms he drew from his extraordinary vocabulary, it has more than one meaning. To "mortify" means to humiliate, to reduce in stature, and that is certainly one of the purposes of the stripping process, even if the reasons for humbling somebody about to enter prison are different from the reasons for humbling somebody about to enter holy orders. To mortify also means to subject somebody to disciplinary austerities, which fits the case here as well. And, finally, to mortify means to "deface" people, to remove the identifying features—hair styles, clothing, adornments—that give them individuality in look and expression.

The mortification process serves several purposes, the most important of them being to place the newcomer in a different master status. For a while, at least, the fact that you are now a convict or an inmate or a postulant over-shadows the other identities that once situated you in the social order. The questions "who are you?" or "what are you?" can no longer be satisfactorily answered by declaring that "I am a Martinez woman" or "I am a mechanic." Those things continue to be the case, of course, but they are simply not that relevant to one's present circumstance. They have slipped into insignificance beneath the dominating fact that one is now something else. Old identities have been filed away to clear a place for the new.

Entering a total institution also involves a symbolic filing away of one's past. Most of us in the everyday world have a good deal of control over the histories that other people know us by, if only because we supply most of the details that those histories are composed of. Kinfolk and schoolmates may embarrass us now and them by dredging up episodes that seem to us better forgotten, but for the most part we are the editors of our own life stories— who we are, where we come from, what has happened to us, and the like. We cannot create new biographical details out of thin air without running the risk of exposure, of course, but we can be selective in what we tell others or include in our dossiers. We are not required to tell others about our most shameful or discreditable moments. That is why I call us *editors* of our life stories rather than *authors*. I must be careful not to stray too far from established fact when I tell you where I was born or how celebrated an athlete I was, but I do not need to tell you about the times I wet my bed or was cruel to my sister or entertained thoughts that might give you reason to wonder how moral or how sane a person I really am. In a prison or mental hospital, however, those are precisely the moments from a life history that matter the most, and the files those institutions keep contain details of just that kind. The dossiers found in mental hospitals will normally focus on times when patients were out of control or hallucinating or being abusive to others, and are not very likely to include information on times when patients exhibited particular competence or behaved in ways that brought them credit. The life histories found in penitentiaries, too, will usually focus on the times when inmates engaged in illegal activity and are not likely to pay attention to the hours and days and years they spent working at jobs, raising children, repairing leaking faucets, and living like everyone else. The sheer fact that a person is now imprisoned or hospitalized, that is, selects out the facts that become relevant to his or her biography.

In general, then, when we undergo important transitions in the flow of our lives we go through a process from which we are likely to emerge changed— acting a bit differently, thinking a bit differently, and having a somewhat revised sense of who we are. For most of us, the process is nowhere near as dramatic as the one experienced by persons on their way to prisons or convents or some other kind of total institution, but the two paths are parallel nonetheless.

Students who enter college from very different life conditions will know what this process is all about, even if the transition they experience is a fairly tame specimen of the genus.

I plan now to provide two examples of the process I have been describing here, not only because they tell us something about this feature of social life, but because, once again, they serve as defining instances of a broader pattern. The first is a description of what can happen when someone leaves civilian society behind and becomes a member of one of the armed forces. It is based on my experience of many years ago, so it is not an accurate look at the modern military, but it illustrates a form of learning found everywhere. The second is a description of what can happen when someone leaves prison behind after a long period of incarceration and tries to re-enter normal social life. It is the story of a man named Harry King who decided to abandon a long career as a safecracker to join what he called "square-John" society. It, too, is of a time long past.

Becoming a Soldier: The Informal Grammar of Military Life

Compared to entering a monastery or a prison, induction into one of the armed forces appears to be a relatively modest business. Recruits are not being asked to shift into a new cultural setting in any important sense of the term, and most of them do not intend to remain there for more than a few years. They are not being required to learn new languages, either (although their vocabulary is likely to be enlarged in other ways!). Their private beliefs and values will remain for the most part unexamined. Yet the dominating assumption of "basic training" or "boot camp" is that those who undertake it might have to go into combat in a relatively short period of time, so it is a very serious matter. Changes of one's inner being are not being asked for, then, but a sizable readjustment of the way one acts and thinks is.

Induction into the army has much in common with the initiation processes of other total institutions, so it fits the pattern of "mortification" described by Goffman well. Basic training involves an abrupt removal from old and familiar surroundings, an interruption of careers either anticipated or under way, and a separation from all those other persons who constitute one's immediate surround. Old decorations of self (what Goffman called one's "identity kit") are systematically stripped away in military settings as they are in monastic and in

penal ones: civilian clothing that reflects a person's individual taste or personality is replaced by institutional clothing that does not, hair styles are cropped
from the heads of the newly arrived with about as much ceremony as fleece is
shorn from the flanks of sheep.

When recruits first enter the army, they usually busy themselves trying to
learn the rules governing what for most of them is a largely unfamiliar terrain.
There are regulations to memorize and skills to learn: how to make one's bed in
the approved army way, how to march in unison, how to disassemble and reas-
semble a rifle, how to stand and walk and eat and dress, how to act when an
officer comes into view. In the early days of basic training, then, it is a matter
of learning what we might call the *formal grammar* of army life, how to live *by
the book*. That experience is hardly unique to military camps, of course, so as
you ponder this account remember that it is meant to serve as a parable of social
life in general as well as the story of a particular setting in the larger human
scene.

After a time, however, recruits come to a slow but sure realization that they
are not actually expected to live by the book. The formal grammar of military
life is impossible to observe all the time. You cannot regularly make beds so
taut that coins bounce on them, no matter how sharply you are instructed to do
so. You cannot always shine boots so well that drill instructors see their reflections in them. You cannot always stand at attention for the length of time you
are ordered to. You cannot react to every one of the directions that pour over
you by the hour. So you have to develop a feel somehow for what is crucial and
what is not. You have to learn where slack is to be found in the system, where a
certain slippage is tolerated. You have to figure out for yourself when an order
means something exact and when it means something broader and more diffuse.
You soon realize, in short, that there is an *informal grammar* of military life as
well. It is not taught. It is not found in regulations. It is not even part of a folklore that can be passed from one generation to another, because the waves of
recruits who preceded you to camp and learned those lessons before you have
moved on to other destinations. But it is there all the same, a sense of how
things are, and newcomers have no choice but to learn it for themselves. They
must discover how to hear the *hidden* language in the process of listening to the
surface language.

In the introduction to this book, I wrote briefly of the time I worked with a
research team studying army squads that had lost one of their members to a

psychiatric ward. I was struck then by the fact that the soldiers diagnosed as psychotic by medical officials seemed to share an inability to move from the formal grammar of army life to the informal grammar. They were living by the book, trying to act precisely as they were told to. A drill sergeant said to one of them, "I want you to scrub that floor until your knuckles bleed," and was then at a complete loss for words when he realized that the recruit was trying to do just that. "I want you to forget about home and concentrate on bayonet practice," said another, and was then dumbfounded when the recruit to whom he said it went into a severe panic because the harder he tried to concentrate on the project of forgetting home the more readily images of home flooded into his mind.

The irony here is that doing exactly as one is told—following instructions down to the last detail, interpreting the words spoken to one as meaning exactly what the dictionary says they do—almost qualifies as a symptom of mental disorder! These recruits appeared disturbed at least in part because they could not do what their fellow squad members could: to understand what is written in the spaces between lines, hear what is said in the silences between utterances, and, in general, sense the lay of the land in ways that no travel account or map or set of regulations can.

The main point to be made here, whether one is speaking of "becoming a person" in the early years or repeating some part of that process later, is that members of a society live by an informal grammar. When children first try to learn the score, their minds have not yet fully matured and their command of the language is not yet complete, so it makes sense to suppose that the learning process may be a bit blurred because the mind going through it is not fully formed. The striking thing about this, however, is that the sanest and most mature of adults go through a process that is every bit as vague. When we are taught a new rule, we soon learn how wide a range of variation other people will tolerate around that mean. When we adopt a new way to behave, we learn how close our approximation must be to the model being set. We are dealing with a very complex matter here.

Examples are almost by definition hard to come by, since our topic is the indistinct edges of social norms rather than their logical centers. Every baseball player knows that the strike zone in any given game is established by the perceptions of the umpire rather than by diagrams drawn in official rulebooks. Every motorist knows that the prevailing speed limit on any given highway has more to do with common sense and the habits of patrolling police officers than it does with posted rules. How many students read every word of the material assigned them with equal attention? Or arrive at every class at exactly the appointed time? To go back to the strike zone: baseball players who think only of official diagrams when at bat are not only playing the game poorly but acting illogically. Drivers who stick doggedly to the posted speed limits no matter what the flows of traffic around them are running a real risk. Students who do everything by the book, who understand only the formal grammar of academic life, are making their lives a great deal harder than is necessary and may even be drawing attention to themselves.

That, too, is part of learning the score. And I will close this discussion by leaving a question floating in the air overhead: How much of that kind of learning is reflected in the way children play and the way they participate in games?

Going Straight

So far, we have been dealing with the processes that occur when people are removed from the larger social order and confined to total institutions. It should be obvious by now that this kind of transition is generally accompanied by large shifts in behavior and mind-set. What may not be so obvious, however, is that to transfer into a prison or monastery or some other kind of total institution can require so complete an unlearning of old habits and ways—so complete a renunciation of old identities—that it becomes difficult to adjust again to the realities of what most people call "normalcy." I am going to tell the story of a career felon who went through exactly that experience. This is an unusual example of what I have called "becoming a person once again" or "resocialization," so it, too, can be seen as an exaggerated sample of a process found throughout the social order.

I will introduce my point, though, by relating the experiences of a group of women who returned to secular life after a period in holy orders. They had been novices when they entered a convent, of course, but they found to their surprise that they were novices all over again when they decided to rejoin society at large. They had expected to feel somewhat at sea when dealing with a world where people were involved in courtship rituals, competed for advantage in the workplace, and negotiated paths for themselves through the intricacies of social life. They knew they were inexperienced in such realms. But they did not expect that their most immediate problems would revolve around tiny things. They were returning to the same social setting from which they had originally come, but they did not know—and could not have known—how much learning they had missed by taking leave of it for a while. They did not know how to shop or dance or handle money or engage in idle chatter. One entered a clothing store: "The salesgirl asked what size I wore, and I just stared at her. I didn't know!" Another went for a job interview: "He asked me what salary I wanted, and I didn't know anything about that." A third was sitting in a tavern for what may have been the first time in her life when the bartender approached: "'What'll you have,' he said, and I couldn't answer. I didn't know one drink from another."

There are sadder tales than that to be told of persons leaving total institutions for life in the "real" world. Of former mental patients who are so uncertain how to act and what to say in the places they now find themselves that they look unbalanced and out of touch with reality even when entirely recovered from their illnesses. Of returning soldiers who feel so disoriented in civilian life that they drift off into homelessness or alcoholism or somewhere else out there on the margins of society without anyone understanding that their problem is one of social adjustment and not one of personal instability.

The story of Harry King is a sad one as well. He was born in the first decade of the 20th century and died in the early 1970s. He was a safecracker by profession, a "box man," and as is the case for most individuals who follow such a trade, he spent a good part of his adult life in prison. The story he narrates about his career as a felon is a relic of times past, so it does not offer a reliable portrayal of the criminal world as it exists now. But the experiences he went through when he tried to return to normal life are exactly as we would find them today. A sociologist named William J. Chambliss met Harry, became his friend, and recorded his life history. The account was edited by Chambliss and appeared in a book that was originally entitled *Box Man: A Professional Thief's Journey,* and was reissued a few years later with the title *Harry King: A Professional Thief's Journey.*

Harry King began his career in crime as a boy, and so was a fifty-year veteran of that way of life when he concluded that the time had come to join "square-John society." He had just completed a five-year sentence in the penitentiary—the "slammer," the "joint"—and did not himself understand where the urge to convert had come from. For Harry, going straight was almost like migrating to a foreign country. It was a move for which he quickly realized that he was poorly equipped. As a psychological matter, he had no feel for it. As a visceral matter, he drew no pleasure from it. As a moral matter, he felt no respect for it. And as a technical matter, he had no idea how to go about it. Like the former nuns we met a moment ago, much of the problem lay in details. In handling money, for example. "I never had any true evaluation of money," he said into Chambliss's tape recorder: "It meant nothing. I can remember when I would pay $250 for a suit of clothes [make that $1,500 in today's money] and get them all greasy and throw them away. I didn't care."

> It's real hard for a thief to plan what you call by the month. If I got a buck in my pocket then I spend the buck. If I ain't got it, then I look around for one. You're trained that way for years. . . . That's why we go broke.

Harry had tried to go straight a few years earlier, so he had advance notice of what it would be like:

> I believe I would have gone straight then if so many people hadn't tried so hard to help me. This is hard to explain. It seemed like every time I turned around they were trying to help me. Nothing could I do for myself. It was "Harry, open a bank account." I couldn't understand why I must have a bank account. I could go straight without a bank account just as easy as I could with one. So I opened a bank account to please them, but it didn't make sense to me. It was "Harry, do this; Harry, do that; Harry, don't associate with this kind; Harry, don't associate with that kind."

So he gave up the effort and was soon back in "the joint." When he was released five years later Harry did go straight, even though, as we shall see, the effort was not without difficulty or pain. He came out of prison thinking that the ideal niche for him in society would have been to serve as a mentor to people like himself—to teach them what he had learned. It was a wonderful idea. He knew things that the pooled wisdom of all the criminologists on earth could not have matched, and he would have been a great tutor to other ex-convicts trying to make the same transition he was.

It was not to happen that way. But I am going to let Harry complete the story in his own words (although the excerpts below are not necessarily presented in the same order as they are in his narrative) because he was wholly correct to suppose that he could explain the nature of the problem we are talking about here better than anyone else.

He wanted to be a teacher. He will be ours now.

When a guy comes out of an institution, especially an old-timer, adjustment to society and what you call a normal life is extremely hard for him. I don't feel that the process sets in for about three months after he gets out. Then he begins to look around. . . . He's trying to understand everything and do everything at one time. He's trying to do his job and get rehabilitated at the same time, and it can't be done very easily so he gets nervous, irritable, and he's tired all the time mentally— maybe not physically, but mentally he's tired all the time.

You must remember that, as a professional criminal, I was not a member of society, was not accepted by society, was rejected by it. So now I have to turn around and change my way of thinking and learn to think the way the people of society do.

I couldn't get adjusted properly. I still thought in black and white. There was no grey, no "perhaps" or "maybe." You do or you don't, that's all there was to it. No in-between of any kind. You liked a person or you didn't like him. I still thought like a criminal. . . . Believe me, there's nothing harder in the world to understand than square-John people. I understand my people. They're a bunch of bums. I know it and they know it, but I don't understand square-Johns.

When I used to steal, why we'd go and visit other thieves, my old lady and I, and we'd visit some other thief and his old lady and maybe there'd be six people then. And we'd sit up there and cut up—what we call "old touches," that's a phrase for discussing old capers, "cutting up old touches"—and we would get a great kick out of it. . . . And I cannot honestly say that I have found anything to laugh about since I became a square-John. Everything's been so serious where I used to laugh a lot. I laughed when I fooled the bulls. I laughed when I pulled a good caper. I'd laugh when I'd sit with friends of mine and talk, and I was happy-go-lucky. But since I turned square-John, why it's been all serious. It's been fighting to under-stand and do like they do. I don't know.

Harry's story has a sad ending. He committed suicide not long after the last of these tapes were recorded. But we don't need so dramatic an ending to emphasize how hard it can be to make the kind of transition Harry had in mind. He spoke the language of the country he wanted to enter and knew its ways, but he simply did not know how to act like the people he hoped to join or think like them or understand what made them happy. In some ways, at least, he was as much a stranger as Moke or Kenge would have been. And in some ways he may have been more of one, because the people he lived among and wanted to join had no way of knowing how strange they seemed to him and thus it never occurred to them to make allowances for that fact.

Creating Divisions

THE FIRST *HOMO SAPIENS* TO STRIDE ACROSS the plains of Africa must have been a rather homogeneous lot. At close range, obviously, the males of the species could be distinguished from the females, and it may have been evident to an onlooker who cared about such things that the human animal, compared to most other creatures who occupied the same landscape, remained immature for a longer span of time near the beginning of the life cycle and lost a good deal of its vigor and endurance as it neared the end. Beyond those contrasts in gender and age, however, distinctions within the human population were few, of little moment, and difficult to detect.

The hunting and gathering life was a spare one. However hard or easy their lives may have been in other respects, people in constant motion are not able to store food in any quantity as a hedge against leaner times, nor are they able to accumulate possessions of the kind that more stationary people learn to view as valuable. So differentials in what we now call "wealth" can only have been very small. Differentials of *any* kind must have been very small, for that matter: members of the band ate the same food, wore the same clothes, slept in the same shelters, were expected to perform more or less the same tasks, and were caught up in the same daily rounds.

That, clearly, is no longer the case. The recent history of our species is in large part a chronicle of the ways in which we have learned to locate ourselves in a whole latticework of classes, estates, orders, and other differentials—none of them having any counterpart in the world of nature. They are all human inventions.

These distinctions are of two quite different but overlapping kinds. The first is the way human beings arrange themselves into hierarchies and gradations based on rank. Every society on record that can be said to have had reserves of wealth and power has allocated them in that manner. Sociologists often call this process *stratification,* having borrowed the term from geology, where it refers to beds of sedimentary rock forming one atop another in layers.

The second has to do with the way human beings sort themselves into other divisions based on gender, occupation, lifestyle, race, and the like. We will call that *differentiation* here. The layers in a stratified structure involve ranking as a matter of definition: lord and commoner, owner and worker, captain and seaman, Brahmin and untouchable. The units in a differentiated structure, however, do not. To distinguish women from men, cobblers from weavers, Croats from Serbs, or Virgos from Aquarians, does not of and by itself assign them to positions in a hierarchy—although, as we shall see, it certainly seems to turn out that way a lot of the time.

I used the term *social geography* in an earlier chapter when we were speaking of the various currents that draw human populations from one place to another. I was dealing at that point with the ways we humans distribute ourselves across *physical* space—patterns of settlement, say, that are quite visible to the eye. But we are dealing now with the ways we humans distribute ourselves across *social* space—patterns involving distinctions that only the mind can see. The two geographies obviously have a decisive influence on each other. Racial prejudices form in the mind, for example, but they result in patterns of residential segregation so easy to see that they may even be visible in those distant reaches where the orbiting stranger keeps a wary eye on our odd comings and goings.

Strata

Some of the things a society comes to value are in limited supply as a matter of fact—parcels of land, heads of livestock, measures of grain, ounces of gold—and for that reason are treated as scarce. Other things a people come to value, however—prestige, honor—are in unlimited supply so far as mother nature is concerned, but they, too, are treated as scarce and rationed accordingly.

If the Queen is so impressed by a service you have done the crown that she awards you a tract of land or a chest full of gold sovereigns, she is giving you something of defined value. She has enlarged your share of the world's finite store of wealth. But if she awards you a knighthood or a titular honor of some other sort, she is giving you something that has no immediate monetary worth at all. She has the authority to issue as many knighthoods as she thinks the merits of her subjects warrant, yet it is quite clear to her, as it would be to anyone, that granting too many honors of that kind debases their currency in almost the same way that printing too much script does the coin of the realm. The value of the title, like the value of the land and the gold, depends on its relative scarcity.

When social scientists talk about "stratification," they are pointing to the process by which things of both tangible and intangible value are apportioned throughout the social order—knighthoods as well as gold sovereigns, status as well as property, power as well as possessions. If there is one rule of thumb that that can be applied throughout the whole of the human universe, it is that things of value are distributed unequally. Andy Warhol may have been correct to suppose that life will afford every one of us fifteen minutes of fame (and whatever leverage comes with that), but the blunt reality is that power in the social order—and especially in our own—is concentrated in the upper levels of the class structure and is largely absent at the lower levels.

That finding is so general, in fact, that it was once argued in sociological circles that inequality must be a natural feature of human society, built into the very fabric of social life. The logic of that line of thought was that inequalities in wealth and honor are essential to the workings of the social order because they assure that persons of ability will be motivated to move into positions of responsibility. Few if any sociologists take the proposition seriously now. It never did make any sense. Most persons of ability would rather be a prime minister than a scullery maid no matter what the difference in take-home pay or in benefits, so why would inducements be required there? And even if that were not the case, why would the CEO of a corporation need to be paid several hundred times the wage of somebody in the accounting office to accept that responsibility? No. Inequality is not society's way of assuring that competencies rise to the top. It is what takes place when other human traits— avarice, pride, and ruthlessness—are given free play. Differentials in wealth and power are found everywhere on the face of the earth, so much so that they can be safely described as universal. Whether they can also be described as *inevitable* is another matter. Karl Marx, anticipating a very different future, would have said no, it need not be so. Max Weber and Durkheim would not have been so sure.

It is common in discussions of the American social scene to think in terms of three—sometimes four—social classes. The first three, of course, are upper class, middle class, and lower (or working) class, a grading as familiar in everyday conversation as it is in academic discourse. The fourth is "underclass," a stratum meant to include people who do not have regular access even to unskilled work, and for that reason seem to live outside the world of opportunity altogether. They have fallen out the bottom, as we noted earlier. They are not a part of the class structure in any meaningful way.

But what does the term "social class" mean as an empirical phenomenon rather than as an abstract concept?

In Theory

Marx, of course, had an answer to that question. He was never all that clear what he meant by "class," nor is there any good reason why he should have been. For him, as we know, everything came down to two opposing assemblies of people—those who control the means of production in society and those who do the actual work of producing things. To Marx, this was the basic division of human society, the central fault line working below the surfaces of social life.

But Marx was drawing an *economic* diagram here, not an *ethnographic* portrait. He knew perfectly well that the ancient world, the medieval world, and the world of his time included any number of people who were neither "workers" nor "owners" in the sense he was employing those terms. He was writing about what he thought to be the principal actors on an economic stage that included a number of other players as well.

Max Weber had an answer to that question too. He shared Marx's view that society was divided into strata that had vastly different degrees of access to the available resources. But he was as interested in an ethnographic portrait as he was in an economic diagram, and it seemed evident to him as he studied the world of his time that class standing was based on many more variables than the two that impressed Marx so much. He assumed, for example—and so have most persons who have studied the subject since—that skilled workers have a different place in the larger economy and thus a different status in the class structure than do unskilled workers, and he assumed as well that persons who share certain life chances or are born to certain privileges have advantages in society quite independent from the amount of money they control or the amount of influence they assert in the economy. A person's class rank, then— "class position," Weber called it—derives from a cluster of attributes, not just wealth but occupation, education, reputation, ability to get things done, and so on.

Most social scientists now accept this more elaborate understanding of what social class actually consists of, and in that sense, we are all Weberians, even those who follow in the tradition of Marx. Marx's argument that the social order is divided into two elemental forces was not that easy to work with even in his own day when the time came to chart the composition of a particular class structure or to assign someone a location in it. And it has become a good deal more difficult since. For one thing, differentials in wealth have grown precipitously in most of the West—an outcome that would have saddened both Marx and Weber but surprised neither of them. And perhaps more to the point, what Marx meant by "owning" the means of production and "working" for those who do has shifted into a new dimension. Some of the wealthiest and most powerful persons on earth now *manage* the means of production for a wage, and are thus technically workers, while the number of persons who qualify as owners now include a massive assembly of individual investors, its numbers changing by the moment throughout the trading day, who own modest shares of stock in different enterprises and draw income from holding companies like pension funds and mutual funds, themselves managed by employees who work for a salary. What would Marx have made of that?

Weber's formulation is much easier to work with in the case of modern economies, since in his view the sheer fact of *ownership* does not count for much of and by itself unless it can be converted into wealth, power, prestige, or some other edge. Successful managers of money may earn billions of dollars a year even though the only means of production they have title to is a laptop computer and a cell phone, and baseball players may earn millions even though the only means of production they actually own outright is a leather glove or two and a few wooden bats. Meantime, owning a few stocks in a corporation does not of itself really confer much in the way of class standing.

An important French sociologist named Pierre Bourdieu has added a new element to recent thinking about stratification by suggesting that class standing is a product not only of the *economic* capital one has at one's disposal but of the *social* and *cultural* capital as well. By "social capital" he meant the kinds of influence individuals can count on to improve their chances in life. And by "cultural capital" he meant personal styles and tastes and scraps of knowledge that give people a certain distinction in the eyes of others.

How we are supposed to deal with those things empirically is a job for hardier souls than me. But if Bourdieu were to undertake a social class audit of the people who live in my university neighborhood, for example, I could imagine him assessing a colleague's status in the following way. She lives on her academic salary and does not have any other resources, so her economic capital is middling. But she has known many students and colleagues over the years who are now in positions of relative power, and even though she has never taken advantage of that source of leverage, it constitutes a line of credit, as it were, on which she could draw if she needed to. Social capital. When Bourdieu interviewed her, moreover, he noticed that she was listening to a composition by Richard Strauss, had placed a volume of poetry by Rainer Maria Rilke on her desktop and a print by Gustav Klimt on the wall of her study. Her choice of words and her diction, moreover, reflected what was once in an earlier epoch called "good breeding." We might be tempted to say of her in English that she "has class," and that is what Bourdieu would have given her credit for in his audit. Cultural capital.

Sooner or later, however, discussions of class are sure to turn to money. There is no question that what Weber meant by "prestige" and what sociologists like Bourdieu mean by "social" and "cultural" capital influence the machinery of social life in important ways. But way down there at the fulcrum of things, wealth is what really matters in modern capitalist and most other economies. Money can almost always purchase power right away, and it can also purchase more illusory goods like esteem in the relatively short term. Money may not be the root of all evil, but it is certainly the root of what we call "stratification" in the United States and most of the industrialized West. And the simple fact is that there is now a huge—*monstrous* might be the only adequate adjective for it—disproportion in the way wealth is distributed across our society and our world, and the evidence all suggests that it is growing by the minute. This is what the surplus I alluded to as a form of "original sin" has wrought.

In Fact

It is remarkably difficult to convey the size of that imbalance. One can try to make the point by reciting stark, impressive figures. For example: individuals who occupy the highest tiers of income distribution in this country take in an average of tens of millions in earnings and investments, while individuals who occupy the lowest tiers take in an average of ten thousand dollars a year in earnings and welfare payments. Does that figure offer an adequate sense of the differential? Numbers like those exist on such different planes, issue from such different spheres of reality, that it is very difficult to know how to find a point of comparison. So we try again. Individuals in the first tier earn as much between breakfast and lunch on any given day of the week as members of the second do in the course of a year. Does that strike a more resonant chord? Or this. An average person in the first tier makes *five thousand times* a year what an average individual in the second tier does. Or to present the same figures in yet another way: it would take the combined incomes of five thousand persons in the second tier—the population of an average town—to equal the income of one person in the first. Sometimes proportions can provide a sharper image. The upper 20 percent of the population, by some estimates, controls 75 percent of the national wealth, while the upper 1 percent controls 50 percent of the privately owned stock.

Sometimes visual representations manage to convey what cold figures cannot. In the 1976 edition of his textbook *Economics,* Paul Samuelson, a wise and not easily excited economist, asked us to imagine the following:

> If we made an income pyramid out of a child's blocks with each layer portraying $1,000 income, the peak would be higher than the Eiffel Tower, but most of us would be within a yard of the ground.

In the 19th edition of the same textbook, published in 1995, Samuelson and his co-author, William Nordhaus, saw an even greater difference:

> If we made a pyramid out of a child's blocks, with each layer portraying $500 of income, the peak would be far higher than Mt. Everest, but most people would be within a few feet of the ground.

As you begin to do the arithmetic here, remember that the dollar values when those figures were drawn are substantially different from those that apply now, so we have to be thinking in proportions rather than in totals here. You should note, too, that the blocks this time are only worth half as much, but you also need to know as you begin your calculations that the Eiffel Tower is 894 feet high and Mt. Everest is 29,029—roughly thirty times higher. If yet another edition was to appear now, what kind of visual image might be required? A pyramid of blocks reaching somewhere into outer space?

Sometimes a striking episode or a telling juxtaposition hits home with unusual force. A writer named Jonathan Kozol once spent time visiting a neighborhood in the South Bronx known as Mott Haven, home to 48,000 people, almost all of them poor. He found a thought-provoking item in the newspaper one day as he was traveling to Mott Haven by subway:

> A Wall Street money manager who had been extremely lucky, or had made some very shrewd decisions, had earnings of more than one billion dollars, which was just about five times the total income of the 18,000 households of Mott Haven. An extra 20 percent tax on his earnings, if distributed in the South Bronx, would have lifted 48,000 human beings—every child and every parent in every family of Mott Haven—out of poverty.

Imagine having that kind of money in a world where so many have nothing! Kozol might have felt better about the vast imbalance he was speaking of when he noticed that the money manager who appeared in the story is one of the most generous philanthropists of our time, named George Soros. But the point itself remains. Many persons who worked around the financial district the same year Soros cleared a billion dollars made enough money to lift the entire populace of Mott Haven out of poverty, and most of them would have had enough left over to live as lavishly as sultans.

The problem with any of these numbers or figures or representations is that they fall so far outside any reasonable sense of human scale. If we hear that a child of five is stuck in a culvert somewhere a thousand miles away or that a kitten is lost and hungry half a block from home, our powers of sympathy, which can fathom such things, will be aroused. But if we hear that thousands of young people in Mott Haven are undernourished and suffer from easily treated illnesses and live in constant fear of the future, we find it difficult to do much more than feel mournful in a somewhat abstract way and sometimes look to the heavens for comfort. Our minds have a hard time processing things on so vast a scale.

As Lived Experience

Class can be a hard concept to come to terms with in a place like the United States because there are no lines out there separating one strata from another—no borders to cross, no walls to breach, no open spaces to traverse. We have to begin on the assumption that gradations of wealth, power, prestige, and all other forms of advantage are spread across a continuous field, with the differing levels shading into one another seamlessly. Those who command a good deal of wealth and power occupy the upper portions of that vertical field. Those who command little of either occupy the lower levels. The rest of us occupy spaces in between.

Class, then, should be visualized as a continuous variable like intelligence or age or weight. Specialists draw lines across that field so as to divide it into more easily visualized groupings—upper class, middle class, lower class—in largely the same way that we might divide a population of people into categories like young, middle-aged, and elderly, or short, medium, and tall. But the lines themselves are nothing more than conceptual contrivances. If we were to study the matter carefully, we might discover that people in the middle ranges of a class structure behave a bit differently and pronounce words a bit differently and dress a bit differently from those in the lower or the upper ranges, but there are no boundaries out there separating one social class from another any more than there are boundaries separating the elderly from the middle-aged. They shade into each other without any visible breaks.

How much actual movement takes place up and down that structure—from class to class, from layer to layer—is a matter observers discuss at considerable length when dealing with contemporary American society. It is fair to assume that the amount of that movement, however one measures such things, is fairly substantial now. We live in fluid times, with many persons moving upward from blue collar jobs into better-paid service positions, and, alas, many drifting downward from the ranks of the regularly employed into a precarious life on the margins of society. It is also fair to assume, however, that there are resistances built into any class structure that simply slow movement down when people born to disadvantage try to climb upward, or when people born to advantage look as though they may slip down. I am not speaking here of visible obstacles that need to be overcome but of inertias built into the very structure of things. It is still a rude fact in the United States that the best predictor of individuals' social standing even now is the social standing of their parents, which means that class position continues to have a way of perpetuating itself.

Where do those inertias reside? What form do they usually take? I taught for most of my professional life in what is often known as an "elite" university, meaning not only that it provides a quality education but that it prepares students for places of special influence in the larger society. I read an article once that made a deep impression on me even though I cannot now remember where I came across it or who wrote it. The title was something like "The Best Schools Have the Least Effect." How frequently, the article asked, do the "best" educational establishments bring about change in the class position of the students who pass through them? Often enough, apparently. But a striking proportion of those who make their way into "elite" universities have parents who attended comparable institutions themselves, who know what a "quality" education can do for one over the long term, who help prepare children for that prospect, and who have the resources to pay for it. Students who start off with those advantages, that is, were on a trajectory heading toward success long before their first exposure to college life. They may learn something useful from the courses they take and the guidance they obtain—professors like me are bound to hope so—but in many ways their college years are part of a steady progression into places of preferment that had been marked out long before.

Inertia of another kind is at work in the lower ranges of the American class structure. Children who grow up in communities where no one really expects very much out of life, where schools slog along as best they can in the absence of adequate resources, and where the mood of everyday life is one of numbed resignation are at a distinct disadvantage when doors of opportunity open a crack. So the poor and unskilled tend to remain where they are. "Tend" is the operative word here.

One reason why poor people do not drift up the class structure in anything like the numbers a random universe would indicate is that they are so likely to develop outlooks—ways of seeing and thinking and behaving—that limit their mobility sharply. Oscar Lewis, you remember, thought that those outlooks constituted a "culture of poverty" that virtually doomed the poor to the lower levels of the social order. Persons attuned to that "culture," said Lewis, are oriented to the present because they have so little confidence in the future, and look out at the world with eyes so glazed and spirits so dimmed that they can scarcely imagine a different condition. Most social scientists have come to feel that "culture" is not really the right word for this, as we saw earlier, but the point cannot be avoided: sustained exposure to poverty works its way deep into the human spirit. It deadens people, numbs them, and makes it all the harder for them to improve their lot. In other writings of mine I have used the term "traumatized" to describe certain of the poor. In that sense, being poor can become a way of life and a source of identity as well as an economic circumstance. It is almost as if the machinery of social life had been calibrated to keep poor people "in their places"—a terrible expression.

I have been speaking of the urban "underclass" here, of course, but the same can be said of working class persons who come to feel that they have been assigned by fate to lives of labor and develop ways of behaving that make it much more likely that they will remain there. Several good studies can be found on sociological shelves dealing with young people growing up in working class communities who learn in subtle ways from their parents, their teachers, their clergy, and their friends not to expect very much out of life and not to aspire to anything beyond easy reach. The lessons one learns in that way can be indirect, but their effect is decisive. Working class youths, who have been told in a hundred oblique ways that education holds little promise for such as they, act in a manner that almost seems calculated to convert that prophecy into reality—neglecting homework on the ground that it is a waste of energy, leaving school as soon as the law permits because earning a pay envelope seems more real and more to the point than earning a high school diploma—thereby helping shape their future without in the least meaning to. They become the authors of their own fate in the sense that they made those decisions themselves, but at the same time they are acting on unspoken instructions that float in the air surrounding them.

In that sense, mobility is not just a matter of how much wealth people can acquire or how fortunate they may become or how wide the gates of advancement open up at any given moment in time. It is also a matter of how people assess their chances in life and how they look at themselves. One of the "hidden injuries of class," to borrow from the title of a good, if dated, book on the topic, is that people so easily regard their own standing near the lower levels of the class structure as evidence that they have not measured up and do not amount to very much. That is one of the things a great disproportion in wealth can do to people. It not only distributes life's chances unequally; it persuades large numbers of people, down to the depths of their beings, that they *belong* in the places fate has set aside for them and that it is not only their destiny but somehow their *doing.* If you listen, you can hear it in the voices of those adults. You can hear it in the voices of children, too. To me, it is one of the saddest and most troubling sounds in the world.

Differentia

I am using the term "differentiation" here to apply to the process by which members of a social order are sorted into categories that are not, on their face, ranked, in contrast to what is generally meant by the term "stratification." A renowned sociologist named Peter Blau was making essentially the same point when he suggested that "inequality" and "heterogeneity" should be viewed as contrasting forms of diversity in the human world. It is a useful difference to keep in mind.

I cited Raymond Williams earlier on the great country houses of England. How can one "think of community," he inquired, when one is contemplating social worlds in which differences of wealth and power and privilege are so enormous? That is a very compelling point. But the gulf that divides the people of the manor house from the people of the village belongs on a vertical plane and is a matter of layers, *strata,* while the differences recognized within the compass of the village belong for the most part on a horizontal plane, a matter of *differentia.* This is not to suggest for a moment that village society is without distinctions of class. They exist, and can be fiercely protected. But the majority of people who live in that social world command similar incomes, live similar lives, and expect to be buried in the same graveyard by the same parish priest reciting the same liturgy. They are differentiated by the families they belong to, the land they are attached to, the work they do, and the roles they play in village life. But seen from even a modest distance, they are of the same level.

The prototype of that kind of social formation may be the classical medieval town. Residents were separated into dozens of specialized trades, each with its own marketplaces, guilds, living quarters, customary dress, and so on. Those are definite human distinctions but they represent diversity without much in the way of layering. The soldiers and peasants, the tanners and coopers, the cobblers and tinsmiths, the street musicians and fishmongers, and everyone else who participated in that colorful street pageant were relatively equal in rank and power and wealth. As Raymond Williams reminds us, we dare not forget for a single moment that this level of equality was contained within a clearly defined and bounded social space. Outside the edges of that space were those who lived in the castles and cathedrals and abbeys who exercised rarely and then only as recreation, and who became flabby of limb, thick of girth, and rich of purse as a result of the exertions of others.

This is something worth thinking about, if only as a footnote in passing. Who built those magnificent cathedrals and castles that still today loom over the towns clustering in their shadow? Who furnished them with silk tapestry, gold plate, carved furniture, and the best of wines? Who paid for the festivities staged in them? Guide books tell us that they were "built" by King Henry or Pope Gregory, Cardinal Richelieu or the Duke of Alba. But none of those worthies ever lifted a stone with their own hands or took a turn at the shovel, and the funds they used to pay the costs of that construction were obtained by raiding other treasuries, exploiting distant colonies, or imposing taxes and tithes on fellow countryfolk, including the poorest of them. Karl Marx, who did not have a very delicate way with words, simply called it "theft." That term might be a bit too blunt and irascible to serve as a useful way of putting it for our purposes, but it does serve to focus our attention differently and to point us in other directions. And theft it certainly was.

The main point to be made in this discussion of sorting people into domains, though, is that humankind has demonstrated a remarkable inventiveness in creating sharp and often humiliating inequalities where the natural world has supplied little more than a few modest *differentia,* if that much. There are no better examples in the life of the social order than the distinctions we have learned to draw (a) between persons of differing "races"; (b) between males and females; and (c) between peoples who view themselves—or are viewed by others—as members of contrasting national and ethnic groups. We will look at issues relating to *race* and *gender* in this chapter. In the chapter to follow, we will turn to ethnic and national identities, which are now the most deadly form of differentiation to be found in our world.

On Race

"Race" has always been a particularly sensitive topic in the United States, of course, and it has figured prominently in the American social sciences. We touched on that subject in the chapter on cities, and for that reason will not go deeply into it now. Our principal concern here will be to consider how "race" should be *conceptualized* and *identified* when seen through a sociological lens. Every time the word "race" appears in this discussion, in fact, it should be read as though it was set off by quotation marks—as it has been in this paragraph. It may well be the murkiest concept in our everyday vocabulary.

Our species is generally thought to have originated in Africa, of course, and to have spread from there over the other surfaces of the earth in migrant currents so slow that they lasted hundreds of millennia. Over that vast a period of time, climate and circumstance have brought about a number of variations in pigmentation and bodily features throughout the human population. Social scientists have no choice but to deal with those variances, not because they explain very much of and by themselves but because the life chances of people out there in the social world have been so influenced by the way fellow human beings view and deal with them. Otherwise, we would probably have to conclude that race is so vague a distinction as to be virtually without useful meaning.

That may sound amazingly naïve at first. Anybody with eyes to see can tell that on average persons from Southern Asia do not look like persons from Central Africa, and that neither look like people from Scandinavia. That observation is so self-evident that it seems almost perverse for anyone to insist that "race" can be better understood as an invention of the social world than as a fact of the natural world. But we should note two things:

First, the range of variation found within racial groupings is so great that the categories themselves seem to fuse into a vast, undifferentiated wash. Norwegians the color of ivory soap, Sicilians the color of almond paste, and Indians the color of dark mahogany are all "Caucasian," and variations in all the other features we generally cite to make "racial" distinctions—texture of hair, shape of eyelids or nostrils, or some other anatomical detail—are just as great among persons who qualify as "Mongoloid" or "Negroid" on this scale or that.

Second, and far more significant in the long term, the issue is not whether there *are* discernible racial differences within the human family but whether those differences *make* a difference. In places like the United States, for example, it is fair to say that our eyes have been trained to exaggerate what nature provides as relatively slight variations in pigment or feature or something else because we have taught one another that they truly *matter.*

Suppose that you and I were to witness a loud and angry exchange between two men on a sidewalk that looked as though it might erupt into a fight. We would be far more likely to remember later that one of the participants in that tense scene was African-American and the other white because we have become so sensitive to that distinction. That is the feature that would draw our attention the most acutely and the one that would lodge in our memory the most clearly. But it is not at all obvious that an Inuit hunter or a Malaysian farmer or a Navajo weaver, differently taught and differently tuned, would pay the same attention to that detail or even notice it. After all, the men squaring off on that sidewalk must have differed in a number of noticeable ways—in tone of voice, in style of dress, in body size, in age, in the way they carried themselves or in some other point of comparison. Why would our eyes concentrate on this detail among all those others? I am not suggesting here that the hunter, the farmer, and the weaver would not *see* what you and I do. Their eyes are as sharp as ours. But among the details their eyes caught and passed on to their brains, a difference in skin color did not register as important, any more than the fact that one of them was wearing blue trousers and the other brown would register with us. We might never have even "seen" that, despite the fact that the visible surface of those garments was many times greater than that of the exposed skin, and the color difference sharper and more distinct by far.

To complicate the example, consider what another creature with good enough vision to make out the distinctions we have been speaking of—a falcon circling overhead or a dog loping by, let's say—would make of that same scene. What details would strike them as particularly interesting or important or worth paying attention to? A minor variance in skin hue would probably rank as vanishingly small.

In that sense, "race" is what sociologists generally describe as a *social construct,* by which we mean that it is a product of the human imagination, a fabrication. We clearly do not mean by this that humankind has *invented* whatever differentials in skin color or in body type can be found out there in the world, but that humankind has invented racial identities by *making something of* those differentials and regarding them as defining.

Think for a minute of the adjectives we often use in everyday speech to identify this thing called "race." I would call myself "white" if asked about my racial identity over the telephone, for example, and would think nothing of it if someone at the other end of the line used the adjective "black." We would just be exchanging information. And in an earlier era, the adjectives "yellow" and "red" might have entered the conversation if the subject of Asians or of Native

Americans (a professional football team in the United States still calls itself "the Redskins") had come up. But none of those words even come close to reflecting the actual color schemes of nature. They imply a degree of differentiation for which there is no warrant in the natural world at all. If someone walked into a classroom of mine who was actually *white* or *red* or *black* or *yellow* as those hues appear on a color chart, I would either think it a prank or call an ambulance.

But what difference does color make in the flow of everyday social life? To deal only with white and black for the moment, the answer is truly staggering. People viewed as "black" are far more likely than people viewed as "white" to die young, to lose children in infancy, to live in poverty, to spend stretches of time in prison, to suffer from a wide variety of illnesses, to be exposed to toxic poisons, to be victims of violent crimes, and to receive an inferior education.

None of these outcomes, with the possible exception of susceptibility to this disease or that one, has anything do with biological endowment. They are all products of social fate. The reasons why the African-Americans among us are more likely to die early or endure a term in prison or develop crippling asthma or live in poverty is that the conditions in which they live are different now and have been different for a long time. With the exception of gender, to which we will turn in a moment, no other distinction having to do with the way the body is formed can divide a human population into such profoundly contrasting realms of experience. Variations in weight or height or eye color? Differentials in strength or skill or intellectual acuity? The only other distinction I can think of that might create as sharp a difference in life chances would be the one dividing individuals of sound constitution from those suffering from serious disabilities. And that comparison might even serve to make the point clearer: To be born black in our society now is to enter life with what can in effect be a disabling handicap. But it is a disability that exists wholly in the eye of the beholder.

On the surface of things, it needs to be said, the position of African-Americans seems to have improved in American society. A black person was elected President of the United States in the first decade of the 21st century. Blacks occupy seats on the Supreme Court, in Congress, and in government offices of substantial influence. They command armies, lead corporations, and play prominent roles in the cultural life of the land. And the same is true, if less dramatically so, for Hispanics and Native Americans.

Below that surface, however, in those more anonymous spaces where the mass of us live out our days, those hopeful signals have much less meaning. Statistics tend toward the slippery there, but the stark and inescapable fact of the matter is that blacks, Hispanics, and native Americans make up a hugely disproportionate share of the poor of this country, and that the disproportion is increasing, particularly for blacks. One estimate is that members of those minorities earn incomes that are on the average but slightly higher than half that of their white countrymen. This yawning gulf means tangible differences so obvious that they could go without saying. The higher people's income, clearly, the better the education and medical care and other life chances they can provide themselves and their children. These are advantages that money can purchase.

But what is not so obvious at first is that the level of people's income has a powerful impact on the intangibles of social life—on their ability to sustain hope, to imagine a better future, to respect themselves, to feel that the children they bring into the world really have a fair chance at life's rewards.

Among the things debated in social science circles and in political forums generally is the extent to which reduced life chances in American society are the result of "class" or the result of "race." Do people in urban slums, say, have a harder time of it because they are poor or because they are black? There are good technical and policy reasons for asking that question, obviously, but the distinction becomes semantic when one is considering the everyday experiences of the people who live there. A vast majority of them are numbingly poor, which explains a good part of their predicament, and a vast majority of them are also discriminated against in dozens of ways because of their race, which explains another part. And in addition to that, their kind have been discriminated against for decades, generations, centuries, which enacts a toll all its own.

The evidence is overwhelming—and has been for some time—that a particular kind of profiling takes place every moment of every day out there in the streets of the real world. We can begin by observing such things as that cab drivers take race into account when they accept fares, and that most of the rest of us, black or white, take race into account when we assess the level of dangers we face in public places. But that only touches the surface of a far more systemic imbalance. It is an established fact that employers take race into account when they hire, that realtors take race into account when they sell or lease, that bankers take race into account when lend, and that police take race into account when they arrest, district attorneys when they prosecute, juries when they convict, and judges when they sentence. In general, the gates of opportunity open much more reluctantly when "people of color" try to pass through them. This can be a result of individual prejudice, obviously, but it can also be a result of rational calculation, since the odds that a poor black person will default on a loan or attract the attention of patrolling police officers are also well known. So the persistent unfairness creates its own logic. Justice would not necessarily be well served well if you or I were to stalk the world with accusing fingers and point them at cab drivers who ignore fares, bank officers who refuse loans, or employers who turn down applicants. Those acts may or may not have issued from motives that can be seen as "racist" at the personal level. But the larger system in which those acts occur can be understood as racist and should be. Persons who come into this social order with the disadvantage of being black are confronted from that moment to the day of their death by expectations on the part of others that do not derive in any way from their own behavior or their own frame of mind. To call that "unfair" or "unjust" does not even begin to describe it.

Charles Blow reflected in the *New York Times* on the police killing of a 16-year-old black youth in Chicago, where the victim was shot 16 times, most of them after he was no longer standing and with his back turned to his assailants:

> Truly, there are many troubling aspects to this case. But having covered so many of those cases in the last couple of years, it strikes me that we may need to push back and widen the lens so that we can fully appreciate and understand the systemic sociological and historical significance of this moment in our country's development. While police departments definitely have distinct cultures, in a way they are simple instruments that articulate and enforce our laws and mores, which are reflections of our values. The only reasons that these killings keep happening is because most of American society tacitly approves or willfully tolerates it. There is no other explanation. If America wanted this to end, it would end.

The editorial ends with a message: "the terrible silence of enough people will continue to sanction this carnage."

Moreover, even if all these forms of discrimination were to end magically at the dot of midnight, the behaviors and outlooks of persons whose lives have been shaped by them over that long, unrelenting past would be unlikely to change soon. Things do not work that way in human life.

No matter where they turn, it would seem, African-Americans are being processed through a different filtering system as they make their way through the housing market, the employment scene, the apparatus of criminal justice, and other ports of entry into a secure place in the world. And there is none of this that cannot be changed. None.

On Gender

On the sixth day of Creation, we read in Genesis, God divided humankind into two categories: "males and females created he them." It was the only form of differentiation then known in the human universe. Many others would follow eventually, of course, but their time had not yet come. There were no tasks to perform or responsibilities to undertake in the Garden of Eden, and thus no need for a division of labor. There were no possessions, and thus no call for a sense of ownership. There were no histories to relate, no genealogies to trace, no misfortunes to account for, no inequalities to explain away, and thus no reasons to parcel blame or give credit for what had happened in the past. There was no past.

This was not to last, as we know. The Lord expelled Adam and Eve from Eden, and decreed in the process that Adam (and the men who came after him) was to "rule over Eve" (and the women who came after her). Adam and Eve were the only people on the face of the earth, and the sole distinction between them—that one was a "he" and the other a "she"—had already been converted into a hierarchy. At the very dawn of history, then, as time is reckoned in this account, a difference in *kind* had become a difference in *rank*.

The project of splitting humankind into categories and of arranging those categories into grades began in earnest soon after the expulsion. Those original refugees now had to face the unfamiliar task of tending herds and tilling fields in order to support life ("from the sweat of thy brow shalt thou eat bread"). The sons of Adam and Eve somehow found wives out there in those ancient shadows—where they came from is not explained in the story—who bore new generations of people, and the distinctions we now know began to emerge.

Similar origin stories are told in other parts of the world, too. They follow different narrative threads, but in one way or another a majority of the ones we know about somehow manage to dignify the status of menfolk at the expense of womenfolk and at least imply that the superiority of the male of the species has been mandated by some higher power, as in the case of Genesis, or is in some other way an undeniable fact of nature.

It is almost inevitable when speaking of differences between male and female in our world that discussion will turn to physical constitutions. After all, anatomical differences were apparent from the start, and they became more apparent millennia later when scientists learned about other details hidden away in the recesses of the human body—the workings of hormones and chromosomes, of reproductive systems and genetic codes, and so on.

There are measurable differences in the way hormones operate, the way genes affect temperament, and maybe even in the way the brain functions. Testosterone is likely to surge more urgently through the bloodstreams of men, and estrogen is likely to be more common in females. But general consensus among specialists is that these differentials do not even begin to account for variations in gender found across the human spectrum. As we noted in our discussion of race a moment ago, the question here is not how natural differences come to influence human affairs, but how those differences come to *make* a difference in human thinking. That is the realm of the cultural.

So we begin with the assumption that virtually every distinction we humans think we sense out there in the world around us—ways of dressing, ways of thinking, ways of acting, ways of dividing up work, ways of assigning ownership to things of value, ways of allotting power and honor and prestige—can only be understood as human inventions. All of these elaborations—millions of filaments spun so thickly around the basic core that the core itself is no longer visible—are our subject matter. Those elaborations are *experienced* as natural by people everywhere, since that is how cultural learning works its way into human thought processes. Every culture has its own stories to relate why it is that women and men behave and think and carry themselves differently, and why those differences seem to be built into the order of things.

In recognition of this fact, sociologists generally make a distinction between *sexual* differences (those that can be attributed to the physical constitution) and *gender* differences (those that can be attributed to the way a society defines what is appropriate for women and for men). Women ovulate and men do not. Sexual difference. Women in most parts of the world have different wardrobes than men. Gender difference. You will not be surprised by now to learn that sociologists tend to place a large number of things in the gender category that people out in the world place in the category of sexual differences.

Most people who read these lines live in a time and place where assumptions about the "place" of men and women in the social firmament are being sharply questioned. One of the excitements of my generation has been that what may really turn out to be a lasting shift in human perceptions of gender has been taking place all around us and looks as though it may be spreading elsewhere—although it is essential to add that this shift we think we can sense has not yet reached vast portions of the rest of the world, including large portions of our own.

But at least we are now in a position to ask the question: where did the notion come from in the first place that the male half of the human species was meant to "rule over" the female half—that men are better equipped as a matter of natural endowment to preside over the human community as leaders, shamans, priests, elders, judges, exemplars, or whatever passed in early times for intellectual elites? Some persons will answer the question without a moment's thought by saying that it was ordained at the beginning by a higher power, but even they have to recognize the fact that Genesis, like most other origin stories, was for the most part recorded by men and recounted by men—exactly those leaders and shamans and priests and elders of whom we just spoke.

Let us suppose for one moment that a writer with the biting satirical sensibility of a Jonathan Swift had created a character named "Nature" and had asked her to speak on that very question. She replies:

Where is it written that men are superior to women? Well, actually, I have to say that men do not count for all that much in the natural scheme of things, and I wonder sometimes where they get the idea that they are so superior. Or even equal, for all of that. The reason I arranged for their presence on earth in the first place is that I need them to produce and pass on the seminal fluid that the survival of the species relies on. I need them to preen their feathers, flex their muscles, display their plumage—to snort and dance and strut their stuff so that females will show at least some interest in them when the time for breeding comes. And I grant you that human males have proven to be very adept at that.

I don't want to be misunderstood here. Men can be very handy creatures to have around. They are good at protecting the campsite and bringing in new forms of protein. But you have to appreciate that the main object of a species is to survive, pure and simple. Everything begins there. So women form the center. It is they who bear the children. It is they who create life. It is they who provide them nourishment, at least in the early going; and (not to put too fine a point on it) it is they who can be counted on to really *care*. The human campsite—the womb, the core, the hearth, the essence—is woman's terrain. The wisdoms that prevail there are the basic human wisdoms.

Well, satire is like that—a blunt, crude, unfair caricature. But its purpose is to peel away the outer layers of convention so that it is easier to peer down into the center of things, and it succeeds to the extent that it allows us to confront something that is otherwise hard to see in those regions of the mind where old cultural reflexes still reside. It is a way of thinking we are asked to understand even as we view it as something worth mocking.

One can imagine "Nature" asking: Is there anything about preparing meals, setting traps, gathering plant life, telling tales, dressing wounds, digging up roots, harnessing oxen to the plow, setting fires, or instructing the young that requires a more advanced set of skills? Is a man throwing a spear demonstrating more dexterity than a woman shaping a pot? More intelligence? More imagination? A more refined sense of morality? More motor skills? More anything? Well, maybe more brute strength—a very useful attribute in the struggle to survive as a species, no doubt, but a limited one nonetheless when we consider the range of adaptive abilities required over time.

People born into the world come to see the way power and privilege are apportioned in social life as part of the very fitness of things. No news there. It is almost as if a sorting of the world's population had taken place in a distant past, before memory, locating some in high estate and others in low, giving some a license to rule and others an obligation to obey. That is one of the things origin stories are about. And it is important to add that those stories are recounted millennia later not only by those who profit from them, but—this being one of those strange chemistries of human life we spoke of earlier—by those who are damaged by them without recognizing that to be so. For untold millennia, women as well as men told those stories to their sons and daughters.

We do not know much about the origin of those origin stories, but we do know what the consequences have been. The roles assigned men and women vary so widely from one culture to another that it is hard to think of any activity that belongs universally in the male or the female domain outside of the responsibilities of child care. Those consequences have been obvious throughout human history and are obvious in the world of our own time. Were we to go into the topic in any detail here, we would turn to gender inequalities that are easy to make out in the marketplace, the political arena, places of privilege and honor, and most of the other visible surfaces on which human life is lived.

But inequalities in the way men and women relate to one another in everyday social life are often harder to get some sense of because they are simply harder to see. Most forms of inequality we have dealt with so far result in fairly visible forms of separation or outright segregation. If he had powerful enough binoculars, our orbiting stranger would notice that people with darker complexions tend to cluster near the urban ghettos of the United States, and that people with more ragged clothing tend to cluster in the *villas miserios* and *bidonvilles* of the less developed world, almost as if they had been drawn there by some form of gravitational pull. People of different stations in life drift into different niches in the social structure, and thus to different locations on the spatial map. In that sense, as we have seen, race and class and other forms of distinction that imply hierarchy can have a geographical dimension.

Things can be a good deal more complicated when it comes to gender, at least below those visible surfaces we have been alluding to—which is, of course, all that the eye of the orbiting stranger can make out even with the aid of those binoculars. Men and women tend to mate in pairs and share the responsibilities of tending to a family, which means that they usually live in the same dwellings or compounds, draw on the same incomes, are subject to the same fate, and in that sense share the same social standing. A sociologist trying to estimate the social class of people by drawing on the usual indices—value of residence, family income, lifestyle—would have little choice but to assume that a married couple shared a common status. In that sense, one might say, the sun shines equally on them both.

But it is evident if one looks at the situation through a more finely focused lens that forms of segregation, even of something approaching a kind of quarantine, are often found *within* household enclosures all over the world. Large inequalities of wealth and leisure can obtain between members of a household even where a fixed volume of money comes in the front door, and differentials of power are all the more easily asserted within the narrow quarters of a home. Acts of dominance and abuse that take place at the breakfast table or in the bedroom or any other corner of the home are almost impossible to take the measure of unless one has access to information of a kind that inquiring outsiders rarely do. It would seem on the face of it as though we are looking at individuals who share the same life chances. But things are rarely that simple, and we need to inquire what role the brute strength we spoke of a moment ago plays in that part of life.

And on that note, I will bring this discussion to a close, having provided many more questions than answers. But this may be one of those times when the way in which I ended that lecture course at Yale makes some sense: if you leave this chapter knowing less than when you began it, I may have accomplished at least part of what I had in mind and what sociology has to offer.

Becoming a People

IN 1991, CIVIL WAR ERUPTED SUDDENLY IN the land then known as Yugoslavia. It was a bitter, savage, sometimes gruesome clash. When the smoke of battle was still hovering over the countryside and echoes of combat were reverberating everywhere, four seasoned experts on the Balkans came together to write a 24-page review of several recent books on what was happening in that war-torn land. They ended their commentary with a question that almost seems to leap from the page, as if it reflected a profound sense of astonishment and perhaps even of exasperation. The "shocking mystery," they wrote—these are among the final words of the review—is "why do human beings take such delight in killing one another?"

These were veteran observers of the human scene, not easily surprised or shocked by news of violence, and the question they were raising is as venerable as the Old Testament: "Why do the nations so furiously rage together?" "From whence come wars and fightings among you?" Still, the most striking thing about that concluding sentence was its seeming naiveté. How often do we hear questions like that asked these days in places where one might reasonably expect them to be: in government offices where decisions about sending young people to war are made, in conference halls where experts in foreign relations gather, in university classrooms where the nature of human existence is discussed? It is generally understood to be an innocent question now, the very opposite of whatever is meant by "realpolitik." The fears and furies that drive human beings to slaughter one another in such vast numbers—think of Rwanda, Cambodia, Sudan, as well as Yugoslavia—are simply *there,* a lethal tendency built into the human grain somewhere that does not require explanation. But the question itself is a wise one and well worth pondering further.

From Whence Come Wars and Fightings Among You?

For many centuries, the accepted answer to that ancient biblical question, at least in the West, has been that the urge to kill issues from natural biological leanings that surge up from some deep inner well in our constitution, whether placed there by divine will or by the workings of evolution or something else. That is what Augustine thought, and so did most of his fellow churchmen in medieval times. That is what Thomas Hobbes thought, as did most of those who pondered the matter in the Age of Reason. That is what Sigmund Freud thought, too, along with many other observers of the late 19th and early 20th centuries when asked where the deadly impulses that burst into human history so often come from. Freud even echoed the famous expression of Hobbes's: human life is "a war of all against all." In some ways, at least, Freud viewed the whole elaborate scaffolding of human society as a device to prevent those dark, innate drives from expressing themselves.

That was the accepted answer in the early years of the social and behavioral sciences as well: warfare and other forms of aggression are built into the very tissues of human life. The psychologist William James—a gentle soul and a resolute pacifist as well as a brilliant thinker—put it bluntly: "Our ancestors have bred pugnacity into our bone and marrow, and thousands of years of peace won't breed it out of us." The seeds of war, that is, are built into our animal nature. We humans are born combative, hostile, and capable of explosive fury. Most social scientists of the time shared that outlook: among those we have encountered so far in this book were Herbert Spencer, William Graham Sumner, and George Herbert Mead.

In the years following World War II, observers of the human scene from a variety of different disciplines began to reconsider that old assumption. For one thing, it seemed only logical to assume that *homo sapiens,* like every other species on record, was likely to have developed inhibitions of some sort against killing creatures of its own biological kind over the course of its evolution. That is the only conclusion that makes any real sense, after all. What species, having as its principal object to assure its own perpetuation, would develop a built-in propensity to kill off its youngest, sturdiest, and most actively breeding members? That would be a remarkably poor survival strategy for any species to adopt as it entered the arena of natural selection.

A good deal of scientific support for that view was offered by naturalists venturing out into the field and coming back with reports that intra-species killing is almost always an aberration in the animal kingdom—a failure of natural processes—and that the savagery we humans have so long attributed to other creatures out there in the wilds has no basis in fact. The notion that nature is "red in claw and tooth," as Tennyson phrased it so famously, may have been an accurate description of the dining habits that prevail when one species feeds on the flesh of another, but it did not accurately describe the way animals of the same kind behave toward one another. They do not kill to promote their own interests or because they have lingering insults to avenge. They have more compelling matters on their agenda. Scientists like Konrad Lorenz, Irenäus Eibl-Eibesfeldt, Niko Tinbergen, and Eric Portman were prominent contributors to that view.

Most animals fight, to be sure. When the season arrives for mating, nesting, and the drawing of territorial boundaries, the sounds of gnashing and snorting, the clatter of antlers and the pounding of hooves and the banging together of skulls are widely heard throughout the animal kingdom. But this is usually a form of ritual combat from which the loser retires with his body (if not necessarily his dignity) intact. For one thing, the rules of that combat allow the loser to surrender and slink away unharmed. For another, the weapons employed in those bouts are the blunt instruments of tournament rather than the lethal instruments of war. Look at the elaborate antlers with which bucks charge one another, for example, or the curved horns with which competing rams clash head to head. It looks as though that natural weaponry was *designed* to avoid lasting damage, and in one sense, at least, that may well be the case. Those ritual tournaments are an elaborate choreography intended to assign males a place in the mating and territorial scheme of things without unnecessary loss of lives. Look at the unicorn, that beautiful, mythical creature, formed with a single sharp horn jutting from its forehead. Combat between two males similarly equipped would clearly have been fatal for one and maybe both if they had charged one another in the manner of a moose or an elk. No wonder it is mythical!

Naturalists were aware of exceptions to that rule. They knew of colonies of ants and other social insects, for example, that fight each other as fiercely as

Cossacks and strew the ground with their dead, and they knew of clans of rats that attack neighboring clans without the slightest concern that they are all members of the same genetic species. But the reigning rule, particularly among the higher primates, was assumed to be otherwise.

What we call "war," then, or any other kind of organized violence in which one band of individuals engages in conflict with another of the same species, was assumed to have no warrant in the world of nature. Sir Julian Huxley, probably the best known natural scientist of the time, announced with magnificent assurance that "war is not a general law of life, but an extremely rare biological phenomenon." And Margaret Mead, probably the best known social scientist of the time, agreed. The slaughter of one set of human beings by another in battle, she wrote with equal assurance, has nothing to do with biological inheritance:

> Warfare is an invention, like any other invention in terms of which we order our lives, such as writing, marriage, cooking our food rather than eating it raw, trial by jury, or burial of the dead.

That conclusion was expressed without a trace of ambiguity in a declaration known as the "Seville Statement," signed by a number of distinguished natural and social scientists in 1986. It read in part:

> It is scientifically incorrect to say that we have inherited a tendency to make war from our animal ancestors. . . . Warfare is a peculiarly human phenomenon and does not occur in other animals. . . . It is scientifically incorrect to say that war *or any other violent behavior* is genetically programmed into our human nature.

That was quite a declaration, particularly that reference to "any other kind of violent behavior" (which I took the liberty of italicizing).

It does not really matter for our purposes here, but I would probably have endorsed the Seville Statement without hesitation back then if anybody had thought me expert enough to solicit my signature. I bring that fact up now because I (and many others who shared that hopeful view of the human prospect) have had to reexamine it in recent years. News reports have been pouring in from everywhere suggesting that we human beings are not as averse to killing one another as that older logic proposes we should be. We live in times when ethnic and national conflicts taking place out there in the killing fields we spoke of earlier involve slaughters that seem to come so easily and with such exuberance that one is tempted to join those Balkan specialists in inquiring: "why *do* human beings take such delight in killing one another?" From what chamber of the human heart do those feelings spring?

As if to rub salt into those already sensitive wounds, moreover, a new generation of naturalists is sending back reports from the field indicating that there may be a good deal more cruelty, brutality, and seemingly pointless killing going on out there in the wilds than anyone imagined a few decades ago—unwelcome tidings for those of us who thought it settled that wanton killing is an anomaly in the animal kingdom. We will return to that later.

So where do we stand now after a thousand years of weighing the human condition philosophically and after a hundred years of studying it scientifically?

Thus far, both the philosophical and the scientific approaches have sought answers to the question "from whence comes . . .?" by drawing conclusions about our biological nature—as if that provided the basic, foundational, bedrock reality. Do we humans share a natural inclination to harm one another? Or does our common specieshood supply its own built-in inhibitions to wanton slaughter? So long as the issue is posed in that way, we may have to conclude that we do not know and cannot know. Our "animal inheritance"—whatever that truly means—has become so submerged under all the social constructs of human time that the question has become moot. The issue is not—never really has been—what natural urges are crouched down in those inner recesses of our being but how life is played out in the social world.

That moves us onto a different conceptual plane altogether where we no longer focus on the essence of the primal *person*—an illusory notion in any event—but on the essence of the *social order* in which we human beings have been enmeshed since the beginning and to which we are adapted. Call it the sociological way of looking. And once on that plane, new questions arise.

If we assume, as William James did, that pugnacity is built into our bone and marrow—that humankind has inherited a mean streak a mile wide—the critical question becomes: how on earth, then, are those violent impulses suppressed and controlled in time of peace? That is the wonder of it. And if we instead assume, as the Seville Statement did, that we are fundamentally a peaceful lot and guided by a built-in aversion to harming our own kind, the critical question—the wonder of it—becomes: how on earth are people induced to slay one another in time of war? How is a willingness to slaughter others coaxed out of the depth of that reluctant spirit? We are no longer asking where those inner urges come from but how they are woven into the fabric of ongoing social life. Where do they fit in the flow of human experience? How are they orchestrated? Patterned? Choreographed? What, in short, is the *social organization* of killing?

Once we move onto that plane, we will note that killing, even at its most horrifying, is almost always a social act. There are exceptions to that rule, to be sure, and we will turn to them later. But in general we may assert that the most violent acts we humans engage in are likely to have as their counterpart equally strenuous acts of caring and even tenderness. Even when a license to kill seems to permeate the atmosphere, as it does in wartime, those who attack with the most concentrated fury generally do so for reasons that can reasonably be called benevolent. If a soldier in combat kills an enemy in cold blood with the thought in mind that he is protecting his comrades, is it an act of savagery or an act of fellow feeling? If a resident of one country slays the resident of another in a moment of icy disdain on the assumption that he is protecting his motherland or his neighborhood at home, is it an act of malice or an act of caring? If a member of a turf gang in New York shoots down a member of a rival gang without so much as a trace of outward remorse, is it an act of brutality or one of brotherhood? The only sensible answer in all those cases has to be "both."

This is what Hobbes, Freud, and others who thought as they did failed to appreciate. It is never a war of *all against all*. It is always a war of *some against some*. The rage with which we human beings are able to shatter the lives of others we dismiss as "they," and the generosity with which we watch over and cherish the lives of those we embrace as "us," are cut from the same emotional cloth, drawn from the same inner depths. They are two halves of the same whole. Feelings of kinship and communality on the one hand and a willingness to kill and do harm on the other are countermoves in the same dance of social life.

And with that recognition, we start over again and reconsider the biblical question from a sociological perspective: from whence come wars and fightings among you?

Our Kind

Human beings have a deep inner need to gather together into social groupings made up of other persons they view as being of like kind. Nature, then, supplies our inclination to sociability. That truly *is* bred into our very bone and marrow. So the social world is our natural habitat. Gathering into communal structures gives us a sense of who we are, where we belong, and what is our place in creation.

But nature does not supply definitions of "like kind" that obtain among any given people at any given moment in time. We humans create them. So even though it is in our nature to seek communion with fellow human beings, the manner in which we go about it, the persons we are drawn to, and the forms of social life that emerge as a result can only be understood as cultural products. Those who view themselves as belonging to "a people" generally speak as though they are linked together by ancient ties of kinship. "We Serbs are of the same lineage." "We Tamils are descended from the same forebears." But even those "peoples" that make the loudest and firmest claims to common ancestry and speak the most passionately about ties of blood are seldom consanguineous in any useful sense of the term. Those ties, when traced historically, prove to be human inventions as well.

Most of us belong to a number of such groupings. To draw again on an image used earlier, these differing aspects of our layered selves can be visualized as concentric circles, radiating out from the individual at their center like ripples in a pond—each of those circles enclosing a "we" in which one feels a sense of belonging. For most persons, the immediate family or household occupies the innermost ring, and as the circles radiate outward in ever widening arcs they may represent an extended family, a village, a neighborhood, a parish, a clan, a tribe, a city, a movement, a region, a people, a nation, a country, a faith, and so on.

We cannot afford to be too precise here. How many circles are given a place on any given concentric map, and which of them should be nested within which others, will vary a good deal from individual to individual, from group to group, and from time to time. Your map will differ in certain details from mine or from anyone else's. In that sense, it is like a signature or a fingerprint. But it will be similar in some ways to those of other people with whom you share an affiliation, and in that sense it is like a group profile.

It is important to note, moreover, that those nested rings represent distinctions that may be far more apparent to observers looking in from the outside than to persons who live out their lives within them. A villager engaged in life's daily rounds is not likely to think of her extended family, her workplace, her parish, her nation, or any of the other domains she lives in as separate constituencies, drawing in a different way on her reserves of devotion, energy, and loyalty. She experiences those realms as part of a continuous social field. She does not see herself a thing of layers. And rightly so. It is we who work in universities and laboratories and the like who divide life into compartments in the hope of seeing the whole better.

To make such a distinction, though, no matter how inexact it must remain, can be a useful way of visualizing human experience because it invites us to focus on a vital matter. People clearly invest more of themselves in some of those concentric domains than they do in others, and the question then becomes: which of them are so crucial to people's sense of belonging and identity that they are willing to kill for them, die for them, or—the acid test—suffer the loss of their own children for them? A Palestinian mother who had recently lost a teenage son to Israeli gunfire said to a reporter: "I will give all my children if that is what it takes to get our homeland back. All of them can become martyrs. It will be a dignity to me."

For the moment, at least, we can term anything that passes so fierce a test a "master identity," drawing on the old sociological concept of "master status." The family, obviously, is an encirclement of that kind, and most of us would defend it at any cost. That reflex is so deep in the human grain—so deep in our animal nature, presumably—that nothing else need be said about it. But what other domain can attract that strong an emotional investment in our time? Most sociologists would nominate *ethnic* or *national* identities for that peculiar distinction as they study the world around them—a pair of adjectives we can collapse into a single term, *ethnonational.* In doing so, we are referring to what happens when a gathering of human beings comes to feel that it constitutes "a people," having been set apart by nature or history or some other inevitable force, and for that reason is entitled to a homeland or to some other special consideration on the earth. This has probably become the most prominent source of group identity in our age. One need only see what has happened in places like the ones I have been drawing attention to—Cambodia, Rwanda, and Sudan, where killings in the hundreds of thousands have been reported; places like Sri Lanka and portions of the Middle East, where vicious waves of hostility have swept over the land and left death and consuming dreams of revenge in their wake; and in places like Catalonia, the Basque region, Belgium, and others, where dark tensions can simmer below the surface and can be summoned to the surface on very little notice.

It was asserted with considerable confidence in social science circles not so long ago that national, cultural, ethnic, and religious differences among the world's peoples were soon to dissolve in the great wash of globalization—that we were all about to become more alike because of the homogenizing effect of mass communications, the diffusion of industrial capital, and the spreading tides of migration carrying persons and customs and ideas across national borders as though they did not exist at all. The reasoning here was that distinctions would have less meaning or even melt away altogether as the peoples of the world began to wear the same clothing, listen to the same music, view the same films, consume the same foods, remain in instant contact with each other through global communication networks—and learn the shapes of reality on the same screens and describe it in the same words. We discussed that in some detail in the chapter called *Worlds Beyond*.

That, clearly, is not how things have worked out. Instead, new forms of nationalism, thought to be on the verge of extinction a few decades ago, have seemed to lurch out from their places of hiding and make themselves heard. An anthropologist named John Comaroff was speaking for a number of his fellow social scientists when he observed: "There seems to be little doubt that ethnic and nationalist struggles—in fact, identity politics *sui generis*—are (re-)making the history of our age with a vengeance." Indeed so. At the same time, though, the landscape on which this is taking place has changed. There is something incongruous in the scene sketched earlier of young Croats and Muslims and Serbs firing at each other across battle lines drawn in the name of ethnonational distinctions while wearing the same caps and jeans and athletic shoes, and having learned how to decorate themselves for combat from an American film called *Rambo*. Serb and Croat and Muslim combatants who had grown up in the same communities were known to call one another on what were then new inventions, cell phones, when the guns were stilled by the approach of darkness to ask about the welfare of persons who had once been neighbors. Why is this happening?

For one thing, globalization can be a frightening prospect, as I noted before. When local and national structures are being washed away by the force of that incoming tide and lose their ability to provide a feeling of shelter and safety for those clustered within them—when tribal lands are absorbed into vast national territories, when states and even empires collapse, and when religious constructs lose some of their coherence—people are likely to feel vulnerable and exposed and to seek new shelter under some other institutional canopy. A considerable majority of the human explosions that have dominated the news in recent years qualify as civil wars, meaning groups of people lashing out at each other who lived in relative harmony under an institutional rubric that seems to be disappearing. The feeling that can come over people when we sense that we have been left alone out there on a bare, empty plain—vulnerable and exposed—can be one of sheer dread.

But why do people who experience that dread turn so often to encirclements based on ethnic and national identity rather than on those based on place, class, and ideology? It would seem fairly obvious that ethnic and national attachments are an appeal to something like kinship—a sense that those who gather together on that basis can depend on one another over the long term because they share a common lineage and are thus "a people." Class and ideology and other potential grounds for connecting may look at first glance as though they would affect people's immediate circumstances more decisively, but relationships that hint at kinship, it would seem, are the human fall-back position.

An anthropologist named Benedict Anderson wrote an immensely influential book in 1982 entitled *Imagined Communities: Reflections on the Origins and Spread of Nationalism,* which had a real impact both on the way social scientists *thought* about the topic and on the way they *spoke* of it. Anderson offered the arresting proposal, as his title indicates clearly, that nations—"peoples"— are *imagined communities,* meaning that they seem to promise the same sense of connectivity one finds in smaller communities. Most sociologists, if invited to undertake a companion inquiry to the one Anderson pursued with the subtitle "Reflections on the Origins of *Community,*" would note that communities are generally viewed by those who live in them as similar to families. We discussed that matter in some detail earlier. So we would not be stretching the syllogism too far if we just concluded that *nations—peoples—*are *imagined families.* The bonds of ethnicity and nationality have much in common with the bonds of family, and share a place in the ecology of the human mind. The terms we use to speak of ethnicity and nationality—of peoplehood in general—would certainly suggest as much. We are brothers and sisters who honor the same ancestors, share a mother tongue, live in a common fatherland or motherland, and so on.

I have been referring rather casually throughout this discussion to "peoplehood" and "kind" and "nationality." Those are vague concepts at best. What is the gravitational force that *brings* them together? What are the connective tissues—the coherencies, similarities—that *hold* them together?

One problem in coming to terms with ethnic and national feelings is that they are so hard to describe using the working vocabularies of the social sciences. What term can even begin to express the feelings of that Palestinian mother toward the cause she embraced with such fierce passion? Shall we say that she felt a "positive valence" toward her people? That she was "strongly disposed" toward her homeland? Poets have a far better time of it. They can write about archaic memories echoing down in the recesses of the mind somewhere and use expressive nouns like "soul" and "spirit" and "blood." But those of us doomed to more cautious forms of discourse may have to settle for the fact that those feelings may be easier to make sense of when they are blurred in shadow than when they are exposed to a bright light. Sigmund Freud once said of himself that he was "irresistibly" drawn to fellow Jews by "many obscure and emotional forces," which are "the more powerful the less" they are "expressed in words." And that is probably where we should leave things as well. Feelings of ethnic and national solidarity—peoplehood, again—do not reside in those regions of the mind where emotions have names, where loyalties can be measured or coded, and where reasons are given. They strike chords of a more mysterious kind.

This might be one reason why ethnonational collectivities are more easily described by what they *are not* than by what they *are*. Words usually come slowly when one is asked to identify those centrifugal pulls, those nameless attractions, that draw humankind together in such powerful clusters. What does it mean to portray oneself as an American, a Muslim, a Ukrainian, a Tamil? Whatever those "obscure and emotional forces" that Freud spoke of really are, the fact appears to be that a collectivity derives its definition and sense of identity less from the positive qualities of a "we" who occupy the center of a group space than from the negative qualities of a "they" who press in on that space from the outside and in doing so mark its boundaries. "They" identify and give substance to "we." It may even be one of the firmer rules of what I earlier called "social geography" that there cannot *be* a "we" without a "they" to give it dimension and contour. The anthropologist Fredrik Barth suggested that it is "the ethnic *boundary* that defines the group, not the cultural stuff that it encloses." And Karl Deutsch drew on an old German saying in making largely the same point: "A nation is a group of people united by a common error about their ancestry and a common dislike of their neighbors."

To the extent that the above is indeed the case, feelings of difference and otherness—even of hostility and antipathy—are the very soul of what is generally meant by nationalism. The drawing of an ethnic boundary involves a process by which persons on one side of the dividing line come to see persons on the other side as so unlike them morally and sometimes even physically that it seems logical to regard them as a different order of being altogether.

This is a crucial distinction in human affairs, so much so that we might well wonder whether "nationalism" is actually the right word for it. With that in mind, I propose now to borrow a concept—a way of seeing things—from elsewhere that speaks of that distinction in a different way. I would like to find a place for that concept in sociological thinking. The discussion will come fairly close to home for me.

On Social Speciation

Erik H. Erikson, my father—a well-known and widely-read psychoanalyst—referred to this process as "pseudospeciation" and defined it thus:

> Humankind from the very beginning has appeared on the world scene split into tribes and nations, castes and classes, religions and ideologies, each of which acts as if it were a separate species created or planned at the beginning of time by supernatural will. Thus each claims not only a more or less firm sense of distinct identity but even a kind of historical immortality. Some of these pseudospecies, indeed, have mythologized for themselves a place and a moment in the very center of the universe, where and when an especially provident deity caused it to be created superior to, or at least unique among, all others.
>
> In times of threat and upheaval the idea of being the foremost species tends to be reinforced by a fanatic fear of and hate of other pseudospecies. The feeling that those others must be annihilated or kept "in their places" by warfare or conquest or the force of harsh custom can become a periodical and reciprocal obsession of humankind.

Similar themes have been sounded by many others, but an anthropologist named David H. Marlowe put it especially well:

> The majority of human groups erect or attempt to erect . . . boundaries which divide "We," the fully human, from "They," the not-quite human, the different, the available for social violence.

It is important to be clear what is being said here. Human beings constitute a single species. That is an obvious and uncontested fact of the natural world. But in the *social* world, where "human" has a moral dimension as well as a biological one, that "fact" is far more ambiguous. If I describe someone as "inhuman," I am far more likely to be speaking of her ethical character than her genetic makeup. The idea that "we" are a special people, sometimes a chosen people, can easily ripen into the notion that the difference between "us" and "they" is built into the design of things. That is what Old Lodge Skins, the fictional Cheyenne chief we encountered in the chapter *Village* had in mind when he called his own people "Human Beings" and implied in doing so that other people—most particularly pale invaders from the East—were made of very different stuff. Old Lodge Skins, remember, said of them: "They are strange and do not know where the center of the world is." And then, speaking of his own people, he added:

> There have always been a limited number of Human Beings, because we are intended to be special and superior. To make this so, there must be a great number of inferior persons. To my mind, that is the function of white men in the world.

It is easy to nod appreciatively at that grave pronouncement. It was written by a white male in the late 20th century, as we know, but it is well tuned ethnographically and placed in the mouth of a very sympathetic character. That pronouncement, however, would have had an entirely different resonance if it had been attributed to a Spanish conquistador in Mexico, a Belgian official in the Congo, or, for that matter, an American cavalry officer on his way to attack the Cheyenne. Imagine General George Armstrong Custer saying to the press as he prepared his troops for a campaign in the West: "White people are intended to be special and superior. That is why there are so many inferior people in the world. We are carrying out a destiny."

Erik H. Erikson and I conferred about the notion of pseudospeciation off and on for two decades or so, and at one point participated in a "debate" on the topic sitting around a conference table, portions of which were later published. Sitting at that table were twenty or thirty colleagues familiar to us both, and it was evident to everyone there that the exchange itself was serious in content but almost tongue-in-cheek in tone. This was not an airing of opposing views, as the term "debate" would suggest, but a re-statement—a re-enactment—of conversations that had brought us to that point.

I had a particular interest in the concept of pseudospeciation—in part because I was in such close touch with its originator, of course, but also in part because I thought it was so relevant to concerns being pursued in sociology. I hoped to bring it across the disciplinary border separating psychoanalysis from sociology. But I had two reservations about the way the concept had been put initially, and I suggested a modest change in *terminology* and one in *emphasis,* as will be clearer soon. He declared that he was comfortable with both.

I should begin by noting that the concepts "pseudospecies" and "pseudospeciation" were introduced by him at a meeting of the Royal Society of London in 1965, so the first audience to hear it was made up for the most part of specialists in the natural and biological sciences. The prefix "pseudo" meant something different to them than it would have to a gathering of sociologists or anthropologists. In the natural sciences, "pseudo" refers to a phenomenon that resembles something else—mimics it—but does not have the same essential qualities. "Pseudoleukemia," for instance, is a disease that often passes for, but is not, leukemia. It is, though, a disease. In everyday English, on the other hand, "pseudo" can have an altogether different ring to it. It comes from the Greek, where it means to cheat, lie, falsify, pretend. A "pseudonym" is a false name. From a biological standpoint, then, "pseudo" would serve as an important modifier because it indicates that the lines one "people" draws to differentiate itself from another issue from the human imagination and not from the natural order. From a social science standpoint, though, "pseudo" almost suggests that the thing being modified is not all that real or substantial, and that would be a strange way to refer to a tendency of such fierce, stubborn force that it can result in the slaughter of millions of people. I feared that it would be misunderstood in that newer setting.

So I proposed that we avoid that potential awkwardness by distinguishing between a natural process to be known as *genetic speciation* and a social process to be known as *social speciation.* The elder Erikson agreed to that phrasing in principle, although he continued "to put things as I did in the past," as everybody involved had assumed he would all along. His last written statement on the subject was published in *The Yale Review*—plot thickens!—at a time when I was its Editor. The original paper in London had been given the equivalent of a biological seal of approval from Julian Huxley, Konrad Lorenz, and others present on that occasion, and this revisiting of the concept in *The Yale Review* twenty years later received a biological seal of approval from Steven Jay Gould, a distinguished expert in human evolution, who offered a written commentary on it. I, meantime, have been planning to return to the notion of social speciation "someday."

I will be speaking of "social speciation" from here on, then, and will begin with the definition I proposed at the time of those original discussions. It is only a slightly revised version of the Royal Society original:

> Social speciation is the process by which one gathering of human beings who form a "people" or a "kind" come to view the members of another gathering as so unlike themselves that they can be treated as if they were another order of being. At its harshest, social speciation can mean that those others are no longer regarded as subject to the normal mercies of human life and become eligible for contempt, exploitation, enslavement, and even slaughter.

That paragraph, obviously, begins with the change in terminology I had initially proposed—social speciation replacing pseudospeciation—but it also accomplishes the shift in emphasis I had in mind at the same time: social speciation refers to an *ongoing process* as well as to an *existing state of affairs*. Those who refer to the way one people manages to diminish the stature of another are usually looking backwards into a long, hard history of human brutality and find themselves writing in the past tense. In doing so, they often give the impression that most of the work of dividing humankind into distinct groups has already taken place. The passage by Erik H. Erikson I quoted a moment ago opened: "humankind from the very beginning has appeared on the world stage split into tribes and nations . . . religions and ideologies." That is certainly the case. The human record is eloquent on that topic. But it was also evident to him, as it has been to many others making similar points, that he was talking of an ongoing human activity, specia*ting,* as well as the established human condition known as specia*tion.*

That distinction really matters when we turn to the shifting nationalisms of our own time, where we can observe the process of *speciating* taking place before our eyes.

Making Nations

Terms like "nation" and "people" have an ancient, biblical sound to them, almost as if they referred to human formations of a distant antiquity. And, indeed, it was a widely accepted notion not so long ago in the West that humankind is naturally divided into nations in much the same way that physical matter is divided into elements and living matter into species. A "nation," according to that way of thinking, is an organic whole with a life of its own. The problem for those who hope to realign the peoples of the world into their natural configuration is to make out the true boundaries of "the" nations underneath all the elaborate scaffoldings that have been imposed on the human landscape by monarchs, chancelleries, parliaments, and all the other agencies that have been drawing artificial borderlines across the surface of the earth for centuries. When those frameworks are stripped away, when all those politically imposed border lines are erased, the true map of humankind—the natural geography of the world—will emerge. That language, of course, is yet another echo from the Age of Reason, and it figured very prominently in what was called a number of years ago the principle of "self-determination." The Allies spoke of it (frequently in the voice of Woodrow Wilson) when they divided up the territories of recently collapsed empires at the close of World War I. Napoleon spoke of it over a century earlier as he carved out new states on lands he had taken over by force of arms. The notion was to make "states" correspond to the homelands of "peoples."

One of the most celebrated expressions of that idea appeared in a lecture delivered by Ernest Renan of the Sorbonne in 1882 and reprinted widely since:

> A nation is a soul, a spiritual principle. Two things, which in truth are but one, constitute this soul or spiritual principle. One lies in the past, one in the present. One is the possession in common of a rich legacy of . . . memories; the other is present-day consent, the desire to live together, the will to perpetuate the value of the heritage that one has received in an undivided form.

Warming to his topic, Renan then declared to his male audience:

> Man, gentlemen, does not improvise. The nation, like the individual, is the culmination of a long past of endeavors, sacrifice, and devotion.

Most observers of the nationalisms of our own time would have been astonished by Renan's comment had he offered it in our day and would suggest instead that we humans are spectacularly adept at exactly the kinds of improvisation Renan was so dubious of, and that "nations" and "peoples" are in a continuing process of formation and re-formation. As we will see in the next (and final) portion of the book, the fall of Yugoslavia in the 1990s was accompanied by something that almost has to be described as the *creation* and *re-creation* of peoples and nations and ethnic formations. It was a time of *speciating*. The same can be said for most if not all of the zones of volatile ethnic tension that reach across our world now. (I have not commented on the explosive unrests taking place in large portions of the Middle East, even though they are much in the news as I write these lines, because I can have no sense of their outcome. But it is well to keep that enigma in mind as we continue to pursue this line of thought.)

This shift in emphasis is reflected clearly in the titles of recent works on nationalism. We have already seen that Benedict Anderson entitled his analysis *Imagined Communities,* while two other distinguished students of the subject, Eric Hobsbawm and Terence Ranger, wrote about "the invention" of national traditions. Expressions like "constructing ethnicity," "creating ethnicity," and "the social construction of nationality" have worked their way into the titles of recent works on nationalism generally, and the conclusions of various studies of specific regions are anticipated by titles like *Medoc, the Making of a Myth; From Peasants to Frenchmen;* and *The Making of the Basque Nation.*

It probably should be added that a "people" does not often invent itself out of whole cloth. Karl Deutsch made the point a number of years ago that national consciousness is not very likely to arise unless there is something out there in the air for people to be conscious of. But most experts would also argue that ethnicities of even the most compelling claim to antiquity have to be seen as emerging from an ongoing social process, as a social construct. When I suggest, as I did a moment ago, that the world was witness to the *creation* or to the *re-creation* of national and ethnic boundaries in the former Yugoslavia, I am stepping onto conceptual territory that has to be negotiated cautiously. I certainly do not mean to suggest that ethnonational distinctions are new to the Balkans—far from it—or, for that matter, that the boundary lines now dividing Tutsi from Hutu in Rwanda or Catholic from Protestant in Northern Ireland or Sunni from Shia in the Middle East are newly drawn.

Those boundary lines are old in the sense that one can easily find traces of them in the historical record. The fissures that opened up in Yugoslavia had long been a part of the Balkan landscape in one sense or another, and for that reason the appearance of new surges of distrust and hostility in the present were "explained" as the flaring up of old fevers. If ethnic suspicions between Protestants and Catholics that threatened to erupt into civil war were to break out suddenly in Louisiana, say, or in some equally unlikely location, it would not be long before commentators began to allude to the long record of conflict between the two religious groups over the centuries and to describe the events in Louisiana as a renewal of those old enmities—ghosts emerging from the rubble of a distant past. That would be a bizarre analysis of the situation, at least to begin with, since the odds are high that few of the principals would have been aware of that history and fewer yet would be ready to claim that it had anything to do with their present frame of mind. Yet it might not take long for that analysis to gain a new currency because we all count on coherent narratives to help us make sense of what is going on around us. That, in any event, is what most experts on the subject think happened in Yugoslavia, as we shall soon see.

For those purposes, the "past" may be best envisioned as an immense storehouse of events, personages, encounters, utterances, suggestive moments, telling details in endless variation. If one passes through that storehouse looking for scraps of evidence that will not only "explain" a particular outcome but make it seem inevitable, the task is not a hard one. Those who seek support for the argument that dark reservoirs of ethnic loathing have been lurking below the surface of the Balkans for centuries, awaiting their chance to emerge, will find something of use to them readily. Those seeking an "explanation" for that hypothetical eruption of bad feeling in Louisiana may have a harder time of it, but they will succeed too. Finding the seeds of discontent is fairly easy work. At the same time, though, if one passes through the storehouse with eyes differently focused and intellectual reflexes differently set, it will be just as simple to assemble details that suggest a far more peaceful narrative.

With one purposeful sweep of the storehouse, that is, one can gather an impressive array of odds and ends, bits and pieces, indicating how old and how intractable the fracture lines are dividing Serb and Muslim in Bosnia, Tutsi and Hutu in Rwanda, Sunni and Shia in the Middle East, or, to draw on our fanciful example one last time, Protestant and Catholic in Louisiana. But with another purposeful sweep one can gather an impressive array of data indicating how recent those fracture lines really are as a historical matter. The details one selects from the storehouse and assembles into a narrative may all be accurate in one sense or another, but the patterns into which they are set and the uses to which they are put amount to a kind of invention, an effort to make the flows of history take on a particular aspect as they drift by. More often than not, many specialists would now insist, the second narrative—the one in which ethnic antagonisms are shown to be of recent vintage—are a more accurate portrayal of modern nationalisms than the first. But the first has a strong and special appeal—not only to individuals caught up in the conflict, since it gives them, often *for the first time,* a logic to explain what they are doing, but also for the rest of us who take comfort in being able to give a coherent shape to what is happening around us in a few deft sentences. "Oh, you know, the Tutsis and Hutus have hated each other since ancient times. This is just African history reasserting itself." "Oh, you know, those people in the Balkans have always been like that. It's inevitable. There's nothing we can do." The foreign policy of several important capitals rested exactly on that assumption. Warren Christopher, then the U.S. Secretary of State, spoke of his country's inattention to the prob- lems of the Balkans in 1991: It is "a tribal feud that no outsider could hope to settle." John Major, then Prime Minister of Great Britain, spoke in exactly that way. So much for that.

One final reflection before we return to these matters.

Most of the raging conflicts we learn of in today's news broadcasts not only involve battle lines of fairly recent coinage, but involve peoples on either side of the line who are very like each other in look, custom, language, and sometimes even in religious conviction. Combatants who confront each other across those new boundaries are looking at faces and hearing voices so like their own that they might as well be staring into a mirror. Our loyal friend, the orbiting stranger, looking down on the earth as it rotates slowly on its own axis and drifts in easy circles around the sun, is likely to conclude that there are no peoples on the planet more alike than Serb and Bosnian Muslim, Tamil and Singhalese, Irish Catholic and Irish Protestant, Flemish and Walloon, Tutsi and Hutu, Catalonian and Castilian. There is good reason for this, of course. It is often the fate of neighbors to have to compete for resources or hegemony or something else even though they are likely to be next-of-kin in the cultural—and even in the genetic— sense. Friction is most easily produced by the rub of adjacent bodies.

That poses a real dilemma. The process of drawing ethnic and national boundaries—the process of speciating—can be an extremely complicated one when the peoples involved cannot easily be distinguished on the basis of their appearance, language, custom, or dress, and when the peoples involved reach back into the same historical record for some sense of who they are and where they came from. The Serbs and Croats and Muslims who fought one another so bitterly during the breakup of Yugoslavia spoke essentially the same language for hundreds of years and were citizens of the same sovereign state for most of (and in the vast majority of cases for all of) their adult lives. The Hutus and Tutsis of Rwanda also speak the same language, observe the same faith, work the same land, and share a common history, which in their case includes a period of grotesque occupation by Belgium. Yet vast numbers of them were hacked to death over a distinction that would not even have been taken seriously by any skilled observer a few years earlier.

The question then becomes: How is this astonishing thing accomplished? How do people who have been navigating by use of the same human map for a long time suddenly divide into national or ethnic segments so antagonistic that they can be viewed as a different order of being? We will see how that process took place in the Yugoslavia of some time ago in the chapter to follow. We will end this one with a few more general thoughts on that subject.

One method for accomplishing that division, tested over many millennia of human history, is to devise new forms of language for describing those newly emerged "others." I noted in the chapter on "Becoming a Person" that the way people *speak* about things has an enormous influence on the way they *visualize* things, and it follows that the words we use to describe other human beings shape the lens through which we see them. A philosopher named Glenn Gray pointed out in a wise and moving memoir of men in battle that we have a tendency to use the definite article when speaking of wartime adversaries. It is never *our* enemy, or *an* enemy, but always *the* enemy—a usage that hints darkly of something fixed and immutable, something abstract and evil. When combatants facing one another across the battle line are strangers in the sense that they come from very different places and live very different lives, that form of demonization comes easily.

In Yugoslavia, Rwanda, and Cambodia, however, to draw once again on examples that have come up frequently so far in this discussion, the demonization of an enemy made up of persons who were once neighbors, fellow townspeople, and compatriots has to begin on an empty slate. Nothing works more efficiently for that purpose than those deadly new weapons of ethnic warfare: newsprint, radio, television, and internet. We will come across a stark example of those new weapons at work when we turn to the example of Yugoslavia. You may know perfectly well that your Serb or Muslim opponent looks exactly like you, but if the media can somehow help you form an image in your mind of a vicious creature who sucks the blood of his victims while gouging out their eyes with gritty thumbnails, the task of drawing ethnic boundaries is made far simpler. The sketch is not really meant to portray the way he actually *looks* but the way he *is*. It is a moral portrait, not a physical likeness.

A Final Thought

It should be evident by now that what I am calling "social speciation" belongs in the realm of the social and the cultural, not in the realm of the biological. It refers to the way we humans come to visualize fellow humans as "they," "them," "of another kind," rather than "we," "us," "our kind." It is not in any way an approach to—never mind a theory of—homicide in general.

I bring this up now because the term "dehumanization" has found its way into discussions of this general topic more often of late, and I would like to draw a contrast between that way of looking at things and the one I have been proposing here. A good example of the new surge of interest in "dehumanization" is the work of an American philosopher named David Livingston Smith. His view of the matter is crisp, decisive, and remarkably assured, so I will enlist him as spokesperson for that emerging point of view.

In a book entitled *Less Than Human: Why We Demean, Enslave, and Exterminate Others,* Smith takes it as a biological given that we human beings are born with "a powerful aversion to harming" one another, "an engrained resistance to killing other humans." The logic of that assumption was discussed earlier in this chapter, of course. But Smith takes a big step further and proposes that nature's way of freeing us from that built-in aversion is to allow us to "dehumanize" other creatures of our biological kind—to demote them from the ranks of the human altogether—and to treat them as another form of life. Our reluctance to harm others is simply eliminated, canceled out, by that mental maneuver. "The function of dehumanization is to override inhibitions against committing acts of violence" toward fellow humans, Smith writes. It is a "precondition" to homicide. And it is a tendency rooted deep in our animal nature—part of "the evolved design of the human species."

A very compelling hypothesis. Evidence to support it can be found everywhere. The historical record simply shudders with occasions when one universe of people has managed to demean the standing of another universe of people to such an extent that those others were treated like loathsome animals. One need only to recall the Holocaust. Or to remember what happened when European powers were colonizing Africa, Asia, and the Americas. Franz Fanon, a black

resident of Algeria at the time of the French occupation and a brilliant observer
of the colonial world more generally, said of the outlook of a typical French
settler in Algeria that

> it dehumanizes the native, or, to speak plainly, it turns him into an animal. In fact,
> the terms the settler uses when he mentions natives are zoological ones. He speaks
> of the yellow man's reptilian motions, of the stink of the native quarter, of breeding
> swarms, of foulness, of spawn, of gesticulations. When the settler seeks to describe
> the native fully in exact terms, he usually refers to the bestiary.

So the human record is awesomely clear on that matter: we are fully capable
of mistreating, enslaving, and slaughtering creatures of our own genetic kind as
if they were of a wholly different order of animal life. "Dehumanization" in that
sense is alive and well in our world. Neat. Simple. Elegant. Mystery solved.

But human life is more complicated than that. It is far too early to wrap up
what little we know about the ways of our kind in so neat a package because the
human record is full of other horrors as well—occasions in which we slaughter
or do harm to others *knowing full well* that they are human, and sometimes—or
so it would sometimes seem—doing so precisely *because* they are human. No
genetic preconditioning required for those atrocities.

To provide examples of what I mean here might turn out to be a misleading
exercise, since focusing on particulars can have the effect of taking one's eyes
from the dimensions of the whole. The point that needs to be made, though, is
that a terrifying share of the violent acts that darken the human scene occur in
circumstances where nothing that can reasonably be called "dehumanization"
takes place at all. A few cases in point:

How often in human history have men (and I mean males here) strutted
across tribal compounds and village greens and city squares boasting of
the fact that they slew other men in combat? They wear medals, display scalps,
cut notches in the handles of their guns, enter parades, and listen with pride
to stories told and songs sung about their heroic exploits. They might have
charged into the battlefield muttering epithets like "dogs," "swine," "rats,"
"snakes," but the sense of accomplishment clearly comes from having slain
another human being. And if a lingering sense of guilt comes later, as we now
know to have been the case for many, that too is a form of recognition that the
slain opponent was indeed human. Many millions have died in civil wars
where there is no evidence at all to suggest that combatants on either side

regarded their counterparts as less than human. The American Civil War is a telling example.

How often in time of war have captive women been raped by men of the other side in clear recognition that they are human? Whether the act itself is provoked by a perverse kind of battlefield lust, a wish to humiliate or demean, an explosion of unspent rage, or something else entirely, the fact that the victim is human— and, not at all incidentally, that her menfolk and other members of her community are human too—is essential to the very meaning of the event. In Bosnia, Muslim women were regularly, systematically, raped by Serb militiamen, and were often informed afterward that the purpose of the violation had been to impregnate them—to plant Serb seed in Muslim wombs, and, by extension, to inject Serb blood into the inner flows of Muslim life. This strategy, clearly, was not very well thought through, since its outcome is likely to mean an increase in the number of persons brought up Muslim who have been taught to hate Serbs. But it does reflect a cunning, furtive, even sinister sense of how human communities sometimes work. It is meant to contaminate the inner tissues of the enemy host as well as damaging it from the outside. It is the ultimate act of sabotage, perhaps. And it is often understood in just that way not only by the women who suffered the assault but by the men who returned from war to their home villages from the front to learn of it. They are, after all, the sons, fathers, brothers, and husbands. This is inhumane by any measure, of course, but it is not brought about by something that even remotely resembles dehumanization. On the contrary, it is an act of aggression we impose on creatures who we recognize as looking, reacting, thinking just like us. We know how they will react because we know that they are at root much like us. In that sense, they *are* us.

And, how often in human life does an individual who is aware of having taken the life of someone else ask himself in the calm of a silent evening afterward, "why did I act as I did?" Or how often is he asked that question by someone else? One answer that can resolve that aching question would be: "well, after all, he was nothing other than a rodent or cockroach or swine." The dehumanizing comes after the fact, not before. It is not a precondition built into our animal nature, our bone and marrow.

So far, we have focused a good deal more attention on the battlefield than the home front, which makes good sense in a chapter on peoplehood and nationalism. But it should be noted as we bring this discussion to a close that a vast majority of the homicides that disturb the public peace at home occur within narrow living spaces. Both the slayers and the slain are from the same neighborhoods. They gather at the same street corners, places of work, parishes, playgrounds, taverns, and, of course, households. No mystery in that. Proximity creates points of friction and irritation. It supplies both an urging to do harm to others and an opportunity to act on it. It is in those narrow spaces that personalities are the most likely to clash, jealousies to develop, idiosyncrasies to rankle, conflicts of interest to arise. And yet those persons are as alike socially, culturally, and probably genetically as human variation allows. Homicide in such close quarters as those can hardly be a result of dehumanization. These persons are the least likely candidates for those mental maneuvers to be found on the face of the earth.

Setting aside for the moment the matter of homicide among neighbors—a subject that would draw us back into the subject of *persons* relating to one another rather than *peoples* relating to one another—the best provisional answer to that old and familiar question "why do the nations so furiously rage together" may well be that we human beings simply operate with a different definition of what constitutes a "species" than natural scientists do. We are on the whole perfectly aware of the distinctions that set our genetic species apart from other genetic species, but the boundary lines that appear to matter the most in the way we view the social landscape are those that sort us into "peoples," "kinds," orders," "strains," genres," "types," "ilks"—all of those terms, let me note a bit slyly, being synonyms for "species" in dictionary English. When Old Lodge Skins spoke of "inferior" white people whose purpose on earth was to demonstrate how "special and superior" his people are, he referred to them as "men" and as "persons." They are human, but not like us. They are human, but made of different stuff. Human, but looking, acting, speaking, thinking quite differently from us.

And there are indications, which I will just let float in the air as we turn elsewhere, that the same may be true for other social creatures.

But this chapter will end as the last one did, raising questions rather than providing answers. Archibald MacLeish has his Hamlet say: "We know the answers, all the answers. It is the questions we do not know." We will take what comfort we can from that.

War Comes to Pakrac

TO OUTSIDERS, AT LEAST, THE PEOPLE WHO lived in the land known as Yugoslavia seemed to form a distinct ethnic enclave. They were quite like each other in look and language and manner, and they were different in exactly those aspects from their immediate neighbors—the Austrians and Hungarians to their north, the Romanians and Bulgarians to their east, the Greeks and Albanians to their south, and the Italians across the Adriatic to their west. One would have thought them natural candidates for peoplehood, and, indeed, the notion that the people of the region belong together in a union of blood and culture and speech has been the prevailing concept behind the two countries called Yugoslavia—the Kingdom established after World War I that lasted from 1918 to 1940, and the Federal Republic established after World War II that lasted from 1945 until 1991. The word "Yugoslavia" means "land of the South Slavs."

In 1991, Yugoslavia splintered into several national fragments like a crystal struck by a hammer. The country had been divided administratively into six different "republics": Slovenia, Croatia, Serbia, Bosnia and Hercegovina, Macedonia, and Montenegro. At first glance, then, the breakup of the country had an almost orderly look because the fracture lines corresponded so closely to the provincial borders. Slovenia, the first to secede, was to be the homeland of the Slovenes; Croatia, the second to secede, was to be the homeland of the Croats; and Serbia, left to its own devices, was to be the homeland of the Serbs. What could be tidier than that?

But things were far messier than that, because those borderlines did not reflect the ethnic distribution of the Yugoslav population at all well. Almost

700,000 individuals who called themselves Serbs lived in Croatia, and close to a million and a half in Bosnia. Some 800,000 Croats lived in Bosnia, and another 200,000 in Serbia. Meantime, something like two million Albanians lived in various locations throughout Yugoslavia, mostly Kosovo, and a number of Hungarians and other ethnic minorities could be found elsewhere. Those border lines, then, appeared to be full of meaning when drawn on a map, but an accurate depiction of the way the population was distributed over space would have asked far too much of that way of portraying reality. A travel writer named Brian Hall asks us to envision the following: a Croat household on a largely Serb street in the Croat neighborhood of a Serb town in Croatia. Pockets within pockets. How might one map that? And to complicate matters, many people, more often found in the cities than in the countryside, identified themselves as "Yugoslav"—as native residents of the land of the South Slavs—rather than as Serbs, Croats, Muslims, or any other ethnicity. So there was a good deal of painful and even deadly sorting out to do.

How that sorting came about has been considered in a number of thoughtful studies, their focus varying with the conceptual height, as it were, from which the authors looked down on the scene.

If one views the Balkan countryside from a considerable altitude—a point of vantage lofty enough for the eye to take in half a continent or so—it makes sense to see the collapse of Yugoslavia as yet another consequence of the splintering of the communist world in 1989. From that high prospect, Yugoslavia was swept up in the same social and economic undertows as many other parts of Eastern Europe, and was thus "part of a more widespread phenomenon of political disintegration," as one expert, Susan Woodward, put it.

If one views that scene from a less commanding elevation, as most correspondents did—a point of vantage from which the eye can take in the region itself—it makes sense to see the fall of Yugoslavia as the work of particular persons or events or policies. Among the *persons* most often nominated as the principal author of the land's troubles was Slobodan Milošević—as worthy a candidate as can be imagined, even if he should not be allowed to occupy that bleak place of honor all alone. Among the *events* most often nominated were the secessions of Slovenia and Croatia from the Republic in 1991. And among the *policies* most often nominated were the decisions of emerging new regimes in Zagreb and Belgrade, capitals of Croatia and Serbia, to rearrange the map of the Balkans along ethnonational lines.

Finally, if one views the Balkan countryside from something closer to ground level—a point of vantage from which the eye focuses on what happens in village greens and church yards, in school rooms and taverns, in homes and barracks, in marketplaces and crossroads—it makes sense to see the death of Yugoslavia as an abrupt shift in the moods and outlooks of its people, whose views on things are seldom included in such studies.

The first and second of those points of vantage can be called *geopolitical* in the sense that they are concerned with the behavior of markets, the deployment of armies, the shifting of populations, the distribution of resources, and the conduct of presidents and parliaments and ministries. It is probably accurate to say that most of what the world has learned about those difficult times, both from news media and from the scholarly ranks, is the product of those angles of vision. The third, though, can be called *psychological* and *social*—we can collapse that into *psychosocial* for the moment—in the sense that it focuses on how people who lived down there at ground level actually *experienced* the conflicts visited upon them from distant markets and distant capitals.

We will be dealing primarily here with that third point of vantage, and we will do so by visiting a particular location on that larger wartime landscape. Croatia and Serbia went to war in the summer of 1991. It was a civil war, to be sure, yet a profoundly complicated one. Croatia seceded from what was left of the original Yugoslavia, which really meant that it was separating from Serbia. And, of course, Croatia was home to hundreds of thousands of ethnic Serbs. Some declared their loyalty to the new Croatia, the land their ancestors had settled on centuries ago, but many others declared their loyalty to the idea of Yugoslavia, which really meant that they were seceding from the new Croatia and recognizing their Serb heritage.

So it was a civil war played out at two wholly different levels. One involved military confrontations between the new nations, Croatia and Serbia. The other involved skirmishes of many kinds, some of them quite deadly, within Croatia itself between fellow countrymen of differing faiths and ethnic identities who had lived together in peace for a long time.

I made a number of research visits to Croatia in the 1990s as the land lay tense and exhausted from the war that had raged—and was still raging—across it. The pages to follow draw on field research that I undertook with three collaborators, one of them a remarkable individual named Eric Markusen who would have served as co-author of this chapter had he lived long enough. The others were Kirsten Schultz, and, in a special way, Randi Markusen. The object of that

effort was to trace the spiral down which a people who had once shared a countryside in relative harmony descended into bitterness and hatred and even acts
of slaughter.

A story that appeared in the *New York Times* on the very last day of 1994
described an incident in which a man, armed with an automatic weapon,
knocked on the door of one of his neighbors and ordered her outside. According
to the woman's account, she said to him: "You know me. You know my husband.
How can you do this to me?" He is said to have replied: "That time is over. I no
longer know you." Whereupon he ordered her, weapon on the ready, to "crawl
along the street as he kicked her repeatedly." He was a Serb and she a Muslim.
That event took place in Sarajevo, the capital of Bosnia, but it offers a very
telling indication of what "neighbor" had come to mean throughout the land of
the South Slavs.

The focus of our research was a town in Croatia called Pakrac (*pock-rots* is
the best I can suggest as a guide to pronunciation). It is situated sixty miles east
and a little south of Zagreb in an area known as Western Slavonia. Pakrac is
of particular interest in this context because its population of something like
25,000 was unusually well-mixed ethnically, being close to 50 percent Serb and
40 percent Croat when active hostilities broke out in 1991. And more telling yet,
a strikingly high percentage of the marriages contracted in Pakrac over the past
few decades had been between a Serb and a Croat, which meant that the population of the town was almost as thoroughly interwoven as circumstances—and
the laws of chance—permit.

We conducted (and recorded) interviews with more than two hundred persons
who had lived in (or in the vicinity of) Pakrac in the time of war. Roughly 50
percent of them were Croats and 40 percent Serbs, reversing the above population numbers—the rest being an assortment of the various minorities that made
their home in the region. For reasons that will become clear as we proceed,
many of the Serbs you will hear from here had to be traced to places of refuge
in other parts of the countryside because they had been driven from home.
Some were located in Serb villages in the vicinity of Pakrac. Others had taken
shelter in the far eastern reaches of Croatia, right up against the border with
Serbia more than a hundred miles away, that were still under Serb control then.
Still others were interviewed in Serbia or in Serb-occupied parts of Bosnia.

The window through which we were looking, then, is a relatively narrow
one, since we were focusing primarily on what happened to the people of a

modest, provincial town. But that window opens onto a vast panorama. Pakrac is not "typical" or "representative" in any of the usual meanings of those terms. It is more than that—a miniature, a concentrated view of events spread across a much wider expanse that could happen anywhere.

Pakrac

War came to Pakrac on August 19, 1991, when Serb irregular troops—soon to be joined by units of what had by then become the Serbian national army—shelled the town from the surrounding hills. Over the next few months, Pakrac changed hands several times as Serb forces swept across it and were repulsed, swept across it and were again repulsed. The streets of the town, on each of those occasions, became scenes of fierce combat. The official casualty rate is that more than a hundred persons lost their lives, several hundred were injured, and many thousands were displaced from their homes. We heard from one Croat official (who had compared notes with his Serb counterpart soon after the fighting had come to a stop) that the casualty figures were considerably higher, and that estimate has to be respected. But all such reckonings, like so many of the "facts" that emerged from those dizzying times, were informed guesses at best. According to yet another estimate, a quarter of the homes in Pakrac were destroyed, half had been struck so hard that they had become uninhabitable for at least the immediate time being, and some of the remaining quarter sustained at least some damage. Those numbers may be too high, but it was visible to the naked eye in the months to follow.

A cease fire was agreed to by both sides in January of 1992, and detachments of the United Nations Protection Force moved in to secure the area. The cease fire had the effect of bringing the shifting tides of war to an abrupt halt, almost as if surges of water had been frozen in mid-motion, and this took place when the line of battle—in a war like this there is not much sense in speaking of a "front"—ran more or less through the middle of the town. For the next four years, a demarcation line separating territory under control of Croat forces from territory under control of Serb forces occupied the very center of Pakrac. Locally, the line was a source of deep pain, since it divided neighbor from neighbor, friend from friend, relative from relative, and even mate from mate and child from parent. Internationally, the line was a source of considerable political and military concern. It was generally assumed, for one thing, that if the war were to break out again, Pakrac might well supply the theater—as indeed turned out to be the case. A writer named Michael Ignatieff visited Pakrac about the time I first did, and his report reflects the tension one could sense then:

> The U.N. checkpoint was a sandbagged Portakabin manned by two Canadian infantrymen guarding a road barrier between the Croat- and Serb-held sections of Pakrac. The road to the checkpoint wound its way between pulverized bungalows, upended cars in the ditches, waist-high grass in abandoned gardens. Just visible in the grass, as we approached the check-point, were two teenage Croatian spotters with their binoculars trained on the Serbian side.

I was at an outdoor café on the Croat side of the demarcation line called the Skorpio on one of my earlier visits to Pakrac, staring out at the rubble across the street, when two men sat down at a nearby table. They were wearing raincoats on a sunny, uncomfortably warm afternoon, and that caught my attention. As they sat down, one could hear the muffled sound of metal objects clanking against one another. We were sitting in the exact center of a demilitarized zone, and it was entirely obvious that they were armed, almost literally, to the teeth. That caught my attention too. A few minutes after that, I crossed the street to take a closer look at those ruins, and when I reached their edge another man charged straight at me, yelling loudly in Serbo-Croatian. That *really* caught my attention, but it turned out to be an act of generosity and gallantry rather than one of hostility. He wanted me—a complete stranger—to know that the ruins had not yet been checked for land mines. I was not about to enter that rubble anyway, but he had no way of knowing that. Tension, obviously, hung in the air.

On May 1, 1995, four years later, war did break out again as Croatian forces overran Serb-occupied sectors of Western Slavonia in a strike called "Operation Flash," so Pakrac became a battlefield yet again. The United Nations force simply stepped aside, as it must in such situations. Available reports were not clear on how much additional damage was done to the town itself. I was there two weeks later and did not think I could see that much of a difference, although it should be added that fresh wounds might have been difficult for a visitor like me to make out in a landscape already as scarred as this one was. But damage to the human spirit was simply tremendous. Vast numbers of Pakrac Serbs, who had been protected on the eastern side of the UN demarcation line for four years, fled in panic, fearing what might be in store for them. We will learn more about them, too.

The situation in the surrounding countryside was very like that in towns like Pakrac. As one drove through the lush pastures and the forested hills of Western Slavonia, one could still encounter peasants dressed in black using scythes and hand-held threshers, and teams of horses dragging plows or hauling wooden carts piled high with hay. But as the road curved around the base of a low hill or dipped into a valley, it was not at all unusual to come across what was once a village of fifty or sixty dwellings but was then little more than a continuous corridor of skeletal remains—the bare husk of a home, the remnant of a wall, the scorched spire of a chimney, or a thick layer of debris lying flat against the ground and slowly being reclaimed by grass and shrubbery. Locals who know about such things point out to visitors who do not that the houses are split open from their hearths, the walls splayed outward from the force of a detonation from within, and the roofs and upper stories collapsed on the floors beneath— evidence that the destruction was not a result of shells dropped in time of war but of explosive charges deliberately set in time of peace. The village signs had been removed, too, as if the place had been erased not only from the surfaces of the land but from memory itself. These were Serb villages in Croat territory. Their exact counterparts could be found on the other side of the demarcation line.

One also passed through villages in which every third or fourth dwelling had been blown apart. They remained there in raw piles of debris, long after the detonations that had brought them down, with splintered bits of furniture, broken dishware, and weathered scraps of cloth peeking out from the remains. Children living on either side of the ruins played near, and sometimes even in them. Adults on their way to places of work or places of worship passed them by. They were once the homes of local Serbs, deliberately destroyed by fellow villagers as a measure of their sense of welcome. Their exact counterpart, once again, could be found on the other side of the line.

That is what war had done to Pakrac and the surrounding countryside. It was a time of corrosive bitterness that comes from the feeling of having been betrayed by people once counted as neighbors.

I am going to pause for a moment now to offer a brief detour that will inter- rupt the flow of the chapter. This detour will be a background sketch of events, telling moments, developments that let up to the collapse of Yugoslavia. It is not a "history" in any useful sense of the term, but a species of trail guide to be read at the beginning of the trip to help locate the story the people will be telling us in time and place.

Background Sketch

In order to really understand the civil war that the people of Pakrac were caught up in, one would need to reach deep into Balkan history for causes. Our reason for taking so close a glance at what happened in Pakrac, though, is that it offers so instructive an example of what can happen to people everywhere swept up in the eddies of a wider war, so we will not go into that history in detail now. Yet you will be hearing occasional echoes of that past in the voices of the people we will be hearing from and will get a sense of some of the tensions they had to live with, so we will need a brief historical sketch.

A fuller account would include a chapter on a distant past when people known as the South Slavs migrated into a largely empty portion of the Balkans in the 6th and 7th centuries. Some of them settled into the western reaches of that land and others into the eastern, which did not became a matter of any relevance until centuries later when the people of the more western regions became Roman Catholic and learned to call themselves "Croat," and those of the more eastern regions became Christian Orthodox and came to call themselves "Serb."

A fuller account would also include a chapter on the many centuries during which the northern portions of the land of the South Slavs became a part of the Habsburg Empire and the southern and eastern portions were entirely submerged under the dominion of the Ottoman Empire. In some respects, at least, it might even be said that the Balkans simply disappeared from European history for those centuries. That need not concern us now, but one consequence of that submergence was that large numbers of persons living under the Ottoman canopy converted to the Muslim faith. Another is that when things settled down over time, the border line separating Croatia from Bosnia became the boundary where the Habsburg Empire met the Ottoman Empire—and, not to be too dramatic about it—where Europe met Asia, where West met East. No trivial detail that! The Habsburgs responded to that setting of the boundary by inviting tens of thousands of Serbs, sworn enemies of the Ottomans and reputed to be fierce warriors, to settle into frontier lands along the Croat side of the line to serve as a kind of armed buffer zone. They were promised freedom of religion and were offered other benefits as well. That outcome might rank as a footnote in in the larger telling of the story, but it matters to us here because those settlers were the ancestors of the Serbs of Pakrac and a majority of the people living in Western Slavonia.

The Ottoman Empire began to withdraw during the second half of the 19th century, and the Habsburg Empire simply disappeared at the opening of World War I in 1916. At the end of that conflict, the various segments of the land of the South Slavs were gathered into a new nation to be called *The Kingdom of Serbs, Croats, and Slovenes* at Versailles in 1919, where the map of much the world was reconfigured. It lasted, if barely, until the beginning of World War II in 1939, when German forces invaded Croatia and installed a government headed by a political faction called the *Ustasha,* made up largely of individuals who seemed to live on a line somewhere between fanaticism and outright derangement. Serbia cast its lot with the Allies. Among the forces under Serbian command at that time were fighters known as *Chetniks,* who were not well-known for their delicacy either, a matter I note now because those two terms, "Ustasha" and "Chetnik," have been a part of the national vocabularies of both Croatia and Serbia in the time since and will appear here as well.

By the end of the war, militias under the command of Marshall Tito were in charge, and he was entrusted with the leadership of a second Yugoslavia as the winning Allies drew new boundaries across vast portions of the earth—at Yalta this time. In some ways, at least, the name of the first Yugoslavia— Kingdom of Serbs, Croats, and Slovenes—was almost an exercise in ambiguity, officially distinguishing three different peoples while gathering them together into a single homeland. Tito's reign can almost be described as a similar exercise, making the most of the fact that Yugoslavia was formed as the land of the South Slavs while apportioning responsibilities and opportunities and benefits by the ethnic backgrounds of his constituents. Yugoslavia began to fracture along ethnic lines soon after Tito died in 1980, and aspirants to positions of power—Slobodan Milošević, once again, comes first to mind—recognized quickly that that the Republic had come on hard times economically and that the most effective card one could place on the table was a nationalist one.

Thus the historical sketch. It is absurdly brief, but even so it may help us understand why observers from other parts of the world began to assume when Yugoslavia did collapse that we were witnessing an eruption of deep ethnic loathings, smoldering underground for generations if not centuries and rushing to the surface as fissures broke the crust of the land to provide an opening. An important writer named Ivo Andrić who won the Nobel Prize for literature in 1961, speaking of the "frenzy of hate" that is supposed to have swept across

Sarajevo after the assassination of Archduke Franz Ferdinand in 1914, expressed that view with frightening clarity:

> Adherents of the three main faiths, they hate one another from birth to death, senselessly and profoundly. . . . Often, they spend their entire lives without finding an opportunity to express that hatred in all its facets and horror; but whenever the established order of things is shaken by some important event, and reason and law are suspended for a few hours or days, then this mob, or rather a section of it, finding at last an adequate motive, overflows into the town . . . and, like a flame which has sought and has at last found fuel, those long-kept hatreds and hidden desires for destruction and violence take over the town, lapping, sputtering, and swallowing everything, until some force larger than themselves suppresses them, or until they burn themselves out and tire of their own rage.

That way of accounting for the troubles that came to plague the region turned out to be a profoundly compelling one. It had a nice gothic ring to it, for one thing, hinting darkly of a land of haunted ruins, festering hatreds, and relentless cycles of violence and retribution—themes that figured prominently in widely read travel accounts like that of Rebecca West, who visited the region shortly before the collapse of the first Yugoslavia. More to the point, perhaps, that argument is appealing because it allows one to see the conflict as the playing out of an inevitable script. We are encouraged to view the conflict as emerging inexorably from the peculiar history of the land or from the peculiar character of its people. Echoes of that argument have been heard so frequently in world capitals, in fact, that they can be said to have informed the foreign policies of several nations, including that of the United States. A Russian army officer serving with the United Nations in Bosnia, speaking to an American correspondent named David Rieff, said:

> You Americans are constitutionally unable to understand what is going on in the Balkans. You're nice boys and girls, so nice. You don't want to see that it's not politics here but blood and history. All you can do is ride out the cycles of killing and try to look after the wounded. For the rest, it's as unstoppable as an earthquake. You have to understand plate tectonics to see what is going on in Yugoslavia.

That Russian observer may or may not have described the temperament of his fellow Slavs accurately, but he was wrong to suppose that Americans in general were slow to appreciate the sad truth he thought he was in possession of. Warren Christopher, then Secretary of State, as we noted earlier, was echoing the view of his President and his government when he called the conflict in Yugoslavia "intractable . . . a tribal feud that no outsider could hope to settle." That was also the view issuing from London, Berlin, Paris, and elsewhere.

There are two tests for such a theory. The first is to consult the experts. They have been virtually unanimous in dismissing it outright. The struggles that were then convulsing the region, Bogdan Denitch wrote, were "not caused by a popular upsurge of national hate." Indeed,

> Serbs and Croats have lived together more or less tolerably for four centuries. . . .
> The hate had to be systematically *created* and maintained. . . . Yugoslavia was not
> destroyed by vast pressures of discontent from below. It was killed by policies
> initiated by the political leadership of the various republics.

Susan L. Woodward was equally emphatic: "To explain the Yugoslav crisis as a result of ethnic hatred," she wrote, "is to turn the story upside down and begin at its end." Ivo Banać put it as sharply: "To define the war as a tribal feud or a civil war is simply an easy way of dismissing the whole thing. . . . It all adds up to a combination of political opportunism and intellectual laziness." These are single voices, chosen because they are such distinguished ones, but they do not stand out in this respect. If we had added other expert voices, we would have gathered a chorus. Consensus reigns here.

The second test, it stands to reason, is to consult the people who lived in the villages and worked the farmlands across which the Yugoslav wars were fought. The theory states that ancient enmities lurk below the surfaces of everyday social life and assert themselves whenever circumstances allow. But lurking where? Unless they are found down in some unconscious chamber of the mind and are acted upon without people being aware of it—an impossible notion to deal with even if we are deeply impressed by the dark mysteries of the Balkans— the enmity is registered somewhere in the conscious mind, and we need only inquire into it. Persons who have been asked that question in various corners of Yugoslavia are for the most part unanimous in reporting that ancient loathings had nothing to do with their participation in the hostilities that swirled around them. Consensus reigns here too.

That brings us to 1991 and the turmoil in Pakrac.

Back to Pakrac

The mood of Pakrac was dark and brooding during my time there as well as electric with a sense of apprehension. And yet every one of the more than two hundred persons we interviewed who had lived in Pakrac before the war agreed that there had scarcely been any history of ethnic hostility there for almost half a century. They remembered a time when neighbors looked out for one another, festivals were shared, and children grew up with far more regard for the locale in which they lived than for the national grouping to which they nominally belonged. Social scientists know from research conducted in other places and at other times that people often find it easy to idealize a past that stands out in such haunting contrast to a painful, horrifying present. Still, when one confronts that degree of unanimity—from Croat and Serb, townsperson and villager, artisan and peasant—testimony like that has to be respected. One local Serb, old enough to remember World War II, offers some historical perspective:

> I will tell you the truth. I was a witness of World War II. I was raised during that war, so I saw the beginning of that new Yugoslavia that everybody now calls the old Yugoslavia. Well, those who were the so-called Ustasha, and those who were Chetniks—for them nationality was very important. For them it was important who was a Serb and who was a Croat. But for the rest of us, for the majority who wanted that new state of Yugoslavia, nationality was unimportant.

And that is how people remember the years since as well. (From here until the end of this chapter, every paragraph indicates a different speaker.) Three Serbs check in, chosen here because they reflect the views of others so well.

> Everybody used to work together. We built each other's houses, celebrated holidays together, visited each other, went to [each other's] churches.

> My parents celebrated Vidovdan every year [an old Serb holiday], but many non-Serbs came to celebrate with us. ... I lived with them and they were everywhere around me. From my earliest childhood we shared everything, good things and bad. We celebrated together, we went to school together, we worked together.

> Twice I was godfather to Croatian children. We went to Catholic churches to attend weddings.

And three Croats, for the same reason:

> There were no tensions between different nationalities. We used to have village festivals, wedding parties, baby showers, different religious holidays. And we were together on those occasions—singing similar songs, having similar customs, the same beliefs.

> When I was young and started to walk with [date] girls—well, maybe this is not appropriate to say in front of my wife, but I dated with Serb and Croat and Czech girls. The nationality was not important at all.

> Before the war, for every holiday and religious festivity Serbs and Croats were together, celebrating and working together. For Christmas and Easter and Saint Peter's Day we used to visit both churches. It was inconceivable for me to celebrate my patron saint without my Serb friends, so thirty or forty of them used to visit me on that occasion. The same was true of Serbs. They were a majority, but they invited us on a regular basis. I can tell you that we used to live like one big family.

We came across a number of persons who did not even know until they were schoolchildren or well into their early teens what their own ethnic identity was.

> I remember a friend of mine who was a Serb. We were asked in school what our nationality is. And she said "Oh, I want to be the same nationality as my friend here." She meant me. And she was told: "OK, then you can say you're a Croat."

> The first time I learned that I am a Croat was in the eighth grade. I was 13 years old. I came home and asked my mother, "What am I?" That's all. She looked at me and asked, "What do you mean?" And I told her that I didn't know what a nationality was. She told me, "Well, you are Croat." It came up because a friend in school asked me: "If America and Russia were in a war, who would you be for?" I said, "for America." And he looked at me with anger and walked away. That is why I asked my mother what that whole thing means. She told me to sit down and explained to me that there are two kinds of people here, one Croat and one Serb. That's what she told me.

> I really didn't know that I am a Croat. When some kids started to talk about that in school, I really didn't know what they were saying. But the kids who were born in 1988 or so, who were two or three years old when the war began, they already knew. When you ask them "who are you?" they know exactly. But I didn't know when I was five years old. Or even ten.

These speakers, of course, were in the minority, and it seems reasonable to assume that the majority of young people knew their nationality even before the approach of the war opened their eyes to new ways of seeing such things. The above remarks suggest as much. But the issue here—something we have had occasion to deal with elsewhere in this book—is not whether people are *aware* of a difference between them but whether people come to feel that the difference *makes* a difference. When war came to Pakrac, even those who had been acutely aware of their ethnic status were learning for the first time that such a thing can truly *matter*—that it can serve as what we earlier called a master identity.

Betrayal

Virtually everyone we talked to, then, agreed that nationality had not mattered much in the Pakrac they once knew. But at the same time, virtually everyone we talked to told of a deep sense of disillusion, even betrayal, that accompanied the souring of those feelings of connectedness. Townspeople were sorting things out, trying to organize an array of bitter wartime memories into a coherent account, to compose a history of the immediate past that might make sense of a bewildering present.

That immediate past had included the emergence of a new Serbia, a new Croatia, and all the other shifts in mood and outlook that brought war to Pakrac. The people of the town, understandably, recall that part of their shared history in differing ways. They do not seem to disagree in any substantial way about the *facts* of the case. For the most part, as lawyers often say, those can be stipulated. But there are major differences in the way people arrange those facts into a narrative sequence, the weight they assign to them, the tone of voice in which they relate them, and the adjectives they choose to modify them. How should people have read such signs of change as these coming in from the world out there?

The language of the newly revised constitution described Croatia as homeland "of the Croat people" rather than as homeland "of the Croatian and Serb peoples," as the earlier version had been careful to. What should one make of that? Is it just an emphatic way of declaring independence? Or is it a meaningful portent, a prelude to the disenfranchisement of Serbs and other minority peoples? It matters what one reads into that.

The new Croatian regime selected for its national emblem a familiar and very telling symbol—a checkerboard shield called the *šahovnica* that had represented Croatia before. It had once been a symbol of the vague and distant glories of medieval Croatia, but it had also been a symbol of the Ustasha, the ruling party of Croatia in World War II when the government was exuberantly fascist and tens of thousands of Serbs had been killed by their Croat countrymen. It is no small matter, obviously, which of those images was conjured up when the new flag was displayed. It was as though a political party in Germany had chosen to be recognized by the swastika and described it as a medieval emblem.

And so it went. The government introduced a form of currency, the *kuna,* that had not been in use since the dreaded days of the Ustasha. It renamed public places to honor the memory of persons who local Serbs saw as bitter antagonists. It instituted something very like a loyalty oath for resident minorities.

Looking back in time, it is entirely understandable that Croats from Pakrac, hearing bulletins like those in the spring of 1990 and identifying with at least some of the nationalist sentiments being expressed in them, would not sense a community problem here. After all, one can love one's country, fly its flag, celebrate its independence, salute its officers, and still cherish one's Serb neighbors, can't one? They are two separate things, two streams of affection that issue from different parts of the mind, aren't they? Well, yes and no.

One Pakrac Croat, reflecting the views of a number of his fellow townspeople, said:

> There were some symbols, some statements, that frightened some of the Serbs. They feared that there were similarities to the Independent State of Croatia during the Second World War. But really, realistically, the government did not do anything that could be compared to that. I mean their [reaction] was irrational, emotional. There were some statements and other stuff, but not really anything concrete. There was absolutely no sign that anybody in Croatia was prepared to do anything against the Serbs. That was paranoid.

A Croat neighbor agreed:

> In May 1991, police officers had to wear legal insignias on their uniforms. The symbol on the cap is the historic coat of arms of Croatia. So the Serbs had no reason to claim it was a Ustasha symbol.

A young Croat woman remembered a scene from school at about that time:

> One of my friends sat at a table and drew the checkerboard symbol. A Serb boy
> came up, took out a toy gun, stamped on the bench, and said: "What are you
> doing?" [My friend] looked up and said, "Oh, I am drawing the symbol of our
> country." [The Serb boy] said: "Erase that immediately!" And they began to fight.
> They were okay before that. They were friends. I really don't know what was
> bothering him.

I then asked her somewhat incredulously: "Do you mean as you sit here now
that you really don't understand what was bothering him?" "No," she said, "I
don't understand."

And yet it may even be easier to appreciate why Serb neighbors—hearing the
same words, seeing the same images, exposed to the same enthusiasms—could
not differentiate the national mood from the local one. Events of the outside
world were increasingly being filtered through different screens as they made
their way into the life of the town. A Serb tried to explain:

> Why were the Serbs frightened when the new government came into power?
> They remembered things from the past, for example the Second World War. When
> the new government came into power and started using symbols like the ones that
> had been used during the Independent State of Croatia, Serbs in Croatia became
> frightened. It seemed that suddenly, overnight, everything became Croatian—
> Croatian grass, Croatian television, Croatian newspapers, Croatian houses,
> Croatian land, Croatian symbols. What then was Serbian? That was a signal
> for the Serbs to create a defense system. We had to protect our political identity,
> culture, education, et cetera. We had to protect all those things that made us
> human.

One young Serb, a gifted linguist speaking here in English, was involved in
a relationship with a Croat man whom she fully expected to marry, and the
astonishment she describes was shared by most and maybe all of her
contemporaries:

> My boyfriend and I went to visit friends in their home. They were also a mixed
> couple. We were talking about ordinary things, and in one moment we saw news on
> TV that today is established a new party in Croatia called the HDZ. It was really
> news for me. I only knew that something was broken in communism. I really didn't
> understand it at all. But that evening I saw flags with that emblem, whatever you

call it. It was the first time I saw politicians and priests together. And they were talking about everything Croatian, you know. Before that time we were talking only about Yugoslavia. Everything was Yugoslavia. Now everything was Croatia. I was very frightened. I can't explain to you what I felt at that moment. A very, very big fear. I had been thinking the next year I would go to Zagreb to study the Serbo-Croatian language. But at that moment it became apparent that this was not possible because our new president, Tudjman, said that "foreign people"—he meant us!—will have to teach their children the Croatian language! So I was really, really afraid, and I was thinking, "this is not happening, this cannot be happening."

If she was surprised, so were linguists of all nationalities. There was no recognizable entity as the "Croatian language." I am going to give this remarkable young woman a fictitious name—Sonja—because we will be hearing from her again. Even in print, one can sense the icy fear that was gathering in her heart and catching in her throat. Sonja felt as though she was being driven out from under the shelter of institutional arrangements that had offered her a degree of safety and belonging, and was being left on a lonely, insecure tract of land. There are few fears sharper than that. For her, the search for new moorages and refuges had just started. And all of this took place months before the war began in earnest.

The most defining moment in that season of growing tensions was a firefight at the Pakrac police station in March of 1991. Historians will presumably record that Serb police officers, a substantial majority of the force, disarmed their Croat colleagues in a lightning coup and flew the Serbian flag from town hall for a day or two before the arrival of police units from Zagreb. The insurgent Serbs exchanged a few rounds of fire without inflicting any casualties, surrendered quickly, turned over their arms, and seem to have been released shortly thereafter. The skirmish was responsible for a brief flurry of excitement across an increasingly more uneasy countryside, but when measured on a scale of significance set by what was soon to take place, it has to be ranked as little more than a passing moment in the history of the times.

The effect of this startling moment on the life of Pakrac, though, was enormous. No townspersons could have foreseen such a thing even in their wildest imaginings, and exactly because it was so hard for people to locate it on any of the familiar frames of reference they usually operated by, they had to look into other and more distant worlds of possibility to find a logic in it.

From that moment on, the Serbs and Croats of Pakrac—and of Western Slavonia as a whole—began to drift apart, almost like molecules being drawn toward contrary poles; and the news media, as we shall see shortly, took to the task of widening those spaces with (quite literally) a vengeance. Reports from Serbs and Croats are essentially alike in describing the new sense of coolness and even menace that found its way into social relations. The voices below, each drawn from a larger chorus—are of two Serbs and three Croats in that order:

There was tension in the air. Everyone could feel it. People started to separate, each to their own side, to those with whom they belonged. Old friendships started to divide.

We began to guard our villages, afraid that Croats would come in. The Croats guarded their villages, afraid that Serbs might try to break in. There was fear on both sides. Communication between Serbs and Croats simply disappeared.

The fact is that relationships started to become rather cool after the attack on the police station. It was no longer possible to talk as we did before. When I came into the office, for example, conversation would just stop, and I knew that they did not want me anymore. And it was like that in other places. You knew then that they did not like you. That they did not want you.

I used to have a lot of friends in the village. When there was a Serbian funeral, all of us went. At one funeral in the spring of 1991, though, I approached one of my friends and she moved away from me. I went to another funeral and everyone turned away from me. I was surprised and embarrassed. It was the house of my next-door neighbor. So I went home. My husband and my son asked me how come I was back home so soon, and I told them what had happened—that my best friend did not want to speak to me and turned her back on me. They said that I was just imagining it. But when there was a funeral of one boy who was killed in a road accident, my husband and my son went, and the same thing happened to them. When they came come, they said, "Mama, you were right." We did not understand why they behaved that way.

Things started to change around 1990. When we approached Serbs, they would stop talking. They were silent. So they started to separate from the rest of us. They were just not as friendly as they used to be. So when, for example, I or some other Croat was around one of those groups, Serbs would just stop all conversation. Something was in the air. Everybody could sense that something was going to happen.

But what did it all mean? Serbs, looking back on those days with moral reflexes sharpened by the war that soon followed, think they can now detect a design that they could not quite make out earlier in the blur of all those speeches and symbols and provocations—that the Croat plan from the start had been the restoration of something like the Ustasha state of Nazi times. And Croats, in their turn, consulting memories that had also gained a new clarity as a result of the painful events that followed, think they can now see the true significance of words and incidents they once found hard to make sense of. In retrospect, those moments appear to have supplied clear evidence—"why didn't we see it then?"—that their Serb neighbors were already plotting, arming, preparing, and in doing so displaying their true ethnic and moral colors. The new mood of suspicion could be expressed in little ways:

> In the hospital, for example, we had a radio, and we used to choose the station with the music that people liked the most. We—I mean not only Serbs but most of us here—were fond of folk music. But when everything started, the Croats did not want to listen to folk music by Serbian or Bosnian performers any longer. It was like that. Pure nonsense. Just like today, the folk music was considered a sign of national belonging. It was weird, very strange, that educated persons could behave in that way, could consider something like that important.

There were gatherings. There were whispers. There were suggestive moments of quiet. There were happenings that people later realized they had been slow to take proper measure of:

> They started to talk about who was who, who was Serb and who was Croat. When Serbs celebrated their religious festivals, they used to fire guns in front of the Orthodox church and to sing loudly. Nobody took any notice of that. Nobody reacted. At the time I did not understand what that was all about. But I understand now.

It seemed evident to many Croats, now that they could see through the surfaces of things to their true underlying meaning, that their Serb neighbors must have been engaged in unimaginable treacheries all along.

> Even four years ago they started to buy tape recorders—that was before the war started—and go with those records and radios to their fields to listen to the

news. And they bought binoculars and walkie-talkies. But we did not pay attention.

About a month before the war started, all the Serbs from our neighborhood–from the entire town—used to leave Pakrac every Friday for Serb villages outside the town. We could not understand the meaning of those trips. They had them three weeks in a row. Later I figured out that Serbs were rehearsing an evacuation out of Pakrac, so that when Serbian troops attacked they would be in a safe place.

There were not so many Serbs around, but they had a secret organization, and it was very powerful. It was like this. Here in Pakrac there were lots of bars, and the owners were mostly Serbs. Every evening the Serbs had some kind of meeting. . . . They used to compose lists of who would be killed and whose houses would be blown up with dynamite. . . . They were building roads through the woods, and when we asked them what those roads were for, they said it was for the Forestry Department. But we soon knew that it was for the [Serbian] Army, and that they were preparing for war.

Local Serbs, too, saw things developing around them, the logic of which made better sense after the fact than before it:

In 1991 we noticed many unfamiliar faces of young men in Pakrac walking and running around. They were brought here so that they could get involved if the opportunity arose. They were all Croats, and you could see them in Pakrac and in the neighboring villages. Many of them were employed by the police. Everyone knew that they were not needed, because we already had an adequate number of policemen. Then twenty times more policemen arrived than were needed. We certainly did not look at them with much sympathy because we thought it was very suspicious.

The countryside in particular became alive with anxiety exactly because villagers had so little idea what was going on around them. Villages that were predominantly Serb or Croat often set up roadblocks and manned them with sentries, while villages that had been ethnically mixed for generations turned tense. In such conditions, of course, another breed of community leader is likely to emerge—younger, brasher, more reckless, less reflective about the political winds gusting about them, more in a hurry to simply *do something*.

On August 19, 1991, as we know, war came to Pakrac in dead earnest. The shelling of the town was fearsome and the combat that followed was equally so.

But that is not what local Croats remember most bitterly. Almost to a person, they take for granted that the Serb residents of the town—their close neighbors, after all—*knew* that an assault was coming and withdrew from the scene of battle without warning them what was in store for them. To the Croats' way of thinking, a sharper form of perfidy is difficult to imagine:

> My neighbors knew what would happen. But none of them warned me about it. On Monday, August 19, 1991, the first mortar grenade was launched on Pakrac. That was at 5:00 a.m. That's when I realized that the war had broken out. And that's when I realized how bad the Serbs are. They betrayed us. I mean, Serbs knew about the war. They evacuated their families from town and just didn't care what happened to our families, to our children. And after that I changed my attitude toward Serbs completely.
>
> You know, the whole thing was prepared. Absolutely. I'm sure of it. I cannot believe that someone I went to school with, someone I've known from the time I was first walking, wouldn't say to me: "Get away. This is not a safe place. Something bad may happen today." Or something like that.
>
> For months before the war, Serbs used to leave Pakrac every weekend with their families. All of those people knew about the attack on Pakrac. They had a very good and very well organized military intelligence. But it was unbelievable that they did not want to tell the truth to any of us so that we could leave Pakrac when the attack started.
>
> I noticed that Serbs sent on weekend trips in large numbers. In a building like mine, such an unusual movement was strange and obvious. Each weekend only Serbs, people we could recognize, went out of town. They used to leave the town for the weekend and with the beginning of the work week they were back. . . . And that was really strange. . . . They were leaving town during those weekends to prepare themselves for the events that soon took place. That was something I could not believe could happen. For me, it was just impossible.

Comments like that reflect the outlooks of virtually every Croat we encountered in Pakrac and surrounding villages. And we know from reports that have come in from other sectors of the Yugoslav war zone that similar views were being developed elsewhere. A journalist named Slavenka Drakulić (who wants her readers to insert quotation marks when they seem appropriate) tells of a conversation she had with a Croat soldier named Josip who came from a village of mixed ethnicities in Bosnia:

That's the hardest thing, he says, the treachery of friends and neighbors who were Serbs and who, all but a couple of them (who are still here), left Sunja on the eve of the first assault because they knew that the village was going to be attacked. . . . They did nothing to warn their neighbors and friends with whom they had lived side by side for many years. Why did they do it to us, says Josip, and shakes his head. There must have been a conspiracy of silence among the Serbs. Why did they say nothing? . . . And how will they ever be able to return to these villages? The way Josip talks about this, I can tell that the memories of the betrayal are fresh.

I need to report, however, that we never once met a Serb survivor of the conflicts in Pakrac who acknowledged knowing anything about the attack beforehand. At this remove in time it is difficult to see why Serbs from Pakrac would think it useful or necessary to be cautious about the matter. Some may hope to return to Pakrac again and know that they will have to explain themselves to old neighbors, but most have relocated elsewhere and have little reason to keep up that kind of pretense.

Moreover, there is a striking inconsistency even in the reports we have heard so far. If Serbs left Pakrac every weekend for outlying villages, as we have just heard three angry witnesses testify, then it would stand more or less to reason that they did not know the date of the attack either. Stories like the following one are told by many Croats as evidence of the betrayal they experienced:

I had very good Serbian friends. The day before the war broke out they came to my house and stayed until midnight. I called them in the morning to find out how they were, to ask if I could help in any way, but my neighbor told me that they had packed their bags right after they left my house and left Pakrac without a word. And we spent the whole evening together! That was very hard for me. I used to work with them. I knew them well. We spent a lot of time together. We were very close. And I did not have a clue about the things that would happen, about the attack and the war.

But if you look at that human scene more closely, it is very easy to imagine that those Serb neighbors, wherever they live now, cite the evening they spent with their Croat friends as evidence that they had no idea in the world about the impending attack. How many of us would while away the few hours remaining before an impending dawn attack drinking *rakija* with friends we knew to be in mortal danger?

This is one of those entanglements that we humans are so adept at spinning. Croats report that Serbs were nowhere to be seen on the day of the attack. It happens that we know a number who *were* in Pakrac that fateful morning, crouched down in cellars like everyone else and trying to keep safe. But they were not very much in evidence after the attack itself—who was?—and were sensible enough to leave town as shortly thereafter as possible:

> On the day the war began, I was supposed to go to work. My shift began at 6:00 a.m. but the shooting began at 5:00. Everyone was running away—to the villages out there or into the forest. I just followed the others to Kraguj, a couple of kilometers from Pakrac.

Most of them were gone by the time the dust settled, so Croat witnesses are easy to believe when they speak of the defection of their Serb neighbors, although it should be added that a considerable number of their Croat neighbors were gone as well. Local Serbs, meantime, report that they would certainly have spread the word had they known of it. That is easy to believe too. Those views of what happened that morning are not at all contradictory when viewed in the calm of half a world away, but it is understandably hard for a Pakrac Croat to think that.

The best guess is that the local Serbs, like most creatures who sense the presence of danger in what had been a safe and familiar world, realized that something was very apt to happen. They could feel it riding on the wind. But they had no way of knowing what that "something" was or when it might take place, and as the summer months lengthened they increasingly spent their weekends in the neighboring Serb villages from which so many of them had come originally. Accumulated vacation days—this was the height of the summer season, after all—were being cashed in. If one hundred Serbs were asked individually why they were away from Pakrac that terrible day, we might hear a hundred different replies. Every one of those replies would ring true to the histories of the families being questioned, presumably, but those hundred scraps of data would together form a pattern: the Serbs of Pakrac simply sensed that it was a good time to be scarce.

> (Did you know something was going to happen?) Well, we knew. But we did not believe that anything like this could happen. We could not believe such a thing. In April of 1991 [the firefight at the police station] we expected some kind of attack,

so for four or five days we did not go to work. And then all of that passed. Nothing happened. So far as I know, we did not expect an attack after that.

Well, I told you. We Serbs heard that something bad was in the making, so it would be better for us not to go to work. We took extended vacations, and after that we did not go to work. It was something like that.

The real troubles began for me when I had to go to work and the shelling began. Actually, I had noticed on the day before that something was going on. People were leaving for the near villages. They did not leave for Serbia or Bosnia or some faraway place. They were just leaving for the villages around the town to be in a safe place until everything passed away. People knew in some way that it would be better for them to be out of town.

One particularly reflective young Croat, an exception to what was otherwise a general rule, saw things in the same way:

Many Serbs left. You know, just disappeared. They just left. (Why do you think they left?) I don't know. Everyone says that it was, like, planned, you know. That they were planning all that for a long time. I don't know. (Do you think that is so?) I think some of them may have known what was going to happen. I don't think they knew the exact date or anything like that, but I think they knew something was going to happen. I think they kind of did know.

I will suggest in a moment why misreadings of this kind loom so heavily in times of crisis. But before turning to that topic, let me note that the conflict in Pakrac and elsewhere in Yugoslavia involved neighbors in a way that is peculiar to civil war.

On Neighbors

On the one hand—this is the good news—there have been a number of reports from war zones in Croatia, Bosnia, and elsewhere of neighbors resisting the worst of the horror building up around them and even risking their own lives to shelter fellow townspeople of a different ethnicity than themselves. If one is looking for evidence of human goodness in that maelstrom, this is where to begin. Pakrac:

During the attack in 1991, for example, when missiles were falling on the town, one Serb covered me with his body in the park saying that if someone should die then let it be him instead of me, a little boy with a lot in front of me.

We were in some basement where they beat us and kicked us very hard. They left us without food and water for eight days. I mean without a drop of water or a single bite of food. . . . I will tell you this, I have a friend, he is a Serb, and he was there. He saved my life. If it was not for him, they would probably have killed me.

When we were imprisoned, some of our former friends did not even look at us. But there were some good people who secretly gave us food. There was one young Chetnik who gave us food and told us the news—what was going on in the battle-fields and that they were preparing to run away. He warned us about other Chetniks. There were some wonderful Serbs up there, some really good persons, and that is how we managed to survive. . . . A few days ago I went to the funeral of one Serb who gave us milk when we were imprisoned in Spanovica.

People of the area often tried to exempt those they knew as neighbors from the more general feelings of anger and distrust that the storms of war and the relentless pounding of the press were generating. An American historian named Christopher Bennett, visiting the region not long after the outbreak of war, wrote:

In Pakrac, both the Serb and Croat militias were largely made up of people from the town itself. Many had lived their entire lives there and knew their adversaries personally. A sense of community persisted and neither side could demonize the other to a level necessary for fighting to break out. But outsiders, who did not have the same sense of community, increasingly took the lead.

That observation would make some residents of Pakrac snort in derision. They have acts of considerable cruelty, sometimes even of outright atrocity, to tell us about:

It was the spitting image of a German concentration camp. We were beaten on a daily basis. Many prisoners were killed and many were taken away and we never heard from them again. . . . The situation was even more difficult because the guards were Serbs from Pakrac and from villages from around the town. For instance, my first neighbor [next-door neighbor] was one of the main killers, and he committed lots of killings. I was raised and went to school with his son.

We have several reports of that kind, and I do not want to minimize for a moment the sheer ugliness of what neighbors sometimes managed to do to one another here. But most residents of Pakrac will testify that Bennett's observation was for the most part correct. As angry as Croats tend to be over the presumed betrayal of their Serb neighbors, most of them take for granted that outsiders were brought in to do the really serious work of killing and terrorizing, and that their neighbors, though made sullen and resentful by the coming of the war, were much less likely to take active roles in the devastation.

But the fact of the matter also is—and the people of places like Pakrac are not likely to forget it anytime soon—that neighbors are usually the only persons who even *know* how to tell Serb from Croat, or, elsewhere, either from Muslim. Think back to the woman driven out onto the sidewalk at gunpoint: who but a neighbor would know that she was a Muslim?

A good deal of screening has to be done in civil wars of this complexity. Who is to be fired upon and who protected? Who should be treated as a civilian and who a combatant? Who should be treated like an ordinary soldier and who a war criminal? Which is another way of asking: who should be disarmed and sent home, and who held for interrogation or even torture? And, finally, most common of all, which dwellings are those of the innocent, and which are those of the guilty? That kind of screening, clearly, requires the assistance of neighbors, since outsiders brought into a community from somewhere else have no way of making those distinctions. The first speaker below is a Croat, whose home was damaged when Serbs were in control of Pakrac; the second is a Serb, who seems to know a thing or two.

> (Well, here's a question which has always interested me. You're talking about "Chetniks" who come from somewhere else, most of them. How did they know that Croats live in your house?) I don't know. I think they knew everything. I guess there were some Serbs from the neighborhood that were in contact with them and telling them.

> I don't know how to explain that to you. It was sufficient that someone pointed a finger at a person and said that the person did something. They were immediately arrested and had to spend several months in jail.

This matters in a number of ways. For one thing, there is now a substantial body of evidence that when people come to feel that the problems plaguing them have been caused by other people rather than a more remote and more abstract fate—and especially so when those other people had been considered up until that time as members of the same general community—they are more likely to suffer symptoms of trauma and less likely to recover from those symptoms in a normal span of time. People in general are certainly no strangers to the feeling of having enemies. But in the imagination, at least, enemies are supposed to sweep in from somewhere over the horizon. They are a visitation from afar, like a plague or storm or some other natural disaster. They can do a tremendous amount of harm, of course, and can leave behind them a lasting dread. But destruction and terror are often what one *expects* from those distant beings, "them," while being attacked by persons from one's own surround— people we count on to have our best interest at heart—leaves in its wake not only the same destruction and dread but a sense of being betrayed that can harm the human spirit in special ways. This is presumably why the assumption by local Croats that they were let down by their Serb neighbors has so bitter a place in their memories of war. And that is presumably why local Serbs look upon the national enthusiasms of their Croat neighbors as a personal affront. The feeling of being betrayed—and the companion feeling that human institutions can no longer be depended on in quite the same way—is palpable throughout Pakrac and other communities like it. A survivor of the siege of Sarajevo wrote about those feelings in a way that civilian victims of war everywhere could relate to:

> I kept staring at my own hands, checking their reality from time to time. One crushing effect of this war on those who actually fared the best—that is, who have not been killed or wounded—is this loss of confidence in reality, or at least in one's ability to experience reality. They lost their world in the way I have lost my house as I looked at it, discovering how beautiful it was.

The following is a fragment of conversation with a young man from Ilok, a town in far eastern Croatia located on a thin sliver of land reaching like a finger into Serbian territory because of an unusual turn in the flow of the Danube. At the time of this interview in 1998, Ilok was full of Serb refugees, many of them from Pakrac—which is why I had visited it in the first place. The young man had been driven out of his home during the Serb advance of 1991, and was about to return to Ilok to recover his family home and holdings.

> (Do the Croats in Ilok have any fears that there will be more Serb invasions from across the river?) No, they are not afraid of the Serbs in Serbia or Bosnia. But a lot of them are afraid of the Serbs who still live in Ilok. (But why? Why would there

be more fear of Serbs who were their neighbors than Serbs who came from a distance?) A lot of people are asking themselves why it is like that. Why are they more afraid of their neighbors than of those from far away? I do not know the answer. If you ask someone from Ilok is he afraid of Serbs, the answer is always no. He is not afraid of those Serbs across the Danube. But if you ask him about his neighbors, the answer would be quite different.

That is a remarkable exchange, an index of the degree to which people can develop a particular fear of those who in normal times live well within the accustomed zone of safety. It involves a kind of inversion, a turning of things inside-out, and for me it is a haunting example of what I once called "the traumatic worldview" in a book I wrote on the subject.

The Media

I have alluded several times so far in this account to the role played by newspaper reports and television broadcasts in stirring up national resentments across Yugoslavia. I do not have time to go into this matter in the detail it deserves, but it is important to recognize that the media have become one of the most lethal weapons of modern ethnic conflict, and that it is difficult to understand what really happened in Pakrac and the rest of Yugoslavia without some sense of how that weapon was deployed. Not long after the crisis of 1991, a number of specialists gathered to evaluate the performance of the Balkan press during that time, and they offered as a hypothesis that "the media themselves were responsible for the war in Croatia." Had those specialists been able to broaden their inquiry to include the war about to break out in Bosnia, they would certainly have come to the same conclusion. In both of those places, the media were in complete control of what a frightened, disoriented, demoralized populace could read or hear or see, and they were free to portray a world of their own invention. Some of those writers may have come to believe that the reports they had seen were literally accurate, but it is fair to assume that most of them were cynically repeating what they knew to be absurd exaggerations. They were, for the most part, city dwellers whose job it was to convey party lines out into the rural countryside.

The presses of both Serbia and Croatia were working overtime to characterize their own sides as a victim of the other—encircled, vulnerable, endangered, on the defensive. A "we" was being given substance by the injuries and betrayals and indignities pressing in on it by a "they."

The news from Belgrade throughout the 1980s had increasingly involved a revisiting of old sufferings and injuries imposed upon Serbs by Croats, bits of this and that drawn from the warehouse we alluded to in the last chapter, and the "genocidal" ambitions those Croats still entertained. And the Zagreb press spoke with equal urgency about the criminal designs that Serbs had always had on Croatian land and Croatian honor. Each a victim of the other.

When active hostilities finally did break out, then, vivid reporting from the front was all the easier to believe. Serbs were the original masters of that art, and the Belgrade press spoke lavishly about "Ustasha hordes" killing, raping, looting, leveling Orthodox churches, defiling Serb graves, building secret gas chambers for the ultimate in ethnic cleansing. The Serbian press described Croat soldiers as "drugged fanatics," "terrorists," and "criminals," while TV Belgrade offered photographic evidence of Croat militia wearing necklaces made of the fingers of Serb children. Croats, eager apprentices in this art, caught the spirit of it soon enough. The Zagreb press described the Serbs who had participated in a shoot-out as "bearded animals on two legs," "beasts in human form," and "bloodsuckers" (an allusion to vampires). Croatian TV spoke of Serb soldiers who "gouged out the eyes before cutting the throats of their Croat victims."

Some of those reports were so improbable that it is hard to imagine how they could have been believed by anyone. But that may be missing the point. A reader or viewer does not need to believe that a news report is accurate in its every detail. The report is not really about an *event* at all ("this is what happened yesterday") but about the moral character of the people who figured in it ("look at the kind of creatures they are"). If we were to object that the necklace was really made of bullet casings and not of human fingers, the reporter might simply shrug a shoulder and say "well, maybe so, but my point is that he is the *kind* of man who could decorate himself with the fingers of children." It is a portrait of the inner person, not of the surface details.

Among the more important tasks of the media was to discount news that might prove inconvenient or embarrassing otherwise. A stunning example was provided by the Bosnian Serbs when seventeen persons were killed by a mortar shell that landed on a public square in Sarajevo. The event was widely reported in the Western press, but the Serbian press calmly announced that the attack had been staged to impress the United Nations, and that the dead bodies—there was no escaping *them*—had been brought in from local morgues and used as props in setting the stage. Later, when a shell landed on a funeral party engaged in the sad project of burying two infants—themselves the victims of Serb sniper fire—Serb television offered the same explanation. Not long afterward, the Croatian press announced that an artillery attack on a Serb settlement in Croatia had been arranged by Serb extremists to slander the Croatian government. A lesson well learned.

Eventually, reports of this kind became so normal that reality itself was transposed. When Serb troops were closing in on an enemy town, for example, and about to crush its defenders, a visiting Serb newsman reported that the local defenders "are trying to threaten the positions of the Serb army." That is worth a pause. When Serb forces had encircled Sarajevo and were shelling the city mercilessly from the surrounding hills, a Serb reporter noted that the inhabitants of the city "are holding Sarajevo under siege from within," and then, since that made no sense at all, added by way of explanation that "the Serbs continue to defend their centuries-old hills around Sarajevo." His words. That is worth a pause too.

One of the most important effects of all this was to create new conceptual languages—new ways of seeing things and classifying them, new ways of ordering the familiar, new screens for filtering the events of everyday life. A good part of that task was accomplished by the simple act of *naming*. Neutral historians looking back on this conflict will write of "armies," "troops," "militias," "forces." Or if they are writing from the point of view of one party to the conflict, of "loyalists" and "insurgents," of "soldiers of the homeland" and of "the enemy," and so on. But in wartime, nouns and adjectives take on a richer tone. In Croatia and Bosnia, troops on the other side of the firing line became "terrorists," "outlaws," "barbarians," "butchers," "criminals," and—we should be expecting this—various forms of animal as the process of speciating begins to enter the picture. One does not need to know the historic meaning of the following words to get the sense of what is happening here. All Serbs, unless specifically exempted from the label, are "Chetniks," all Croats are "Ustasha," and all Muslims are "Turks" or "Islamic fundamentalists" or something of the sort—which means as a factual matter that the users of those terms are demonstrably wrong virtually all the time. But there, too, accuracy has nothing to do with it. All three of the national groups that entered the Yugoslav conflict were "genocidal." Croats were "fascist" and

"German." Serbs were "fascist" and "Bolshevik." And Muslims were "fascist" and "Islamic fanatics." These pairings involve a heroic disdain for historical detail, but, after all, they are meant not as descriptions but as epithets.

An important figure in the Serb opposition, himself no stranger to stirring up national troubles, said: "UN peace-keeping forces should occupy Belgrade's and Zagreb's television stations because they are keeping two half-mad and warlike regimes in power." People from other parts of the world dare not take much comfort from the thought that there is something peculiarly Balkan about this state of affairs. A Serb journalist named Miloš Vasić issued a challenge to Americans to "imagine a United States with every little TV station everywhere taking exactly the same editorial line—a line dictated by David Duke [an extreme racist who was much in the news then]. You, too, would have a war in five years."

Pakrac, One Last Look

What was Pakrac like in the years to follow? The war ended in 1995, and an uneasy peace settled over the land. I was last there in 2003, so the report you are reading now is of a time past. A number of Serbs had remained in Pakrac or its outlying villages throughout the war, and they were trying to make a place for themselves in the new world. A number of others hoped to return and to reclaim their old homes and their old places in the community. But it was not at all clear what kind of response they could expect.

Most of the Croats of the town had by then developed emphatic views on "Serbs" as a national group, no matter how those views were likely to be expressed in their encounters with old neighbors:

> What can I say? I spent three years in a concentration camp. Each day someone was killed. There were severe beatings and tortures all the time. My hands were covered with wounds from the wire they used to tie us up with. They broke four of my ribs. My skull is cracked. I do not know what to say to you. We are supposed to live together again. It should be like that. But we do not have to talk or say hello to each other. The kind of life that existed before the war is now over for good. That is the way I see things.

> Yes, it will be possible to live again together. But it cannot be the same as it was before the war. Never again. They lied to us. They betrayed us. We do not want to

take revenge on them, to harm them. But we do not have to accept them. They do not deserve it.

Serb people? For me they do not exist any longer. Listen to me. They were beating us up there when we were in prison. They killed us. So I cannot talk with them anymore. I do not want to do any harm to anyone or kill anyone, but I do not have to live with them or communicate with them. They did a lot of very bad things to me.

And, finally, a young Croat speaking in somewhat awkward but very emphatic English: "I do not judge him, Serbs. I do not trust him, Serbs. Personally, I do not love him very much. And I do not trust him one hundred percent."

Many Croats, however, make a distinction that may be of considerable significance for the future—between Serbs who cast their lot with Serbia and thus betrayed their fellow townspeople, and Serbs who continued to think of themselves as members of their original communities and did not become involved in the hostilities. An outsider can be forgiven for wondering how that distinction is made. When we would ask about it, we would generally receive an astute look that seemed to imply "we townspeople know such things." And so they might. But the outsider is hard pressed to learn what kinds of local knowledge support such assertions as the following:

Yes, we all knew. For example, my neighbor living in the fourth house on the right was a sniper and almost killed my mother. The Chetniks used to meet at his house. When the first bombs started falling, he left.

(If you were at home now with the people you grew up with, would you know who the Serbs were that fired on you?) Yeah, I would know. Most people would. It's not secret, you know. Everything you do leaves some trail behind you.

It is difficult to avoid the impression that for many local Croats the sheer fact that a Serb neighbor left town is evidence of guilt: "Those who remained, for me they are not enemies. I still work in Serb villages. Every year I go there for the harvest. But why did the others run away?" Another young Croat from a town near Pakrac came even closer to suggesting that his neighbors' absence was itself equated with villainy: "Some of my classmates were out of town, so the word was around that they were up in the hills shooting at us in Daruvar. It's a small town, you know. The rumor was that they refused to become citizens of the new Croatia."

Whether or not the line that separated loyal Serbs from enemy ones was being drawn accurately, the fact that it was being drawn at all is significant. If I ask Croats from Pakrac about "Serbs," I am inviting them to think in terms of a general class of others, an abstract group, and in doing so I am running the risk of imposing my way of organizing reality upon them. To speak of "Serbs" is to summon up a "them." To speak of persons with familiar names and faces and histories is to summon a quite different set of associations:

> Well, of course my attitudes and opinions are different concerning those people. It would be strange if they had remained the same. We cannot believe them anymore. That is it. Most probably I will never be a friend with those who were shooting at us and did all those things. But I will not go after them. I am not looking for revenge. I just want to live a normal life. Of course even now I have Serb friends who did not take arms against us, who did us no harm. But for those on the other side, I just pay no attention to them, as if they did not exist at all.

> With those Serbs who remained here, we have good relationships. We are living together. But those Serbs who started the war, with them we do not want to work. If I should meet one of them on the street, I would just pass him by as if he was just a lamp post. You have to understand us on this issue. We do not want to harm other people. But those who wanted to hurt us, who were evil to us—it is better for them to get out of our sight.

Local Serbs who visited Pakrac after the war to learn the lay of the land encountered a variety of reactions from the Croats they once called "neighbors." For most, it was a flat rejection:

> He stood there, just twenty meters from me, and I said: "Good afternoon, neighbor." I was on the street. He just glanced in my direction, and when he recognized me he turned away and went into his house. We used to be good neighbors. Why did he not return my regards? Because I am a Serb. I cannot think of any other reason. I did nothing to him. There is no reason to blame me. We were the same, completely equal.

> Well, the Croats are already here, in the street. They are fixing their houses, and they do not want to talk to us, not even to say hello. It's as if we do not exist at all. They are obviously against the Serb people.

> I had an apartment here in Pakrac, and I left the key with my neighbor to watch it for me and to use it. He is a Croat, a war invalid. [When I came back] I could not

enter my apartment because it was by then the property of a Croat soldier. [An official] told me that there was no job or place for me in the town. If I wanted to stay, then it was my problem. It did not concern him. And that situation remains the same today. I am paying off my debt for an apartment that does not belong to me. For five years I have been an outcast in my own town.

There are moments of special poignancy to report here involving kinship or something very like it spiritually. "My father went to Pakrac to collect his pension," said a young Serb," and when he tried to visit his sister—she was married to a Croat who died during the war—she would not let him in, probably because she was afraid what her neighbors might say." And another Serb native of Pakrac, quoted earlier because he had twice been godfather to Croat children, lamented that "my godchild's daughter does not even know me. She passes by my house every day. Her mother [must have] told her that she should not meet me."

Others, however, receive a more ambivalent reception, one that reflects all the pain that has been experienced, all the anger that has been expressed, all the emotions that have been sharpened—and yet at the same time also reflects an unwillingness for that to be the measure of everything. The Serb woman who felt like an outcast in her own town spoke of one such moment:

> It was awful. One year ago was the anniversary of my graduation day. Thirty years. Croats came. I came. And the most pleasant person to me was a guy who had been beaten and tortured. He was very kind. He begged me not to go over those old insults and everything. But the ones who didn't lose anything in the war wouldn't talk to me. They were the worst kind.

"Look," said a Serb man who hoped that he and his old neighbors might yet find a middle ground on which they could meet one day,

> it is not possible that every Croat is Ustasha and that every Serb is Chetnik. [One] is responsible only for his deeds and cannot be blamed for the things others did. Some of my colleagues from work, some of my friends, are now just passing me by. They pretend that I am a stranger, or, worse, that I have no business around here, that this is not my place anymore. . . . For them all individuals from some nation or some minority are just all the same.

The chief of Pakrac police, whose official task it is to provide security for whatever Serbs decide to return (and whose personal hope is that the old community can be restored in part) said:

People are slowly returning to Pakrac. The process is very slow because many houses are destroyed or someone else lives in them. Despite everything, I can sense a high level of optimism among the people. They believe that return is possible. However, laughter and happiness are still very much lacking from people's faces. Before the war the Catholics and Orthodox used to celebrate holidays together. They intermarried and they laughed together. This is very different now. It will take a long time to achieve this once again.

The young Serb woman I have been calling Sonja, who had a Croat boyfriend when we first met her, returned to Pakrac for a visit right after the war. She was a skilled linguist, you may remember, and spoke in English:

I saw my house. At first I couldn't find it because the street is so different and the houses are all broken. Then I found it because there is still a house number on one wall. It was the wall of my room. I just felt a big and very cold wall between me and my house. I stayed on the street for five minutes, looking at it. And then suddenly I had a big need to—not to cry, but to scream and to yell out bad words.

And then a short time later that day:

On the street I saw my ex-boyfriend's father. I told him that I was wrong to say hello to him without him saying hello to me first, because sometimes it is bad for them to have that happen. But it was my only day [in Pakrac] and I like him very much. I said: "Mr. X, I just wanted to say hello." And he said to me, "Oh, it's so nice to have a hello from such a nice girl, but, miss, I don't know who you are." And I said, "you really don't know who I am?" He was looking at me and thinking hard. He couldn't imagine that [a Serb from the old days] could appear there, you know. I told him, "I'm Sonja." And he said, "That's you? That's my dear child?" I said "Yes." And then he started to talk. Talk, talk, talk—very fast. He was confused, telling me things I couldn't understand. He's on a pension. My ex-boyfriend is now married. His wife and he are building a house. News, news, news. Very ordinary news of very ordinary life. He did not ask where I was [living]. And then it really sank in to him who he was talking to. I was thinking, "How many years are on my face? How many years are in me and in him?" Before we were so close. But what to say now? "Please, write me a letter?" "Why don't you come to visit me or call?" What, really? It's not possible anymore. Everything is broken. We both knew that we could have been family, but we are not, and will not be. So it doesn't make any sense to be in contact. But we needed to say something to each other, and he kept saying, "My dear, you are so pretty." His expression said that he was only trying to say something nice, something human. I was not pretty then. It was one of the worst times in my life. But he kept repeating, "You're so nice, you're so pretty." And then I just blurted out, "I wish none of this had happened." And he started to cry out loud. "Me too." And then in a moment he just pushed me and turned his back and walked away. Awful. Awful experience.

We may never hear a more telling account of what civil war can do to people caught up in it. There was a wide gulf now dividing Sonja from a man she once loved and thought would become a second father to her. The striking thing about that gulf, though, is not only how wide it had become but how small the differences were between the two persons who found themselves arrayed on either side of it. They were separated now by an ethnic divide that had meant nothing to them earlier. What makes this scene so haunting is that the shove that marked the line dividing those former neighbors might, under different circumstances, have been a gunshot.

In 1991, when Sonja first saw those frightening images on television with the young Croat man she intended to marry, she sensed that something important was about to happen to her and everyone else. She turned to her father for counsel:

I said to him, "Father, I think there will be a war here." He said, "Yes, there will." "Please explain to me," I asked him, "who will shoot who? Who will fight with who?" He said, "you will see." I said, "explain to me on which side will my friend Eva be?" He said, "I don't know, but when it begins everyone will know for themselves." I was so afraid that summer of 1991.

She asked the same question of another friend—it might have been Eva—and got the same answer: "She was smiling, and she said: 'When this is over, everyone will know what side they are on.'" By 1999, Sonja had found her way to Belgrade and had learned all too well what side she was on:

When you learn which side you feel safe, that is your side. When you feel so in danger that you think you will be killed, then you find a side where you will feel safety. That's it. How other people found their side, I don't know. I don't know how people from mixed families decided which is the safer side for them. I don't know. For us, we were Serbs and we felt safe with Serbs. You need to be with other people and to try to survive somehow.

Sonja had *become* a Serb. She had always been one, of course, for purposes of filling out census forms, but now it was a source of meaning, a master identity.

This was happening all over the land. A writer named Slavenka Drakulić, who we heard from earlier, complained in terms that vast numbers of others could identify with that "being a Croat has become my destiny. . . . Along with millions of other Croats, I was pinned to the wall of nationhood. . . . That is what the war is doing to us, reducing us to one dimension: the Nation." Nationality had become not only the principal source of individual identity but the principal shelter into which one can retreat for safety. A Bosnian Muslim said to an American reporter named David Rieff, who we also heard from earlier:

> First, I was a Yugoslav. Then I was a Bosnian. Now I'm becoming a Muslim. It's not my choice. I don't even believe in God. But after two hundred thousand dead, what do you want me to do? Everybody has to have a country [probably "norod," meaning nation, people] to which he can belong.

Back once again to Pakrac, then, as we bring this story to a close, where the process of learning a new ethnic and national geography—a new way of positioning oneself in place—was well under way. These voices speak for themselves:

> The changes began in 1989 when the first explosions occurred in Pakrac [the episode at the police station]. We started to think about nationality then, about who is who, about who is Serb and who is Croat, about the things that were taking place.

> Until 1990, I declared myself a Yugoslav. But my decision was changed under the influence of Croatian propaganda. Croats were talking about "clean Croatian air," and there was no place for me in that environment. So I took a Serbian identity. My forefathers have been living in this land for seven centuries!

> After that bloody weekend everything started. I really felt my nationhood. I felt like a Croat.

> Well, it was not easy for me at the beginning. I had never expressed aloud the fact of my Croat nationality. But when the environment changed, my attitude changed as well. I became rather stubborn in the course of events, in fact. I felt that my feelings of belonging to the Croat nation were growing stronger.

> After the crisis in 1991, there were three different groups of local people. One group was the Serb side. Another was the Croat side. And a third group just went on about their business thinking that a war would not occur. I belonged to that third group. So did most people. Now it is the aftermath of that war. The Serbs

were responsible for it. So now I am a Croat. That third group lost all its charm. It doesn't exist anymore.

To fully appreciate the meaning of the comment below, it will be useful to know that Aunt Mira is a Serb and Uncle Toma, her husband, a Croat.

There is one thing I will never forget. This happened just before the war. I had a very good friend in our village. She and her husband were both Serbs. One day I went to their house and their youngest child suddenly asked me: "Aunt Mira, what are you?" I said: "I am just that, Aunt Mira." Then he asked, "what is Uncle Toma?" And then he inquired about Marica, a Croat woman from the village, and my answer was again the same, "she is simply Aunt Marica." This was the moment when I realized that nothing was any longer the same as it used to be. How could it be that even little children were inquiring about people's ethnic background?

So the first step in this fateful business is to draw the line, and then to locate oneself firmly on one or another side of it. And when that task has been accomplished, the time has come to assess what those others—only yesterday your neighbors, classmates, in-laws—are really like. Knowing their true character, among other things, provides a point of contrast against which one can know one's own.

These things, the destruction of schools and churches, never happened before, not even in World War II. That's how we learned how bad the Serbs are. Until then we did not hate them. But afterward we came to understand the difference between Croats—a people with culture—and those savages.

The Serb people are not expansionist or aggressive. Serbs love their culture, their peaceful Orthodox religion, their creative instincts. Creation and love are Serbian traits that show through our hospitality. The Croats, on the other hand, do everything out of malice. The Serb people are always prepared to forgive. I do not think Croats are capable of that. We want to live surrounded by beauty and culture. The other side produces bombs and tanks.

Serbs are brought up in a different way. It is a custom among them to give a gun as a present for a newborn child. For the same occasion, Croats give a holy token, a relic. And 90 percent of Serbs are raised with a hatred toward Croats. Croats are different. Serbs are raised to hate. Croats are not raised that way. I am speaking out of my own experience.

Serbs are not that kind of people. We are willing to negotiate. Serbs are not that hard.

It is very hard to explain the transformation. It was like a miracle. How to understand it? It looks like Serbs have nourished some sort of hatred inside themselves for a long time. It is different with Croats. We do not have that in ourselves.

You may have noticed that the speakers above are, in order, a Croat, a Serb, a Croat, a Serb, and a Croat. To me, two things stand out in those expressions. The first is that the sheer naiveté of what people are saying would seem to suggest that these are relatively new concepts to the persons who are uttering them—lines spoken without the seasoned cadence that familiarity and repetition lend. The second is that each side detects in the other exactly the same faults that the other detects in it. And why not? Those who confront one another across the new boundary line are looking at visages so like their own that they might as well be looking into a mirror.

The same could be said for most of the spilling of blood that took place then in the land of the South Slavs, and we will close this discussion with an observation by Charles Dickens: "When men unnaturally fight against their own countrymen, they are always observed to be more unnaturally cruel and filled with rage than they are against any other enemy."

Postscripts

Two brief observations as the book comes to a close, very different both in subject matter and in tenor.

I

First, I want to take a moment now to offer a few excerpts from notes I took during one of my visits to wartime Yugoslavia. They are more detailed than field notes usually tend to be, since my purpose in writing these out so fully was to share a sense of what that landscape and its peoples looked and felt like with my family as well as offering a sense of what field work is like more generally. I will ask you to appreciate that those five days of observing and interviewing were unusually productive, which is, of course, why I am offering them now. I was truly fortunate in that respect. But it is not always like that out in the field, as those who venture out there will want you to know. It often involves long stretches of emptiness and silence.

Saturday

I flew from Copenhagen to Zagreb and then drove to Pakrac, about sixty miles to the southeast. I met with Eric there, and we decided to take our first look at Jasenovac, a town about fifteen miles south. It had been the site of a gruesome concentration camp in World War II where as many as 150,000 persons were executed—Gypsies, Jews, but mostly Serbs living in Croatia. Fellow citizens, in other words. Elaborate pains had been taken in the time since to obliterate most traces of the camp, leaving in its place an empty field now being taken over by scrubby plant life. There was once a small museum near the entrance to the site, but it is now in ruins as a result of recent fighting. A decaying monument stands in the middle of the field, consisting largely of wooden ties from the railroad line that once brought prisoners into the camp. No one tends it now. A tough underbrush is forcing its way through every crack in the structure, and the concrete blocks that supported it are crumbling. All that neglect makes the monument seem even more haunting than the original designer must have had in mind.

Sunday

In the morning, we drove to a village a few miles from Pakrac named Batanjani that had been roughly 70 percent Serb and 30 percent Croat before the conflict. I knew those figures from census data, but they could have been estimated from the look of the village itself. Two-thirds of the dwellings had been systematically flattened six years earlier, those being the homes of local Serbs who had been driven away, and most of those stark ruins still lay there untouched. Bit by bit, they were being taken over by that same harsh, dogged underbrush, curling around bits of debris, asserting itself. It must be the most resilient form of life to be found in these parts. The Serb cemetery was so overgrown with it that you could barely see the top of the larger gravestones. The Croat cemetery looked as though it had been tended half an hour earlier like a local garden.

The man we went to see was a farmer with a neat, sturdy house facing the road. The houses on either side of him had been destroyed, both of his neighbors having been Serb, so he lived surrounded by crumbling ruins. He spoke of how much he missed those neighbors, even though he also told us of having been imprisoned and beaten by people of their kind. I asked him if he knew the persons who had done that to him, and he just nodded vaguely and stared at me as if he had recollections there was no point in trying to share.

I told him that I was driving the next day to Ilok, a town on the far eastern edge of Croatia which was still under Serb control and serving as a place of refuge for Serbs from the Pakrac area. He brightened measurably with the thought that I might run across his neighbors and be able to convey his warm wishes to them. The odds of that actually happening, as he surely knew, had to be in the range of several hundred to one, but even that thin wisp of hope encouraged him.

I later went prowling with a tape recorder and an interpreter, and we found an old woman of 87 dressed entirely in black from the soles of her feet to the top of her head. I asked her the usual set of questions, and I thought the interview was going well. After about forty minutes of that, however, she turned to me abruptly and asked me to turn off the tape recorder. I thought I was about to hear something special and leaned forward. But no, she had a joke to offer and did not think it was suitable for tape. "There is something all men have and want to share with women. Johnson [meaning Lyndon] has a longer one than Tito. The Pope has one but never uses it. What is it?" A tense silence reigned for a moment, and when she could stand it no longer she cried out "*a surname!*" and broke into a laugh so shrill that it alarmed the chickens outside the screened kitchen door. There could not have been more than five or six teeth in that wondrous, smiling mouth. I asked her if I might take her photograph so that I could show my family the new friend I had made in Batanjani, but she held up a pair of worn, leathery hands as if to ward off the devil. She was smiling as she did so, but she was in dead earnest—and I should have known better. There are parts of the world where one does not take photographs of persons.

Later that day I interviewed a young mother in her home whose husband was in the Croatian army. A dozen or more neighbors had drifted in to see what was going on—a familiar occurrence to me by then—and we had been in conversation for half an hour when the front door burst open as if it had been hit by a violent gust of wind and the local priest stormed in. He took a seat directly across the room from me, leaned forward, stared fiercely at me for a long moment so that the villagers would get a sense of the gravity of what he was about to do, and launched into one of the most inane reviews of recent history I have ever heard—and this in a land and at a time when bizarre accounts of what was going on is a regional specialty. He was blaming Americans—in the person of me—for preventing Croatian armed forces from sweeping across the whole of Bosnia and claiming it for Croatia. It was not only foolish as a practical matter but reckless to a degree that would probably have unnerved Mussolini. Not exactly what one would expect from a gentle shepherd tending his flock.

My interpreter that day was a thoughtful, sensitive, intelligent young man I will call Stjepan. He was clearly unnerved by this. Toward the end of my conversation with the priest, he even picked up the gauntlet himself on occasion, joining the argument on his own behalf in words I could not make out, a brave venture for a 17-year-old sitting among villagers who knew his parents. At one point I turned to Stjepan, who was sitting next to me, and asked in a whisper whether he and I were the only ones there who knew English. He nodded, and I asked him—again in a whisper—how he would feel if I said to the priest that we had more important things to do and would now take our leave. He passed that on to the priest without even answering my question, and within a few seconds I was following him out the door to a numbing silence. One does not speak that way to a priest. Once on our way down the street, Stjepan noted that he hated that kind of talk—meaning the slashing bullying of the priest—and added that any time he wanted to hear that kind of thing all he had to do was go home. In an effort to soften the moment, I said "he came in like Operation Flash, didn't he?"—meaning the lightning military strike that had driven the Serbs out of that part of Croatia six years before. "Yes," he said without a pause, "but he was louder and took longer." Seventeen years old! If persons like him are to be Croatia's future, all may be well.

Monday

The road to eastern Croatia took us into Serb-occupied territory. The license plates of the car we were driving indicated clearly that it was from Zagreb, recently enemy territory, and it seemed to attract attention. We watched the road carefully. There were signs warning that the unpaved shoulders had not been cleared of mines, and that accidents had been reported.

We stopped at Vukovar on the western bank of the Danube separating Croatia from Vojvodina, a part of Serbia. It was shelled mercilessly during the early months of the war, and occupied by Serb forces shortly thereafter. It looks like Dresden must have at the end of WWII. Our destination was Ilok. The village was once the home of Croats, driven westward by Serb forces coming across the Danube, and it would soon become so again as the result of a treaty. For the time being, however, those unoccupied homes were serving as places of refuge for Serbs driven eastward from other parts of Croatia. They knew they would have to leave soon. To go where? They had no idea.

Tuesday

I visited a site on which Serb refugees—many of whom did not have enough to eat—and were soon to leave the area in any case—were helping to construct an Orthodox church. I talked to a man who was introduced to me as a Bishop. He spoke English, and I asked him—without really thinking about what I was saying—why they were erecting a place of worship when the Serbs would soon be gone and the incoming Croats might well destroy it. I thought he was avoiding the question and was about to ask it again when it dawned on me that I may have been blundering into the right answer without meaning to. Can it be that all that human energy was being invested into the building of a church *because* it might be blown up? It would be yet another sin to add to the thousands already registered in the ledger of Croat villainy, another outrage calling for revenge. I was wondering what to say next when the Bishop was called away.

Not long after that I met the priest in charge of the building project itself. He spoke English as well. He poured two glasses of rakia and waved a large wooden cross over them in a vacant gesture. "Holy water," I ventured. "Yes," he said laughing, "but only if I do it." I liked that and thought for a moment that I might be in for an unusually informative interview as well as a pleasant time. But, alas, that promising beginning was followed by yet another of those endless, inept history lessons. He later told me his story. He had been driven out of his home village near Pakrac and had watched his home burned to the ground. I asked him what he would like to do next, and he replied that his main responsibility now was to take care of his children. But, he added ominously, were it not for that, "I would go back and sacrifice myself before my enemies." I wrote that on the back of my mind and transferred it to paper as soon as I could. "What does that mean?" I asked. He gave me a look that meant "you know," and I guess I did. He meant that he would charge into the ranks of his enemies, get killed in the process, and in that way contribute his death to that already over-stuffed book of dark Croat accounts. His revenge would be to offer himself up as a reason for revenge. Would he have done that? Did he mean it? I have no idea. But it was the mind-set that impressed me. Both the Bishop and the priest, if I was reading them correctly, were speaking the language of martyrdom.

Our last visit of the day was to the building that once housed the local Fire Brigade. The motto printed above the entrance was translated to me as "The fire will go out as soon as everything is burned." They should post that on every border station in the land. There is a large room in the building that once served as a refuge for twenty Serbs or more and now holds six. A table takes up the center of the room, covered with loaves of bread. That is far more than the six residents can eat, but it is the only food they have on hand. Cots were spread around the room as well as neat stacks of military blankets. Winter would arrive soon. A small tin stove that looked as though it would not heat a closet provided the only protection they had against the cold. It does not work, they noted, but that scarcely matters because they have no fuel in any case. Lying on one of the nearby cots was a young woman curled up into the fetal position and staring blankly at nothing. "Nerves," her mother explained. A gaunt, elderly man walked into the room so slowly and carefully and deliberately that he looked as though his whole body machinery had been placed on very slow motion. His face was as grey as cold ashes, and when he first sat down and was motionless for an instant I shuddered with the thought that I was witnessing a death. He moved slightly, to end that thought. But, in a way, I probably was.

Wednesday

Interviews today. The first of them was with a Serb woman who had taken refuge in Ilok with her two children. The story I am about to relate is a lot grimmer than most of the others I have offered here, but I am passing it on because it illustrates—far too well—a problem that often comes up in this kind of work. I begin most encounters with the obvious disadvantage that I do not know the language and have to conduct conversations with the help of someone else who does. That is almost bound to be a local person, often one who has been caught up in the same historical currents as the people I am talking to. Everyone in the room, then, shares a world of experience that I would like to understand better but will never belong to or get a true feel of.

I was asking questions of the mother—her children sitting directly across the room from me—about her retreat from what had been home. My interpreter for the day was a young Serb, herself a refugee, and, as usual, the room was full of neighbors who had drifted in. The mother was speaking of the time she and a group of other evacuees were in a forest somewhere, making their way down a narrow dirt road. She paused for a long moment, and I, wholly insensitive to what was going on, asked the kind of question that is almost a matter of reflex for an interviewer trying to keep a flow of words going. "And what happened next?" She said something very softly, barely audible. The interpreter next to me bent over in pain and tried to muffle a cry, and everyone else in the room went pale. I was looking at the children, and it seemed to me that they had almost stopped breathing and turned into stone. The abrupt change in atmospheric pressure was palpable, and yet I was the only person in the room who had no idea what had just been said! When the interpreter was able to regain her voice, she offered a faint translation of what everyone else had heard earlier: "and then the Ustasha came out of the woods and killed my husband with an axe." I was still looking at the children out of the corner of my mind as I heard that, and it was my turn to lose it and to go pale. "Were *they* there?" I blurted out, gesturing toward the children. It took another moment for everyone else there to hear what I had just said, of course, because it, too, had to be translated. But there was no reply. The answer was obvious; they knew that I was expressing shock in my own way.

So here I am, an expert from afar, having come to the edges of someone else's war and knowing less about what is going on than anybody within a radius of hundreds of miles.

II

In 1973, Erik H. Erikson, from whom we have heard more than once in this book, was invited to present a set of talks known as the annual Jefferson Lectures. He later expanded those lectures into a book entitled *Dimensions of a New Identity.* He ended the lectures, as he did the book, with two words, printed in capital letters for emphasis: TAKE CARE.

The sentence that preceded that stark ending explained: "There is a greeting going around these days which, used casually, seems to suggest not much more than we should be careful, or take care of ourselves. I would hope that it could come to mean more than that, and I therefore want to conclude these lectures with it."

I was very impressed by that closing then, and I would like to borrow it now as well. What the elder Erikson meant then, as he made quite clear, was that we should all be taking care of the people in our immediate surroundings, and, most particularly, those we bring into the world and into the family hearth. He had in mind as well that taking care of oneself is almost a precondition for taking care of others. But he noted in passing that we are obliged to take care of people in what he called "our sector of the world," and I would like to turn there.

We are social creatures to the core, as has been pointed out from the start of this book. Taking care of others, then, is not only built into our bone and marrow. It is the adhesive, the connective tissue, that has brought our kind together into sturdy wholes that survive (and thrive) handsomely where a scatter of separate individuals could not. Our sector of the world? That clearly means more than our own comfortable neighborhoods or communities but extends to the people of the urban slums and other barren places across our landscape.

And we should be looking beyond our part of the world to a time and place when we actively seek places of safety and comfort for everyone—those inns and resting places of the human soul—not only for "our kind" but for all of those we recognize as human across the surfaces of the planet. He thought so too.

It seemed to me that my country and parts of my world were taking some strange turns as this book went to press, and the advice I am about to close with becomes all the more relevant in times of fear and doubt and the closing in of boundaries. So, TAKE CARE.

SOURCES

View from the Fourteenth Floor

"The supreme awareness we can have . . ." Stanley Kunitz, "The Life of Poetry," *Antaeus* (Spring 1980): 153.

"Sociology is a new science . . ." Sir Ernest Gowers, ed., *Fowler's Modern English Usage,* 2nd ed. (Oxford: Oxford University Press, 1988), pp. 569–70.

"the remorseless pursuit of what everybody knew all along . . ." Murray Kempton, *New York Post,* 31 August 1960. Reprinted in "Social Notes (on the A.S.A. Meetings)," *Sociological Inquiry* 31, no. 2 (1961): 180.

"the familiar envelope of circumstances . . ." Henry James, *Portrait of a Lady* (Boston: Houghton Mifflin, 1963), p. 172.

The Individual and the Social

"Thou shall not . . ." W. H. Auden, "Under Which Lyre: Reactionary Tract for the Times," W. H. Auden *Collected Poems*, NY: Random House, 1976.

"O sweet spontaneous," e. e. cummings, *The Dial* 68, no. 5 (1920).

"The first fruit of that imagination . . ." C. Wright Mills, *The Sociological Imagination* (New York: Oxford University Press, 1959), p. 5.

Knowing the Place for the First Time

"We shall not cease . . ." T. S. Eliot, "Little Giddings," *Four Quartets*, T. S. Eliot New York: Houghton Mifflin Harcourt, 1936.

"Kenge, a young man . . ." The dispute in the Ituri Rain Forest is described by Colin Turnbull in *The Forest People* (Garden City, NY: Anchor, 1962). It appears on pp. 118–19 and is paraphrased here. (It may be worth noting that Turnbull's book has been the subject of a number of questions about its accuracy, but none of them bear on Moke or on the story told here. See Alex Liazos, "The 1950s Mbuti: A Critique of Colin Turnbull's *The Forest People*.")

"Once, when the Kiowa were at war . . ." The Kiowa story is repeated here exactly as it appeared in Jane Richardson, *Law and Status Among the Kiowa Indians* (New York: J. J. Augustin, 1940), p. 44.

"carried out at a lonely crossroads . . ." Starling Lawrence, *Montenegro: A Novel* (New York: HarperCollins, 2006), p. 111.

"A man started running through the village . . ." Leo W. Simmons, ed., *Sun Chief: The Autobiography of a Hopi Indian* (New Haven: Yale University Press, 1960), pp. 118–19.

Excerpts from court records, repeated here in their original form, are from two different sources: *Records of the Governor and Company of the Massachusetts Bay in New England,* ed. Nathaniel Shurtleff, printed by order of Massachusetts Legislature, 1853–1854; and *Records and Files of the Quarterly Courts of Essex County,* 1636–1683, ed. George Francis Dow, Essex Institute, several volumes variously dated.

"There was a youth . . ." The sad story of Thomas Granger is quoted here from William Bradford, *Of Plimouth Plantation.* The original appeared in 1648. The edition used here is: William Bradford, *Of Plymouth Plantation, 1620–1647,* ed. Samuel Eliot Morison (New York: Knopf, 1952), pp. 320–21.

Disaster at Buffalo Creek

This chapter adapted from Kai Erikson, *Everything in Its Path: Destruction of Community in the Buffalo Creek Flood* (New York: Simon & Schuster, 1976).

"like a pool of gravy in a mound of mashed potato . . ." Harry M. Caudill, "Buffalo Creek Aftermath," *The Saturday Review,* 29 August 1976, p. 16.

Human Origins

"Most of our knowledge of him . . ." Loren Eiseley, *The Immense Journey* (New York: Vintage, 1957 [1945]), p. 88.

"The first man who, having enclosed a piece of land . . ." Jean-Jacques Rousseau, "Discourse on the Origin of Inequality: The Second Part," *The Social Contract: & Discourses,* trans. G. D. H. Cole (London: J. M. Dent and Sons, Limited, 1920), p. 207.

Discovering the Social

"the patient silent struggles . . ." Marc Bloch, *French Rural History,* trans. Janet Sondheimer, Berkeley, CA: University of California Press, 1970, p. 170.

"the weapons of the weak," James C. Scott, *Weapons of the Weak,* New Haven: Yale University Press, 1985.

"war of every one against every one . . ." Thomas Hobbes, *The Leviathan,* ed. C. B. MacPherson (London: Penguin Books, 1985), pp. 189. The quote is found in Part 1: Of Man, Ch. XIV.

"solitary, poor, nasty, brutish, and short . . ." Hobbes, *Leviathan,* p. 186. The quote is found in Part 1: Of Man, Ch. XIII.

"Man is naturally good . . ." Rousseau's statement is from a 1762 letter to Malesherbes. The full passage reads: "Oh, Monsieur, if I had ever been able to write a quarter of what I saw and felt under that tree, with what force would I have exposed all the abuses of our institutions, with what simplicity would I have demonstrated that man is naturally good, and that it is by these institutions that men have become wicked." Quoted in the introduction to Jean-Jacques Rousseau, *On the Social Contract,* ed. Roger D. Masters, trans. Judith R. Masters (New York: St. Martin's Press, 1978), p. 8.

"The first man who . . ." Jean-Jacques Rousseau, "Discourse of the Origin of Inequality: The Second Part," *The Social Contract: & Discourses,* trans. G. D. H. Cole (London: J. M. Dent and Sons, Limited, 1920), p. 207.

"Man is born free, but . . ." Rousseau, *On the Social Contract,* p. 46.

"the regeneration of the human race . . ." Alexis de Tocqueville, *The Old Regime and the Revolution,* trans. John Bonner (New York: Harper and Brothers, 1856), p. 27.

"inns and resting places . . ." Edmund Burke, *Burke's Reflections on the Revolution in France,* ed. F. G. Selby (London: MacMillan and Co., Limited, 1906), p. 222.

Coming to Terms with Social Life

"Society is no more decomposable . . ." Auguste Comte, *System of Positive Polity, Vol. 2,* trans. Frederic Harrison (New York: Burt Franklin & Co., 1875), p. 153.

"repulses friendships . . ." Edmund Wilson, *To the Finland Station: A Study in the Writing and Acting of History* (New York: Farrar, Straus and Giroux, 1972), p. 116.

"in the womb . . ." Karl Marx, "Marx on the History of His Opinions (Preface to *A Contribution to the Critique of Political Economy*)," *The Marx-Engels Reader,* 2nd ed., ed. Robert Tucker (New York: W. W. Norton and Company, 1978), p. 5. The entire passage reads: "The bourgeois relations of production are the last antagonistic form of the social process of production—antagonistic not in the sense of individual antagonism but of one arising from the social conditions of life of the individuals; at the same time the productive forces developing *in the womb* of bourgeois society create the material conditions for the solution of that antagonism." Emphasis added.

"The mode of production in material life . . ." Marx, "Marx on the History of His Opinions," p. 4.

"opinions seemed always to have been arrived at . . ." Wilson, *To the Finland Station,* p. 180.

"It is impossible to read *Das Kapital* . . ." Wilson, *To the Finland Station,* p. 361.

"that tempering of character, that heightening of life . . ." Steven Lukes, *Émile Durkheim: His Life and Work* (London: Penguin, 1973), p. 40.

"a small society, compact and cohesive . . ." Lukes, *Durkheim,* p. 40.

"by a progressive analysis of his thought and the facts . . ." Marcel Mauss, in Lukes, *Durkheim,* pp. 30, 67.

"sums up and implies a whole new order of ideas . . ." Émile Durkheim, *The Rules of Sociological Method,* ed. Steven Lukes, trans. W. D. Halls (New York: Free Press, 1982), p. 195. Originally published in 1903 as "Sociologie et sciences sociales." *Revue philosophique* 55:465–97.

"determine our behavior from without . . ." Durkheim is quoted in Lukes, *Durkheim,* p. 35.

"His long, thin body was enveloped in a large dressing-gown . . ." Lukes, *Durkheim,* p. 367.

"Every time a social phenomenon is . . ." Émile Durkheim, *The Rules of Sociological Method,* ed. George E. G. Catlin, trans. Sarah A. Solovay and John Mueller (Glencoe, IL: Free Press, 1938), p. 104.

"we can be certain that in the entire course of social evolution . . ." Lukes, *Durkheim,* p. 105.

"the totality of beliefs and sentiments common to the average citizens . . ." Émile Durkheim, *The Division of Labor in Society,* trans. W. D. Halls (New York: Free Press, 1982), p. 38.

"lost in the whole . . ." Raymond Aron, *Main Currents in Sociological Thought,* vol. 2, trans. Richard Howard and Helen Weaver (New York: Doubleday Anchor, 1970), p. 17.

"air is no less heavy because we do not detect its weight . . ." Durkheim, *Rules,* p. 5.

"a category of facts with very distinctive characteristics . . ." Durkheim, *Rules,* p. 3.

"a new variety of phenomena . . ." Durkheim, *Rules,* p. 3.

"The first and most fundamental rule is . . ." Durkheim, *Rules,* p. 14.

"If there is any fact whose pathological character appears incontestable, that fact is crime . . ." Durkheim, *Rules,* p. 65.

"a factor in public health . . ." Durkheim, *Rules,* p. 70.

"is bound up with the fundamental conditions . . ." Durkheim, *Rules,* p. 70.

"as a formidable intellectual armed with doctrine . . ." Lukes, *Durkheim,* p. 364.

"perhaps the greatest single book of the twentieth century . . ." Randall Collins and Michael Makowsky, *The Discovery of Society,* 2nd ed. (New York: Random House, 1978), p. 107.

"If we have taken primitive religion as the subject . . ." Émile Durkheim, *The Elementary Rules of the Religious Life,* trans. Joseph Ward Swain (London: George Allen and Unwin, Ltd., 1915), pp. 1–2.

"The division of the world into two domains . . ." Durkheim, *Elementary Rules,* p. 37.

"In the last analysis, [human beings] have never worshipped . . ." Aron, *Main Currents in Sociological Thought,* p. 50.

"The believer is not deceived. . . ." Durkheim, *Elementary Rules,* p. 225.

"It is from a chair like that . . ." Lukes, *Durkheim,* p. 370.

"a mixture of severe authority and anxious affection . . ." Davy in Lukes, *Durkheim,* p. 367.

"I want to see how much I can stand . . ." Quoted in Dennis Wrong, *Max Weber* (Englewood Cliffs, NJ: Prentice-Hall, 1970), p. 4.

"demonic . . ." Wrong, *Weber,* p. 4.

"if one wants to settle with this devil . . ." Wrong, *Weber,* p. 6.

"When I come to die, there is no one better . . ." Donald MacRae, *Max Weber* (New York: Viking Press, 1974), p. 18.

"to be ill . . . was then an alternative vocation . . ." MacRae, *Weber,* p. 30.

"Not summer's bloom lies ahead of us . . ." Max Weber, "Politics as a Vocation," *From Max Weber: Essays in Sociology,* ed. and trans. H. H. Gerth and C. Wright Mills (New York: Oxford University Press, 1946), p. 128.

"to substitute a one-sided materialistic . . ." Max Weber, *The Protestant Ethic and the Spirit of Capitalism,* trans. Talcott Parsons (New York: Charles Scribner's Sons, 1958), p. 183.

"An ideal type is formed by the one-sided accentuation . . ." Max Weber, "'Objectivity' in Social Science and Social Policy," *Methodology of Social Sciences: Max Weber,* ed. and trans. Edward Shils and Henry A. Finch (New Brunswick, NJ: Transaction, 2011), p. 90.

"One does not need to be Julius Caesar . . ." MacRae, *Weber,* p. 18.

"that successfully claims the monopoly of the legitimate use of violence . . ." Max Weber, "Politics as a Vocation," p. 78.

Aron, *Main Currents,* p. 271.

The Journey of Piotr and Kasia Walkowiak

William I. Thomas and Florian Znaniecki, *The Polish Peasant in Europe and in America,* vols. 1 and 2 (New York: Alfred A. Knopf, 1927).

"had been born and bred here for centuries, like a tough and hardy plant . . ." Emile Zola, *The Earth,* trans. Douglas Parmee (Harmondsworth: Penguin, 1980), p. 48.

"To the peasant the State is more distant . . ." Carlo Levi, *Christ Stopped at Eboli: The Story of a Year,* trans. Frances Frenaye (New York: Farrar, Strauss, and Giroux, 2006), p. 76.

"Late at night . . ." Ewa Morawska, *For Bread with Butter: Life-Worlds of East Europeans in Johnstown, Pennsylvania, 1890–1920,* London: Cambridge University Press, 1985, 125.

"It was terrible hard work . . ." Morawska, *Bread and Butter,* p. 1.

Places

"powerful forces [are] transforming *community* into *society* . . ." Edward A. Ross, *Social Control: A Survey of the Foundations of Order* (Cleveland: Case Western Reserve University, 2001), p. 482.

Robert Redfield, *The Little Community* and *Peasant Society and Culture* (Chicago: University of Chicago Press, 1956).

Village

"On reading Gans's descriptions of the patterns of life . . ." Jack E. Weller, *Yesterday's People* (Lexington: University of Kentucky Press, 1965), p. 4.

"My view of the West Ender's self . . ." Herbert J. Gans, *The Urban Villagers: Group and Class in the Life of Italian-Americans,* rev. ed. (New York: The Free Press, 1982), p. 100. Gans was speaking of Daniel Lerner, *The Passing of Traditional Society* (Glencoe, IL: The Free Press, 1958).

"It is fashionable to admire . . ." Raymond Williams, *The Country and the City* (New York: Oxford University Press, 1965), p. 105.

"Community is a fusion of feeling and thought . . ." Robert A. Nisbet, *The Sociological Tradition* (New York: Basic Books, 1966), p. 48.

"Most villages have a love . . ." Richard Critchfield, *Villages* (Garden City, NY: Anchor Doubleday, 1981), p. 454.

"Almost every rise of ground . . ." John McPhee, *The Crofter and the Laird* (New York: Farrar, Strauss, and Giroux, 1970), p. 53.

"I identify with that dirty hole . . ." John Baskin, *New Burlington: The Life and Death of an American Village* (New York: New American Library, 1976), p. 46.

"They are unmistakably poor children . . ." Robert Coles, *Children of Crisis* (Boston: Little, Brown, and Company, 2003), p. 270.

"include a high proportion of factual incorrectness . . ." McPhee, *Crofter and the Laird*, p. 100.

"The village people brought things up . . ." Baskin, *New Burlington*, p. 46.

"One of the conditions . . ." Baskin, *New Burlington*, p. 240.

"New Burlington was like a medieval society . . ." Baskin, *New Burlington*, p. 44.

"In New Burlington, everyone had a place . . ." Baskin, *New Burlington*, p. 44.

"We had all these things . . ." Baskin, *New Burlington*, p. 243.

"The Gemeinschaft, to the extent that it is capable of doing so . . ." Ferdinand Tönnies, *Community and Society (Gemeinschaft und Gesellschaft)*, trans. and ed. Charles P. Loomis (New Brunswick, NJ: Transaction, 2004), pp. 164–65.

"My mother died in 1945 . . ." Ronald Blythe, *Akenfield: Portrait of an English Village* (New York: Pantheon, 1969), p. 95.

"We all have our own pattern . . ." Blythe, *Akenfield*, p. 148.

"The old men will tell you . . ." Blythe, *Akenfield*, p. 265.

"The men . . . worked perfectly . . ." Blythe, *Akenfield*, p. 58.

"I have sometimes dared to question . . ." Blythe, *Akenfield*, p. 73.

"They'll talk all day . . ." Blythe, *Akenfield*, p. 108.

"Here . . . we touch upon . . ." Julian A. Pitt-Rivers, *The People of the Sierra*, 2nd ed. (Chicago: University of Chicago Press, 1971), p. 49.

"They are a hard people . . ." Blythe, *Akenfield*, p. 75.

"Most of these villages, of course . . ." Baskin, *New Burlington*, p. 197.

"The deities of the State . . ." Carlo Levi, *Christ Stopped at Eboli: The Story of a Year*, trans. Frances Frenaye (New York: Farrar, Strauss, and Giroux, 2006), p. 77.

"community . . . seems never to be used unfavorably" Raymond Williams, *Keywords: A Vocabulary of Culture and Society* (New York: Oxford University Press, 1976), p. 66.

"the idiocy of village life . . ." Karl Marx, "Manifesto of the Communist Party," *The Marx-Engels Reader*, 2nd ed., ed. Robert Tucker (New York: W. W. Norton and Company, 1978), p. 477.

"these idyllic village communities . . ." Karl Marx, "The British Rule in India," *Orientalism: A Reader*, ed. A. L. Macfie (New York: New York University Press, 2000), pp. 16–17. Originally published under the same title in the *New York Daily Tribune* on 25 June 1853.

"In all that great Mississippi Valley . . ." Sherwood Anderson, *Poor White* (New York: Viking Press, 1966), pp. 44–45.

"You quit the large roads . . ." George Wilson Pierson, *Tocqueville in America* (New York: Doubleday Anchor, 1959), pp. 151–52.

City

"It was a most heavenly day . . ." Thomas De Quincey, *Autobiographical Sketches* (New York: Hurd and Houghton, 1876), pp. 204–7.

"an instrument . . . [for] the extraction and concentration . . ." V. Gordon Childe is quoted in Lewis Mumford, *The City in History* (Harcourt, Brace, and World, 1961), p. 89.

"pestilential to the morals . . ." Thomas Jefferson, letter to Benjamin Rush, *The Papers of Thomas Jefferson,* vol. 32: *1 June 1800–16 February 1801,* ed. Barbara B. Oberg (Princeton, NJ: Princeton University Press, 2005), pp. 166–69.

"the city is a state of mind . . ." Robert Ezra Park and Ernest Burgess, *The City* (Chicago: University of Chicago Press, 1925), p. 1. See also "The Metropolis and Mental Life," Georg Simmel, *The Sociology of Georg Simmel,* ed. Kurt H. Wolff (New York: Free Press, 1960), pp. 409–24.

"the great tidal wash . . ." Robert Fishman, *Bourgeois Utopias: The Rise and Fall of Suburbia* (New York: Basic Books, 1987), p. 191.

Douglas Massey and Nancy Denton, *American Apartheid: Segregation and the Making of the Underclass* (Cambridge, MA: Harvard University Press, 1993).

Donald Braman, *Doing Time on the Outside: Incarceration and Family Life in Urban America,* (Ann Arbor: University of Michigan Press, 2004).

Oscar Lewis, *La Vida: A Puerto Rican Family in the Culture of Poverty* (New York: Vintage, 1968).

"Homely filth begrimes him . . ." Charles Dickens, *Bleak House* (London: Bradbury and Evans, 1853), p. 452.

"white spaces" Elijah Anderson. "The White Space," *Sociology of Race and Ethnicity,* 2015: vol 1 (1), pp. 10–21.

William Julius Wilson, *When Work Disappears: The World of the New Urban Poor* (New York: Knopf, 1996).

"The once lively streets . . ." Wilson, *When Work Disappears,* p. 5.

John J. DiIulio Jr., "When Decency Disappears," *National Review* 49, no. 1 (1997): 53–55.

Jonathan Kozol, *Amazing Grace: The Lives of Children and the Conscience of a Nation* (New York: Harper Perennial, 1996).

"They were now on the outskirts of the city . . ." Michael Thelwell, *The Harder They Come* (New York: Grove Press, 1980), pp. 120–21.

"fed by methone from . . ." John Macionis, *Sociology,* Englewood Cliffs, NJ: Prentice-Hall, 1997, p. 291.

"at the end of the day . . ." Mike Davis, "Planet of the Slums," *New Left Review* 26 (March–April 2004): 26.

"the real governments of the slums . . ." Davis, "Planet of the Slums," p. 30.

Worlds Beyond

"that successfully claims the monopoly of the legitimate use of violence . . ." Max Weber, "Politics as a Vocation," p. 78.

"We will not make Britain's mistake . . ." Ludwell Denny, *America Conquers Britain: A Record of Economic War* (New York: A. A. Knopf, 1930), pp. 406–7.

"We might say that everything . . ." Amin Maloof, *In the Name of Identity: Violence and the Need to Belong,* trans. Barbara Bray (New York: Arcade Publishing, 2001), p. 92.

"The internet . . . [is] an ectoplasmic monster . . ." Maloof, *In the Name of Identity,* p. 126.

"Markets abhor frontiers . . ." Benjamin R. Barber, *Jihad vs. McWorld: How Globalism and Tribalism Are Reshaping the World* (New York: Ballantine Books, 1995), p. 13.

"Never have men had so many things . . ." Maloof, *In the Name of Identity,* p. 93.

"one thing that is not happening . . ." Jonathan Friedman, "The Hybridization of Roots and the Abhorrence of the Bush,"*Spaces of Culture: City, Nation, World,* ed. Mike Featherstone and Scott Lash (London: Sage, 1999), p. 241.

"people and peoples would rather murder . . ." Letter from Erik H. Erikson to Roger Fisher, editor, *Daedalus,* October 1962. It was originally intended for publication in the magazine *Daedalus,* but was later withdrawn and reserved for "private circulation." Portions of it are reprinted in Carol Hoare, *Erikson on Development in Adulthood: New Insights from Unpublished Papers* (New York: Oxford University Press, 2002).

It Seemed Like the Whole Bay Died

"We've fetched up hard . . ." J. Steven Picou, Duane A. Gill, and Maurie Cohen, eds., *The Exxon Valdez Disaster: Readings on a Modern Social Problem* (Dubuque, IA: Kendall/ Hunt, 1997), p. 3.

"A thick layer of black crude oil . . ." Rick Steiner, "Probing an Oil-Stained Legacy," in Picou et al., *Exxon Valdez,* pp. 111–15.

"This is a way of life for us . . ." This quotation, like all of those here attributed to an Alaska Native—as well as two brief remarks made by non-Native observers—appeared in one or both of two writings I am the author of: Kai Erikson, Foreword, in Picou, Gill, and Cohen, *Exxon Valdez*; and Kai Erickson [*sic*], "Social Effects of the *Exxon Valdez* Oil Spill on the Native Villages in Alaska," Prepared for Cohen, Milstein, Hausfeld, & Toll, and Sonosky, Chambers, Sachse, Miller & Munson, March 1993. The vast majority of those quotes were drawn from the following sources:

Braund, S. R., and Associates, *Effects of the Exxon Valdez Oil Spill on Alutiiq Culture and People,* February 1993

Impact Assessment, Inc., *Social and Psychological Impacts of the Exxon Valdez Oil Spill, Third Interim Report of the Oiled Mayors Study,* 13 August 1990

Impact Assessment, Inc., *Economic, Social, and Psychological Impacts of the Exxon Valdez Oil Spill,* Oiled Mayors Subcommittee, Alaska Conference of Mayors, 15 November 1990

Minerals Management Service, *Social Indicators Study of Alaskan Coastal Villages,* Parts One and Two. Anchorage, Alaska, Department of the Interior, 1993

Meganack, Walter, Sr., "Coping with the Time the Water Died," *Anchorage Daily News,* 5 August 1989

Palinkas, Lawrence, A. John S. Petterson, John Russell, and Michael A. Downs, "Community Patterns of Psychiatric Disorders After the Exxon Valdez Oil Spill," *American Journal of Psychiatry,* 150, no. 10 (1993), pp. 1517–23

"When the *Exxon Valdez* ran aground . . ." Palinkas et al., "Community Patterns," p. 1522.

Becoming a Person

"a blooming, buzzing confusion . . ." William James, *Principles of Psychology,* vol. 1 (New York: Henry Holt and Company, 1890), p. 488.

"For the most part . . ." Walter Lippmann, *Public Opinion,* Piscataway, NJ: Transaction, 1946, p. 81.

"We walked down the path . . ." Helen Keller, *The Story of My Life,* ed. Candace Ward (Mineola, NY: Dover, 1996), p. 12.

"These include snow that is falling . . ." Hugh Brody, *The Other Side of Eden: Hunter-Gatherers, Farmers, and the Shaping of the World* (London: Faber and Faber, 2001), p. 50.

"The same principle applies . . ." Brody, *Other Side of Eden,* p. 197.

Kenge, out in the open countryside, was first described by Colin Turnbull in *The Forest People* (Garden City, NY: Anchor, 1962), pp. 251–53.

George Herbert Mead, *Mind, Self, and Society: From the Standpoint of a Social Behaviorist,* ed. Charles W. Morris (Chicago: University of Chicago Press, 1934).

"O wad some Pow'r the giftie gie us . . ." Robert Burns, "To a Louse," *The Works of Robert Burns,* vol.1, ed. Alan Cunningham (Boston: Hilliard Gray and Co., 1834), p. 475.

"making countermoves in the same game . . ." Joseph Conrad, *The Secret Agent* (Garden City, NY: Doubleday Anchor, 1916), p. 82.

"Products of the same machine . . ." Conrad, *Secret Agent,* p. 110.

William A. Cordero, *The Sociology of Childhood,* 4th ed. (Los Angeles: Sage, 2015).

"the words I learn now . . ." and other quotes from Eva Hoffman are from her *Lost in Translation: A Life in a New Language* (New York: Vintage, 1998), pp. 75, 104–8.

Erving Goffman, *Asylums: Essays on the Social Situation of Mental Patients and Other Inmates* (Garden City, NY: Doubleday Anchor, 1961).

"The salesgirl asked . . .," "He asked me what salary. . .," " 'What'll you have . . ." Lucinda SanGiovanni, *Ex-Nuns: A Study of Emergent Role Passage* (Norwood, NJ: Ablex Publishing Corporation, 1978), pp. 90–91.

Harry King, *Box Man: A Professional Thief's Journey,* as told to and edited by Bill Chambliss (New York: Harper Torchbooks, 1972).

"I never had any true evaluation . . ." and other quotes from Harry King are from Harry King and William J. Chambliss, *Harry King: A Professional Thief's Journey* (New York: John Wiley, 1984), pp. 18, 20–21, 124, 128.

Creating Divisions

Pierre Bourdieu, "The Forms of Capital," *Handbook of Theory and Research for the Sociology of Education,* ed. John G. Richardson (New York: Greenwood, 1986), pp. 241–58.

"If we made an income pyramid . . ." Paul Samuelson and Peter Temin, *Economics,* 10th ed. (New York: McGraw-Hill, 1976), p. 84.

"If we made a pyramid out of a child's blocks . . ." Paul Samuelson and William Nordhaus, *Economics,* 15th ed. (Boston: McGraw-Hill, 1995), p. 359.

"A Wall Street money manager who had been extremely lucky . . ." Jonathan Kozol, *Amazing Grace: The Lives of Children and the Conscience of a Nation* (New York: Harper Perennial, 1996), p. 111. The reference to Soros is on p. 265.

Richard Sennett and Jonathan Cobb, *The Hidden Injuries of Class* (New York: Vintage, 1972).

"truly, there are many . . ." James Blow, "Laquin McDonald and the System, *New York Times* opinion section, 30 November 2015.

Becoming a People

"why do human beings take such delight in killing one another? . . ." Gale Stokes, John Lampe, Dennison Rusinow, Julie Mostov, "Instant History: Understanding the Wars of Yugoslav Succession," *Slavic Review* 55 (1996): 136–60.

"Our ancestors have bred . . ." William James, "The Moral Equivalent of War," *Memories and Studies* (London: Longmans, Green, and Co., 1911), pp. 267–96.

"war is not a general law of life . . ." Julian Huxley, "War as a Biological Phenomenon," *Man in the Modern World* (London: Chatto and Windus, 1947), p. 181.

"Warfare is an invention, like any other . . ." Margaret Mead, "Warfare Is Only an Invention— Not a Biological Necessity," *Asia* 40 (1940): 402–5, quote on p. 402.

UNESCO, *Seville Statement on Violence, 1986,* available at http://ringmar.net/politiskai-deer/index.php/seville-statement-on-violence-1986.

"I will give all my children . . ." Michael Finkel, "Playing War," *New York Times Sunday Magazine,* 24 December 2000.

"There seems to be little doubt . . ." John Comaroff, "Ethnicity, Nationalism, and the Politics of Difference in an Age of Revolution," in *Perspectives on Nationalism and War,* ed. John Comaroff and Paul Stern (Amsterdam: Overseas Publishers Association, 1995), p. 244.

"irresistibly" drawn by "many obscure and emotional forces . . ." Sigmund Freud is quoted in Walker Connor, *Ethnonationalism: The Quest for Understanding* (Princeton, NJ: Princeton University Press, 1994), p. 203. Connor notes that he drew on two different translations here.

"the ethnic boundary that defines the group . . ." Fredrik Barth, *Ethnic Groups and Boundaries: The Social Organization of Culture Difference* (Boston: Little, Brown and Company, 1969), p. 15.

"A nation is a group of people united by a common error . . ." Karl Wolfgang Deutsch, *Nationalism and Its Alternatives* (New York: Knopf), p. 3.

"Humankind from the very beginning . . ." Erik H. Erikson, "Reflections on Ethos and War," *The Yale Review* 73 (1984): 481–86.

"The majority of human groups . . ." David H. Marlowe, "Violence and Aggression: A Look at Confoundations and Entanglements," unpublished, undated paper.

"They are strange . . ." and "There have always been a limited number . . ." A fictional Cheyenne chief in Thomas Berger, *Little Big Man* (New York: Dell, 1989), p. 91.

"humankind from the very beginning . . ." Erik Erikson, "Reflections on Ethos and War," p. 481.

Portions of the debate on pseudospeciation were later published in Kai Erikson, "On Pseudospeciation and Social Speciation," in *Genocide, War, and Human Survival,* ed. Charles B. Strozier and Michael Flynn (Lanham, MD: Rowman & Littlefield, 1996), pp. 51–57.

"A nation is a soul . . ." Ernest Renan, "What Is a Nation?," in *Becoming National: A Reader,* ed. Geoff Eley and Ronald Grigor Suny (New York: Oxford University Press, 1996), p. 52.

"a tribal feud that no outsider . . ." Quoted in Thomas L. Friedman, "Bosnia Reconsidered," *New York Times,* 8 April 1993, p. A1.

On use of the definite article when speaking of wartime adversaries, see J. Glenn Gray, *The Warriors: Reflections on Men in Battle* (Lincoln: University of Nebraska Press, 1998), pp. 133–34.

"a powerful aversion to harming . . ." David Livingstone Smith, *Less Than Human: Why We Demean, Enslave, and Exterminate Others* (New York: St. Martin's Press, 2011), p. 250. Elsewhere in this paragraph: "an engrained resistance to killing," p. 61; "The function of dehumanization," p. 264; "the evolved design," p. 101.

"it dehumanizes the native . . ." Franz Fanon, *The Wretched of the Earth* (New York: Grove Press, 1966), p. 34.

War Comes to Pakrac

"part of a more widespread phenomenon . . ." Susan Woodward, *Balkan Tragedy: Chaos and Dissolution After the Cold War* (Washington, DC: Brookings Institution, 1995), p. 3.

"You know me. You know my husband . . ." Roger Cohen was the correspondent who reported the episode in the *New York Times*. He described it again in his *Hearts Grown Brutal: Sagas of Sarajevo* (New York: Random House, 1998), p. 221.

"The U.N. checkpoint . . ." Michael Ignatieff, *Blood and Belonging: Journeys into the New Nationalism* (New York: Farrar, Strauss, and Giroud), p. 3.

"Adherents of the three main faiths . . ." Ivo Andrić, *Gospodjica,* 1961, quoted in Lenard Cohen, *Broken Bonds: The Poisoning of Yugoslavia* (Los Angeles: Westview, 1993), p. 330.

"You Americans are constitutionally . . ." David Rieff, *Slaughterhouse: Bosnia and the Failure of the West* (New York: Touchstone, 1995), p. 75.

"intractable . . . a tribal feud . . ." Quoted in Woodward, *Balkan Tragedy,* p. 307.

"not caused by a popular . . ." Bogdan Denitch, *Ethnic Nationalism: The Tragic Death of Yugoslavia* (Minneapolis: University of Minnesota Press, 1994), pp. 63–64.

"To explain the Yugoslav crisis . . ." Woodward, *Balkan Tragedy,* p. 15.

"to define the war as a tribal feud . . ." Ivo Banać in "Separating History from Myth: An Interview with Ivo Banac," in *Why Bosnia? Writings on the Balkan Wars,* ed. Rabia Ali and Lawrence Lifschultz (Stony Creek, CT: Pamphleteer's Press, 1993), p. 136.

"That's the hardest thing . . ." Slavenka Drakulić, *The Balkan Express: Fragments from the Other Side of War* (New York: Norton, 1993), p. 63.

"In Pakrac, both the Serb and Croat militias . . ." Christopher Bennett, *Yugoslavia's Bloody Collapse* (New York: NYU Press, 1995), p. 150.

"I kept staring at my own hands . . ." Dzevad Karahasan, *Sarajevo, Exodus of a City* (New York: Kodansha International, 1994), p. 27.

"the traumatic worldview" Kai Erikson, *A New Species of Trouble: Explorations in Disaster, Trauma, and Community* (New York: Norton, 1994).

"the media themselves were responsible . . ." Marjan Malešič, ed., *The Role of Mass Media in the Serbian-Croatian Conflict,* Psykologist Forsvar Report 164, Stockholm, 1993.

"imagine a United States . . ." Milos Vasik, quoted in Noel Malcolm, *Bosnia: A Short History* (New York: NYU Press, 1969), p. 252. I have not identified the quotes used over the past several pages because this list of references would be littered with citations. Most (maybe all) of the material Marjkan cited, though, comes from four sources. Malesic, Role of Mass Media; Jasmina Udovici and James Ridgeway, *Yugoslavia's Ethnic Nightmare* (New York: Lawrence Hill Books, 1995); Mark Thompson, *Forging War: The Media in Serbia, Croatia, and Bosnia-Hercegovina* (London: Article 19, 1994); and Norman Cigar, *Genocide in Bosnia* (College Station: Texas A&M University Press, 1995).

"being a Croat has become my destiny . . ." Slavenka Drakulić, *Balkan Express: Fragments from the Other Side of War* (New York: Norton, 1993), pp. 50–51.

"First, I was a Yugoslav. Then . . ." Rieff, *Slaughterhouse,* p. 12.

Charles Dickens, *A Child's History of England* (Oxford: Oxford University Press, 1987), p. 338.

ACKNOWLEDGMENTS

THE SOCIOLOGIST'S EYE HAS BEEN MANY YEARS in the making, and that is bound to result in a rather long list of persons to whom I feel particularly indebted. It is also bound to result in a fairly awkward list in the sense that the book has been a major preoccupation of mine for decades, and it is not as clear to me now as it has been for other writing projects I have been engaged in where the line belongs between those who have made a special contribution to the manuscript itself and those who have enriched the outlook and the sensibility I brought to the task.

The book first took life in a graduate seminar I presided over at Yale in the 1980s and 1990s. It had a more formal title, but it was widely known then and has been remembered since as "the writing seminar." And that is what it was. Students brought written work to our class sessions and shared them with one another. And so did I. The seminar was ongoing, paying no attention at all to the coming and going of academic semesters or even school years, so quite a number of students were in attendance for a matter of years as they wrote dissertations and continued their apprenticeships in sociology. I mention that now to help explain how it was possible for book-length manuscripts to be reviewed and discussed in class meetings over time.

An early draft of what later become this book was one of them. When I first turned the draft in to the Yale University Press, it was accompanied by letters from Nancy Ammerman, Michael Bell, Daniel Chambliss, Jeffrey Olick, Diane Pike, Francesca Polletta, Barry Seltzer, Jeffrey Swanson, and Beau Weston—all of whom had read what was then the entire manuscript. Other members of that ongoing seminar who contributed in important ways to the manuscript—I am running a substantial risk by relying solely on memory here—were Lee Cuba, Patricia Ewick, Willian Freudenberg, Bernice Pescosolido, David Stevenson, Paul Wolpe, Diane Vaughn, and Susan Watkins. I need to set aside a particularly grateful sentence to Michael Rowe, who was a student then and a particular help in the book project but has continued in that role over the years and become a valued friend and colleague. I also need to note that Nancy Ammerman, Daniel Chambliss, and Diane Pike have continued to be wise advisers in the time since. Diane deserves a place of her own on that chart for her willingness to be consulted over and over again on matters where her sensitivity to matters of particular concern to me were incalculable.

I have resisted the temptation here to speak of teachers and mentors who had a particular meaning to me in the years before this project even began for fear of cluttering this section with too many names, but I would like to mention three individuals who I never met in a classroom but who were honored elders (if not that much older) and important teachers in the years I was formulating this book. Ray L. Birdwhistell, Erving Goffman, and Robert K. Merton all saw portions of the book in its earlier stages and offered lasting advice.

The current draft of the manuscript was read and commented on by a number of colleagues, to my immense profit. Alice Fothergill, Steve Kroll-Smith, Harvey Molotch, Immanuel Wallerstein, and Eviatar Zerubavel read the whole of the book, and particularly sensitive portions of it were read by Michael Brown, Stanton Burnett, Michael Carey, William Corsaro, Duane Gill, Timothy Goldsmith, Jan Gross, Jerome Kagan, Thomas Kohut, Joseph La Palombara, Wayne Meeks, Charles Perrow, and John Stephen Picou.

I want to acknowledge my very special debt to Lori Peek, whose name belongs prominently on the last of colleagues who have read the manuscript more than once with remarkable care and has supplied me with many valuable suggestions. That is reason enough for endless thanks, but she also arranged for it to be read and commented on by two rare and thoughtful students at Colorado State, Meredith Dickinson and Brock Rauzi, which made a real difference.

Lori Peek was also responsible for putting me in touch with Meghan Mordy, who began her association with me as a technical assistant but quickly became a valued partner and adviser.

I once offered portions of the manuscript to students enrolled in an introductory sociology class at Williams College. The students knew as they enrolled in the class that these chapters would constitute a considerable portion of the homework assigned them and that they would be asked to comment on them in writing as the course proceeded. So they were in on what sounds a little like a conspiracy from the start. Those comments made a real difference to me—as I hope they did to at least some of them—and I have turned to them many times as the final draft of the book took form. I will not list those students for fear of submerging the thought under an avalanche of names, but they taught me as a class, a group—a village, I am tempted to propose—and I will thank them in the same way.

A special note is necessary for the field visit that brings the book to a close. It begins one day in the village of Stadtschlaining on the eastern edge of Austria. I was teaching a summer course in what was then called the European University Center for Peace Studies. James M. Skelly, one of the directors of that program and a close friend of long standing, asked me one morning whether I might be free for a while. He wanted to show me something. I asked how long we might be away. Well, he said, if we drive hard we might be back this time tomorrow. We drove across two sensitive borders to Pakrac, many miles to the south. I had never heard of the place before, but that Jim, he knew exactly what he was doing. Thanks are very much in order there. The work that followed in Pakrac and in what had recently been Yugoslavia would never have taken place without the financial support—and, far more to the point, the intellectual support—of the Copenhagen Peace Research Institute, COPRI, and the extraordinary person who was then its Director, Håkan Wiberg. Most of my travels to wartime Croatia both began and ended in Copenhagen, where I reported my findings to scholars there. Håkan, who is no longer with us, is remembered widely and profoundly for his work in the interests of peace, and he became a cherished comrade as well as a wise teacher. I mentioned Eric Markusen in my chapter on Pakrac, but I also owe considerable debts to Ivo Banać, Bogdan Denitch, and Susan Woodward on this side of the Atlantic, and to Goran Božičevi and Bartol Letica in Croatia itself. Jasmina Bešerivić-Regan, who grew up in Bosnia and knows the sound and the feel of wartime was helpful to me in ways she only half knows.

I have left four names out of this accounting so far because my debts to them simply belong on a rather different plane. Kenneth Allan has been tutoring me for some time now on matters of sociological theory in particular and the uses of social narrative in general. His generosity of spirit is reflected throughout. Christopher Erikson read every word of this long manuscript with his keen editorial instincts, and in doing so has changed not only the texture of the language but the wisdom of the contents. Charles Lemert read the first draft of this for the Yale University Press a decade and a half ago but has been in on every draft in the time since. It gives a special meaning to the term "colleague." John Ryden's name appears last on this list as a matter of alphabet, but he belongs first in more ways than one. He was Director of the Yale University Press when I signed up there earlier, and he has been my counselor in everything having to do with the process in the time since. He has read every line of the book—and often more than once—with rare intelligence and with a care that comes both from rich literary skills and true friendship.

In an earlier book of mine published in 1966, I noted: "I read the first draft of this study over several evening sessions to the most important group of critics I know—Joan Erikson, Erik H. Erikson, and Joanna Erikson." The first two are long gone, but the third, Joanna, constitutes that irreplaceable group by herself. Without her, there would be nothing.

INDEX

abstract reasoning, 68, 275, 278, 280, 281

Age of Exploration (also Age of Discovery), 234

Age of Reason, 83–92, 106, 321, 335. *See also* Enlightenment

agriculture
  age of, 76, 161
  and empty land, 235–36
  and family size, 220–21
  and land, 78, 139, 144, 176, 186, 198, 218, 235–36, 282, 354
  migrant farm workers, 8, 82, 141, 219, 228
  and modernization, 185, 221, 224
  and Native life, 254
  surplus, 187–88
  and transformation, 144, 184–85
  See also countryside; land

Akenfield (East Anglia, England), 166, 173–76, 179

Alaska, 138, 228, 252–64

Alcalá de la Sierra (Spain), 166, 179–80, 197

alienation, 91, 97–98, 113, 195

Allan, Kenneth, 93

Alutiiq people, 8, 252–64

American Civil War, 342

Anderson, Benedict, 329, 336

Anderson, Elijah, 210

Anderson, Sherwood, 179–80

Andrić, Ivo, 352

anomie, 91, 111

anxiety, 51, 195, 363

Appalachia, 8, 43–44, 165–66, 168, 170, 180, 280. *See also* Buffalo Creek flood (West Virginia)

Aron, Raymond, 93, 110, 118, 135

Auden, W. H., 23

Australia, 117–18

autonomy, 25, 86, 110

Balkans
  and colonialism, 233
  and ethnonational distinctions, 336–38, 345
  geopolitical viewpoint of, 345–46
  and the media, 371–74
  pre-1991 history of, 351–54
  psychosocial viewpoint of, 346
  and reason for war, 320, 324
  See also Bosnia and Hercegovina; Croatia and Croats; Serbia and Serbs; Slovenia; Yugoslavia

Banać, Ivo, 354

Barber, Benjamin R., 245